HOW CAN I KNOW IF I AM ONE OF GOD'S ELECT?

HOW CAN I KNOW IF I AM ONE OF GOD'S ELECT?

UNDERSTANDING AND APPRECIATING THE DOCTRINES OF ELECTION AND PREDESTINATION

RELIANT PUBLISHING
A DIVISION OF REDEMPTION PRESS

GENE GOBBLE

Published by Reliant Publishing, an imprint of Redemption Press, PO Box 427, Enumclaw, WA 98022.

Toll-Free (844) 2REDEEM (273-3336)

Redemption Press is honored to present this title in partnership with the author. The views expressed or implied in this work are those of the author. Redemption Press provides our imprint seal representing design excellence, creative content, and high-quality production.

ISBN: 978-1-68314-959-0 (Paperback)
978-1-68314-960-6 (ePub)
978-1-68314-961-3 (Mobi)

Library of Congress Catalog Card Number: 2020905848

The information for the individual names seen throughout the book was obtained from various resources online. The following list is offered as examples of these resources.

https://ammooni.ga/file-ready/second-helvetic-confession
http://apostles-creed.org
https//www.apuritansmind.com
https://www.blueletterbible.org
www.britannica.com
https://www.crcna.org
www.cslewisinstitute.org
Dictionary.reference.com
www.encyclopedia-titanica.org/titanic-victim/john-harper.html.
http://www.flowingfaith.com
http://www.generationword.com/bible_school_notes/30.html
https://godandmath.com
http://gracegems.org
http://higherpraise.com/preachers/shields.htm
www.history.mcs.st andrews.ac.uk/history/Mathematicians/Bernoulli_Johann.html
http://www.hsbchurch.com
www.merriam-webster.com
https://www.monergism.com
https://openlibrary.org/publishers/Ages_Software
www.PocketCollege.com
https://reformationhistory.org
https://www.salon.com
http://www.sbcec.net
https://sbcvoices.com
https://www.scribd.com
SermonIndex.net
http://www.solid-ground-books.com
https://theancientpaths.org
www.theopedia.com
www.thisday.pcahistory.org
http://en.wikipedia.org
https://www.wikipedia.org
https://www.1689.com/confession.html

CONTENTS

INTRODUCTION AND INVITATION

How Can I Know if I Am One of God's Elect?

Dear Friend,

If you are by God's providence looking at this book or reading about it online, and you are asking yourself, "Why spend the time to read through another long, dry book on one aspect of theology or drudge through another publication dealing with the various controversies regarding the biblical doctrines (systems) of election and predestination?" Please let me provide a few reasons for you to consider:

1. Maybe you will discover whether or not you are one of God's elect. That alone would make reading this worth your time.
2. The book is full of many flavors and variances of rich theology.
3. The book is full of all kinds of deep and stimulating philosophy.
4. The book is overflowing with rich history, including biblical history, European history, American history, and political history.
5. The book brings into focus the ongoing struggle between spiritual powers and political powers, which continue to this day.
6. Finally, the book contains many interesting and incredible true stories about different Christian people throughout the ages who have testified how God's

sovereign grace, through the knowledge of election and predestination, helped them endure the severest of trials and see their works for the kingdom of Christ made effective and fruitful for His glory. Some of these stories will give you goose bumps, some will thrill your soul, and some will make you wish you were more committed to the work of Christ on earth.

If you just love good theology and deep philosophy, you will enjoy the book. If you are captivated by all kinds of history, you will enjoy the book. If you take pleasure in theology, philosophy, and history—then I believe you will certainly appreciate the content. If powerful testimonies encourage you, then you will be inspired.

If you risk buying the book and actually take the time to carefully read through it slowly and attentively, saving your final conclusions about the content until you have finished every chapter and the appendix (which is one of the most vital pieces in the whole book) and you then have buyer's remorse—please let me know, and I will do everything in my power to refund the cost to you. I know for that to happen, I would still have to be alive, and I would have to have the financial means at that time to refund the purchase price to you, but I am willing to trust the Lord to help me do so at the time because I know you sincerely read the entire book and genuinely considered the points made on behalf of historical Christian orthodoxy regarding election and predestination.

Back in the mid-1980s, a man named Edgar Whisenant wrote a book called *88 Reasons Why the Rapture Will Be in 1988*. Whisenant was a former NASA engineer and a diligent Bible student.[1] He was convinced that the rapture of the church would occur sometime between September 11 and September 13, 1988. He seemed to be very sincere at the time, because he was able to raise enough money to mail 300,000 free copies of his book to pastors, preachers, and ministers across America, but he was also went on to sell 4.5 million copies in bookstores and other venues.

After his book came out and was being consumed by the public, some wealthy individual contacted Mr. Whisenant and offered to make an incredible deal with him. The man told him that he would purchase every one of the books available right then if Mr. Whisenant would buy them all back from him if the rapture did not occur when Mr. Whisenant predicted. I think this man may have made his offer after Mr. Whisenant made this comment, "Only if the Bible is in error am I wrong and I say that to every preacher in town."[2]

---

[1] Gregory J. Sheryl, "Can the Date of Jesus's Return Be Known?," Bibliotheca Sacra (2012), vol. 169, no. 163:27.

[2] Gregory J. Sheryl, "Can the Date of Jesus's Return Be Known?"

Mr. Whisenant refused the offer and the rest is history. Why would I share this unrelated story with you about the selling and buying of books? My reason is to let you know that I did not publish this book to try and make money. I wanted to publish this book in gratitude for my own salvation, to honor the Word of God, and to see if the content of the book could help people visualize the truths of election and predestination from as many perspectives as possible. The Bible does not need my help at all, but it sure is a joy to write about eternal truths that cause me to rejoice every day.

The premise for this book comes from Romans 9:11–18 (NASB), which is listed below:

> For though the twins were not yet born and had not done anything good or bad, so that God's purpose according to His choice (election) would stand, not because of works but because of Him who calls, it was said to her, "The older will serve the younger." Just as it is written, "Jacob I loved, but Esau I hated." What shall we say then? There is no injustice with God, is there? May it never be! For He says to Moses, "I will have mercy on whom I have mercy, and I will have compassion on whom I have compassion." So then it does not depend on the man who wills or the man who runs, but on God who has mercy. For the Scripture says to Pharaoh, "For this very purpose I raised you up, to demonstrate My power in you and that My name might be proclaimed throughout the whole earth." So then He has mercy on whom He desires, and He hardens whom He desires.

From these verses, please note how God clearly explains how He does what He wants to do, which would be a natural thing for a sovereign God. He says, "I will do this and I will do that." Specifically, He says these four things:

"I will have mercy on whom I have mercy."
"I will have compassion on whom I have compassion."
"He has mercy on whom He desires."
"He hardens whom He desires."

The Bible is filled with examples of God doing what He wants to do and sometimes having to do what He did not want to do, but felt compelled to, even though it grieved Him to do so.

In God's four statements above, there is a natural cause-effect relationship seen in the "I will" and "I have." God wanted to do something and He did it. It is so simple. If we put the "I will's" together in one sentence, as we look back through biblical history (His-Story), it looks like this: "I have had mercy and compassion on the ones whom I wanted to have mercy and compassion on and I have hardened the ones who I wanted to harden."

What was our sovereign God talking about when He explains having mercy and compassion on the ones whom He wanted to have mercy and compassion on? From an eternal perspective, God was referring to the salvation of the elect. Even though God did manifest temporal mercies in many different forms, upon many different people throughout biblical history (such as physical healing, monetary blessing, the ability to bear children, family relationships, issues of worship, etc.), His primary mercy and compassion is seen in the gift of personal redemption and salvation in the lives of individual people (from all people groups) through election and predestination. Not much really matters if you have only a blessed life here on earth, but die and go to an eternal hell. So while it is a wonderful and blessed thing to experience God's mercy and compassion in real and tangible ways during your short life here on earth, how much more wonderful is it to experience God's mercy and compassion throughout eternity? This is what election and predestination does for you!

This book was compiled with the hope and prayer that it would help you understand, appreciate, and be deeply grateful for what our all-powerful God has done—in saving you *from hell* and *for heaven* through the life, death, and resurrection of our Lord Jesus Christ.

When God chose to save you in Christ, before the creation of the universe, He chose you to:

1. Be saved from sin, from Satan, from yourself, and from eternal hell.
2. Be set apart from the ways of the world.
3. Be conformed to the moral and spiritual image of the Lord Jesus Christ.
4. Be Christ's representative in this world to every person you will ever meet.
5. Strengthen the body of Christ by serving others to your greatest potential with your spiritual gift from Romans 12.
6. Join the Lord in heaven at the time of your physical death.
7. Worship and glorify God throughout the rest of eternity.

Thank you in advance if you take the precious time to read the following pages!

Yours in Christ,

Gene Gobble

1 ✒

A Controversial but Providential Doctrine

The doctrines of election and predestination are two of the most interesting doctrines in the Bible, and yet two of the most misunderstood, controversial, and divisive. These doctrines have the ability to exalt and glorify God when understood in a comprehensive and balanced approach, but when only partially understood or interpreted out of context, these doctrines have birthed some of the most divisive controversies in the history of the universal church.

I call these concepts controversial but providential because *beyond* the divisiveness caused by misunderstanding God's purpose and power in them (the doctrines), when properly understood, they provide the understanding believer with more comfort, peace, and freedom than any others—save the wonder of God's marvelous grace in the atoning sacrifice of Jesus Christ! Properly understood, these doctrines will set you free! If you want more peace, more comfort from God's truth, and more understanding of the depths of our God's amazing character and the blessings He bestows upon those who believe, read on!

Throughout church history, Christian leaders on opposite sides of interpreting these doctrines have opposed and fought with each other for years and *never resolved* their differences. One well-known disagreement in the early church was the confrontation between Augustine and Pelagius culminating in the condemnation of Pelagianism (as interpreted by Augustine) at the Council of Ephesus in 431.

Since the 1500s it would be hard to list all of the people who opposed John Calvin and his explanations of election and predestination, which became known as Calvinism. In the 1700s George Whitefield and John Wesley, who were best friends and ministry partners for many years, ended up separating their ministries over their different beliefs about election and predestination (see the letter from Whitefield to Wesley in appendix 1 of this book. Please don't fail to read it).

Controversies over defining the *correct* or *best* interpretation of election and predestination continue to this day without producing much fruit for the glory of God. Just spend some time interacting with believers on Facebook, for example, and you'll observe some vehement arguments over it. Friendships have been lost, Bible study groups divided, and even whole denominations have split into one or more sub denominations entirely over a group's particular convictions about election and predestination.

Because God is infinite and eternal, any truths revealed by Him are of the utmost importance to all humanity. These truths bring salvation, identity, morality, spirituality, a sense of destiny, and manifold blessings into our lives. Therefore, we must step up to the *study plate* and do our best to discern and grasp these truths. Election and predestination can help form the needed foundation for understanding almost every other doctrine in the Bible. Through comprehensive and balanced insights into election and predestination, we can understand the purposes of creation, history (His-Story), the development of languages, the rise and fall of nations, prophecy, evangelism and missions, and the unique roles of Jews and Gentiles in God's plan.

Therefore, the purpose of this book is to attempt to make these two doctrines as simple as possible, whereby the reader can see and appreciate the biblical purpose of and the value to humanity of election and predestination. This understanding can be an immediate revelation or perhaps an epiphany to the believer's soul or such understanding may come slowly—through a diligent, thorough, and prayerful study of Scripture. Consider Paul's exhortation to all Christians in 2 Timothy 2:15: "Be diligent to present yourself approved to God as a workman who does not need to be ashamed, accurately handling the word of truth" (NASB).

For genuine spiritual worship to occur in our hearts, we must feel a genuine gratitude to God. If we do not feel grateful, we will not worship in truth and spirit. Election can be the key to establishing permanent gratitude in our minds and hearts, which will become the foundation of our worship. A right perspective of election and predestination will bring great joy into our hearts and will produce great praise from our lips to God. My prayer for you as a reader is found in Ephesians 1:18 (NASB): "I pray that the eyes of your heart may be enlightened, so that you will know what is the hope of His calling, what are the riches of the glory of His inheritance in the saints."

So again, the goal of this book is to lay out the meanings of election and predestination in the simplest ways possible, so those who are open to it can embrace these truths and rejoice in gratitude and praise. For you as a reader of this book, freedom lies in the providence of God's choices and the grace He bestows upon us through these marvelous truths. The goal is not to present in great detail the many variations of interpretation, which have surfaced since the first century, or to share the many challenges to the historical orthodox definition of election and predestination. While a few examples of controversies will be mentioned for illustration sake, the goal is to unveil the simplest expressions of these two doctrines that best match the scriptural revelation when taken at face value (the simplest reading).

When a person becomes a Christian, reads Genesis 1, 2, and 3 for the first time, and simply accepts what the verses reveal about God's creation of the universe, it is natural for him or her to conclude that God created everything that exists in six literal days. Similarly, when a person becomes a Christian and reads the biblical texts referring to election and predestination for the first time, what conclusions do he or she come to on their own without outside influences? When new Christians read Ephesians 1 and Romans 8 for the first time, they usually conclude that God chose them to be saved, that the chosen ones became the elect, and that predestination brought the chosen ones (the elect) to salvation. Such is the plain, straightforward reading of the text, which causes a new or young Christian to rejoice exceedingly. This was my experience.

As a new Christian, I had never read any commentaries about Romans or Ephesians, nor had I read any systematic theology books on election and predestination, or topical books on the various attributes of God. I was simply devouring as much Scripture as I could, as one of those new born babes, craving the pure spiritual milk of the Word—which quickly turned into the solid spiritual meat of the Word.

Therefore, my convictions came from the Scriptures and not from commentaries. I really did not even know what a commentary was when I first got saved. Of course, as I grew in the faith, got involved with a church, and sat under the preaching and teaching of spiritual leaders, I began to hear about commentaries, Bible Dictionaries, and other useful study tools, but in the beginning, it was just the Holy Spirit teaching me from the Word itself. I would personally recommend this approach to any new Christian.

If you just came to Christ and want to experience solid spiritual growth, then please just read through the Bible two or three times on your own before considering the thoughts and words of men. Give the Holy Spirit the opportunity to be your exclusive teacher and tutor, like the apostle Paul did when he went out into the Arabian desert for three years just to be taught and mentored by Christ Himself (see Galatians 1:11–17).

My Story

I grew up in the First Christian Church (Disciples of Christ). My parents faithfully took me to Sunday School and church every week. I went to our church camp each summer. When I was twelve years of age, I went through our weeklong confirmation classes taught by our pastor. These classes were designed to help us understand the basic teachings of the church necessary to profess our faith in Christ and be baptized. At the end of these classes, we were each asked if we understood and believed what we had been taught and if we wanted to be baptized. Each of us in this small group affirmed our belief in what we had been taught and we were baptized. After baptism, we were allowed to take communion each week. All of these experiences make you feel like you are a Christian and a true member of the church. I have no way of knowing what was going on in the hearts and minds of my peers, who went through these classes with me, but something was still missing in my life, even though I did not realize it at the time.

I continued faithfully participating in our church throughout my high school years, but when my college years began, I fell away from morality and a presumed spirituality. My intellectual confessions of faith, baptism, church membership, communion, and acquired knowledge of the Bible did not dominate my life. My lusts took over as I pursued the pleasures of the world. I rarely went to church and never read my Bible. I got thoroughly acquainted with the world and loved it. I abused alcohol, drugs, and moral standards. After all of those years in a church environment, Christianity now had no hold on me. By my lifestyle and value system, I demonstrated that I was what the Bible calls "lost" in my sin. I never felt like I really knew the Lord personally anyway (I just knew what I had learned about Him), and my worldly pursuits took me further and further away from what I believed the Christian life should look like.

After trying to attend college for three semesters, my party life caused me to flunk out. The same semester I received my walking papers (the invitation from the college administration to not come back for at least a year).

Then the lottery system used by the military to draft people into service was initiated. My lottery number was nine, which meant I would be taken in the very first round of drafts. Out of a fear of getting drafted and sent to Vietnam, I worked up the courage to go down to my local army reserve unit and enlist in the US Army Reserves.

After attending boot camp and participating in eighteen months of weekend meetings and summer camps, my wild and rebellious ways caused me to fall out of grace with our local fulltime sergeant who managed our reserve unit. I was in constant trouble and I was certainly not enjoying it. I finally decided that I could not take another four and half years of this kind of bondage. So I boldly went into our sergeant's office and told him I wanted to volunteer for active duty, get out of my reserve status, and take my chances (as to where they might send me). The sergeant was already so disgusted with me that he told me he *would not* activate me. In other words, I was stuck with him. He did not refuse to activate me because he wanted me around or valued my service. He just did not like me and wanted to keep me in my misery. So he told me he would not activate me.

How did I respond? In all my wisdom, I told him on the spot that I was quitting and would never come back again. I walked out in a huff (AWOL). Nine months later, I received this huge yellow envelope in the mail. I had sincerely concluded that this sergeant and the army had forgotten about me and that I was home free, but this big yellow envelope told a different story. The very sight of it made my heart skip a beat. I finally mustered up the courage to read what were orders from Washington, DC, to report to Fort Dix, New Jersey, on a particular date to be flown to West Germany for two years of service.

As this news sunk in, I actually began to rejoice, and I actually remember thanking God for this news. Rather than my worst fears coming true (going to war in Vietnam), my greatest dream came true (getting to live in Europe for two years). I really got excited and somehow was able to give God all the credit for this opportunity, even though I was totally lost.

When I got to Germany, I was chosen by the captain of a Military Police Unit in Ansbach, Germany (close to the larger city of Nuremberg in Bavaria), to serve in his unit as a truck driver and supply clerk. I learned (about a year after getting to Ansbach) from a friend of mine also serving there, that some clerk in the states had accidentally put down in my records that I already had earned 115 semester hours of college, which would make me only five hours short of graduation, when in reality I only had about thirty hours of credit and had flunked out earlier. So I think this captain presumed I had promise. I got along great with him, worked hard for him, and was grateful to be in a good duty station.

When I arrived in Frankfurt, had my first German beer, and put my first coins into a slot machine on the base, I thought I had died and gone to heaven. I could not believe where I was and how much I liked it. From that first day in Deutschland, I pursued my pleasures and lusts with every bit of energy I had. Wine, women, and song were my life, and I traveled all over Europe and the Holy Land. From a worldly perspective, it was the best two years of my life. It was one constant party. I never went to church and I never had a discussion with any Christian.

About halfway through my tour in Germany, the Holy Spirit (completely on His own accord without human instruments involved) began convicting me in the deepness of my heart and spirit that I was a real sinner, separated from God, and could die and go straight to hell. I became conscious of my sin, my sin nature, and my rebellious ways as never before. The fear of God fell upon me as I began to realize how lost I was and how controlled I was by my fleshly and sinful ways. It got so bad that I would go back to my room in the barracks at night, after partying as hard as I could, and fall asleep crying over my sinfulness, begging God to have mercy on me.

I would tell God that I was lost and confessed that I did not know him, but I wanted to and I did not want to die and go to hell. The more I cried out to God during that last year in Germany, the deeper the conviction of the Holy Spirit got . . . to the point I thought I would die if I did not find out how to get right with God and find forgiveness and salvation. I thought many times about everything I had learned in church growing up and all my experiences with the church, but there was nothing in those memories to set me free, except the knowledge that Jesus Christ was the Savior according to the Bible. I also knew my grandmother had always prayed for me, but I did not know how to come to Jesus. I did not know how to ask for salvation and forgiveness.

This may seem like a simple thing, but when you are lost, you are lost. I was spiritually blind, deaf, lame, and mute. All that I did know (through the sovereign work of the Holy Spirit apart from any effort of other people, save the prayers of my grandmother and she had no idea what I was going through) was that I was totally lost and separated from God and that I wanted to be saved more than anything else in the world.

God in His wisdom allowed me to go on suffering in my lost state until the end of my tour in Germany. When it was time to be released and return home, I hoped that somehow the change in lifestyles and being back in my home environment might make things better, but it was not to be. The convictions and guilt only increased, and my crying out to God reached its zenith. I was either going to die or find the Lord. Finally four months after getting home and resuming college, one of my best friends growing up came back to town and made a point to contact me. Oscar Houchins (now Dr. Oscar Houchins) wanted to see me and catch up, but his real purpose was to let me know that he himself had become a Christian during my time overseas and he wanted to share the gospel with me.

Oscar had no idea about God's sovereign work of conviction in my life and how I had been crying out for the knowledge of how to be saved for the previous eighteen months. So he set about to explain the gospel in its fullness from Genesis to Revelation from 9:00 p.m. on a Friday night until 1:00 a.m. Saturday morning. After four hours of sharing what seemed to be every single Scripture related to becoming a Christian, he finally stopped and asked me if I wanted to call upon the Lord and be saved.

I told Oscar that I had been anxiously waiting the entire time for him to ask me this. So we both got down on our knees in his parents' living room and prayed together. He led me in a traditional sinner's prayer that many people are familiar with. I personally asked Jesus Christ to save me from my sinfulness, to forgive me for all my sins, and I begged Jesus to take over my life and be my Lord. I knew immediately in my spirit that Jesus had responded and cleansed me from all guilt and shame and had made me into that new creature that Paul talks about in 2 Corinthians 5:17. I have never been the same since. For the first time in my twenty-three years, I felt alive and free.

As I have thought about my salvation experience over the years, I am always overcome with such gratitude to God for how He interrupted my life of sin and pursuit of worldly pleasures and sovereignly produced (within the deepest parts of my soul and spirit) the proper fear of God, the deepest hunger, and thirst for righteousness possible. And then, just at the right time, He brought this good friend back into my life with the good news He had prepared my heart for. It was a divine experience from start to end and it would have never happened had God not taken the initiative. God also protected me from dying without Christ all those years I lived without Him. In my wild and rebellious ways, I was in near-death experiences three different times (that I'm aware of). I would have died, woken up in hell, spent the rest of eternity there, and as the Scriptures teach, I would have deserved it (Eph. 2:1–10), but God's mercy and grace protected me from dying as a lost person until He brought me to Christ.

As I read through Romans and Ephesians for the very first time as a baby Christian, I could clearly see how God had chosen me before the foundations of the world, faithfully worked to protect me along the way, and brought me to Christ just at the right time through the ministry of personal evangelism. It was a glorious revelation that has been the sweetest truth to my soul ever since. I pray that these glorious truths (doctrines) will become crystal clear and precious to your soul as you read through this book. The next chapter will be our diving board into the deep waters of election and predestination.

2 🙖

Basic Definitions

If you have an interest in exploring the concepts of election and predestination, you will find it an edifying pilgrimage—spiritually, morally, intellectually, and emotionally. This pilgrimage will not be a dry academic exercise. Election and predestination are two of the most fascinating and challenging doctrines in the Bible. Once a person understands the saving grace of God through Christ Jesus and recognizes His sovereign actions in drawing that person to Himself through the truth of the Word and the power of the Holy Spirit, these doctrines bring enormous comfort. Knowing that God loved you before the foundations of the world were set, that He sovereignly chose you in eternity past to live and worship Him for the rest of eternity, and that Jesus' death paid the just penalty for your sinful nature and sins in God's sovereign plan brings not only comfort, but a new recognition of freedom, reassurance, and liberty.

To help pave the way for your pilgrimage, certain definitions will be helpful. Therefore, this chapter offers basic, but critical definitions of those concepts directly related to the doctrines of election and predestination. Appropriate Bible verses are given along with each definition. After establishing these definitions, the following chapters are intended to help the reader grasp a practical understanding and appreciation of these difficult ideas. The more time a person takes studying the definitions, the more sense the remaining chapters will make.

The words *election* and *predestination* are used interchangeably in many places, but there is a scriptural difference in the two concepts. The two concepts complement each other, and will be explained and illustrated. Election lays the foundation for predestination and predestination fulfills election.

The specific words defined below will be seen throughout the book in various Scriptures, illustrations, and applications. The many Bible verses listed throughout the book are listed specifically for the reader to see how the Bible addresses these doctrines in such detail.

"Election"

Elect (*eklektos*) means picked out or chosen by God to obtain salvation through Christ. Christians are called the "chosen or elect" of God (*The NAS New Testament Greek Lexicon*).

Election refers to the choice God (referring to the Triune Godhead) made before the creation of the universe to save particular individuals among the billions who would live throughout history. His choices were made completely according to His own wisdom and pleasure. His choices had nothing to do with any intrinsic value of those chosen (the elect). His choices ensure the unconditional salvation of these individuals through the logistics of predestination.

The doctrine of election, as seen throughout the Bible from Genesis to Revelation, is applied to angels, the nation of Israel, and individual people. The simplest definition of election is that God decided beforehand (before He created anything) what He wanted to do regarding His dealings with angels, the nation of Israel, and individual people throughout history. Predestination carries out the plans needed for the elect to be saved. Both election and predestination are a part of God's eternal decree. His eternal decree established the framework for how history would be played out in a way that God's perfect will (from an eternal perspective) would be accomplished.

Several verses describe election:

How blessed is the one whom You choose and bring near to You to dwell in Your courts. We will be satisfied with the goodness of Your house, Your holy temple. (Psalm 65:4)

Remember the former things long past, for I am God and there is no other. I am God and there is no one like Me, declaring the end from the beginning, and from ancient times things which have not been done, saying, "My purpose will be established and I will accomplish all My good pleasure, calling a bird of prey from the east and the man of My purpose from a far country. Truly I have spoken. Truly I will bring it to pass. I have planned it. Surely I will do it." (Isaiah 46:9–13)

For many are called, but few are chosen. (Matthew 22:14)

Unless those days had been cut short, no life would have been saved, but for the sake of the elect those days will be cut short. (Matthew 24:22)

You did not choose Me, but I chose you and appointed you that you would go and bear fruit and that your fruit would remain, so that whatever you ask of the Father in My name He may give to you. (John 15:16)

What then shall we say to these things? If God is for us, who is against us? He who did not spare His own Son, but delivered Him over for us all, how will He not also with Him freely give us all things? Who will bring a charge against God's elect? God is the one who justifies. Who is the one who condemns? Christ Jesus is He who died, yes, rather who was raised, who is at the right hand of God, who also intercedes for us. Who will separate us from the love of Christ? Will tribulation or distress or persecution or famine or nakedness or peril or sword? (Romans 8:31–35)

For though the twins were not yet born and had not done anything good or bad, so that God's purpose according to His choice (election) would stand, not because of works but because of Him who calls, it was said to her, "The older will serve the younger." Just as it is written, "Jacob I loved, but Esau I hated." What shall we say then? There is no injustice with God, is there? May it never be! For He says to Moses, "I will have mercy on whom I have mercy, and I will have compassion on whom I have compassion." So then, it does not depend on the man who wills or the man who runs, but on God who has mercy. For the Scripture says to Pharaoh, "For this very purpose I raised you up, to demonstrate My power in you and that My name might be proclaimed throughout the whole earth." So then, He has mercy on whom He desires, and He hardens whom He desires. (Romans 9:11–18)

In the same way then, there has also come to be at the present time a remnant according to God's gracious choice. But if it is by grace, it is no longer on the basis of works, otherwise grace is no longer grace. What then? What Israel is seeking, it has not obtained, but those who were chosen obtained it and the rest were hardened. (Romans 11:5–7)

Just as He chose us in Him before the foundation of the world, that we would be holy and blameless before Him. (Ephesians 1:4)

So as those who have been chosen of God, holy and beloved, put on a heart of compassion, kindness, humility, gentleness and patience. (Colossians 3:12)

Paul and Silvanus and Timothy, To the church of the Thessalonians in God the Father and the Lord Jesus Christ: Grace to you and peace. We give thanks to God always for all of you, making mention of you in our prayers, constantly bearing in mind your work of faith and labor of love and steadfastness of hope in our Lord Jesus Christ in the presence of our God and Father, knowing, brethren beloved by God, His choice of you. (1 Thessalonians 1:1–4)

Paul, a bondservant of God and an apostle of Jesus Christ, for the faith of those chosen of God and the knowledge of the truth which is according to godliness. (Titus 1:1)

But you are a chosen race, a royal priesthood, a holy nation, a people for God's own possession, so that you may proclaim the excellencies of Him who has called you out of darkness into His marvelous light. (1 Peter 2:9)

Consider *Morning and Evening: Daily Readings* by C. H. Spurgeon (©2008 Wilder Publications) and his short devotion called "His Chosen Ones," based on Psalm 48:14:

In the very beginning, when this great universe was in the mind of God, like unborn forests in a cup of acorns, long before the echoes walked in the quiet solitudes, before the mountains were brought forth, and long before the light flashed through the sky, God loved His chosen men and women.

Before there were men and women—when the heavens were not yet fanned by an angel's wing, when space itself did not exist, when there was nothing but God alone. Even then, when there was only that deep quiet and depth of Deity, His heart moved for His chosen ones. Their names were written on His heart and they became dear to His soul. For this God is our God for ever and ever and He will be our guide even to the end.

"Predestination"

The English word *predestination* is made up of two words. The first part is "pre," which means "before or beforehand." The second part of the word is *destination* which means "the climax, end, or farthest extent." The word *pre* has to do with something beforehand. The word *destination* has to do with the farthest extent of a planned trip. The precise meaning of *predestination* conveys something beforehand along with the farthest end of a process or trip in mind.

The English word *predestination* comes from the Greek word *proorizo*, which occurs six times in the New Testament, each time demonstrating that God is the one who is bringing about certain events according to His foreknowledge. Predestination refers to all of the plans, processes, and providential care, planned beforehand and executed in time, needed to bring the elect to eternal salvation in Jesus Christ. When God ordained the salvation of the elect, He also ordained the means to bring them to saving faith in Christ. Predestination includes *all* of those means.

In the passage below we see *election* in the phrase "for those who He foreknew." God foreknew the elect because He chose them. Once He chose them, they were forever known to Him as the elect. The rest of the precious words in this passage, after the phrase "for those whom He foreknew," refer to *predestination* or all of the plans and processes (the means) involved in bringing the elect to salvation. Several verses describe this:

And we know that God causes all things to work together for good to those who love God, to those who are called according to His purpose. For those whom He foreknew, He also predestined to become conformed to the image of His Son, so that He would be the firstborn among many brethren and these whom He predestined, He also called and these whom He called, He also justified and these whom He justified, He also glorified. What then shall we say to these things? If God is for us, who is against us? He who did not spare His own Son, but delivered Him over for us all, how will He not also with Him freely give us all things? Who will bring a charge against God's elect? God is the one who justifies. Who is the one who condemns? Christ Jesus is He who died, yes, rather who was raised, who is at the right hand of God, who also intercedes for us. Who will separate us from the love of Christ? Will tribulation or distress or persecution or famine or nakedness or peril or sword? Just as it is written, "For Your sake we are being put to death all day long. We were considered as sheep to be slaughtered." But in all these things we overwhelmingly conquer through Him who loved us. For I am convinced that neither death, nor life, nor angels, nor principalities, nor things present, nor things to come, nor powers, nor height, nor depth, nor any other created thing, will be able to separate us from the love of God, which is in Christ Jesus our Lord. (Romans 8:28–39)

Yet we do speak wisdom among those who are mature, a wisdom, however, not of this age nor of the rulers of this age, who are passing away. But we speak God's wisdom in a mystery, the hidden wisdom which God predestined before the ages to our glory, the wisdom which none of the rulers of this age has understood, for if they had understood it they would not have crucified the Lord of glory. (1 Corinthians 2:6–8)

In love, He predestined us to adoption as sons through Jesus Christ to Himself, according to the kind intention of His will, to the praise of the glory of His grace, which He freely bestowed on us in the Beloved. (Ephesians 1:5–6)

Also, we have obtained an inheritance, having been predestined according to His purpose who works all things after the counsel of His will, to the end that we who were the first to hope in Christ would be to the praise of His glory. In Him, you also, after listening to the message of truth, the gospel of your salvation—having also believed, you were sealed in Him with the Holy Spirit of promise, who is given as a pledge of our inheritance, with a view to the redemption of God's own possession, to the praise of His glory. (Ephesians 1:11)

But we should always give thanks to God for you, brethren beloved by the Lord, because God has chosen you from the beginning for salvation through sanctification by the Spirit and faith in the truth. It was for this He called you through our gospel, that you may gain the glory of our Lord Jesus Christ. (2 Thessalonians 2:13–14)

Peter, an apostle of Jesus Christ, to those who reside as aliens, scattered throughout Pontus, Galatia, Cappadocia, Asia, and Bithynia, who are chosen according to the foreknowledge of God the Father, by the sanctifying work of the Spirit, to obey Jesus Christ and be sprinkled with His blood. May grace and peace be yours in the fullest measure. (1 Peter 1:1–3)

"Foreknowledge"

Foreknowledge comes from the Greek words translated *foreknow* (the verb *proginosko)* and *foreknowledge* (the noun *prognosis).* The verb *proginosko* has the basic meaning of "to know beforehand" or "to know in advance" and the noun *prognosis* simply means "foreknowledge" (cf. Bauer, Arndt, Gingrich, *A Greek-English Lexicon of the New Testament and Other Early Christian Literature*). Reformed scholar Loraine Boettner[3] makes the point that what is foreknown is foreordained:

Now if future events are foreknown to God, they cannot by any possibility take a turn contrary to His knowledge. If the course of future events is foreknown, history will follow that course as definitely as a locomotive follows the rails from New York to Chicago. The Arminian doctrine, in rejecting foreordination, rejects the theistic basis for foreknowledge. Common sense tells us that no event can be foreknown unless by some means, either physical or mental, it has been predetermined. Our choice as to what determines the certainty of future events narrows down to two alternatives—the foreordination of the wise and merciful heavenly Father or the working of blind physical fate.

---

[3] Loraine Boettner (March 7, 1901–January 3, 1990) was an American theologian, teacher, and author in the Reformed tradition. He is best known for his works on predestination, Roman Catholicism, and postmillennial eschatology.

Millard Erickson[4] expands upon the idea that what is foreknown is foreordained and relates it to human freedom:

It should be noted that if certainty of outcome is inconsistent with freedom, divine foreknowledge, as the Arminian understands that term, presents as much difficulty for human freedom as does divine foreordination. For if God knows what I will do, it must be certain that I am going to do it. If it were not certain, God could not know it; He might be mistaken (I might act differently from what He expects). But if what I will do is certain, then surely I will do it, whether or not I know what I will do. It will happen! But am I then free? In the view of those whose definition of freedom entails the implication that it cannot be certain that a particular event will occur, presumably I am not free. In their view, divine foreknowledge is just as incompatible with human freedom as is divine foreordination. This line of theological reasoning can be illustrated in the following syllogism:

- What is foreknown is fixed.
- What is fixed is certain.
- What is certain is predestined.
- What is foreknown is predestined.

Jesus Christ was crucified according to the foreknowledge of God (1 Peter 1:20; Acts 2:23). Does foreknowledge in this context mean that God had no absolute plan or no causative personal relationship to the mission of the Second Person of the Trinity, Jesus Christ? It would be absurd to deny causation here. In the same way, divine foreknowledge as it relates to any element of God's predetermined purpose, must relate to God's active involvement in bringing the event to pass. God's foreknowledge demonstrates His love. Just as Jesus Christ was "foreknown" by God (1 Peter 1:20) in the sense that God has eternally set His love upon Him, believers have been foreknown by God in that He has eternally set His love upon them (Romans 8:29). God's foreknowledge demonstrates His sovereignty. God's omnipotent sovereignty entails more than His omniscience. God is not simply "looking ahead" and planning His course accordingly. His plan is unconditional and complete according to His good pleasure (cf. Ephesians 1:2ff).

God's foreknowledge demonstrates His personal care. Predestination apart from foreknowledge might imply impersonal fatalism. However, God is not a God of impersonal fatalism, but a God who is intimately involved with His creation and in His plans for it.

---

[4] Millard J. Erickson (June 1932—) is a Protestant Christian theologian, professor of theology, and author. He has written the widely acclaimed 1,312-page systematics work, *Christian Theology* as well as over twenty other books. Currently, Erickson is Distinguished Professor of Theology at Western Seminary in Portland, Oregon.

Below are some verses that talk about foreknowledge:

Known unto God are all his works from the beginning of the world. (Acts 15:18, KJV)

This Man, delivered over by the predetermined plan and foreknowledge of God, you nailed to a cross by the hands of godless men and put Him to death. (Acts 2:23)

And we know that God causes all things to work together for good to those who love God, to those who are called according to His purpose. For those whom He foreknew, He also predestined to become conformed to the image of His Son, so that He would be the firstborn among many brethren. (Romans 8:28–29)

For as many as are the promises of God, in Him they are yes; therefore, also through Him is our Amen to the glory of God through us. (2 Corinthians 1:20)

He made known to us the mystery of His will, according to His kind intention which He purposed in Him. (Ephesians 1:9)

This was in accordance with the eternal purpose which He carried out in Christ Jesus our Lord. (Ephesians 3:11)

"Decree"

God's *decree* is also called His *counsel* to signify consummate wisdom. Each is called God's *will* to show He was under no external controls, but acted according to His own pleasure and wisdom. God was alone when He made His decree and His determinations were not influenced by any external cause. There was no one else around. He was free to decree or not to decree, and to decree one thing and not another. This liberty and freedom flow from the only eternal being who has ever existed and who is supreme, independent, and sovereign in His nature and in all His doings.

The Lord of hosts has sworn saying, "Surely, just as I have intended so it has happened, and just as I have planned so it will stand." (Isaiah 14:24)

Who has directed the Spirit of the Lord or as His counselor has informed Him? With whom did He consult and who gave Him understanding? And who taught Him in the path of justice and taught Him knowledge and informed Him of the way of understanding? (Isaiah 40:13–14)

The execution of God's eternal decree is absolute and unconditional. It does not depend upon any condition which may or may not be performed. In every case where God has decreed an end, He has also decreed every means needed to bring about that end. The One who decreed the salvation of His elect also decreed to work out the needed faith in them.

> But we should always give thanks to God for you, brethren beloved by the Lord, because God has chosen you from the beginning for salvation through sanctification by the Spirit and faith in the truth. (2 Thessalonians 2:13)

> Declaring the end from the beginning and from ancient times things which have not been done, saying, "My purpose will be established, and I will accomplish all My good pleasure." (Isaiah 46:10)

God's wisdom is always associated with "His will" in His divine proceedings. Therefore, God's decree is said to be "the counsel of His own will" in Ephesians 1:11. Ephesians 1:11–12 says, "Also, we have obtained an inheritance, having been predestined according to His purpose who works all things after the counsel of His will, to the end that we who were the first to hope in Christ would be to the praise of His glory."

The decree of God always relates to future things throughout the scope of history, so that whatever is done in time, was foreordained before time began. God's purpose was concerned with everything, no matter how big or small, or how seemingly great or insignificant.

God's eternal purposes are as comprehensive as the logistics implemented to fulfill them. They extend to all creatures and all events including our life and death, our time in history, and our state in eternity. As God works out all things according to the counsel of His own will, we learn His counsel from His works, just as we would evaluate a ship builder's plan by inspecting the ship that was constructed according to his directions and blueprint.

The next chapter studies the connection between God's attributes and the doctrines of election and predestination.

3

How God's Power and Attributes Relate to the Doctrines of Election and Predestination

As the previous chapter introduced the basic doctrines themselves in a brief manner, so we should continue to explore scriptural truths that unearth the treasures of God's nature as His attributes and actions form the necessity of the doctrines. Once any believer begins to realize that these doctrines of election and predestination are necessary truths required by God's very being, nature, and attributes as taught in the Scriptures, then the person's spirit is freed from the old ways of thinking, and that freedom results in a freeing of the person's spirit to serve the great, mighty, and sovereign God.

"Prophecy"

Prophecy is the verbal or written expression (manifestation) of God's eternal and perfect foreknowledge within His divine omniscience. Prophecy is the prediction of a future event that is revealed to a designated prophet, so that the prophet can either speak the prophecy to a targeted audience or send the prophecy in written form to a targeted audience.

2 Peter 1:20–21 (NASB) says, "But know this first of all, that no prophecy (*propheteia*)

---

of Scripture is a matter of one's own interpretation, for no prophecy was ever made by an act of human will, but men moved by the Holy Spirit spoke from God."

In the verse above the English word "prophecy" is translated from the Greek word *propheteia*. The Greek word refers to the divine gift of communicating revealed truth. *Strong's Greek Concordance* provides the following information on the word *propheteia*:

> *Prophēteía* comes from *prophḗtēs* (prophet), which is derived from *pró* (meaning "before") and *phēmí* (meaning to make clear or assert as a priority)—properly, what is clarified *before*hand; *prophecy* which involves divinely empowered *forthtelling* (asserting the mind of God) or *foretelling* (prediction).

Dr. Paige Patterson explains prophecy like this:

> The word prophecy arises from a combination of "speak" (phemi) and "before" (pro). An important use of the word essentially means to "speak for God before." *Before what?* is an appropriate question. One sense of the preposition (pro) would be to speak about an event before it happens. Another sense would be to speak before listeners of the purpose and acts of God. (*Revelation: An Exegetical and Theological Exposition of Holy Scripture,* New American Commentary [B & H Publishing 2012], p. 346.)

Scripture reveals and affirms that those who become believers were in fact chosen in Christ before the world began and given grace to repent of their sinfulness and commit their lives to the Lordship of Jesus Christ.

> Blessed be the God and Father of our Lord Jesus Christ, who has blessed us with every spiritual blessing in the heavenly places in Christ, just as He chose us in Him before the foundation of the world, that we would be holy and blameless before Him. In love, He predestined us to adoption as sons through Jesus Christ to Himself, according to the kind intention of His will, to the praise of the glory of His grace, which He freely bestowed on us in the Beloved. (Ephesians 1:3–6)

> Therefore, do not be ashamed of the testimony of our Lord or of me His prisoner, but join with me in suffering for the gospel according to the power of God, who has saved us and called us with a holy calling, not according to our works, but according to His own purpose and grace which was granted us in Christ Jesus from all eternity, but now has been revealed by the appearing of our Savior Christ Jesus, who abolished death and brought life

and immortality to light through the gospel, for which I was appointed a preacher and an apostle and a teacher. (2 Timothy 1:9)

"Omniscience"

The Greek word for *omniscience* is "πάνσοφος" pronounced *pansofos*. In Latin, "omnis" means "all" and "sciens" means "knowing." "Omniscience" is the capacity to know everything that there is to know. Some theologians make a distinction between "inherent omniscience" and "total omniscience."

Inherent Omniscience is the ability to know anything that one chooses to know. In this scenario, God chooses to limit His omniscience in order to preserve the freewill and dignity of His creatures.

Total Omniscience is actually knowing everything that can be known. In this scenario, God is omniscient in the total sense without interfering with the free will and dignity of His creatures.

I believe the concept of *total omniscience* is the biblical model, as the following Scripture passages demonstrate:

If there is famine in the land, if there is pestilence, if there is blight or mildew, locust or grasshopper, if their enemy besieges them in the land of their cities, whatever plague, whatever sickness there is, whatever prayer or supplication is made by any man or by all Your people Israel, each knowing the affliction of his own heart, and spreading his hands toward this house; then hear in heaven Your dwelling place, and forgive and act and render to each according to all his ways, whose heart You know, for You alone know the hearts of all the sons of men, that they may fear You all the days that they live in the land which You have given to our fathers. (1 Kings 8:37–40)

Do you not know? Have you not heard? The Everlasting God, the Lord, the Creator of the ends of the earth does not become weary or tired. His understanding is inscrutable. (Isaiah 40:28)

O Lord, how many are Your works! In wisdom, You have made them all. The earth is full of Your possessions. (Psalm 104:24)

Great is our Lord and abundant in strength. His understanding is infinite. (Psalm 147:5)

O Lord, You have searched me and known me. You know when I sit down and when I rise up. You understand my thought from afar. You scrutinize my path and my lying down and are intimately acquainted with all my ways. Even before there is a word on my tongue, Behold, O Lord, You know it all. You have enclosed me behind and before and laid Your hand upon me. Such knowledge is too wonderful for me. It is too high. I cannot attain to it. (Psalm 139:1–6)

He counts the number of the stars. He gives names to all of them. Great is our Lord and abundant in strength. His understanding is infinite. (Psalm 147:4–5)

Behold, the former things have come to pass. Now I declare new things. Before they spring forth I proclaim them to you. (Isaiah 42:9)

Remember the former things long past, for I am God, and there is no other. I am God and there is no one like Me, declaring the end from the beginning and from ancient times things which have not been done saying, "My purpose will be established and I will accomplish all My good pleasure, calling a bird of prey from the east, the man of My purpose from a far country. Truly I have spoken. Truly I will bring it to pass. I have planned it. Surely, I will do it." (Isaiah 46:9–11)

Oh, the depth of the riches both of the wisdom and knowledge of God! How unsearchable are His judgments and unfathomable His ways! For who has known the mind of the Lord or who became His counselor? Or who has first given to Him that it might be paid back to him again? For from Him and through Him and to Him are all things. To Him be the glory forever. Amen. (Romans 11:33–36)

For by Him all things were created, both in the heavens and on earth, visible and invisible, whether thrones or dominions or rulers or authorities—all things have been created through Him and for Him. (Colossians 1:16)

Just as God's prophetic power and His omniscient nature point to His *ability* to know and to prophesy the future work of Christ, the believer's election to salvation, and make these truths known through His revelation in the Holy Scriptures and the life and works of Jesus Christ, so also His other attributes point to the necessity of His election of His saints to such salvation. These truths become necessities because of His nature, as we shall continue to unearth the "treasures" of His divine character from His Word.

"Omnipotence"

The original Greek word for *omnipotence* is παντοκράτωρ translated "all mighty" or "omnipotent." The Latin word for *omnipotence* comes from *Omni Potens* meaning "all *power*" or "unlimited power." Another biblical word conveying the unlimited power of God is "almighty." Therefore, some of the Scriptures below are those where God is referred to as "God Almighty" revealing that His might or power has no limits.

Now when Abram was ninety-nine years old, the Lord appeared to Abram and said to him, "I am God Almighty. Walk before Me and be blameless." (Genesis 17:1)

May God Almighty bless you and make you fruitful and multiply you, that you may become a company of peoples. (Genesis 28:3)

And I appeared to Abraham, Isaac, and Jacob, as God Almighty, but by My name, Lord, I did not make Myself known to them. (Exodus 6:3)

I know that You can do all things and that no purpose of Yours can be thwarted. (Job 42:2)

Let all the earth fear the Lord. Let all the inhabitants of the world stand in awe of Him. For He spoke, and it was done. He commanded and it stood fast. (Psalm 33:8–9)

All the inhabitants of the earth are accounted as nothing, but He does according to His will in the host of heaven and among the inhabitants of earth and no one can ward off His hand or say to Him, "What have You done?" (Daniel 4:35)

Behold, I am the Lord, the God of all flesh! Is anything too difficult for Me? (Jeremiah 32:27)

This is the plan devised against the whole earth and this is the hand that is stretched out against all the nations. For the Lord of hosts has planned and who can frustrate it? And as for His stretched out hand, who can turn it back? (Isaiah 14:26–27)

Thus says the Lord, your Redeemer and the one who formed you from the womb, "I the Lord, am the maker of all things, stretching out the heavens by Myself and spreading out the earth all alone." (Isaiah 44:24)

Moreover, the sound of the wings of the cherubim was heard as far as the outer court, like the voice of God Almighty when He speaks. (Ezekiel 10:5)

For since the creation of the world His invisible attributes, His eternal power and divine nature, have been clearly seen, being understood through what has been made, so that they are without excuse. (Romans 1:20)

As it is written, "A father of many nations have I made you" in the presence of Him whom he believed, even God, who gives life to the dead and calls into being that which does not exist. (Romans 4:17)

And He is the radiance of His glory and the exact representation of His nature, and upholds all things by the word of His power. When He had made purification of sins, He sat down at the right hand of the Majesty on high. (Hebrews 1:3)

We give You thanks, O Lord God, the Almighty, who are and who were, because You have taken Your great power and have begun to reign. (Revelation 11:17)

And they sang the song of Moses, the bondservant of God, and the song of the Lamb, saying, "Great and marvelous are Your works, O Lord God, the Almighty. Righteous and true are Your ways, King of the nations!" (Revelation 15:3)

And I heard the altar saying, "Yes, O Lord God, the Almighty, true and righteous are Your judgments." (Revelation 16:7)

And I heard as it were the voice of a great multitude and as the voice of many waters and as the voice of mighty thunderings, saying "Alleluia," for the Lord God omnipotent reigneth. (Revelation 19:6, KJV)

I saw no temple in it, for the Lord God the Almighty and the Lamb are its temple. (Revelation 21:22)

At this point you may feel more freedom in your belief in the work of Christ on your behalf, His sacrifice of His blood on that cross at Calvary to satisfy God's wrath, and that He paid the penalty God required for your reconciliation to Him. These things were necessary to satisfy God's very holy nature and His omniscient and all-powerful character, since apart from His work on our behalf, we would never have believed. We are shown God's nature and His plan from before Creation to glorify Himself through the work of His Son. These are very satisfying truths that reveal His great love for His chosen people. Let's continue to explore His nature and attributes to further our understanding of His plan and its reflection of His character.

"Omnipresent"

The Greek words for *omnipresent* are πανταχού παρών pronounced "pantachou paron." The Latin words for *omnipresent* are "*omni*present." "Omnipresent" means being present everywhere at the same time. God's "omnipresence" is mostly understood through the presence of the Holy Spirit throughout the universe. The Spirit of God, as the third personality of the Triune Godhead, is everywhere outside of the created universe and everywhere inside of the created universe. He is simply everywhere at the same time. We refer to God and His Spirit as infinite or without any finite or measurable limits.

Rev. Thomas Tyree, Jr.[5] is a pastor respected for his detailed teachings from the original languages. He sums it up this way:

> Omnipresence does not imply that God is spread out or diffused throughout the universe in that only part of Him is everywhere. This is erroneous thinking. He is wholly present as fully as if He were in only one place. God completely fills the entire universe and all aspects of it without diffusion, expansion, multiplication, or division. The Father, Son, and Holy Spirit are fully present in every minute part of His infinite dominion. This is known as God's immanence. God is everywhere and in all things simultaneously in His totality and with all of His perfect attributes. Whether it is the atmosphere, stratosphere, ionosphere, or throughout space, God is there. No matter how far you go out in space or even into heaven, God is there. God is in His heaven. God is throughout space. God is throughout our stratosphere, our ionosphere, and our atmosphere. God is everywhere, even in the depths of the ocean and in the depths of the earth. You cannot hide from God and God never hides from any of us.

---

[5] Thomas Tyree, Jr. is Pastor-Teacher of the Grace Bible Church of Costa Mesa, California, which he founded in 1972. Pastor Tyree received his academic preparation at Biola College with graduate work at Talbot Theological Seminary. Prior to completing his theological training, he served his country in the US Air Force during the Korean War. With his academic training, Pastor Tyree teaches from the Scripture based on the original languages of the Bible. Through his continual studies over the past 30 years, he has developed a teaching style that emphasizes the application of Bible truth to the believer's spiritual way of living. Pastor Tyree considers the preaching and teaching of God's Word an inestimable privilege and he has faithfully endeavored to communicate Bible doctrine accurately as the divinely inspired inerrant Word of God for mankind.

The following verses refer to the "omnipresence" of God:

But will God indeed dwell on the earth? Behold, heaven and the highest heaven cannot contain You, how much less this house which I have built! (1 Kings 8:27)

For the eyes of the Lord move to and fro throughout the earth that He may strongly support those whose heart is completely His. (2 Chronicles 16:9)

For His eyes are upon the ways of a man and He sees all his steps. There is no darkness or deep shadow where the workers of iniquity may hide themselves. (Job 34:21–22)

The Lord is in His holy temple. The Lord's throne is in heaven. His eyes behold. His eyelids test the sons of men. (Psalm 11:4)

Where can I go from Your Spirit? Or where can I flee from Your presence? If I ascend to heaven, You are there. If I make my bed in Sheol, behold, You are there. If I take the wings of the dawn, If I dwell in the remotest part of the sea, even there Your hand will lead me and Your right hand will lay hold of me. If I say, "Surely the darkness will overwhelm me and the light around me will be night, even the darkness is not dark to You and the night is as bright as the day. Darkness and light are alike to You." (Psalm 139:7–12)

The eyes of the Lord are in every place, watching the evil and the good. (Proverbs 15:3)

"Am I a God who is near, declares the Lord, and not a God far off? Can a man hide himself in hiding places so I do not see him?" declares the Lord. "Do I not fill the heavens and the earth?" declares the Lord. (Jeremiah 23:23–24)

The God who made the world and all things in it, since He is Lord of heaven and earth, does not dwell in temples made with hands, nor is He served by human hands, as though He needed anything, since He Himself gives to all people life and breath and all things. And He made from one man every nation of mankind to live on all the face of the earth, having determined their appointed times and the boundaries of their habitation, that they would seek God, if perhaps they might grope for Him and find Him, though He is not far from each one of us. For in Him we live and move and exist, as even some of your own poets have said, "For we also are His children." (Acts 17:24–28)

The word "od" (noun) is kind of an illustration from nature of God's "omnipresence." The word "od" (also listed as "ohd") is defined as a hypothetical force formerly held to pervade all nature and to manifest itself in magnetism, mesmerism, chemical action, etc . . . The term "od" was coined by the German chemist and philosopher Karl Ludwig von Reichenbach as a name for his hypothetical force. He proposed the name "od," because he thought a short word starting with a vowel would be more easily combined in compound words. Reichenbach's concept of "the Odic force" was an impersonal force like gravity, whereas the Holy Spirit and His omnipresence are completely personal, with all of the attributes of the Triune God, applied to every spiritual, moral, psychological, and physical element in the created order.

I would like to use an illustration from twenty-first century cell phone/satellite technology as a very simple analogy of God's Omnipresence. I have enjoyed using an iPhone for many years now and one of the most fascinating things for me, is to be able to punch a button and ask Siri for directions, for the location of certain facilities, the weather, the time, or whatever. People have also been highly entertained on long road trips by asking Siri silly questions just to see how she will answer. Below are a few examples:

Siri, where do you live?
Siri, do you love me?
Siri, when are we going to get married?
Siri, how old are you?
Siri, how many languages can you speak?

(You get the point—if you have an iPhone, you have likely done this in some form or fashion.)

On my last road trip, I needed to ask Siri if she could tell me how much time it would take to drive to my next stop. As Siri was answering me, I was getting out of my car at a gas station, and I noticed about three, maybe four other people close by who were all talking to Siri about their own unique need for whatever.

And then it hit me. How easy it is for anyone in the world with an iPhone to talk to Siri anytime day or night at the exact same time anyone else was talking with Siri (and you thought she was just sitting there waiting for you to ask her something), wherever they were in the world, all because of constant technology continually in use around the world and always available to iPhone users. Right there before me, three or four different people who did not know each other, were all talking with Siri at the same time and getting different answers according to their needs. I was captivated by it. It was like Siri had her own form of omnipresence. From there of course, my thoughts were overwhelmed with how easy it is for our sovereign, omnipotent, omniscient, omnipresent God to hear every person in the world, at the same time, and respond to them according to their needs.

If you are at home, not traveling and don't need your iPhone, you can use Google to do the same and get written answers to your questions. The Lord can place His answer to you in your thoughts (your mental inbox), whisper it in your ear (your spiritual hearing aid), or speak audibly to you or speak through another person to you or write His answer in the clouds for you to read, if He chose to do so. It is all up to how He chooses to communicate with you when you talk to Him.

Psalm 34:15 (NASB) says, "The eyes of the LORD are toward the righteous and His ears are open to their cry," and 1 Peter 3:12 (NASB) says, "For the *eyes* of the LORD are toward the righteous, and His *ears* attend to their prayer, but the *face* of the LORD is against those who do evil" (emphasis mine).

I really hope, sometime, a Christ-led and Spirit-filled geek will research and write a huge book on all of the ways he or she can find how twenty-first century technology illustrates God's mighty attributes. Each technology has its own special focus and uniqueness, which illustrate a little minute part of one of God's attributes, while God has them all and in full force at all times. His divine intelligence flows down into and is revealed by every aspect of discovered and developed technologies, as mankind continues to take dominion over the earth (and now a little slice of space)—as commanded in Genesis, "Be fruitful and multiply and take dominion over the earth (and its resources)." What a read that would be.

Take heart, my friend—the Lord can hear you! The next chapter addresses which attribute of God makes the doctrine of election possible?

4 ✦

The Ultimate Attribute of God Making the Doctrine of Election Possible: "Sovereignty"

We have observed the amazing knowledge, power, and presence of God in His cosmos—His creation, including His actions before the creation. Now we shall unearth the ultimate treasure to complete our overview of the most relevant attributes of God's character that support the doctrines of election and predestination, in this case, His rulership of the entire cosmos. He is Lord over all!

The Hebrew word *adonai,* translated "Lord," and the Greek word *kurios,* also translated "Lord," both express the concept of "sovereignty" as we see in 1 Timothy 6:13–16:

> I charge you in the presence of God, who gives life to all things, and of Christ Jesus, who testified the good confession before Pontius Pilate, that you keep the commandment without stain or reproach until the appearing of our Lord Jesus Christ, which He will bring about at the proper time—He who is the blessed and only Sovereign, the King of kings and Lord of lords, who alone possesses immortality and dwells in unapproachable light, whom no man has seen or can see. To Him be honor and eternal dominion! Amen.

The Greek word *dunastēs* is translated "sovereign" (in the above verse). *Dunastēs* means ruler or potentate. The word *dunastēs* come from the root word *dunamai,* which is defined by the *NAS New Testament Greek Lexicon* as:

- strength, power, ability
- inherent power, power residing in a thing by virtue of its nature, or which a person or thing exerts and puts forth power for performing miracles
- moral power and excellence of soul
- the power and influence which belong to riches and wealth
- power and resources arising from numbers
- power consisting in or resting upon armies, forces, hosts

The English word "dynamite" also comes from the Greek word *dunamai. Webster's Collegiate Dictionary* lists these definitions of "sovereignty":

a. supreme power, dominion
b. undisputed ascendancy, dominance
c. unlimited extent, absolute
d. autonomy, independence, absolutely free
e. superlative quality, excellent
f. unqualified, unmitigated, unconditional

Sovereignty means that God, as the creator and ruler of the universe, has the absolute *right* to do whatever He wants with His creation. He is in complete control over everything that happens. Nothing happens without His direction or His permission.

His sovereignty represents His ability to exercise His holy will or supremacy. As the Most High God and Lord of heaven and earth, He has unlimited power to do what He has resolved. God is absolutely independent and does as He pleases. Nothing can deter Him or hinder Him. Romans 8:28 tells us in the NASB that "we know how God causes all things to work together for good for those who love Him and for those who are called according to His purpose." This concept could simply not be true if God was not totally sovereign. It just wouldn't work. If He does not control everything and have power over everything, He just could not make all things work for good for any of us. Being 99% sovereign, like a monarch having control over 99% of his country, would not work. The 1% that a monarch did not have control over could thwart his ability to do as he pleases or thought best for his country and his subjects. If God only had control over 99% of His creation (the universe and its inhabitants), then the 1% He did not control could thwart His plans for the 99% He did control. His total sovereignty is the basis of His ability to fulfill Romans 8:28 in our lives.

Many years ago, I had the opportunity to study the Bible with a forty-year-old Hispanic man I had led to the Lord in south Texas. As we were studying Romans 8 together one night and got to verse 28, he had the pleasure of reading this verse for the very first time in his life. This Hispanic man was overcome with awe and he immediately explained how he had been taught a Spanish proverb growing up that seem to say the same thing as Romans 8:28, but in a reversed approach. The proverb says, "Something bad happens to you to keep something worse from happening to you." To phrase it in biblical terms, God allows something to happen to you that seems bad at the time, but it actually keeps something worse from happening to you at the time or in the future. This is a wonderful application of Romans 8:28. Give it a chance to sink in and see if it does not bless you and give you a new perspective the next time something happens to you that seems bad right when it happens.

Consider these insights from www.theopedia.com:

God works not just some things, but all things according to the counsel of His own will. His purposes are all-inclusive and are never frustrated or thwarted. Nothing ever takes Him by surprise. The sovereignty of God is not merely that God has the power and right to govern all things, but that He does so, always and without exception. In other words, God is not merely sovereign de jure (in principle), but sovereign de facto (in practice).

Consider the thoughts of J. Hampton Keathley, III, a former professor at Moody Bible Institute, a Dallas Seminary graduate, and current writer for Bible.org:

One of our problems today is that we have lost the biblical perspective of the majestic greatness of God and we have a completely wrong focus on God. As J. B. Phillips points out in his book, *Your God Is Too Small*, people today see God as: (a) the resident police-man; (b) the grand old man; (c) a parental hangover, or some other short-sighted, twisted view of God. The sovereignty of God may be defined as the exercise of His supremacy, His infinite rule, His authority and power. Being infinitely elevated above the highest creature in authority, nature, and being, He is the Most High Lord of heaven and earth and all creation whether angels or the heavenly hosts.

Basically, God's sovereignty means that He is the Supreme Ruler who immanently and personally rules over all the affairs of the universe—and this includes our personal lives both as individuals and as a local body of believers. God's sovereignty is a place of rest for the child of God, as well as a cause of worship (cf. Ps. 48:1; 95:3, 6). One particular place of rest and application in relation to God's sovereignty and rule is His guidance and work to accomplish His purposes for our lives individually and corporately.

Paul has this in mind, at least in part, in Philippians 1:6 when he says: "I am confident of this very thing, that He who began a good work in you will perfect it until the day of Christ Jesus." (Compare also Eph. 1:11–12.) Such actions of God's sovereignty are seen in the life of Naaman the leper as God worked to lead this man to Himself. Of course, men may resist and fail to respond to God's grace, but even then God rules and uses them for His own purposes as He did with Pharaoh (cf. Prov.16:5).

The following Bible verses are a few of those supreme expressions of God's sovereignty:

Now see that I, even I, am He, and there is no God besides Me. I kill and I make alive. I wound and I heal. Nor is there any who can deliver from My hand. (Deuteronomy 32:39, KJV)

Then Jonathan said to the young man who was carrying his armor, "Come and let us cross over to the garrison of these uncircumcised. Perhaps the Lord will work for us, for the Lord is not restrained to save by many or by few." His armor bearer said to him, "Do all that is in your heart. Turn yourself and here I am with you according to your desire." Then Jonathan said, "Behold, we will cross over to the men and reveal ourselves to them. If they say to us, 'Wait until we come to you,' then we will stand in our place and not go up to them. But if they say, 'Come up to us,' then we will go up for the Lord has given them into our hands and this shall be the sign to us." When both of them revealed themselves to the garrison of the Philistines, the Philistines said, "Behold, Hebrews are coming out of the holes where they have hidden themselves." So the men of the garrison hailed Jonathan and his armor bearer and said, "Come up to us and we will tell you something." And Jonathan said to his armor bearer, "Come up after me, for the Lord has given them into the hands of Israel." Then Jonathan climbed up on his hands and feet, with his armor bearer behind him, and they fell before Jonathan and his armor bearer put some to death after him. That first slaughter which Jonathan and his armor bearer made was about twenty men within about half a furrow in an acre of land. And there was a trembling in the camp, in the field, and among all the people. Even the garrison and the raiders trembled and the earth quaked so that it became a great trembling. (1 Samuel 14:6–15)

Yours, O Lord, is the greatness and the power and the glory and the victory and the majesty. Indeed—everything that is in the heavens and the earth is yours. Yours is the dominion, O Lord, and You exalt Yourself as head over all. Both riches and honor come from You and You rule over all and in Your hand is power and might. And it lies in Your hand to make great and to strengthen everyone. (1 Chronicles 29:11–12)

For the Lord is a great God and a great King above all gods, in whose hand are the depths of the earth. The peaks of the mountains are His also. The sea is His, for it was He who made it, and His hands formed the dry land. Come, let us worship and bow down, let us kneel before the Lord our Maker. For He is our God and we are the people of His pasture and the sheep of His hand. (Psalm 95:3–7)

But our God is in the heavens. He does whatever He pleases. (Psalm 115:3)

The plans of the heart belong to man, but the answer of the tongue is from the Lord. All the ways of a man are clean in his own sight, but the Lord weighs the motives. Commit your works to the Lord and your plans will be established. The Lord has made everything for its own purpose, even the wicked for the day of evil. (Proverbs 16:1–4)

All the inhabitants of the earth are accounted as nothing, but He does according to His will in the host of heaven and among the inhabitants of earth and no one can ward off His hand or say to Him, "What have You done?" (Daniel 4:35)

Remember this and be assured. Recall it to mind, you transgressors. Remember the former things long past, for I am God and there is no other. I am God and there is no one like Me, declaring the end from the beginning, and from ancient times things which have not been done, saying, My purpose will be established and I will accomplish all My good pleasure, calling a bird of prey from the east, the man of My purpose from a far country. Truly I have spoken. Truly I will bring it to pass. I have planned it, surely I will do it. (Isaiah 46:8–11)

For My thoughts are not your thoughts, nor are your ways My ways, declares the Lord. For as the heavens are higher than the earth, so are My ways higher than your ways and My thoughts than your thoughts. (Isaiah 55:8–9)

On the contrary, who are you, O man, who answers back to God? The thing molded will not say to the molder, "Why did you make me like this," will it? (Romans 9:20)

We have obtained an inheritance, having been predestined according to His purpose who works all things after the counsel of His will. (Ephesians 1:11)

And a voice came from the throne, saying, "Give praise to our God, all you His bondservants, you who fear Him, the small and the great." Then I heard something like the voice of a great multitude and like the sound of many waters and like the sound of mighty peals of thunder, saying, "Hallelujah! For the Lord our God, the Almighty, reigns." (Revelation 19:5–6)

And I saw heaven opened and behold a white horse and He who sat on it is called Faithful and True and in righteousness He judges and wages war. His eyes are a flame of fire and on His head are many diadems and He has a name written on Him, which no one knows except Himself. He is clothed with a robe dipped in blood, and His name is called The Word of God. And the armies which are in heaven clothed in fine linen, white and clean, were following Him on white horses. From His mouth comes a sharp sword, so that with it He may strike down the nations and He will rule them with a rod of iron and He treads the wine press of the fierce wrath of God, the Almighty. And on His robe and on His thigh He has a name written, "KING OF KINGS, AND LORD OF LORDS." (Revelation 19:11–16)

It is possible that no one in the last 100 years has summed up the sovereignty of God any better than theologian Arthur W. Pink. He lived from 1886 to 1952 and wrote well-known and respected books about the sovereignty of God, the attributes of God, and election and predestination. Here are a few selected thoughts of his on the sovereignty of God taken from chapter 1 of *The Sovereignty of God* (Whitaker House, 2016):

The Sovereignty of God is the key to history, the interpreter of Providence, the warp and woof of Scripture, and the foundation of Christian theology. The sovereignty of God is the supremacy of God, the kingship of God, the godhood of God. To say that God is sovereign is to declare that God is God. To argue that man is a free moral agent and the determiner of his own destiny, and that therefore he has the power to checkmate his Maker, is to strip God of the attribute of Omnipotence.

In a word, to deny the sovereignty of God is to enter upon a path which, if followed to its logical terminus, is to arrive at blank atheism.

The sovereignty of the God of Scripture is absolute, irresistible, and infinite. When we say that God is sovereign we affirm His right to govern the universe, which He has made for His own glory, just as He pleases. . . . We affirm that He is under no rule or law outside of His own will and nature, that God is a law unto Himself, and that He is under no obligation to give an account of His matters to any.

Sovereignty characterizes the whole being of God. He is sovereign in all His attributes. He is sovereign in the exercise of His power. His power is exercised as He wills, when He wills, where He wills. . . . God is sovereign in the exercise of His mercy. Necessarily so, for mercy is directed by the will of Him that showeth mercy. Mercy is not a right to which man is entitled. . . . God is sovereign in the exercise of His love. When we say that God is sovereign in the exercise of His love, we mean that He loves whom He chooses. God does not love everybody; if He did, He would love the devil. If then there is nothing in any member of the human race to attract God's love, and if, notwithstanding, He does love some, then it necessarily follows that the cause of His love must be found in Himself, which is only another way of saying that the exercise of God's love toward the fallen sons of men is according to His own good pleasure.

In the final analysis, the exercise of God's love must be traced back to His sovereignty, or, otherwise, He would love by rule; and if He loved by rule, then is He under a law of love, and if He is under a law of love then is He not supreme, but is Himself ruled by law. "But," it may be asked, "Surely you do not deny that God loves the entire human family?" We reply, it is written, "Jacob have I loved, but Esau have I hated" (Rom. 9:13). If then God loved Jacob and hated Esau, and that before they were born or had done either good or evil, then the reason for His love was not in them, but in Himself. . . . God is sovereign in the exercise of His grace. This of necessity, for grace is favor shown to the undeserving, yea, to the hell-deserving. Grace is the antithesis of justice. Justice demands the impartial enforcement of law. Justice requires that each shall receive his legitimate due, neither more nor less. Justice bestows no favors and is no respecter of persons. Justice, as such, shows no pity and knows no mercy. But after justice has been fully satisfied, grace flows forth. Divine grace is not exercised at the expense of justice, but "grace reigns through righteousness" (Rom. 5:21), and if grace "reigns," then is grace sovereign.

The next chapter identifies that one incredible attribute of God, which penetrates the sinfulness we were born with and opens our eyes to our spiritual need.

5 ✥

"Irresistible Grace" or "The Spirit's Effectual Call to You"

The "irresistible grace of God" refers to God's supernatural ability and infinite wisdom to convince and motivate any creature to do His perfect will. The Holy Spirit effectually applies grace (desire, motivation, understanding, and power) to elect sinners. Any and all resistance of an elect sinner will be overcome in the right place at the right time, so that he or she will respond to the gospel message. His or her response to the gospel will include genuine repentance and faith in Jesus Christ. The Holy Spirit works on the inside of a sinner's mind and heart as well as in through outward circumstances to bring him or her to repentance and faith. Through the unconditional love of God, elect sinners are drawn into a willing relationship with Jesus Christ.

Here are the words of a few wise and powerful preachers from the past on God's "irresistible grace":

John Calvin (1509–1564)

John Calvin said, "God's intervention is not violent, so as to compel men by external force, but is a powerful impulse of the Holy Spirit, which makes men willing who formerly were unwilling and reluctant" (*Institutes of the Christian Religion* by John Calvin, first published in 1536 and revised and enlarged by Calvin in several editions before the definitive edition was published in 1559.)

Jonathan Edwards (1703–1758)

The Calvinistic notion of sovereign and arbitrary grace, whereby some, with the very same sincerity of endeavors and the same degree of endeavors and the same use of means, shall have the success which is denied others and although all things are exactly equal in both cases, both as to their persons and their behavior, yet one has that success by sovereign grace and God's arbitrary pleasure that is denied another. (*An Autobiography: A Personal Narrative*, by Jonathan Edwards in 1738. Edwards was the primary figure in America's first Great Awakening in the 1700s.)

George Whitefield (1714–1770)

Whitefield was a British evangelist who helped spread America's first Great Awakening throughout the American colonies during the 1700s. Below is an excerpt from Whitefield's sermon on 1 Corinthians 1:30 titled "Christ: The believer's Wisdom, Righteousness, Sanctification, and Redemption":

For my part I cannot see how true humbleness of mind can be attained without a knowledge of the doctrine of election and though I will not say that everyone who denies election is a bad man. Yet I will say, with that sweet singer, Mr. Trail, it is a very bad sign. Such a one, whoever he be, I think cannot truly know himself. For if we deny election, we must partly at least, glory in ourselves. But our redemption is so ordered that no flesh should glory in the Divine presence and hence it is, that the pride of man opposes this doctrine, because, according to this doctrine and no other, "he that glories must glory only in the Lord."

But what shall I say? Election is a mystery that shines with such resplendent brightness, that, to make use of the words of one who has drunk deeply of electing love, it dazzles the weak eyes even of some of God's children. However, though they know it not, all the blessing they receive, all the privileges they do or will enjoy, through Jesus Christ, flow from the everlasting love of God the Father. O come, come, see what it is to have eternal life. Do not refuse it.

Haste, sinner, haste away. May the great, the good Shepherd, draw your souls. Oh! If you never heard his voice before, God grant you may hear it now . . . O come! Come! Come to the Lord Jesus Christ. To him I leave you . . . Amen.[6]

---

[6] https://www.blueletterbible.org/Comm/whitefield_george/Sermons/witf_044.cfm

John Gill (1697–1771)

John Gill was the first great Baptist theologian in Britain who wrote at the same time as the English Puritans, but was distinctive in his Calvinism as a Baptist. His commitment to the doctrines of grace is evident in this paragraph from his commentary on John 6:44 in his *Exposition of the Bible*:[7]

> This act of drawing is an act of power, yet not of force. God in drawing of the unwilling, makes willing in the day of His power. He enlightens the understanding, bends the will, gives a heart of flesh, sweetly allures by the power of His grace, and engages the soul to come to Christ, and give up itself to Him. He draws with the bands of love. The drawing, though it supposes power and influence, does not always involve coercion and force. Music draws the ear, love draws the heart, and pleasure draws the mind.

Charles Spurgeon (1834–1892)

Spurgeon was an internationally recognized British preacher, pastor, evangelist, and author who was referred to as the "Prince of Preachers." As you will see from his words below, he was very effective in his articulation of God's grace. Excerpt adapted from Steven Lawson's *The Gospel Focus of Charles Spurgeon* from Reformation Trust, February 27, 2012:

> Irresistible grace is the sovereign work of the Holy Spirit, who convicts, calls, draws, and regenerates elect sinners. This work unfailingly results in the faith of all those chosen. All whom the Father chose in eternity past and all those for whom the Son died are those whom the Spirit brings to faith in Jesus Christ. None whom the Father elected and for whom Christ died fail to believe. The Holy Spirit grants repentance and faith to these elect sinners and ensures their conversion. This irresistible call is distinct from the general call of the gospel. The former is extended only to the elect and cannot be resisted. The latter is extended to all who hear the gospel and is resisted apart from the Spirit's effectual call. The general call of the gospel is like the common "cluck" of the hen which she is always giving when her chickens are around her. But if there is any danger impending, then she gives a very peculiar call, quite different from the ordinary one, and the little chicks come running as fast as they can, and hide for safety under her wings. That is the call we want, God's peculiar and effectual call to His own. his effectual call always secures its desired effect—the salvation of God's own.

Charles Spurgeon also wrote "Subdued by Sovereign Love!" (based on John 6:37: "All that the Father gives me shall come to me"):

---

[7] *Exposition of the Old and New Testament*, by John Gill, [1746-63], at sacred-texts.com

This declaration involves the doctrine of election. There are some whom the Father gave to Christ. It involves the doctrine of effectual calling. These who are given must and shall come, however stoutly they may set themselves against it, yet they shall be brought out of darkness into God's marvelous light. It teaches us the indispensable necessity of faith. For even those who are given to Christ are not saved except they come to Jesus. Even they must come, for there is no other way to heaven but by the door, Christ Jesus. All that the Father gives to our Redeemer must come to him, therefore none can come to heaven except they come to Christ. Oh the power and majesty which rest in the words "shall come." He does not say they have power to come, nor they may come if they will, but they "shall come." The Lord Jesus does by His messengers, His Word, and His Spirit, sweetly and graciously compel men to come in that they may eat of his marriage supper. And this He does, not by any violation of the free agency of man, but by the power of His grace. Jehovah Jesus knows how, by irresistible arguments addressed to the understanding, by mighty reasons appealing to the affections, and by the mysterious influence of his Holy Spirit operating upon all the powers and passions of the soul, so to subdue the whole man, that whereas he was once rebellious, he yields cheerfully to His government, subdued by sovereign love! But how shall those be known whom God has chosen? By this result that they do willingly and joyfully accept Christ and come to him with simple and sincere faith, resting upon him as all their salvation and all their desire. Reader, have you thus come to Jesus?" (*Morning and Evening: Daily Readings*, by C. H. Spurgeon, Wider Publications)

R. C. Sproul (1939–2017)

Sproul was an ordained Presbyterian pastor and a respected reformed theologian. He founded the Ligonier Ministries named for the Ligonier Valley just outside Pittsburgh, where the ministry started as a study center for college and seminary students. Sproul also helped produce the Ligonier Statement on Biblical Inerrancy, which would eventually grow into the 1978 Chicago Statement on Biblical Inerrancy.

In historic Reformation thought, the notion is this: *regeneration precedes faith*. We also believe that regeneration is monergistic. Now that's a three-dollar word. It means essentially that the divine operation called rebirth or regeneration is the work of God alone. An erg is a unit of labor, a unit of work. The word *energy* comes from that idea. The prefix *mono* means "one." So *monergism* means "one working." It means that the work of regeneration in the human heart is something that God does by His power alone—not by 50 percent His power and 50 percent man's power or even 99 percent His power and 1 percent man's power. It is 100 percent the work of God.

He, and He alone, has the power to change the disposition of the soul and the human heart to bring us to faith. In addition, when He exercises this grace in the soul, He brings about the effect that He intends to bring about. When God created you, He brought you into existence. You didn't help Him. It was His sovereign work that brought you to life biologically. Likewise, it is His work and His alone that brings you into the state of rebirth and of renewed creation.

Hence, we call this "irresistible grace." It's grace that works. It's grace that brings about what God wants it to bring about. If indeed we are dead in sins and trespasses, if indeed our wills are held captive by the lusts of our flesh and we need to be liberated from our flesh in order to be saved, then in the final analysis, salvation must be something that God does in us and for us, not something that we in any way do for ourselves.

However, the idea of irresistibility conjures up the idea that one cannot possibly offer any resistance to the grace of God. However, the history of the human race is the history of relentless resistance to the sweetness of the grace of God. Irresistible grace does not mean that God's grace is incapable of being resisted. Indeed, we are capable of resisting God's grace and we do resist it. The idea is that God's grace is so powerful that it has the capacity to overcome our natural resistance to it. It is not that the Holy Spirit drags people kicking and screaming to Christ against their wills. The Holy Spirit changes the inclination and disposition of our wills, so that whereas we were previously unwilling to embrace Christ, now we are willing and more than willing.

Indeed, we aren't dragged to Christ, we run to Christ and we embrace Him joyfully because the Spirit has changed our hearts. They are no longer hearts of stone that are impervious to the commands of God and to the invitations of the gospel. God melts the hardness of our hearts when He makes us new creatures. The Holy Spirit resurrects us from spiritual death, so that we come to Christ because we want to come to Christ. The reason we want to come to Christ is because God has already done a work of grace in our souls. Without that work, we would never have any desire to come to Christ. That's why we say that regeneration precedes faith. I have a little bit of a problem using the term *irresistible* grace, not because I don't believe this classical doctrine, but because it is misleading to many people. Therefore, I prefer the term *effectual* grace, because the irresistible grace of God effects what God intends it to effect." (*What Is Reformed Theology?: Understanding the Basics*, by R. C. Sproul, 1997)

Donald Allister (1952–Present)

Rev. Allister is a respected bishop in the Church of England and has this to say:

What predestination and election are all about is God's grace. He chooses us though we are far from attractive to him. He loves us when we do not deserve it. He is faithful to us when we are unfaithful. He ensures our salvation by not only calling us, but calling us effectively, with words of love and a gospel of power that we cannot refuse. He promises never to let us go when we come to Christ. He keeps us secure in Christ for all eternity. As Paul put it in Romans 8:30–39, "Those He predestined, He also called; those He called, He also justified; those He justified, He also glorified. What, then, shall we say in response to this? If God is for us, who can be against us? . . . Who will bring any charge against those whom God has chosen? . . . [nothing] in all creation will be able to separate us from the love of God that is in Christ Jesus our Lord." Praise him for His electing grace![8]

Here are a few more awesome verses referring to the "irresistible grace of God":

All that the Father gives Me will come to Me and the one who comes to Me I will certainly not cast out. For I have come down from heaven, not to do My own will, but the will of Him who sent Me. This is the will of Him who sent Me, that of all that He has given Me I lose nothing, but raise it up on the last day. (John 6:37–39)

No one can come to Me unless the Father who sent Me draws him and I will raise him up on the last day. It is written in the prophets, "And they shall all be taught of God." Everyone who has heard and learned from the Father, comes to Me. (John 6:44–45)

It is the Spirit who gives life. The flesh profits nothing. The words that I have spoken to you are spirit and are life. But there are some of you who do not believe. For Jesus knew from the beginning who they were who did not believe and who it was that would betray Him. And He was saying, for this reason I have said to you, that no one can come to Me unless it has been granted him from the Father. As a result of this many of His disciples withdrew and were not walking with Him anymore. (John 6:63–66)

When the Gentiles heard this, they began rejoicing and glorifying the word of the Lord and as many as had been appointed to eternal life believed. (Acts 13:48)

A woman named Lydia, from the city of Thyatira, a seller of purple fabrics, a worshiper of God, was listening and the Lord opened her heart to respond to the things spoken by Paul. (Acts 16:14)

---

[8] Donald Allister, chapter 6, article 17, "Predestination & Election," in *A Commentary on the 39 Articles*, 14–16. Donald Spargo Allister is a Church of England bishop. He was the Archdeacon of Chester from 2002 to 2010 and on November 5, 2009, was nominated as the next Bishop of Peterborough.

And we know that God causes all things to work together for good to those who love God, to those who are called according to His purpose. For those whom He foreknew, He also predestined to become conformed to the image of His Son, so that He would be the firstborn among many brethren and these whom He predestined, He also called and these whom He called, He also justified and these whom He justified, He also glorified. (Romans 8:28–30)

For God has not given us a spirit of timidity, but of power and love and discipline. Therefore do not be ashamed of the testimony of our Lord or of me His prisoner, but join with me in suffering for the gospel according to the power of God, who has saved us and called us with a holy calling, not according to our works, but according to His own purpose and grace which was granted us in Christ Jesus from all eternity, but now has been revealed by the appearing of our Savior Christ Jesus, who abolished death and brought life and immortality to light through the gospel, for which I was appointed a preacher and an apostle and a teacher. (2 Timothy 1:7–11)

"Infralapsarianism" Verses "Supralapsarianism"

During the Reformation, some considered God's election to have occurred after the fall of Adam and Eve in response to human sin. This was called "infralapsarianism." Others saw God's election to have occurred before the creation week and the fall of Adam and Eve. This was called "supralapsarianism." Nonetheless, all Reformed confessions of faith include election and some people feel that the Canons of Dort[9] do so in the greatest detail. I personally believe in the "supralapsarianism" approach to election based upon Ephesians 1:4–6, which you can read below:

For He chose us in him before the creation of the world to be holy and blameless in His sight. In love He predestined us for adoption to sonship through Jesus Christ, in accordance with His pleasure and will—to the praise of His glorious grace, which He has freely given us in the One He loves.

---

[9] The Canons of Dort came from an international synod of Reformed Christians held in Dordtrecht, Netherlands in 1618–19. One of its main goals was to settle a theological controversy (Arminianism) concerning the way in which believers receive the benefit of Christ. The canons articulate Calvinistic beliefs in direct rebuttal of Arminianism.

Amyraldism

Amyraldism is traced back to Moses Amyraut[10] (1596–1664). It also known as "hypothetical universalism" or "post-redemptionism" or "moderate Calvinism" or "four-point Calvinism." It primarily refers to a modified form of Calvinist theology that rejected one of the five points of Calvinism, which was the doctrine of limited atonement. This school of thought favored an unlimited atonement similar to that of Hugo Grotius. In simple terms, Amyraldism teaches that God has provided Christ's atonement for all alike, but seeing that none would believe on their own, He then elected those whom He will bring to faith in Christ, thereby preserving the Calvinist doctrine of unconditional election. This doctrine is still viewed as a variety of Calvinism, because it maintains the particularity of sovereign grace in the application of the atonement. However, detractors like B. B. Warfield[11] have termed it "an inconsistent and therefore unstable form of Calvinism."

"Calvinism" Versus "Arminianism"

The Reformed theological tradition known as Calvinism addresses all of the traditional topics of Christian theology, but the word Calvinism is usually known to refer to the reformed views on salvation, election, predestination, and the sovereignty of God. These are summarized in the five points of Calvinism (TULIP) and those following these tenets are referred to as Calvinists. TULIP stands for:

1. Total Depravity
2. Unconditional Election
3. Limited Atonement
4. Irresistible Grace
5. Perseverance of the Saints

The doctrinal expressions that people tend to associate with John Calvin (1509–1564), because of his abilities to express these tenets, really go back to the apostle Paul's writings in the New Testament. There are many biblical passages throughout the Old Testament and

---

[10] Moses Amyraut September 1596—January 8, 1664) was a French Protestant theologian and metaphysician. He is remembered for his modifications to Calvinist theology regarding the nature of Christ's atonement, which is referred to as Amyraldism or Amyraldianism.

[11] Benjamin Breckinridge Warfield (November 5, 1851—February 16, 1921) was professor of theology at Princeton Seminary from 1887 to 1921. He served as the last principal of the Princeton Theological Seminary from 1886 to 1902. Many conservative Presbyterians consider him to be the last of the great Princeton theologians before the split in 1929 that formed Westminster Theological Seminary and the Orthodox Presbyterian Church.

the New Testament referring to the sovereignty of God in salvation, but many of the most well-known verses are found in Romans and Ephesians (written by Paul under the inspiration of the Holy Spirit). Therefore, many people embracing Calvinism (including myself) prefer to see ourselves as embracing Paulinism, referring back to the original doctrines or teachings of the apostle Paul.

Arminianism is based on the theological ideas of the Dutch Reformed theologian Jacobus Arminius (1560–1609). His supporters were known as the *Remonstrants*. It is known as a soteriological sect of Protestant Christianity (Soteriology is the study of salvation). Dutch Arminianism was originally articulated in the *Remonstrance* (1610), which was a theological statement signed by forty-five ministers and submitted to the States-General of the Netherlands. The Synod of Dort (1618–1619) was called by the States General to consider the Five Articles of Remonstrance. They asserted that:

1. Election (and condemnation on the day of judgment) was conditioned by the rational faith or non-faith of man (e.g., free will).
2. The Atonement, while qualitatively adequate for all men, is efficacious only for the man of faith.
3. Unaided by the Holy Spirit, no person is able to respond to God's will.
4. Grace is resistible.
5. Believers are able to resist sin, but are not beyond the possibility of falling from grace.

The centerpiece of *Remonstrant Arminianism* is found in the assertion that human dignity requires an unimpaired freedom of the will. Arminian theology usually falls into one of two groups: *Classical Arminianism* (drawn from the teaching of Jacobus Arminius) and *Wesleyan Arminian* (drawing primarily from John Wesley). Both groups overlap substantially. The dominant theme in Arminian thinking is that election is individual and based on God's foreknowledge of faith. This means God looked down throughout history and could see (foreknow) who would believe in Christ. Therefore, God chose (elected) those whom He saw would use their free will to choose Christ. Below is a simple chart comparing Calvinism to Arminianism.

Calvinist Theology Compared to Arminian Theology

From the Online Bible School at http://www.generationword.com/bible_school_notes/30.html.

Issue	Calvinist	Arminian
Sin Nature	Total depravity	Weakness inherited from Adam
Human Will	In bondage to sin	Free to do spiritual good
Grace	• Common grace for all • Saving grace for the elect	• Enabling grace given to all • Saving grace given to those who believe • Persevering grace given to those who obey
Predestination	God caused it	God knew it
Regeneration	Holy Spirit alone through election & irresistible grace	God and man work together
Atonement	Jesus died as a substitute for man and to pay the penalty of sin	Jesus' death was accepted by God instead of a penalty on man
Who Will Be Saved	Only the elect	Salvation is available to all
How does Salvation Come	By the Holy Spirit according to God's will	By the Holy Spirit in response to the will of the man
Order of Salvation Events	1. election 2. predestination 3. calling 4. regeneration 5. faith 6. repentance 7. justification 8. sanctification 9. glorification	1. calling 2. faith 3. repentance 4. regeneration 5. justification 6. perseverance 7. glorification
Eternal Security	The elect cannot lost their salvation	• Those who believe continue in salvation if they are obedient • Persevering grace given to those who obey

Each of the definitions reviewed in this chapter, individually and corporately, demonstrate that our salvation is totally embedded in election and predestination. The next chapter addresses the core issue of why election and predestination are absolute necessities for anyone to be saved.

6

Why Election and Predestination Are Absolute Necessities for Anyone to Be Saved

The Word of God is the divinely inspired record of the creation of the universe and the early history of man from Adam through Jesus Christ and the early church through the end of the first century AD. The Bible, as the inspired (God-breathed) and infallible Word of God, clearly teaches the total depravity of mankind.

This total depravity of the human heart and mind began with the first sins of Adam and Eve. Their innocent natures changed after they sinned and experienced what is referred to as the *fall out of grace*, which means they fell out of the natural relationship with God with which they had been created. When they rebelled against God's one commandment (limitation in the Garden of Eden), their natures became innately sinful, selfish, disobedient, and rebellious. When they had children, their children were born into the world with the same kind of sinful nature, illustrated when Cain murdered his brother Abel. This total depravity has been passed down to every person ever born into the world since then, except Jesus Christ.

We observe one of the greatest demonstrations of total depravity expressed through the sinful nature in the persistent human inability to honor limitations. We inherited this struggle from Adam and Eve when they failed to honor the singular God-given limitation in their lives (e.g., "Do not eat the fruit growing on the tree of the knowledge of good and evil"). This struggle is manifested from the time we are born, continues throughout life, and can only be overcome by becoming a new creation in Christ Jesus.

It is easier to relate to this as an observer, rather than to admit our own struggles with it. If you have children, you well remember how many times you told one of your children not to do something before walking away, only to turn around and see them do that very thing you told them not to do. The expressed limitation itself stirs up their desire to do it. They don't like being told they can't have something or they can't do something. It rubs their sinful natures the wrong way and they always want to test any limits put on them.

One of the most serious examples of this is the old rule "don't play in the street," no ifs, ands, or buts! This one command (limitation) is given with one thing in mind. The parent or caretaker does not want the child to be hurt or killed by a passing car, which takes us right back to God's loving motivation in the Garden of Eden. He did not want Adam and Eve or their descendants to experience death (spiritual death and the physical death that would follow physical death), which is exactly what He expressed to them. Satan convinced them that the only limitation God gave them (in their entire lives) was unfair. Eve fell for it, Adam willingly went along with her, and the rest is history. How would you like it, if there was only one thing in the entire world you could not do during your life? Would you think that was a great deal? Would you see that as a lot of freedom?

As children mature, their struggle with limitations continues and intensifies. That struggle works its way into everything they face in life, including their educational environments, social circles, relationships with the opposite sex, work environments, political environments, etc. As we progress through life, we are told "for our own good (usually)" by those in various authority structures, that we should not look at certain things (a limitation), listen to certain things (a limitation), touch certain things (a limitation), go to certain places (a limitation), or eat and drink certain things (a limitation). It can get to the point where one feels like life is just one big limitation and human nature rebels against this, even when the limitations are totally justified and motivated by the desire to protect.

People who struggle with election and predestination either have not faced up to their own total depravity, or they do not accept it, but the Bible is very clear and explicit about the innate sinful nature of human beings. To help you understand the depravity of mankind, which is essential to understanding the necessity of election and predestination, please review the following biblical passages. Admittedly, there are many Bible verses below, but they must be understood and accepted as truth, in order to be able to grasp the moral and spiritual depravity of mankind. Once this principle is accepted as truth, the necessities of election and predestination (for even one person to ever be saved) become very clear. As noted in chapter 1—unless otherwise indicated, all Scripture passages cited are from the New American Standard Bible (NASB).

> Then the Lord God took the man and put him into the Garden of Eden to cultivate it and keep it. The Lord God commanded the man, saying, "From any tree of the garden you may eat freely, but from the tree of the knowledge of good and evil you shall not eat, for in the day that you eat from it you will surely die." (Genesis 2:15–16)

> Now the serpent was more crafty than any beast of the field which the Lord God had made. And he said to the woman, "Indeed, has God said, 'You shall not eat from any tree of the garden'?" The woman said to the serpent, "From the fruit of the trees of the garden we may eat; but from the fruit of the tree which is in the middle of the garden, God has said, 'You shall not eat from it or touch it, or you will die.'" The serpent said to the woman, "You surely will not die! For God knows that in the day you eat from it your eyes will be opened, and you will be like God, knowing good and evil." When the woman saw that the tree was good for food, and that it was a delight to the eyes, and that the tree was desirable to make one wise, she took from its fruit and ate; and she gave also to her husband with her, and he ate. Then the eyes of both of them were opened, and they knew that they were naked; and they sewed fig leaves together and made themselves loin coverings. They heard the sound of the Lord God walking in the garden in the cool of the day, and the man and his wife hid themselves from the presence of the Lord God among the trees of the garden. Then the Lord God called to the man, and said to him, "Where are you?" He said, "I heard the sound of You in the garden, and I was afraid because I was naked; so I hid myself." And He said, "Who told you that you were naked? Have you eaten from the tree of which I commanded you not to eat?" The man said, "The woman whom You gave to be with me, she gave me from the tree, and I ate." Then the Lord God said to the woman, "What is this you have done?" And the woman said, "The serpent deceived me, and I ate." The Lord God said to the serpent, "Because you have done this, Cursed are you more than all cattle, and more than every beast of the field. On your belly you will go and dust you will eat all the days of your life and I will put enmity between you and the woman and between your seed and her seed. He shall bruise you on the head and you shall bruise him on the heel." To the woman, He said, "I will greatly multiply your pain in childbirth and in pain you will bring forth children. Yet your desire will be for your husband and he will rule over you. Then to Adam He said, "Because you have listened to the voice of your wife and have eaten from the tree about which I commanded you, saying, 'You shall not eat from it,' cursed is the ground because of you. In toil you will eat of it all the days of your life. Both thorns and thistles it shall grow for you. And you will eat the plants of the field. By

the sweat of your face you will eat bread, till you return to the ground, because from it you were taken. For you are dust and to dust you shall return." Now the man called his wife's name Eve, because she was the mother of all the living. The Lord God made garments of skin for Adam and his wife and clothed them. Then the Lord God said, "Behold, the man has become like one of Us, knowing good and evil, and now he might stretch out his hand and take also from the tree of life and eat and live forever." Therefore, the Lord God sent him out from the garden of Eden to cultivate the ground from which he was taken. So, He drove the man out and at the east of the garden of Eden He stationed the cherubim and the flaming sword which turned every direction to guard the way to the tree of life. (Genesis 3)

The verses above explain how sin and innate sinfulness entered into the human race through the first sin (the disobedience and transgression) of Adam and Eve. The Old Testament and New Testament passages below confirm and illustrate the effects of Adam and Eve's sin upon all of humanity. Genesis 6:5 says, "Then the Lord saw that the wickedness of man was great on the earth and that every intent of the thoughts of his heart was only evil continually."

God's observation led to Noah's Flood, which cleansed the entire earth. Then after the flood, He reflected in Genesis 8 as follows:

The Lord smelled the soothing aroma and the Lord said to Himself, "I will never again curse the ground on account of man, for the intent of man's heart is evil from his youth, and I will never again destroy every living thing as I have done." (Genesis 8:21)

We see the theme of mankind's estrangement from the creator throughout the Wisdom Literature.

How then can a man be just with God? Or how can he be clean who is born of woman? If even the moon has no brightness and the stars are not pure in His sight, how much less man, that maggot and the son of man, that worm! (Job 25:4–6)

Behold, I was brought forth in iniquity and in sin my mother conceived me. (Psalm 51:5)

Indeed, there is not a righteous man on earth who continually does good and who never sins. (Ecclesiastes 7:20)

This is an evil in all that is done under the sun, that there is one fate for all men. Furthermore, the hearts of the sons of men are full of evil and insanity is in their hearts throughout their lives. Afterwards they go to the dead. (Ecclesiastes 9:3)

We continue to observe the depravity of man and the resulting magnified separation from God throughout the prophetic literature:

The heart is more deceitful than all else and is desperately sick. Who can understand it? (Jeremiah 17:9)

Can the Ethiopian change his skin or the leopard his spots? Then can you do good who are accustomed to doing evil? (Jeremiah 13:23, NIV)

For all of us have become like one who is unclean and all our righteous deeds are like a filthy garment. And all of us wither like a leaf and our iniquities, like the wind, take us away. There is no one who calls on Your name, who arouses himself to take hold of You. For You have hidden Your face from us and have delivered us into the power of our iniquities. But now O Lord, You are our Father, we are the clay and You our potter and all of us are the work of Your hand. (Isaiah 64:6–8)

In the Gospels, we see the theme continued with the authoritative words of Jesus Himself:

For from within, out of the heart of men, proceed the evil thoughts, fornications, thefts, murders, adulteries, deeds of coveting and wickedness, as well as deceit, sensuality, envy, slander, pride and foolishness. All these evil things proceed from within and defile the man. (Mark 7:21–23)

This is the judgment, that the Light has come into the world, and men loved the darkness rather than the Light, for their deeds were evil. (John 3:19)

No one can come to Me unless the Father who sent Me draws him; and I will raise him up on the last day. (John 6:44)

But there are some of you who do not believe. For Jesus knew from the beginning who they were who did not believe and who it was that would betray Him. And He was saying, "For this reason I have said to you, that no one can come to Me unless it has been granted him from the Father." (John 6:64–65)

Jesus answered them, "Truly, truly, I say to you, everyone who commits sin is the slave of sin." (John 8:34)

Finally, we observe the critical theological writings of the apostle Paul:

What then? Are we better than they? Not at all, for we have already charged that both Jews and Greeks are all under sin. As it is written, "There is none righteous, not even one. There is none who understands. There is none who seeks for God. All have turned aside, together they have become useless. There is none who does good, there is not even one. Their throat is an open grave. With their tongues, they keep deceiving. The poison of asps is under their lips, whose mouth is full of cursing and bitterness. Their feet are swift to shed blood. Destruction and misery are in their paths and the path of peace they have not known. There is no fear of God before their eyes." (Romans 3:9–18)

For all have sinned and fall short of the glory of God. (Romans 3:23)

For the mind set on the flesh is death, but the mind set on the Spirit is life and peace. Because the mind set on the flesh is hostile toward God, it does not subject itself to the law of God, for it is not even able to do so. And those who are in the flesh cannot please God. (Romans 8:6–9)

But a natural man does not accept the things of the Spirit of God, for they are foolishness to him and he cannot understand them, because they are spiritually appraised. (1 Corinthians 2:14)

And you were dead in your trespasses and sins, in which you formerly walked according to the course of this world, according to the prince of the power of the air, of the spirit that is now working in the sons of disobedience. Among them we too all formerly lived in the lusts of our flesh, indulging the desires of the flesh and of the mind, and were by nature children of wrath, even as the rest. (Ephesians 2:1–3)

For we also once were foolish ourselves, disobedient, deceived, enslaved to various lusts and pleasures, spending our life in malice and envy, hateful, hating one another. (Titus 3:3)

Because of the way sin entered into Lucifer (the devil) and then into humanity through Adam and Eve's transgression, election and predestination were an absolute necessity if there was to be eternal redemption (salvation) for even one lost soul. With every single person born into the world in a state of total sinful depravity, with no way to save himself or herself or even understand their need to be saved, God (in His mercy) had to choose to initiate the plan and process of salvation in the lives of individual sinners. God made the choice to do this before He created anything. Election and predestination were absolutely necessary to ensure anyone ever got saved (redeemed from sin, self, and eventual hell).

God created the universe and human beings in a state of perfection with Adam and Eve created into a relationship with God that would go on forever, if they simply obeyed one command. With their obedience to this one command, their children, grandchildren, and all of their descendants (all the way down to you and me) would have been born into a natural and eternal relationship with God and needing no salvation. This was God's desire and plan. He never wanted Adam and Eve to sin and bring humanity into a state of sin and depravity and separation from Him.

God's original plan included everyone, but He wanted people to have true "free will." He wanted Adam and Eve to freely choose to love Him and honor His one command (one and only one limitation). So He had to allow them to carry out their choices. He knew that if they sinned, it would affect all of their offspring until the end of history. If people were to have true "free will" and be responsible for their choices and actions, there was no other way to do it. Anything short of this would have meant that Adam and Eve needed to be created with some kind of mechanical obedience.

Once their transgression occurred, all of future humanity was separated from God and the need for redemption (salvation) and restoration was in place. People would still have their free will, but their free will was corrupted by their sinful nature. They would only be able to choose (use their free will) within the limitations of their sinful nature. Any creature can only make choices according to its nature. You can domesticate a pig and train him to do certain things that might impress you and entertain you, but if (after all the training) you ask that pig to make a choice of what college he should attend and what degree program he should pursue, that pig would not have a clue what you were talking about. The pig simply would not understand or respond appropriately to you. Those decisions and choices are beyond a pig's nature. The pig is incapable of choosing such things. And after your discussion with him about the value of higher education and virtue of academic excellence, that pig would be glad to get back to its pig sty.

Dogs make wonderful pets and companions. My wife and I have two Yorkies that we enjoy immensely, but as much as we adore them, we could not talk to them about a relationship with God and their need to seek out a personal relationship with the Lord Jesus Christ. Their natures just don't allow them to consider such choices. Their choices are limited to their canine instincts. We do talk to them throughout each day and they understand many things we say, but when we say things they cannot relate to, they just turn their cute little heads at a funny angle and look at us with this sense of bewilderment as an expression of "Say what?"

Some of you may be thinking that the two illustrations above (the limited choices belonging to the free will of pigs and dogs) are over simplistic and cannot realistically illustrate the complexities of human nature. Please just focus on the main point, that the free will of any creature is always limited to the type of nature it has. Sinners have sinful natures and left to themselves can only make choices within the confines of that nature. Sinners always operate according to their instincts. Only when supernatural power comes in from without and empowers a sinner to consider and understand things beyond their natures, can they do so.

If you have been an active witness for the Lord Jesus Christ, you have no doubt experienced many times the frustration of trying to explain to a non-Christian their need for God and salvation. They listen to you, but your words just don't penetrate their minds and hearts. They will look at you like a calf looking at a new gate: "What the heck is that?" Without the enlightenment and empowerment of the Holy Spirit working upon the lost and depraved nature of the sinner you are talking to, he or she will never understand or respond to you. In fact, they may get very angry with you and demonstrate hostility toward you, because of their inherit pride and stubbornness.

One time I picked up a hitchhiker for the purpose of sharing the gospel with him between the place I picked him up and the place he wanted to be dropped off. As soon as I began the conversation about the Lord and the need to be saved, he confessed to be an alcoholic with the implication being that it was just a sickness and not something he had a responsibility or accountability for. So I told him the Bible actually said he was a drunk, not an alcoholic (it is better to be a drunk than an alcoholic because you don't have to go to all those meetings), and that he could repent of his drunkenness, but he would never repent as long as he saw himself as an alcoholic (a victim of alcohol). Immediately his faced turned red with anger and he yelled at me to stop the car, so he could get out. I stopped the car and he got out in a storm of anger and walked off.

As a young man in college, I had the chance to work all summer at an oil refinery during what is called a "turnaround" when annual maintenance is done throughout the facility. My responsibilities were to manage the tool room where welders, pipe fitters, electricians, and other kinds of trade specialists would come and check out needed tools and then return them when finished. I felt led to keep a supply of Pocket New Testaments and evangelistic tracts on the front counter where these workers would come and request tools and supplies. I wanted to give as many of them away as possible to anyone who would receive them before the summer was over.

As you can imagine, the many people I engaged with in that environment, responded across the board with a multitude of emotions from gratitude to anger and hatred. As I attempted to give one older gentleman a tract and New Testament, he responded with, "Why you _____, _____, _____, _____, (taking God's name in vain with many other expletives), of course I am a Christian. I am a Mason!" As he walked off, I thought, How sad! It was obvious, to me at least, that this gentleman had not embraced the gospel in a way that it affected his disposition!

As an active witness, I have also experienced the joy of explaining to a non-Christian his or her need for God and salvation when all of a sudden, I saw the light bulb going off in the person's mind and heart (through the enlightenment and empowerment of the Holy Spirit) and he or she responded by the grace of God and called upon the Lord to save them. I witness with amazement one of the elect (chosen ones) being born again into the family of God right before my eyes, like the amazement any father has who has had the chance to be with his wife when she gives birth to their child. I hope the story below will encourage many readers to be faithful in sharing the gospel at every opportunity, knowing that God is always at work in the life of elect sinners, preparing them to receive Christ.

Good Old Door-to-Door Gospel Witnessing

For many years, my full time ministry was going house to house in various small towns. I knocked on doors, with the hope of sharing the gospel, distributing evangelistic tracts and New Testaments, and hoping to begin home Bible studies with those who responded. When I had approached one home, which was only a few houses down from where I lived, I had the privilege of leading the wife living there to the Lord. She was anxious for me to meet her husband and share the truth with him.

After several attempts to catch him at home during the evenings after work (but missing him, as he was a busy building contractor), I felt the Lord leading me to knock on his door at eight a.m. on a Saturday morning. Sure enough, after a couple of minutes, he answered his door. He was a large man and looked frustrated and stressed out. I had to think twice about beginning a conversation with a large, frustrated, and stressed out homebuilder on a Saturday morning at eight a.m. in his own house, but the Holy Spirit gave me peace to proceed.

I asked him if I could spend just a few minutes talking with him about God and spiritual things. To my surprise and delight, he said yes, and he invited me into his living room.

Within thirty minutes he bowed his head and prayed with me and asked the Lord Jesus Christ to save him from his sin and become his personal Lord and Savior. As he raised his head from prayer, I saw the relief in his face as he experienced the cleansing of all guilt and shame through the blood of Jesus Christ.

He and his wife immediately began weekly Bible studies with me, demonstrating a real hunger to learn as much as possible about God, the Bible, and living the Christian life. When we were into our third month of weekly Bible studies together, this man decided to share with me the context of our first encounter at his front door that Saturday morning almost three months earlier. He explained how he had just been released from our county jail that morning, where he had to go before a judge for his arrest for drunkenness and disorderly conduct the night before.

He had gone to a large bar and lounge on Friday night, gotten pretty drunk, gotten into a fight with another man, and was arrested for being the aggressor. After spending Friday night in the county jail (his very first time behind bars), he had the chance to think about his life (which he had never done before) and the way it was going morally and spiritually (even though he had a college education and was a successful building contractor). Early Saturday morning, he had to go before the judge and receive whatever punitive action there would be, which could be fines and more jail time. There were also forty-nine other men who had been arrested that Friday night and also had to go before the judge. My new friend was the last in line, number fifty.

He had to sit there and listen to the judge deal with forty-nine other transgressors of the law and see them receive the consequences of their actions. Many of them received serious punitive decisions from this judge. My new friend was very nervous and worried about his situation, but when he finally got up before the judge and the judge listened to the circumstances of his arrest and the charges against him, the judge unpredictably voiced a very merciful decision on his behalf, which—in purely human terms—my friend still does not understand to this day, except that it got him home in time to meet me that morning.

Having put his faith in Christ later that morning, he now does understand it as a part of God's mercy and providence over his life. The judge told him that he was going to fine him $50.00 and let him go with the warning not to ever come before his court again. My friend walked out in shock and drove the thirty minutes to his house. He walked in and then heard me knock on his door to talk to him about God and spiritual things. The rest is history, but what a wonderful experience it was for me, to see how God supernaturally prepares people to hear the gospel and respond to it with gratitude.

With the ability to only make choices based upon their innate sinfulness, people are incapable of seeking out redemption and restoration with God. By nature, we run from

God, just as Adam ran and hid in the garden the first time God came down to visit with him after he sinned. The human race has been running from God ever since Adam's first jog (game of hide and seek) in the Garden of Eden. This means no one would ever come to God on their own. Left to ourselves, we run from God. The only way any person can be saved (redeemed & restored to God) is for God to pursue the sinner (as He did with Adam) and initiate the relationship with/through "irresistible grace."

Once again, irresistible grace means that the Holy Spirit pours all of the energy and effort into a relationship that is needed, and for as long as needed, to overcome all of the stubbornness, resistance, rebellion, and natural enmity found in the heart of a man (or woman) toward God. Without this "irresistible grace," every person would choose to go on his or her way (freely and happily without God and Jesus Christ) and plunge into hell without a second thought (until they got there). Now let's observe a passage that further illustrates what I've been describing:

> In Him we have redemption through His blood, the forgiveness of our trespasses, according to the riches of His grace which He lavished on us. In all wisdom and insight, He made known to us the mystery of His will, according to His kind intention which He purposed in Him with a view to an administration suitable to the fullness of the times, that is, the summing up of all things in Christ, things in the heavens and things on the earth. In Him also we have obtained an inheritance, having been predestined according to His purpose who works all things after the counsel of His will, to the end that we who were the first to hope in Christ would be to the praise of His glory. In Him, you also, after listening to the message of truth, the gospel of your salvation—having also believed, you were sealed in Him with the Holy Spirit of promise, who is given as a pledge of our inheritance, with a view to the redemption of God's own possession, to the praise of His glory. (Ephesians 1:7–14)

Beginning with the birth of Adam and Eve's first child (Cain), who murdered his brother Abel, every person has been born into this world spiritually dead. We come into the world with physical life and with an eternal soul, but with no spiritual life. Our spiritual life is in a negative or minus state. It is completely dead, and we have no ability to relate to God or connect with Him.

Spiritually, we are like Lazarus in John 11, lying in the grave after four days. Physically and biologically Lazarus was completely dead. He had no more physical powers or abilities. His body lay there completely helpless and in a state of decay. If left to himself, he would never be a part of this world again, but Jesus had other plans. The Lord stood outside his tomb, called to Lazarus by name, told him to rise up, come out of that tomb, and come out of his state of physical death. The irresistible power of Jesus' words caused Lazarus to get up, come out of that tomb, and resume his life here on earth.

Such is the case with every one of us sinners when we are in a state of complete spiritual death. We have no ability or power to rise up out of our spiritual grave and join Jesus and the family of God. Jesus has to call out to us by name with irresistible power (grace) and give us the desire and power to acknowledge our sinfulness to God (repentance) and ask the Lord to personally save us, forgive us, and to restore us to God. Without this process, initiated by the Lord, salvation does not happen. If God had not chosen to pursue a certain number of specific sinners with His irresistible power (grace), no one would have ever been saved and restored spiritually to Him. We would have all gladly gone to hell ("gladly," until we got there). There are no people in hell who are glad to be there. They all want out, but there is no escape. Their position in hell is called "eternal damnation" and is an existence of unending punishment and suffering. Significantly, the core of that suffering is in the eternal nature of it, and the constant realization of the opportunities the sinner had experienced in this life to seek the Lord. Further realization on the part of the suffering souls in hell is the comprehension that they will never get the opportunity to be restored to God through the power of Jesus's purchase of redemption on the cross at Calvary! Imagine!

The Lord Jesus commanded that the gospel (how to be saved through faith in Him) be preached all over the world to every nation, tribe, language group, and ethnic group. As the gospel is preached, those who hear have the opportunity to understand their need to be saved and how to be saved. As people exercise their corrupted free will, they naturally reject the truth, and continue on in their spiritual lostness. If people were not totally depraved and spiritually ignorant, they would respond to the gospel message. They would want to be saved and go to heaven forever and ever. Who in their right mind would want to go to hell for all of eternity? But—as the masses of humanity around the world in every generation continue to reject the gospel and seek to fulfill their evil desires, they prove their total inability to understand their need to be saved and restored to God on their own.

For the "elect" the Holy Spirit mercifully continues to pursue them individually until they are overcome by His irresistible power (grace), see their need, repent, and commit themselves to the Lordship of Jesus Christ. For everyone else, God simply lets them go their way, do as they please, and they inherit the consequences. Let us close out this chapter with an excellent article, "Whom Chose Whom?"[12] by Don Fortner, illustrating how necessary it was for God to do the choosing.

---

[12] Published in *Disciple Cry*, Sunday, August 29, 2010. Don Fortner has pastored Grace Baptist Church of Danville, Kentucky, for over twenty-five years.

"The decision is yours . . . Now it is all up to you . . . God has done all He can to save. The rest is up to you. You must choose Christ for yourself. You must make the final decision."

How often we have all heard statements like those above? I want to raise a question regarding this matter of eternal salvation: Whose choice is it? Our Lord Jesus Christ has answered the question very plainly: "You have not chosen me, but I have chosen you" (John 15:16). Divine election is a very humbling and at the same time it is a very encouraging and blessed doctrine of Scripture.

It is humbling to know that we would never have chosen Christ. Our needs were so many, our hearts were so hard, that we would never have sought the Lord. Yet, it is exceedingly comforting to hear our Savior say, "I have chosen you." Our Lord Jesus Christ loved us long before we ever loved Him. He loved us even when we were dead in sin. Had He not loved us, we would never have loved Him. Had He not chosen us, we would never have chosen Him. Language could not be clearer. Our Savior tells us that man, by nature, will never choose Christ. It is true, in one sense, that every believer chooses Christ. This is the result, not the cause, of Christ's choosing him.

The natural ear is so deaf that it cannot hear. The natural eye is so blind that it cannot see. The natural heart is so hard that it cannot feel. Man sees no beauty in Christ. He feels no need of Christ. He has no desire for Christ.

Only after God by almighty grace opens the blind eye, unstops the deaf ear, quickens the dead heart, and gives strength to the withered hand is the sinner made willing to seek Christ and given the strength of faith to embrace Him. All who believe on the Lord Jesus Christ in time, were chosen by God in eternal love, and that choice of them secures their faith and holiness in Christ.

What does the term "election" mean? Accurate statements on this doctrine are essential. No doctrine in the Bible has suffered so much damage from the erroneous views of its foes and the inaccurate statements of its friends. Election may be defined this way: God has been pleased from all eternity to choose certain men and women, whom He has determined to save by the righteousness and shed blood of Christ. None are finally saved, except those whom He has chosen. Therefore the Word of God calls His people "the elect." And the choice, or the appointment of them to eternal life, is called "the election of God." All those whom God was pleased to choose in eternity were redeemed by Christ at Calvary. All who were chosen and redeemed are (in due season) called to salvation and eternal life by the Holy Spirit.

He convinces them of sin.
He leads them to Christ.
He works repentance and faith in them.
He keeps them by His grace from falling entirely away.
He brings them all safely to eternal glory.

In short, election is the first link in the chain of salvation, of which eternal glory is the end. All who are redeemed, justified, called, born again, and brought to faith in Christ are elect. The primary and original cause of the saint's being what he is, is God's eternal election. What does the Word of God teach about election? God's election of men to salvation is gracious and free, absolute and sovereign. It is an unconditional act of sovereign mercy. He did not choose us because He foresaw that we would repent and believe on Christ. Our repentance and faith is the result of God's election, not the cause of it (John 10:16, 26; 15:16; Acts 13:48). God's election is personal. He chose not a mass of nameless faces, but individual sinners, calling them His sons and daughters. This election of grace is also eternal and immutable (Ephesians 1:4). When the Triune Godhead existed alone in glorious self-sufficiency, we were chosen in covenant mercy. God chose us because of His eternal love and sovereign pleasure, simply because He would be gracious. We were chosen in Christ Jesus.

Behold God's strange choice! He chose not the noble, but the common. He chose not the wise, but the foolish. He chose not the righteous, but the wicked. He chose us, "that no flesh should glory in His presence . . . that according as it is written, 'He that glories, let him glory in the Lord'" (1 Corinthians 1:29–31). Let all who are born again confess, "By the grace of God, I am what I am" (1 Corinthians 15:10). Let us sing of electing love:

> Tis not that I did choose Thee,
> For, Lord, that could not be;
> This heart would still refuse Thee,
> But Thou hast chosen me.
> My heart owns none before Thee;
> For thy rich grace I thirst;
> This knowing, if I love Thee,
> Thou must have loved me first.

—Josiah Conder

In the next chapter, we will look at some of the things God had to decide before He created anything.

7

God's Choices before Creation

Before God decided to create anything in what we refer to as "eternity past," He had infinite choices about if He would create or not create, what He would create if He did create, when He would create, and how He would create what He chose to create. He had no limitations, restrictions, or hindrances of any kind. He was free to do anything He wanted to do. These choices God enjoyed are very important to keep in mind as we think about election and predestination.

Within the counsel of the Godhead (Father, Son, and Holy Spirit), the decision was made in eternity past to create two kinds of creatures to worship and serve the Godhead. We know these two kinds of creatures as angels and humans. The other created kinds, including animals, birds, insects, and marine life were created for the needs and pleasures of mankind and for the glory of God. There are no alien life forms anywhere in the universe. There are only angels, demons, and human beings.

God had the pleasure of choosing what kind of natures, intellect, and bodies to give angels and humans. He chose to create angels with spiritual bodies with incredible intellect and great power. He chose to create humans with physical bodies with incredible intellect and limited power (compared to angels). He chose to give both angels and humans what has become known as "free will," which means they have the ability to make truly free choices according to their natures. They can understand, analyze, feel, and choose to do anything within their powers, which is a miraculous thing. But by definition "free will" meant there would have to be moral choices based upon the character of the creator and sustainer of the universe. Angels and humans would have to be able to choose what was right according to the creator, which means they would also have the ability to choose what was wrong according to the creator. Without this baseline freedom, there could be no true worship of God, which is one of the main reasons angels and humans were created. One of the foundational tenets of true worship is recognizing and honoring the wishes of the one being worshipped. Choosing to honor the creator for who He is and to obey His commands is worship. Therefore, one must have true "free will" to really be able to worship God and glorify God.

God could have decided to create life forms that would mechanically obey Him, mechanically serve Him, and mechanically give Him praise, but there would have been no pleasure in that regard for God or for the created beings. So He did not go this route. He desired creatures with free moral agency who could choose to recognize Him as their creator, honor Him as their Lord, serve Him as their master, and love Him for who He is and for the love given to them.

God could have created the world order in a way where there would have never been an opportunity for one's free will to be tested in choosing right over wrong, good over evil, or obedience over disobedience to divine revelation. The Bible says that where there is no law, God does not count sin against us. As Romans 5:13 (NLT) tells us: "Yes, people sinned even before the law was given. But it was not counted as sin because there was not yet any law to break."

If there was no opportunity for failure, then sin would have never entered the world and bring death into existence and a need for hell. This would have been fantastic, but again there would have been a mechanical relationship between God and His created beings. Angels and humans would not have had the opportunity (chance) to freely offer their love, their faith, and their obedience to God. There would have been no purpose to life if created beings just wandered around the universe never accomplishing any moral or spiritual purpose (like an eternal ant hill with lots of busy work, but no eternal purpose). God desired the pleasure and the glory that He would get from freely offered love, praise, faith, and obedience (i.e., worship). God also wanted His created beings to experience the pleasure of freely offering up their worship (love, obedience, praise, and gratitude) to a perfect and holy creator. This is a win-win situation for God and His created beings, but it required true free will in His created beings with the ability to say "yes" or "no" to their creator.

We know that one-third of the angels said "no" to their creator, following the lead of Lucifer. Lucifer and one-third of the angels fell from their position in heaven and became evil beings called demons, with Lucifer as the head demon we now know as Satan or the devil. They were cast out of heaven. Some of them now inhabit the earth as the unseen agents of evil, carrying on their rebellion to God by trying to do everything within their power, to keep human beings in a similar state of rebellion to God—while others are locked up in a spiritual dungeon until the Great White Throne Judgment. It does appear that Satan and perhaps a number of demons have access to God in heaven whenever God allows it, but Satan seems to use these occasions for accusatorial purposes, where Satan's goal is to accuse and criticize select people on earth. Note the following passages as examples.

> In whose case the god of this world has blinded the minds of the unbelieving, so that they might not see the light of the gospel of the glory of Christ, who is the image of God. (2 Corinthians 4:4)

> And angels who did not keep their own domain, but abandoned their proper abode, He has kept in eternal bonds under darkness for the judgment of the great day. (Jude 1:6)

> Now there was a day when the sons of God came to present themselves before the Lord, and Satan also came among them. The Lord said to Satan, "From where do you come?" Then Satan answered the Lord and said, "From roaming about on the earth and walking around on it." The Lord said to Satan, "Have you considered My servant Job? For there is no one like him on the earth, a blameless and upright man, fearing God and turning away from evil." Then Satan answered the Lord, "Does Job fear God for nothing? Have You not made a hedge about him and his house and all that he has, on every side? You have blessed the work of his hands, and his possessions have increased in the land. But put forth Your hand now and touch all that he has; he will surely curse You to Your face." Then the Lord said to Satan, "Behold, all that he has is in your power, only do not put forth your hand on him." So Satan departed from the presence of the Lord. (Job 1:6–12)

Some angels (referred to as the elect angels) were protected by God's grace from rebelling with Lucifer (Satan), while the others were allowed to make their choice in following Lucifer (Satan) in his attempt to overthrow the throne of God.

> How you have fallen from heaven, O star of the morning, son of the dawn! You have been cut down to the earth, you who have weakened the nations! But you said in your heart, "I will ascend to heaven. I will raise my throne above the stars of God. And I will sit on the mount of assembly in the recesses of the north. I will ascend above the heights of the

clouds. I will make myself like the Most High." Nevertheless, you will be thrust down to Sheol, to the recesses of the pit. (Isaiah 14:12–15, NASB)

The seventy returned with joy, saying, Lord, even the demons are subject to us in Your name. And He said to them, "I was watching Satan fall from heaven like lightning. Behold, I have given you authority to tread on serpents and scorpions, and over all the power of the enemy, and nothing will injure you. Nevertheless, do not rejoice in this, that the spirits are subject to you, but rejoice that your names are recorded in heaven." (Luke 10:17–20 NASB)

After Satan's rebellion, he and his demon followers have never been offered the opportunity for redemption. Jesus Christ did not die to obtain the salvation of fallen angels (demons). He died to bring God's plan of redemption into place for those human beings chosen (before the creation of the universe) to be a part of the elect. This makes God's preserving grace to those angels He protected from following Lucifer even more incredible. They were saved from acting in a way that would have brought eternal damnation upon them with no remedy, while the others were allowed to carry out their own choices along with the devil.

Adam and Eve were allowed to make their choices. Their choices brought them and all of their human descendants throughout the rest of history into a state of spiritual separation from the Godhead. But in mercy, the Godhead executed a plan of redemption (decreed before anything was created), which would bring about the eternal salvation of millions or even billions of selected individuals. The individuals are referred to in the Bible as "the elect":

And you were dead in your trespasses and sins, in which you formerly walked according to the course of this world, according to the prince of the power of the air, of the spirit that is now working in the sons of disobedience. Among them we too all formerly lived in the lusts of our flesh, indulging the desires of the flesh and of the mind and were by nature children of wrath, even as the rest. But God, being rich in mercy, because of His great love with which He loved us, even when we were dead in our transgressions, made us alive together with Christ (by grace you have been saved), and raised us up with Him and seated us with Him in the heavenly places in Christ Jesus, so that in the ages to come He might show the surpassing riches of His grace in kindness toward us in Christ Jesus. For by grace you have been saved through faith and that not of yourselves. It is the gift of God, not as a result of works, so that no one may boast. For we are His workmanship, created in Christ Jesus for good works, which God prepared beforehand so that we would walk in them. (Ephesians 2:1–10)

There is no better way to express praise to God for His indescribable mercy and grace than the words penned by Fanny Crosby in her famous 1875 hymn titled: "To God Be the Glory."

To God Be the Glory
Text: Fanny J. Crosby
Music: William H. Doane

To God be the glory, great things he hath done!
So loved he the world that he gave us his Son,
who yielded his life an atonement for sin,
and opened the life gate that all may go in.

Refrain: Praise the Lord, praise the Lord,
let the earth hear his voice!
Praise the Lord, praise the Lord,
let the people rejoice!

O come to the Father thru Jesus the Son,
and give him the glory, great things he hath done!
O perfect redemption, the purchase of blood,
to every believer the promise of God;
the vilest offender who truly believes,
that moment from Jesus a pardon receives.
(Refrain)

Great things he hath taught us, great things he hath done,
and great our rejoicing thru Jesus the Son;
but purer, and higher, and greater will be
our wonder, our transport, when Jesus we see.
(Refrain)

The excerpt below is from C. H. Spurgeon is an inspiring confirmation of Fanny Crosby's hymn above.

Election on a Grand Scale!

From: Spurgeon's sermon called "Free Grace":

The motive for the salvation of the human race is to be found in the breast of God and not in the character or condition of man. Two races have revolted against God—the one angelic, the other human. When a part of this angelic race revolted against the Most High, justice speedily overtook them. They were swept from their starry seats in heaven and henceforth they have been reserved in darkness unto the great day of the wrath of God. No mercy was ever presented to them, no sacrifice ever offered for them, but they were without hope and mercy, forever consigned to the pit of eternal torment.

The human race, far inferior in order of intelligence, sinned just as atrociously. However, the God who in His infinite justice passed over "some angels" and forced them forever to expiate their offenses in the fires of hell, was pleased to look favorably upon man. Here was election on a grand scale—the election of manhood and the reprobation of fallen angels.

But God, who does as He wills with His own and gives no account of His matters, but who deals with His creatures as the potter deals with his clay, took not upon Him the nature of angels, but took upon Him the seed of Abraham and chose "sinful men" to be the vessels of His mercy. God sees us—abandoned, evil, wicked, and deserving His wrath. If He saves us, it is His boundless, fathomless love that nothing whatever in us deserves.[13]

In the next chapter, we get into the nuts and bolts of election and predestination by identifying the three underlying principles of these doctrines.

---

[13] Sermon No. 233. Delivered on Sabbath Morning, January 9, 1859, by the Reverend C. H. Spurgeon at the Music Hall, Royal Surrey Gardens. Copyright © 2001 by Phillip R. Johnson. All rights reserved.

8 ❧

Three Basic Principles of Election and Predestination

Chapter 8 will identity three principles of election and predestination, which give you the heart or the spirit of the matter—that is, the truth, the doctrine, the system, etc.

Principle 1

Election is unconditional

Principle 1: Election Is Unconditional

Election is unconditional, which means that it did not depend (nor can it) upon any foreseen faith or good works of any person chosen before the foundations of the world. God did not look forward into the future (throughout history) and see some kind of faith in certain persons that pleased Him and which caused Him to choose those people as His elect. God did not need to look into the future to see what would be in the heart of every person ever born. He already knew what would reside in the heart, spirit, and soul of every person who ever lived. He knew that evil would be the moral condition of every individual, whether male or female. He knew that total depravity would be the spiritual condition of every individual, whether male or female. He knew that no person would have faith on his or her own to be saved. He knew every person would be willfully lost and that the only way for any person to ever be saved was through unconditional election. Consider Acts 13:48 from the following translations:

> When the Gentiles heard this, they began rejoicing and glorifying the word of the Lord, and as many as had been appointed to eternal life believed. (NASB)

> This message made the Gentiles glad and they praised what they had heard about the Lord. Everyone who had been chosen for eternal life then put their faith in the Lord. (CEV)

> And when the Gentiles heard this, they were glad and glorified the word of the Lord, and as many as were ordained to eternal life believed. (KJ21)

> And when the Gentiles heard this, they were glad and glorified the Word of the Lord, and as many as were ordained to eternal life believed. (KJ21)

> When the Gentiles heard this, they were glad and honored the word of the Lord, and all who were appointed for eternal life believed. (NIV)

> And when the Gentiles heard this, they rejoiced and glorified (praised and gave thanks for) the Word of God, and as many as were destined (appointed and ordained) to eternal life believed (adhered to, trusted in, and relied on Jesus as the Christ and their Savior). (AMP)

> When the Gentiles heard Paul say this, they were happy [rejoiced] and gave honor to [praised] the message [word] of the Lord. And the people who were chosen [destined; appointed] to have life forever believed the message [believed]. (EXB)

The Gentiles living in Pisidian Antioch had just heard Paul explain that God had included Gentiles (and not only Jews) in His plan of salvation. They became very excited and believed in the gospel of salvation through Jesus Christ. But notice the cause-and-effect process in this verse. The ones who believed and were saved were those who had been appointed to eternal life before the creation of the universe. The appointment to eternal life was the cause and the believing in Christ for salvation was the effect. This is the way it is with every person who ever gets saved through their belief in the atoning work of Jesus Christ on the cross. The Lord starts the dominos falling in the right direction for each elect person and the sequence does not stop until that person is saved.

Cause and effect refers to the philosophical concept of causality in which an action or

event will produce a certain response to the action in the form of another event. Causality (also referred to as causation) is the relationship between an event (the cause) and a second event (the *effect*) by which the second event is understood as a consequence of the first. In common usage, causality is also the relationship between a set of factors (causes) and a phenomenon (the *effect*). Anything that affects an effect is a factor of that effect. A direct factor is a factor that affects an effect directly, that is, without any intervening factors. Intervening factors are sometimes called "intermediate factors." The connection between a cause and an effect in this way can also be referred to as a *causal nexus*.

The chart below puts cause and effect into a biblical/spiritual framework.

God's CAUSE	God's EFFECT
Eternity Past	
God Chose You	
Universe Created	You believe in Christ and experience salvation at just the right time and place.
Your Birth in Timeline of History	
Work of Grace upon Your Heart	

Principle 2: Election Is Irresistible

Principle 2

Election is irresistible

Election is irresistible, which means that God can and does exert such an influence upon a human heart and mind to make it willing and glad to repent and accept Jesus Christ as Lord and Savior. God has the power and the wisdom to help any person understand his/her moral depravity and his or her spiritual lostness, and to see his or her need for salvation from sin, self, the devil, and eternal hell. God has the power and the wisdom to help any person see that Jesus Christ was crucified on a terrible Roman cross for his or her sinfulness and that His shed blood provides the payment for his or her sinfulness and sins. God's irresistible grace enables a person to see his/her need and embrace Christ in genuine faith. Consider Philippians 2:13 from the following translations:

For it is God who is at work in you, both to will and to work for His good pleasure. (NASB)

God is working in you to make you willing and able to obey Him. (CEV)

For it is God which worketh in you both to will and to do of His good pleasure. (KJV)

For it is God who worketh in you, both to will and to do of His good pleasure. (kj21)

For it is God who works in you to will and to act in order to fulfill His good purpose. (NIV)

For it is God who is all the while effectually at work in you [energizing and creating in you the power and desire], both to will and to work for His good pleasure and satisfaction and delight. (AMP)

Because God is working in you to help you want to do and be able to do (both to will/desire and to work) what pleases Him. (EXB)

Throughout the Bible there are examples of people who were completely opposed to God, His will, and His plans. These people thought they could do as they pleased without any human or deity stopping them. Some of them thought they were in the place of God within their own domains. They saw themselves as the sovereign ruler over their own lives, families, and kingdoms. They did not recognize the true God as existing and as the supreme ruler over the universe. But in the end, each learned who was really God and saw the will and plan of God accomplished. These people demonstrated God's ability to change hearts and minds and see His desires (will) done.

Pharaoh, Moses, and the Children of Israel

God, through Moses, told Pharaoh to let the Israelites leave Egypt. Pharaoh did not want to lose all of the slave labor his nation had been enjoying and he refused to let them go. Here is Pharaoh's response to Moses in Exodus 5:1–2:

> And afterward Moses and Aaron came and said to Pharaoh, "Thus says the Lord, the God of Israel, 'Let My people go that they may celebrate a feast to Me in the wilderness.'" But Pharaoh said, "Who is the Lord that I should obey His voice to let Israel go? I do not know the Lord and besides, I will not let Israel go."

God told Moses He would pour out major plagues or calamities, known as judgments, upon Egypt that would eventually motivate Pharaoh to let them go. After the tenth judgment (the death of the firstborn child in each family throughout Egypt), Pharaoh urgently commanded Moses to take the Israelites and leave Egypt. Pharaoh did not really want to do this, but he was afraid God would eventually kill everyone in Egypt. So he let them go, only to have such regrets that he pursued them in the wilderness, only to see his entire army drowned in the Red Sea. God demonstrated His supernatural ability to convince a proud, ungodly ruler to do His will. Romans 9:17–24 (NASB) addresses God's dealings with Pharaoh:

> For the Scripture says to Pharaoh, "For this very purpose I raised you up, to demonstrate My power in you, and that My name might be proclaimed throughout the whole earth." So then, He has mercy on whom He desires, and He hardens whom He desires. You will say to me then, "Why does He still find fault? For who resists His will?" On the contrary, who are you, O man, who answers back to God? The thing molded will not say to the molder, "Why did you make me like this," will it? Or does not the potter have a right over the clay, to make from the same lump one vessel for honorable use and another for common use? What if God, although willing to demonstrate His wrath and to make His power known, endured with much patience vessels of wrath prepared for destruction? And He did so to make known the riches of His glory upon vessels of mercy, which He prepared beforehand for glory, even us, whom He also called, not from among Jews only, but also from among Gentiles.

Joshua and the Israelites Begin to Capture Palestine

Joshua and the Israelites fulfilled God's will toward these Palestinian cities (and their people) and at the same time inherited God's promise to them (the land for their use).

Joshua 11:1–23: Then it came about, when Jabin king of Hazor heard of it, that he sent to Jobab king of Madon and to the king of Shimron and to the king of Achshaph and to the kings who were of the north in the hill country and in the Arabah—south of Chinneroth and in the lowland and on the heights of Dor on the west—to the Canaanite on the east and on the west and the Amorite and the Hittite and the Perizzite and the Jebusite in the hill country and the Hivite at the foot of Hermon in the land of Mizpeh. They came out, they and all their armies with them, as many people as the sand that is on the seashore, with very many horses and chariots. So all of these kings having agreed to meet, came and encamped together at the waters of Merom, to fight against Israel. Then the Lord said to Joshua, "Do not be afraid because of them for tomorrow at this time I will deliver all of them slain before Israel. You shall hamstring their horses and burn their chariots with fire." So Joshua and all the people of war with him came upon them suddenly by the waters of Merom, and attacked them. The Lord delivered them into the hand of Israel, so that they defeated them and pursued them as far as Great Sidon and Misrephoth-maim and the valley of Mizpeh to the east and they struck them until no survivor was left to them. Joshua did to them as the Lord had told him. He hamstrung their horses and burned their chariots with fire. Then Joshua turned back at that time and captured Hazor and struck its king with the sword. For Hazor formerly was the head of all these kingdoms. They struck every person who was in it with the edge of the sword, utterly destroying them. There was no one left who breathed. And he burned Hazor with fire. Joshua captured all the cities of these kings and all their kings and he struck them with the edge of the sword and utterly destroyed them, just as Moses the servant of the Lord had commanded. However, Israel did not burn any cities that stood on their mounds, except Hazor alone, which Joshua burned. All the spoil of these cities and the cattle, the sons of Israel took as their plunder, but they struck every man with the edge of the sword, until they had destroyed them. They left no one who breathed. Just as the Lord had commanded Moses his servant, so Moses commanded Joshua, and Joshua did. He left nothing undone of all that the Lord had commanded Moses. Thus, Joshua took all that land, the hill country and all the Negev, all that land of Goshen, the lowland, the Arabah, the hill country of Israel and its lowland from Mount Halak, that rises toward Seir, even as far as Baal-gad in the valley of Lebanon at the foot of Mount Hermon. And he captured all their kings and struck them down and put them to death. Joshua waged war a long time with all these kings. There was not a city which made peace with the sons of Israel except the Hivites living in Gibeon. They took them all in battle. For it was of the Lord to harden their hearts, to meet Israel in battle in order that he might utterly destroy them, that they might receive no mercy, but that he might destroy them, just as the Lord had commanded Moses. Then Joshua came at that time and cut off the Anakim from the hill country, from Hebron, from Debir, from Anab and from all the hill country of Judah and from all the hill country of Israel. Joshua utterly destroyed them with their cities. There were no Anakim left in the land of the sons of Israel, only in Gaza, in Gath, and in Ashdod some remained. So Joshua took the whole land, according to all that the Lord had spoken to Moses, and Joshua gave it for an inheritance to Israel according to their divisions by their tribes. Thus, the land had rest from war.

God had promised this land to the children of Israel hundreds of years earlier (including what is now the Gaza Strip and the West Bank). By the way, God could only promise this land to the Israelites and give it to the Israelites as a gift if He owned it in the first place. Does not Psalm 24:1–2 say, "The earth is the LORD's and all it contains, the world and those who dwell in it. For He has founded it upon the seas and established it upon the rivers."

The inhabitants of the land had finally reached the full measure of their sin where God was no longer willing to allow these people to live and occupy this land. He planned the arrival of the Israelites from Egypt just at the right time to execute His judgment upon these cities/kingdoms. Joshua and the Israelites fulfilled God's will toward these cities (and their people) and at the same time inherited God's promise to them (the land for their use). The Scriptures above state how God specifically hardened the hearts of these city or regional kings to join together in fighting Israel, so that God could give the Israelites a complete victory over them and save time. God allowed these city or regional kings to think that they could join together and defeat Israel, rather than realizing it was a hopeless cause and that they should flee for their lives. This incident is very similar to how God hardened the heart of the Egyptian pharaoh to pursue the Israelites into the Red Sea where they drowned.

Nebuchadnezzar, King of Babylon

God made Nebuchadnezzar the greatest king on earth during his day. He ruled the known world from 605–562 BC. Rather than honoring and praising God for His great blessings upon Nebuchadnezzar, he became proud and arrogant and gave himself credit for everything he had and everything he had accomplished. God sent Daniel to warn Nebuchadnezzar to humble himself before God and give God the credit for his life and accomplishments. Nebuchadnezzar ignored the warning. A year later God took away Nebuchadnezzar's sanity and drove him into the wilderness to live like an animal for seven years. During those seven years, God kept him from dying or being killed, so he could complete God's plan for his life. During that time, Nebuchadnezzar was humbled before God. After seven years God restored Nebuchadnezzar's sanity and kingdom. This is what Nebuchadnezzar had to say after this experience. As you read Nebuchadnezzar's testimony below, keep Proverbs 21:1 (NIV) in mind: "The king's heart is in the hand of the Lord. He directs it like a watercourse wherever he pleases."

> But at the end of that period, I, Nebuchadnezzar, raised my eyes toward heaven and my reason returned to me and I blessed the Most High and praised and honored Him who lives forever. For His dominion is an everlasting dominion and His kingdom endures from generation to generation. All the inhabitants of the earth are accounted as nothing, but He does according to His will in the host of heaven and among the inhabitants of earth. And no one can ward off His hand or say to Him, "What have You done?" At that time, my reason returned to me and my majesty and splendor were restored to me for the glory of my kingdom and my counselors and my nobles began seeking me out. So I was reestablished in my sovereignty and surpassing greatness was added to me. Now I, Nebuchadnezzar, praise, exalt, and honor the King of heaven, for all His works are true and His ways just and He is able to humble those who walk in pride. (Daniel 4:34–37)

Once again God demonstrated His supernatural ability to convince another proud, ungodly ruler to do His will.

In the New Testament, one of the best-known stories of God changing a person's heart, who was completely opposed to His will and plans, is Saul of Tarsus who became known as the apostle Paul after his conversion. As a totally dedicated Jewish religious leader from the respected group known as the Pharisees, Saul was convinced that Christians were heretics. In the name of preserving the Jewish faith, Saul felt compelled to pursue, persecute, imprison, and even try to have Christians put to death (even though these were fellow Jews and their only fault in his eyes was believing in Christ).

But God Almighty had other plans for Saul of Tarsus and Jesus Christ struck Saul down with something similar to a bolt of lightning as he was walking on a road from Jerusalem to Damascus. The Lord Jesus spoke out loud to Saul and told him that he was a chosen vessel to carry the Christian message to the Gentile world (whom the Jewish nation despised). Saul met Jesus Christ personally on that dusty road and immediately became a committed Christian who would spiritually shake the Roman world and who would write more of the New Testament books than anyone else. Review his conversion testimony recorded in Acts 9:1–18:

Now Saul, still breathing threats and murder against the disciples of the Lord, went to the high priest, and asked for letters from him to the synagogues at Damascus, so that if he found any belonging to the Way, both men and women, he might bring them bound to Jerusalem. As he was traveling, it happened that he was approaching Damascus and suddenly a light from heaven flashed around him and he fell to the ground and heard a voice saying to him, "Saul, Saul, why are you persecuting Me?" And he said, "Who are You, Lord?" And He said, "I am Jesus whom you are persecuting, but get up and enter the city and it will be told you what you must do." The men who traveled with him stood speechless, hearing the voice but seeing no one. Saul got up from the ground, and though his eyes were open, he could see nothing and leading him by the hand, they brought him into Damascus. And he was three days without sight and neither ate nor drank. Now there was a disciple at Damascus named Ananias and the Lord said to him in a vision, "Ananias." And he said, "Here I am, Lord." And the Lord said to him, "Get up and go to the street called Straight, and inquire at the house of Judas for a man from Tarsus named Saul, for he is praying, and he has seen in a vision a man named Ananias come in and lay his hands on him, so that he might regain his sight." But Ananias answered, "Lord, I have heard from many about this man, how much harm he did to Your saints at Jerusalem and here he has authority from the chief priests to bind all who call on Your name." But the Lord said to him, "Go, for he is a chosen instrument of Mine, to bear My name before the Gentiles and kings and the sons of Israel, for I will show him how much he must suffer for My name's sake." So Ananias departed and entered the house and after laying his hands on him said, "Brother Saul, the Lord Jesus, who appeared to you on the road by which you were coming, has sent me so that you may regain your sight and be filled with the Holy Spirit." And immediately there fell from his eyes something like scales and he regained his sight and he got up and was baptized and he took food and was strengthened. Now for several days he was with the disciples who were at Damascus and immediately he began to proclaim Jesus in the synagogues saying, "He is the Son of God." All those hearing him continued to be amazed and were saying, "Is this not he who in Jerusalem destroyed those who called on this name and who had come here for the purpose of bringing them bound before the chief priests?" But Saul kept increasing in strength and confounding the Jews who lived at Damascus by proving that this Jesus is the Christ.

The Lord Jesus did not ask Saul if he wanted to serve Him and take His message to the Gentiles. Jesus just told Saul that he was a chosen instrument and would do His will. Saul immediately submitted to Jesus Christ as his personal Lord and Savior and began obeying His Word. The experience on the Damascus Road only took a few minutes, but it produced probably the greatest Christian who has ever lived, illustrating the power and ability of God to do whatever He wants with any human being.

The following Bible verses also testify to God's sovereign power and ability over human hearts and minds.

The Lord said to him, "Who has made man's mouth? Or who makes him mute or deaf or seeing or blind? Is it not I, the Lord?" (Exodus 4:11)

The Spirit of God has made me and the breath of the Almighty gives me life. (Job 33:4)

Not to us, O Lord, not to us, But to Your name give glory because of Your lovingkindness, because of Your truth. Why should the nations say, "Where, now, is their God?" But our God is in the heavens. He does whatever He pleases. (Psalm 115:1–3)

For I know that the Lord is great and that our Lord is above all gods. Whatever the Lord pleases, He does in heaven and in earth, in the seas and in all deeps. He causes the vapors to ascend from the ends of the earth and makes lightnings for the rain and brings forth the wind from His treasuries. He smote the firstborn of Egypt, both of man and beast. He sent signs and wonders into your midst, O Egypt, upon Pharaoh and all his servants. He smote many nations and slew mighty kings, Sihon, king of the Amorites, And Og, king of Bashan, and all the kingdoms of Canaan. And He gave their land as a heritage, a heritage to Israel His people. (Psalm 135:5–12)

It is He who changes the times and the epochs. He removes kings and establishes kings. He gives wisdom to wise men and knowledge to men of understanding. It is He who reveals the profound and hidden things. He knows what is in the darkness and the light dwells with Him. (Daniel 2:21–22)

The Lord of hosts has sworn saying, "Surely, just as I have intended so it has happened and just as I have planned so it will stand, to break Assyria in My land and I will trample him on My mountains. Then his yoke will be removed from them and his burden removed from their shoulder. This is the plan devised against the whole earth and this is the hand that is stretched out against all the nations. For the Lord of hosts has planned and who can frustrate it? And as for His stretched out hand, who can turn it back?" (Isaiah 14:24–27)

That men may know from the rising to the setting of the sun that there is no one besides Me. I am the Lord, and there is no other, the One forming light and creating darkness, causing wellbeing and creating calamity. I am the Lord who does all these. (Isaiah 45:6–7)

Before I formed you in the womb I knew you and before you were born I consecrated you. I have appointed you a prophet to the nations. (Jeremiah 1:5)

For I know the plans that I have for you, declares the Lord, plans for welfare and not for calamity and to give you a future and a hope. (Jeremiah 29:11)

Ah Lord God! Behold, You have made the heavens and the earth by Your great power and by Your outstretched arm! Nothing is too difficult for You. (Jeremiah 32:17)

Moreover, I will give you a new heart and put a new spirit within you and I will remove the heart of stone from your flesh and give you a heart of flesh. I will put My Spirit within you and cause you to walk in My statutes and you will be careful to observe My ordinances. (Ezekiel 36:26–27)

For God has put it in their hearts to execute His purpose by having a common purpose and by giving their kingdom to the beast, until the words of God will be fulfilled. (Revelation 17:17)

The following commentary, *The Nature of Effectual Calling*, by Thomas Boston, also helps us grasp God's sovereign power and ability over human hearts and minds. Thomas Boston was a respected Scottish church leader, theologian and philosopher. An excerpt follows:

Effectual calling is the first entrance of a soul into the state of grace, the first step by which God's eternal purpose of love descends unto sinners, and we again ascend toward the glory to which we are chosen. And upon the matter, it is the same with conversion and regeneration.

Negatively. It is neither the piety, parts, nor seriousness of those who are employed to carry the gospel call to sinners, 1 Cor. iii.7. Indeed, if moral suasion were sufficient to bring sinners back to God, men that have the art of persuading, and can speak movingly and seriously could not fail to have vast numbers of converts. But that work is not so brought about, Luke xvi. ult. Hence said Abraham to the rich man in hell, "If they hear not Moses and the prophets, neither will they be persuaded though one rose from the dead." Never did these, conjunctly or severally, appear in any, as in any, as in Christ, who "spake as never man spake." But behold the issue, John xii. 37, 38. "But though he had done so many miracles before them, yet they believed not on him: that the saying Esaias the prophet might be fulfilled, which he spake, 'Lord, who hath believed our report? and to whom hath the arm of the Lord been revealed?' Neither is it one that uses his own free will better than another does," Rom. ix. 6. "It is not of him that willeth, nor of him that runneth, but of God that sheweth mercy." For every man will be unwilling till the power from another quarter make him willing, John vi. 44. If it were so, one man should make himself to differ from another in that grand point. But hear what the apostle Paul says, 1 Cor. iv. 7. "Who maketh thee to differ from another?" Men are dead in trespasses and sins, and such cannot difference themselves.

Positively. We may say in this case, "Not by might, nor by power, but by the Spirit of the Lord." It is the Spirit of the Lord, accompanying the call of the word, that makes it effectual, John vi. 63. Hence days of the plentiful effusion of the Spirit are good days for the take of souls, and contrary wise, when the Spirit is restrained, Psal. cx. 3. Therefore, Isaiah resolves the question thus, "Who hath believed our report? and to whom is the arm of the Lord revealed?" The report may reach the ears, but it is the arm of the Lord that must open the heart.[14]

Principle 3: In Utilizing Election, God Cannot Be Charged with Injustice

Principle 3

Election is not chargeable with injustice

Election—that is, God's use of it—is not chargeable with injustice. We can speak of injustice only when one party has a legitimate claim on another party. When some critics consider election and predestination, they tend to evaluate the doctrines based on their own limited concept of human fairness, which is shallow, faulty, and inconsistent. They cannot see the beginning from the end. They are not able to grasp all of the factors involved in creation, the fall, and the eternal plan of redemption. Most critics do not consider the rights of creation possessed only by God. And more than anything, such skeptics have a hard time accepting the total depravity of man, which makes election and predestination an absolute necessity for even one person to be saved and restored to a relationship with God.

Biblical revelation makes it very clear that no created being has ever had a legitimate claim against the Creator. Consider Romans 9:19-24

You will say to me then, "Why does He still find fault? For who resists His will?" On the

---

[14] Excerpt from *A Complete Body of Divinity, Volume 1*, by Thomas Boston (Charleston, South Carolina: Nabu Press, 2010).

contrary, who are you, O man, who answers back to God? The thing molded will not say to the molder, "Why did you make me like this," will it? Or does not the potter have a right over the clay, to make from the same lump one vessel for honorable use and another for common use? What if God, although willing to demonstrate His wrath and to make His power known, endured with much patience vessels of wrath prepared for destruction? And He did so to make known the riches of His glory upon vessels of mercy, which He prepared beforehand for glory, even us, whom He also called, not from among Jews only, but also from among Gentiles.

Romans 9 identifies several situations where parties might have thought they had a claim on God, but it was not so, illustrated by the following cases.

The first case involves the Israelites who thought they had the right to be the eternal children of God, because they were the biological descendants of Abraham. But Paul negates that claim and explains that the true children of God are those who are referred to as the children of the promise. There is an analogy here between Abraham's children who came into the world through natural means when Abraham and Hagar had Ishmael together and Abraham's children who came into the world through supernatural means with Abraham and Sarah having Isaac together at their advanced ages. Abraham was ninety-nine and Sarah was ninety. Sarah had passed the age of bearing children on her own. God had to empower Sarah to conceive, which He did.

Paul uses this scenario to illustrate the difference in Jews who were considered God's people through biological means (as descendants of Abraham and Sarah) and Christians who are God's children through supernatural means (born again through the power of the Holy Spirit). The Jews have historically seen themselves as God's children in this world who have a claim on God as their Father, as the biological descendants of Abraham. The Jews told Jesus in John 8:32 that they were Abraham's descendants and had never been enslaved to anyone. So they could not understand how He could tell them that they could become free from sin through faith in Him and be born again spiritually into the family of God.

Rather than trying to grasp how they could become true children of God for all of eternity by accepting Jesus Christ as God and as their Lord and Savior, they focused on their claim and right to be God's children as biological descendants (children) of Abraham. They had no claims on God or rights to anything and they could not charge God with injustice because of any Gentiles He chose to save and bring into the kingdom of God.

The second case involves Esau and Jacob. Although they were twins born to Isaac and Rebecca, Esau was born first. As the first born, he inherited certain traditional privileges and rights, which he became fully aware of as he was growing up. No one knows if the twins were made of aware of God's Word to Isaac and Rebecca before they were born, but God declared (as their creator) that contrary to their tradition, the older would serve the younger, that He had already made a choice to love Jacob and hate Esau, and that this choice had nothing to do with the good or bad of either child, because the choice was made before they were born.

When the Scripture declares that God chose to hate Esau, this really rubs the carnal mind the wrong way. What God was communicating here, in context of all Scripture, was that He had chosen beforehand to let Esau go his own way and do his own thing, which resulted in Esau living a selfish, stubborn, and sinful life, which God hated and rejected. Jacob was just as bad in his lying, deceiving, manipulating, and contriving ways, but God chose beforehand to pursue Jacob with His grace, overcome his carnal ways, and turn him into a man of faith who followed God. Therefore, God could declare beforehand, "Jacob have I loved," or if I can paraphrase like this, "I love Jacob and what Jacob will become through My power and grace."

God exercised His sovereign choice as creator to let Jacob inherit the blessings of the first born and to establish His covenant with Jacob. Esau had no claims on God's decision and Esau had no basis for charging God with injustice. Paul uses this story as an illustration of God's right to choose those who would be saved throughout history before anyone came into existence and did anything good and bad. As Paul so eloquently put it in Romans 9:11, "So that God's purpose according to His choice would stand, not because of works but because of Him who calls." Consider these words from Spurgeon's sermon titled, "Jacob and Esau":[15]

> Jacob have I loved, but Esau have I hated. (Romans 9:15). *There is a man up in the gallery there, that, work as hard as he likes, he cannot earn more than fifteen shillings a week. And here is another man that gets a thousand a year.* What is the reason of this? One is born in the palaces of kings, while another draws his first breath in a roofless hovel. What is the reason of this? God's providence—God puts one man in one position, and another man in another. Here is a man whose head cannot hold two thoughts together. Here is another man who can sit down and write a book and dive into the deepest of questions. What is the reason of it? God has done it. Do you not see the fact that God does not treat every man alike? He has made some eagles and some worms. He has made some lions and some creeping lizards. He has made some men kings and some are born beggars. Some are born with gigantic minds and some verge on the idiot. Why is this? Do you murmur at God for it?

---

[15] "Jacob and Esau," preached at the New Park Street Pulpit on January 16, 1859, and adapted from the C. H. Spurgeon Collection, Version 1.0, Ages Software.

No. You say it is a fact and there is no good in murmuring. What is the use of kicking against **facts**? It is only kicking against the pricks with naked feet and you hurt yourself and not them.

Well then—election is a positive **fact**. It is as clear as daylight, that God does, in matters of religion, give to one man more than to another. He gives to me opportunities of hearing the word, which He does not give to the Hottentot. He gives to me, parents who, from infancy, trained me in the fear of the Lord. He does not give that to many of you. He places me afterward in situations where I am restrained from sin. Other men are cast into places where their sinful passions are developed. He gives, to one man a disposition which keeps him back from some lust, and to another man he gives such impetuosity of spirit, and depravity turns that impetuosity so much, that the man runs headlong into sin. Again, he brings one man under the sound of a powerful ministry, while another sits and listens to a preacher whose drowsiness is only exceeded by that of his hearers. And even when they are hearing the gospel, the fact is God works in one heart when He does not in another. Though, I believe to a degree, the Spirit works in the hearts of all who hear the Word, so that they are all without excuse, yet I am sure He works in some so powerfully, that they can no longer resist Him, but are constrained by His grace to cast themselves at his feet and confess him Lord of all, while others resist the grace that comes into their hearts and it does not act with the same irresistible force that it does in the other case and they perish in their sins, deservedly and justly condemned.

Are not these things **facts**? Does any man deny them? Can any man deny them? What is the use of kicking against facts? What then, is the use of our discussing any longer? We had better believe it, since it is an undeniable truth. You may alter an opinion, but you cannot alter a fact. You may change a mere doctrine, but you cannot possibly change a thing which actually exists. There it is—God does certainly deal with some men better than He does with others. I will not offer an apology for God. He can explain His own dealings and He needs no defense from me. There stands the fact. Before you begin to argue upon the doctrine just recollect, that whatever you may think about it, you cannot alter it and however much you may object to it, it is actually true that God did love Jacob and did not love Esau.

Why did God love Jacob? Because of His sovereign grace. There was nothing in Jacob that could make God love him. There was everything about him that might have made God hate him, as much as He did Esau, and a great deal more. But it was because God was infinitely gracious that He loved Jacob, and because He was sovereign in his dispensation of this grace, that he chose Jacob as the object of that love. "He will have mercy on whom he will have mercy." And rest assured, the only reason why any of us can hope to be saved is this—the sovereign grace of God. There is no reason why I should be saved or why you should be saved, but God's own merciful heart, and God's own omnipotent will.

The third case involves what God explained to Moses about His dealings with Pharaoh, which is Romans 9:13: "For the Scripture says to Pharaoh, 'For this very purpose I raised you up, to demonstrate My power in you and that My name might be proclaimed throughout the whole earth.' So then, He has mercy on whom He desires and He hardens whom He desires."

God raised Pharaoh up to show that He has control over all circumstances in the universe. Pharaoh thought he was the one in control of his life, his family, and his nation. He thought he could do as he pleased with anyone or anything, including the Israelites. God executed a plan to show Pharaoh and all of the Egyptians that there was only one God and it was not Pharaoh. God's plan was to command Pharaoh to let the Israelites leave Egypt with the threat of plagues if he didn't obey. God knew He was going to allow Pharaoh to just harden his heart and not agree to anything.

With each judgment, Pharaoh hardened his heart even more so he refused to do what God said. God continued to pour out judgments upon his nation where everyone in Egypt could see the God of Israel was the true God and the only God. As Pharaoh continued to harden his heart and disobey, God had the chance to display His power over nature, angelic forces, false gods, the magicians of Egypt, and all humanity. God knew Pharaoh would not agree (obey) to let the Israelites go until Pharaoh finally lost his firstborn son and was afraid he was going to lose his own life. After the death angel killed all the firstborn children in Egypt, Pharaoh chased Moses and the Israelites out of Egypt. But God was not through demonstrating His power, and He stirred up the heart of Pharaoh to send his army after the Israelites in the wilderness in a feeble attempt to bring them back or kill them in the trying. God staged the last act of this saga to issue His final judgment upon Egypt, the destruction of the entire Egyptian army in the Red Sea.

In Romans 2:4 Paul explained a very important principle. He wrote, under the inspiration of the Holy Spirit, that the goodness of God leads people to repentance. When God desires to lead a person toward repentance and faith, He generally pours out His goodness, in one form or another, upon that person to motivate them to consider their life and their need for salvation. This principle is the exact opposite of the principle God used with Pharaoh. God told Moses that He was going to harden the heart of Pharaoh. How did God harden Pharaoh's heart? God poured out one plague (judgment) after another upon the nation of Egypt. With each plague or judgment, Pharaoh's heart got harder toward God, Moses, and the Israelites. His stubbornness reached its peak when he told Moses that he would kill him if he ever saw him again (and it was only the power of God that kept Pharaoh from killing Moses in the very beginning of the exchanges between the two). Moses agreed that they would never meet again and that God was going to judge Pharaoh's arrogance and stubbornness by killing the firstborn child of every family in Egypt including the firstborn of Pharaoh.

After that dreadful night when the death angel passed through every home in Egypt and killed the firstborn child in each family that was not covered with the blood of a lamb upon the door, Pharaoh ordered the Israelites to quickly leave Egypt. Pharaoh did not agree to this, because he had a change of heart and wanted to obey and honor God. He only agreed to let the Israelites depart, because he and his people were afraid they were all going to die if the Israelites didn't go. Once again God demonstrated in the most public of ways that He has the power to get people to do what He wants, either through His goodness or through His raw power. Pharaoh had no basis for claiming injustice with God. Once again Romans 9:16–18 reaffirms this: "So then, it does not depend on the man who wills or the man who runs, but on God who has mercy. For the Scripture says to Pharaoh, "For this very purpose I raised you up, to demonstrate My power in you and that My name might be proclaimed throughout the whole earth." So then, He has mercy on whom He desires and He hardens whom He desires."

The fourth case involves the relationship of a potter with his clay as an analogy of God's relationship with His created beings. Paul expresses the analogy in these words in Romans 9:20–21, "The thing molded will not say to the molder, 'Why did you make me like this,' will it? Or does not the potter have a right over the clay, to make from the same lump one vessel for honorable use and another for common use?"

For illustration sake, Paul uses the absurd idea of a piece of clay rising up and saying to its potter, "Why did you make me like this?" This is absurd for several reasons. First, a potter has sovereign rights over his clay. Second, a potter has all authority over his clay. Third, a potter has total power over his clay. He can do as he pleases with his own clay. Fourth, the clay has no right, authority, or power to question the potter and anything he does with the clay. The potter can make the clay into any shape or form he wants. The potter can make his clay into something beautiful for noble use or he can make his clay into a common bowl or cup or vase. The potter can make a piece of clay into something and then decide to throw it away or tear it down and make it into something completely different. There are no limitations to what a potter can do with his own clay.

A lump of clay simply has no ability or power to resist the potter or to even question the potter. The analogy may be hard for some people to accept, but the message is very clear. Human beings are God's clay. He has the right to do with us as He pleases. As a master potter, God shaped and made Adam out of dirt and He had the right to do with Adam as He pleased. We came from Adam and, as such, we are also God's clay and He has the right to do with us as He pleases. None of us has a basis for charging God with injustice. Romans 9:22–24 states, "What if God, although willing to demonstrate His wrath and to make His power known, endured with much patience vessels of wrath prepared for destruction? And He did so to make known the riches of His glory upon vessels of mercy, which He prepared beforehand for glory, even us, whom He also called, not from among Jews only, but also from among Gentiles."

The fifth case involves the relationship God establishes with those who were not considered His people. Paul refers back to Hosea in Romans 9:25–26 (NASB) when he quotes, "I will call those who were not My people, 'My people,' and her who was not beloved, 'beloved.' And it shall be that in the place where it was said to them, 'you are not My people, there they shall be called sons of the living God.'" This scenario refers to the contrast between Jews and Gentiles. Jews historically have only recognized two classes of people on earth, themselves (all true Jews) and everyone else (Gentiles). Jews have always seen themselves as God's chosen people, but Paul explained in Romans 9 that the eternal children of God are those whom God has chosen among Jews and among Gentiles. Gentiles were not seen as God's people, but God revealed that He had chosen many Gentiles to be saved and become His true children through their faith in Jesus Christ. With His choice of untold numbers of Gentiles, God cannot be charged by Jews of injustice. God has the right to grant grace and faith to anyone He chooses anywhere in the world from any ethnic group. In fact, God makes it very clear that unless He had chosen a specific number of Jews to be saved, none of them would end up in heaven, even though they had been a part of God's chosen nation on earth.

The Holy Spirit expressed it though Paul like this, "Though the number of the sons of Israel be like the sand of the sea, it is the remnant that will be saved, for the Lord will execute His Word on the earth, thoroughly and quickly" (Romans 9:27). Though the Jews multiplied into millions and millions of people since Abraham fathered this unique people's group, it is only the remnant of specific individual Jews who were chosen by God to become His eternal children. "Remnant" in this verse is a very precise phrase representing the elect from among all the Jews who will ever live. Many Jews may find this hard to believe, but the Word of God is clear. God offered the good news of salvation through Jesus Christ to the nation of Israel first. Those who had been chosen responded to the gospel and committed their lives to the Lordship of Jesus Christ. The others used their corrupted free wills to reject Christ and continue on their path of unbelief and self-righteousness, believing they would go to heaven simply because they were Jews by birth. God allowed them to make their choices and go their way. Some Jews have to come to Christ throughout each century since the church began, showing themselves to be a part of that remnant chosen by grace. The final Jews will be saved during the Great Tribulation period when God pours out His grace upon every Jew living at that time. He will open all of their eyes and they will see Jesus Christ really is the Son of God who died for their sins on that Roman cross in the first century. They will all accept Christ as their Lord and Savior, and as it says in Romans 11:26, all Israel will be saved in a moment's time as the deliverer comes and removes all ungodliness from Jacob.

Paul made this additional comment quoting Isaiah, "And just as Isaiah foretold, unless the Lord of the Sabbath had left to us a posterity, we would have become like Sodom and would have resembled Gomorrah." This comment applies to Jews and Gentiles. If the Lord had not preserved a certain number of true believers in the nation of Israel, the entire nation would have become totally depraved like Sodom and Gomorrah. Sodom and Gomorrah threw off all moral restraints, along with the acknowledgment of God, and plunged themselves into a state of total sexual perversion. They became so evil that God rained fire and brimstone down upon them. They were completely eliminated from the earth as a warning to anyone else who would ever learn of this destruction.

Likewise, if the Lord had not preserved, by grace, a certain number of true believers around the world, from the day Noah and his family got off of the ark and began repopulating the earth, all of humanity would have again become totally degenerate like Sodom and Gomorrah, deserving total annihilation (as was seen in the worldwide flood). Election has been the only thing that has allowed humanity to continue. Without God's preserving grace, every individual in every single community around the world would become totally degenerate, deserving God's wrath and destruction. Humanity would not have survived until this day or a day beyond without the preserving grace expressed through election and predestination.

In Matthew 20:1–16, Jesus shared a parable that illustrates in a very practical way how God cannot be charged with injustice because of the sovereignty of God through the doctrine of election:

> For the kingdom of heaven is like a landowner who went out early in the morning to hire laborers for his vineyard. When he had agreed with the laborers for a denarius for the day, he sent them into his vineyard. And he went out about the third hour and saw others standing idle in the market place and to those he said, "You also go into the vineyard and whatever is right I will give you." And so they went. Again, he went out about the sixth and the ninth hour and did the same thing. And about the eleventh hour he went out and found others standing around and he said to them, "Why have you been standing here idle all day long?" They said to him, "Because no one hired us." He said to them, "You go into the vineyard too." When evening came, the owner of the vineyard said to his

foreman, "Call the laborers and pay them their wages, beginning with the last group to the first." When those hired about the eleventh hour came, each one received a denarius. When those hired first came, they thought that they would receive more, but each of them also received a denarius. When they received it, they grumbled at the landowner, saying, "These last men have worked only one hour and you have made them equal to us who have borne the burden and the scorching heat of the day." But he answered and said to one of them, "Friend, I am doing you no wrong. Did you not agree with me for a denarius? Take what is yours and go, but I wish to give to this last man the same as to you. Is it not lawful for me to do what I wish with what is my own? Or is your eye envious because I am generous?" So the last shall be first, and the first last.

The workers who were hired first around six in the morning believed they had a claim of injustice against the vineyard owner, because they worked all day for a *denarius,* which was the going rate for a day's work, and the workers hired around five (one hour before the work day was over) also got paid a *denarius.* To these workers who had put in a full day's work (around twelve hours including breaks) it just did not seem fair (just) that those workers hired later on in the day got paid the exact same thing they were paid, a *denarius.* They reasoned among themselves that surely the vineyard owner would either pay them more for working a full day or pay the other workers less who worked shorter shifts, depending on what time of the day they were hired.

The workday usually began around 6:00 a.m. and lasted until six in the evening, close to sunset. The vineyard owner went back into the marketplace three more times during the day to see who was there. He went there at the third hour (9:00 a.m.), at the sixth (12 noon), at the ninth hour (3:00 p.m.) and the eleventh hour (5:00 p.m.). Each time he found workers waiting there, trying to find work for the day. Each time he decided to hire the workers, he found and sent them to work in his vineyard. Even at five, when he found men there still waiting and hoping for work, even though the day was almost over, he exercised mercy and hired them to finish the workday in his vineyard.

When the day was over around six, all the men gathered around to be paid for their one day's work. The owner of the vineyard (the employer) paid each worker, no matter what time they were hired, a *denarius,* which was a fair day's wage. He was completely honest, just, and fair with those he hired at 6:00am in the morning, but for those hired throughout the day, he was merciful and generous. In all reality, the vineyard owner rewarded those men who kept themselves available for work throughout the day even though their hope of gaining any work faded more and more as the day went on. The men who kept themselves available throughout the day, especially until the later hours of 3:00 p.m. and 5:00 p.m., were amazing. The vineyard owner seemed very impressed that these men did not give up hope and go home and sit around feeling sorry for themselves. He also knew that each of these men had families to take care of and who were waiting for these men to bring home food for the night and following day. These men had the same needs as the men hired at 6:00am or 9:00am or noon and these men did not give up trying to find work. They kept themselves available to the very end of the day. Therefore the vineyard owner really rewarded them more for their availability than any work they completed, which was his right and choice to do.

The workers hired first thing in the morning felt cheated, that they put in all that work during the heat of the day, and got paid the same thing as those who only worked for one hour at the end of the day. To them this was unjust and they sincerely thought they had a claim against their employer. But the vineyard owner didn't see it that way. He told them he paid them exactly what he promised and exactly what they had agreed upon. He told them to take their money and go home and that he was free to pay the others whatever he wanted and that they should not complain about his generosity to those who had similar needs. He posed the question to them that sums up the principle. "Is it not lawful for me to do what I wish with what is my own?"

This parable has many practical applications for everyday life and the work environment, but it also has applications for eternal life, election, and predestination. To start with, some people live sinful, irresponsible lives and then get saved right before they die (like the workers who worked for one hour and got paid a full day's wage). Then they go to the same heaven as those who got saved as a child and served the Lord in faithfulness all their lives (like the workers who worked all day). There will be a difference in eternal rewards given out at the judgment seat of Christ (the awards platform in heaven called the Bema) based upon faithful service and sacrifice, but in the context of the parable, we all get to go to the same heaven, whether we got saved at 6:00 a.m. or 5:00 p.m.

People can only come to Christ and get saved when the Holy Spirit works upon their heart and draws them to Christ. The Lord in His wisdom brings "elect individuals" to salvation at the times He has planned and then He rewards those individuals with the same eternal life as every other elect person, no matter if they were saved a few minutes before they died (as the converted thief on the cross with Christ) or they were saved 100 years before they died. It is lawful for the Lord to do what He wishes with His own.

In purely human reasoning, some people look at this judgment as unfair when others live in sinful pleasure all their lives and then get saved at the last moment, die, and still get to go to heaven. Such reasoning might be considered an inadvertent acknowledgment that they wished they could have indulged in sinful pleasures for as long as possible and still get saved and get to go to heaven (like the workers who labored all day wished they could have been hired at 5:00 p.m. and still got a full day's wage). But what kind of spiritual attitude is that? This attitude does not recognize the effects of sin in this life upon anyone living in it, whether they go to heaven or not. And it does not recognize the danger of dying in one's sin during all of those sinful years and going to hell. No one really knows they are going to get saved until it happens. For a person to think he or she can live in sin for a determined period of time and then get saved at the last minute is pure presumption and presumption of the worst kind. This attitude also fails to recognize the pleasure, the satisfaction, and the blessings which come through living a pure and righteous life by the grace of God. There is nothing better in this life than living in an intimate fellowship with Jesus Christ and the Holy Spirit.

In the next chapter, we will connect the dots between election and predestination and five of the most important truths in the Bible that spring from election and predestination.

9

Election and Predestination: The Foundations of Many Biblical Truths

Election and predestination provide the foundation of many truths evangelical Christians hold dear to their hearts, but many Christians have not made the connection between these truths and election and predestination. Consider the relationship between election and predestination and the following five subjects.

Salvation

The previous chapters have gone into great detail about the absolute necessity of election and predestination for anyone throughout history to ever be saved. Because of the total depravity of man, no one would ever choose to be saved on his or her own. We would all choose self and sin over salvation and righteousness and willingly go to hell (not believing we would really end up there). God in His mercy and through His irresistible grace had to pursue (literally chase down and tackle so to speak) elect sinners to save them (the chase was framed by His love and executed with His grace to win the heart and mind of the sinner). This would be a good place to list the famous acronym TULIP, which sprang up during the famous Reformation period as a summation of Calvinistic teachings about election and predestination, even though John Calvin never used this term. Most of the points have been addressed already, but are listed here as a summation related to the acronym "TULIP."

The acronym called TULIP was created by a theological student who was trying to devise a way to help him remember the big five points of Calvinism.[16]

1. Total Depravity (also known as Total Inability and Original Sin)
2. Unconditional Election
3. Limited Atonement (also known as Particular Atonement)
4. Irresistible Grace
5. Perseverance of the Saints (also known as Once Saved Always Saved)

These five categories do not comprise Calvinism in totality. They simply represent some of its main points. John Calvin, along with many of the Reformers, tried to apply all of the Bible to every area of life (believing that is its purpose).

Total Depravity

Sin has affected all parts of man. The human spirit, heart, emotions, will, mind, and body are all affected by sin. We were born completely sinful. Any individual may not be as sinful as he or she could be, but we were all affected by the fall of Adam and Eve into their sinful state (spiritual condition). On the other hand, there seems to be no limit to how sinful any one person can become. If you take a gallon of pure, clean, transparent water and squirt some black or brown food coloring in it then shake it up real good—what happens? Every molecule of that water is then tainted with some degree of the black or brown food coloring. The more food coloring you pour in, the darker the taint becomes. All of our spiritual water was tainted from birth. One man was trying to expose the fallacy in that old saying, which says, "Every now and then, I mess up and do something wrong." The man explained that the truth of the matter is that every now and then we mess up and do something right. Kenny Rogers wrote and sang a song many years ago that has this main thrust, "I just dropped in to see what condition my condition was in." Have you ever sincerely just dropped in to see what condition your spiritual condition was in?

The doctrine of total depravity is derived from many Scriptures that reveal the inherent flaws in human nature. Consider the following verses from the New American Standard Version:

For there is no man who does not sin. (I Kings 8:46)

---

[16] For a very interesting explanation of this, please see: http://www.thisday.pcahistory.org/2013/09/origina-tor-of-the-t-u-l-i-p-acrostic.

Man's heart is spiritually and morally sick. (Jeremiah 17:9)

Man's heart is evil. (Mark 7:21–23)

Man is a slave of sin. (Romans 6:20)

Man does not seek for God. (Romans 3:10–12)

Man cannot understand spiritual things. (1 Corinthians 2:14)

Man is by nature a child of wrath. (Ephesians 2:3)

Man is at enmity with God. (Ephesians 2:15)

Humans, being slaves to sin, can only break away from their slavery by God's work, which we will now study. God brings us out of our slavish devotion to sin and our flesh by His unconditional love.

Unconditional Election

God does not base His election on anything He sees in any individual. He chose the elect according to the kind intention of His own will (Ephesians 1:4–8 and Romans 9:11) without any consideration of merit within the individual, nor does God look into the future to see who would pick Him and base His choice on their choice. I call that theory "secondhand election." God saw that you would choose Him, so He chose you. That just does not work biblically.

Specific individuals are elected to salvation in Jesus Christ, while others are not (Romans 9:15, 21). Consider these thoughts from C. H. Spurgeon from his comments on Acts 18:10: "I have many people in this city,"[17] and in his devotional:

This should be a great encouragement to try to do good, since God has among the vilest of the vile, the most reprobate, the most debauched and drunken, an elect people who must be saved. When you take the Word to them, you do so because God has ordained you to be the messenger of life to their souls, and they must receive it, for so the decree of predestination runs. They are as much redeemed by blood as the saints before the eternal throne. They are Christ's property and yet perhaps they are lovers of the ale house and haters of holiness. But if Jesus Christ purchased them he will have them. God is not unfaithful to

---

[17] *Morning and Evening: Daily Readings for December 4* by C. H. Spurgeon © Wider Publications.

forget the price which His Son has paid. He will not allow His substitution to be in any case an ineffectual, dead thing.

Tens of thousands of redeemed ones are not regenerated yet, but regenerated they must be and this is our comfort when we go forth to them with the quickening Word of God. No, even more, these ungodly ones are prayed for by Christ before the throne. "Neither pray I for these alone," says the great Intercessor, "but for those also who shall believe on me through their word." Poor, ignorant souls, they know nothing about prayer for themselves, but Jesus prays for them. Their names are on his breastplate and before long they must bow their stubborn knee, breathing the penitential sigh before the throne of grace. The predestinated moment has not struck, but when it comes, they shall obey, for God will have His own. They must, for the Spirit is not to be withstood when He comes forth with fullness of power. They must become the willing servants of the living God. "He shall justify many." "He shall see the travail of his soul." "My people shall be willing in the day of my power."

Limited Atonement

Jesus died only for the elect. Though Jesus's sacrifice was sufficient for all, it was not efficacious for all. Jesus only bore the sins of the elect. *Merriam-Webster* defines *efficacious* as having the power to produce a desired effect. Support for this position is drawn from such Scriptures as Matthew 26:28 where Jesus died for "many", John 10:11–15 that says that Jesus died for the sheep (not the goats as explained in Matthew 25:32–33), John 17:9 where Jesus in prayer interceded for the ones given Him and not those of the entire world, Isaiah 53:12 which is a prophecy of Jesus's crucifixion where He would bear the sins of many (not all), Hebrews 9:28 where Christ was offered once to bear the sins of many, and John 15:13 where Christ laid down His life for His friends (His chosen friends). If you are now a Christian, you are truly a friend chosen by Christ. People who do not believe in election and predestination (in the historical way) emphasize other Scriptures that refer to Jesus dying for the sins of all, such as John 3:16 where God so loved the world that He gave His only begotten Son, 2 Corinthians 5:15 where it says He died for all, 1 Timothy 2:4–6 where it says God desires all men to be saved and that Jesus gave Himself as a ransom for all, 2 Peter 3:9 where it says the Lord does not want any to perish and wants all to come to repentance, and 1 John 2:2 where it says Christ is the propitiation for the sins of the whole world.

Whether Christ died and shed His holy blood for the sins of every person ever conceived in the womb throughout history or He died specifically and only for the elect, the end result is the same. Only the elect end up experiencing salvation. If a prospective mother prepared an appropriate outfit for her expected child and the child was stillborn, the outfit had already been prepared just as if the child had lived. Christ's work was prepared and completed in its entirety on the cross. The elect are born again and inherit the salvation attire which had been prepared. The rest are stillborn spiritually (so to speak). 1 Timothy 4:10 has an interesting angle to this: "For therefore we both labor and suffer reproach, because we trust in the living God, who is the Savior of all men, specially of those that believe."

This verse seems to be very clear in teaching that in its sufficiency the atonement of Christ is universal. Provision is made for all mankind in totality. But in its efficiency the atonement is limited to those who believe, which are those who are effectually (effectively) drawn to Christ in repentance and faith by the power and grace of the Holy Spirit (the elect).

Irresistible Grace

When God calls His elect into salvation, all of their resistance is ultimately overcome. The wisdom and ability of the Holy Spirit overcomes their resistance and rebellion and successfully motivates them to repent and accept Jesus Christ as their Lord and Savior. God offers the gospel message to all people as the good news preached to general populations around the world. This is referred to as the "external call." But to the elect, God extends an "internal call," which, in the end, will not be resisted. It is the Holy Spirit who works in the hearts and minds of the elect to effectually bring them to repentance and regeneration, whereby they willingly and freely come to God. Some of the verses used to support this teaching are Romans 9:16 where it says that "it is not of him who wills nor of him who runs, but of God who has mercy", Philippians 2:12–13 where God is said to be the one working salvation in the individual, John 6:28–29 where faith is declared to be the work of God; Acts 13:48 where God appoints people to eternal life, and John 1:12–13 where being born again is not by man's will, but by God's will.

Jesus summed up the point in John 6:37: "All that the Father gives Me shall come to Me and the one who comes to Me I will certainly not cast out." In Romans 10:13, the apostle Paul explained how faith comes by hearing and hearing by the "word" of God. In this particular verse, the Greek rendering for "word" is *rhema*, not *logos*. *Rhema* represents the personal revelation of God to a person as that person hears or reads the *logos*. When an elect sinner hears the gospel message (e.g., the Word of God in written or spoken form) and it is the right time for conversion, that elect sinner will hear God speaking to them personally through the *logos*. That personal revelation is called a *rhema*. That person was enabled (spiritually quickened) by the grace of God to hear, understand, and respond to the calling of God to salvation in Jesus Christ. If you are already a Christian, you can certainly remember that time when you heard God speaking directly to you, giving you the desire and the power to acknowledge your sinfulness, and put all of your faith in Christ's finished work on the cross. After experiencing salvation, God continues to speak to and direct His children through *rhemas* as they read and meditate upon the *logos* (the revealed Word) of God. 2 Timothy 3:16–17 states that "All Scripture is inspired by God and profitable for teaching, for reproof, for correction, for training in righteousness—so that the man of God may be adequate—equipped for every good work." Once again we see the urgent need for each child of God to personally read, memorize, and meditate on various parts of Scripture each and every day. God wants to speak to us through His *Logos* with *rhemas*. Don't be satisfied with secondhand *rhemas* (things God has taught His other children).

Let God teach, guide, inspire, and speak directly to you each day through the *rhemas* He wants to reveal to you. After you have heard from "the original source," then it is great to also hear what He has taught your brothers and sisters in Christ and compare notes, but you need to give the Lord the chance to speak to you directly first. How would you have felt growing up, if every time your dad wanted to say something to you, he would first say it to one of your siblings, and then tell that sibling to go share it with you. You would always hear it second hand. You would miss the interaction. Would you not much rather be able to go straight to your dad each time and share what was on your mind and hear your dad respond directly back to you in person? So let your heavenly Father do that with you. Jump into His Word and let Him speak to you personally!

Perseverance of the Saints

An elect believer who has been saved cannot lose his or her salvation. All members of the Trinity are involved in the salvation of the elect. The Father elects, the Son redeems, and the Holy Spirit applies salvation to the elect and seals them until the day of redemption. Those who are saved are eternally secure, because the Holy Spirit provides sufficient grace whereby the elect are able to persevere through all the circumstances involving the trials and tribulations of life that test the faith of believers. In those tough situations where believers would be tempted to give up their faith and turn back to the world, they do not do so because of the persevering grace of God given to them as needed. We can all look back to a time where we sincerely knew we could not hold on to our faith (that rope of our faith holding us up to God above) for another hour or another day because of severe trials, overwhelming discouragements, intense physical suffering, or situations that have become what the world would call hopeless. Eventually we reach that point where we cannot go on another minute and we decide to give up and let go of that faith rope and do whatever. We try to let go and to our surprise, we find out we cannot let go. We just can't do it. Something won't let us. Then we look down and see that the almighty hand of God is holding us to the bottom of the rope. Once we see that, God's grace helps us, one pull at a time, to climb back to the very top of our rope of faith and we continue on in life with a deeper, richer, fellowship with Christ.

Some of the verses for this position are John 10:27–28 where Jesus said His sheep will never perish; John 6:47 where salvation is described as everlasting life (you cannot lose an eternal gift that was freely given to you, and is eternal, not temporal or temporary), Romans 8:1 where it is said that elect believers have passed out of judgment, 1 Corinthians 10:13 where God promises to never let elect believers be tempted beyond what they can handle, and Philippians 1:6 where God is the one who is faithful to perfect the faith of elect believers until the day of Jesus's return.

Once again, consider these insights from C. H. Spurgeon from his devotion called "Our Pilot" (from *Multitudinous Thoughts and Sacred Comforts* #883) delivered on Sunday morning, August 1, 1869, at the Metropolitan Tabernacle, Newington:

Remember that your way is ordered by a higher power than your will and choice. The eternal destiny of God has fixed your every footstep. Believe that wisdom, not blind fate, but God's wisdom, has ordained the bounds of your life and fixed your position and your condition so definitely that no fretfulness of yours can change it for the better. In the decree of God, all your history is fixed, so as to secure His glory and your soul's profit. Your present sorrow is the bitter bud of greater joy. Your transient loss secures your ultimate and never ceasing gain.

How I rejoice to believe that the Lord shall choose my inheritance for me! All things are fixed by my Father's hand, by no arbitrary and stern decree, but by his wise counsel and tender wisdom. He who loved us from before the foundations of the world, has immutably determined all the steps of our pilgrimage! Why then, should you worry yourself? There is a hand upon the helm which shall steer your vessel safely enough between the rocks, and by the quicksands, and away from the shoals and the headlands, through the mist, and through the darkness, safely to the desired haven. Our Pilot never sleeps, and his hand never relaxes its grasp.

It is a blessed thing, after you have been muddling and meddling as you ought not to do with the affairs of providence, to leave them alone and cast your burden upon the Lord. I charge you, therefore, children of God, in times of dilemma, to roll your burdens upon God, and He will sustain you and make you to rejoice in beholding His wisdom and His love.

The next chapter will get us into that foundation of biblical truth referred to as "the security of the believer."

10 ⚘

The Foundations of Biblical Truth: The Security of the Believer

The elect believer experiences the security of his or her salvation, because of election and predestination. When God made His choices for those who would become His elect, He made those unconditional choices within Himself without anything depending on the object of His choices, referring to those believers who would end up being saved at the right time and place. Therefore it is His choice that guarantees the salvation of each elect believer and nothing else.

Elect believers could not do anything on their own to gain their salvation in the first place and they cannot do anything to lose their salvation, because their salvation never depended on them. It is God's choice to include a person among the elect who guarantees his or her salvation and eternal life. Therefore once people are saved (born again) through their faith in Christ, they are eternally secure in their relationship with God and can never undo their election to salvation established before the creation of the universe or lose the free gift of eternal life God gave them or undo their spiritual birth into the family of God. Consider the confirmation of this truth in Romans 8:28–29:

> And we know that God causes all things to work together for good to those who love God, to those who are called according to His purpose. For those whom He foreknew, He also predestined to become conformed to the image of His Son, so that He would be the

firstborn among many brethren and these whom He predestined, He also called and these whom He called, He also justified and these whom He justified, He also glorified. What then shall we say to these things? If God is for us, who is against us? He who did not spare His own Son, but delivered Him over for us all, how will He not also with Him freely give us all things? Who will bring a charge against God's elect? God is the one who justifies. Who is the one who condemns? Christ Jesus is He who died, yes, rather who was raised, who is at the right hand of God, who also intercedes for us. Who will separate us from the love of Christ? Will tribulation or distress or persecution or famine or nakedness or peril or sword? Just as it is written, "For Your sake we are being put to death all day long. We were considered as sheep to be slaughtered." But in all these things we overwhelmingly conquer through Him who loved us. For I am convinced that neither death, nor life, nor angels, nor principalities, nor things present, nor things to come, nor powers, nor height, nor depth, nor any other created thing, will be able to separate us from the love of God, which is in Christ Jesus our Lord.

These verses clearly express the eternal security of each true believer who was elected to salvation before the creation of the universe or anything in it. Those whom God foreknew, because He chose them, were called and predestinated to be conformed to the perfect moral and spiritual image of Jesus Christ. Those who were chosen and then predestined and then called into salvation were justified and declared eternally righteous and perfect in Jesus Christ. Those chosen ones (the elect) who were justified are guaranteed glorification. Glorification refers to the resurrected and glorified physical bodies each believer will receive in heaven. These bodies will be like the resurrected and glorified body of Christ.

Paul makes the logical case that no one can stand against an elect believer who has been chosen, predestined, called, justified, and glorified by God. Paul asks who or what can separate an elect believer from the love of God in Christ Jesus? No one or nothing can come between God and His elect. By the grace of God and the power of the Holy Spirit the elect are able to more than conquer anything they will ever face. The elect are secure in God the Father, in Jesus the Son, and in the Holy Spirit, not to mention to the guidance, provision, protection, deliverance, comfort, and assistance they get from those mighty angels assigned to them (see Hebrews 1:14).

The Lord Jesus clearly enunciated the security of each elect believer in John 6:39 where He said, "This is the will of Him who sent Me, that of all that He has given Me, I lose nothing (none), but raise it up on the last day." An expanded paraphrase of this verse would read, "My Father who sent me has willed that of all the specific individuals He has given me (as the reward for my sacrifice on the cross), I will not lose a single one, but will raise each one of those individuals up on the last day or the day of the final resurrection." This verse explains some very important points that confirm election and the eternal security of believers at the same time. First, Jesus said that His Father gave to Him, as a gift for His sacrifice on the cross, a specific number of elect believers. Second, not one of those elect believers promised to Jesus will be lost. Each one will be delivered into His hands. Jesus will successfully raise each one of them up in the resurrection to spend the rest of eternity with Him. Thirdly, the fulfillment of this promise is identified as the will of God the Father who sent Jesus the Son into the world. If you are now a born-again Christian, then you can know that God the Father promised you to Jesus before the creation of the universe. Praise God!

I had the joy and privilege of working for Dr. Rochunga Pudaite and his lovely wife Mawii, founders of Bibles for the World, for about four years. On one particular flight we took together, I had the chance to ask Dr. Ro this question, "What is the most profound thing you have ever learned about God?"

His reply was so insightful into the eternal relationship each Christian has with God. He said, "The deepest and most profound thing I have ever learned about God is that there is nothing I can ever do to cause God to love me less and there is nothing I could ever do to cause God to love me more."

If you are a born-again child of God, you are simply in "the eternal love of God." When one realizes this truth, it usually results in a lifetime of joyful thanksgiving as we'll see next.

Joy Unspeakable

When Christians realize that they are part of the elect, who were chosen before the universe began, it causes them to rejoice and praise God from the depths of their spirits. As they contemplate the fact that God made His own personal specific choice to save them (before He created anything) and make them one of His eternal children, it overwhelms them. They sit in wonder and amazement and try to figure out why God chose them. They are never really able to answer this question, but nonetheless, they cannot help thinking about how supernatural it is and how unworthy they are. The fact that God chose to make them the object of His eternal mercy, grace, fellowship, and blessings is incomprehensible! All one can do is rejoice as it says in 1 Peter 1:8, "Whom having not seen, ye love, in whom though now ye see Him not, yet believing, ye rejoice with joy unspeakable and full of glory" (King James Bible [Cambridge Ed.]).

Consider the words of high praise and deep gratitude expressed by the apostle Paul in Ephesians 1:1–14, as one of the chosen, who understood election and predestination as well as any human being who has ever lived:

Paul, an apostle of Christ Jesus by the will of God, to the saints who are at Ephesus and who are faithful in Christ. Grace to you and peace from God our Father and the Lord Jesus Christ. Blessed be the God and Father of our Lord Jesus Christ, who has blessed us with every spiritual blessing in the heavenly places in Christ, just as He chose us in Him before the foundation of the world, that we would be holy and blameless before Him. In love He predestined us to adoption as sons through Jesus Christ to Himself, according to the kind intention of His will, to the praise of the glory of His grace, which He freely bestowed on us in the Beloved. In Him we have redemption through His blood, the forgiveness of our trespasses, according to the riches of His grace which He lavished on us. In all wisdom and insight He made known to us the mystery of His will, according to His kind intention which He purposed in Him with a view to an administration suitable to the fullness of the times, that is, the summing up of all things in Christ, things in the heavens and things on the earth. In Him also we have obtained an inheritance, having been predestined according to His purpose who works all things after the counsel of His will, to the end that we who were the first to hope in Christ would be to the praise of His glory. In Him, you also, after listening to the message of truth, the gospel of your salvation—having also believed, you were sealed in Him with the Holy Spirit of promise, who is given as a pledge of our inheritance, with a view to the redemption of God's own possession, to the praise of His glory.

Also, consider the words of high praise and deep gratitude expressed by the Psalmist who was a true Jewish believer and understood God's work of grace in his own life in Psalm 149:1–6:

Praise the LORD! Sing to the LORD a new song and His praise in the congregation of the godly ones. Let Israel be glad in his Maker. Let the sons of Zion rejoice in their King. Let them praise His name with dancing. Let them sing praises to Him with timbrel and lyre. For the LORD takes pleasure in His people. He will beautify the afflicted ones with salvation. Let the godly ones exult in glory. Let them sing for joy on their beds. Let the high praises of God be in their mouth and a two-edged sword in their hand.

Rejoice again in these eloquent words of C. H. Spurgeon from his sermon called "A Basket of Summer Fruit":[18]

I am persuaded that the doctrine of predestination is one of the "softest pillows" upon which the Christian can lay his head and one of the "strongest staffs" upon which he may lean, in his pilgrimage along this rough road. Cheer up Christian! Things are not left to

---

18 "A Basket of Summer Fruit" by C.H. Spurgeon ©2002–2018 SermonIndex.net.

chance! No blind fate rules the world! God has purposes and those purposes are fulfilled! God has plans, and those plans are wise, and never can be broken! Your trials always come to you at the right moment. The language of your faith should be, "Great God, I leave my times and seasons in your hand, for well I know if you smite me again and again, and again, it is that you may multiply blessings to me, that my manifold trials may produce in me manifold blessings."

So be of good cheer, my hearer. He knows when your strength is spent and you are ready to perish. For then shall the Sun of Righteousness arrive with healing beneath His wings. Your deliverances from trouble shall always come to you in time enough, but they shall never come too soon, lest you be proud in your heart. Learn, believer, to be resigned to God's will. Learn to leave all things in his hand. Tis pleasant to float along the "stream of providence." There is no more blessed way of living, than the life of faith upon a covenant-keeping God. To know that we have no care for He cares for us and that we need have no fear, except to fear Him. To know that we need have no troubles, because we have cast our burdens upon the Lord, and are conscious that He will sustain us.

In the next chapter, we will study an all-important foundation of biblical truth, which is one of the ordained "means" used to bring the salvation of the elect to completion and how Christians participate in it.

11 🌿

The Foundation of Biblical Truth: Evangelism

Note: This is admittedly a long chapter because it has many true stories of God's sovereign providence working through evangelism to bring the elect to Christ. If you will persevere and finish this chapter, I believe you will be very encouraged. Thank you in advance!

True biblical evangelism is one of those amazing tools that God created to bring the elect to salvation. God ordained the eternal salvation of the elect. He also ordained the means necessary to bring the elect to salvation. Evangelism is the process whereby faithful Christians approach non-Christians and share the gospel (good news of salvation in Christ) with them. As the gospel and plan of salvation are communicated to a non-Christian, the Holy Spirit works upon that non-Christian according to God's will. If the non-Christian is one of the elect, the Holy Spirit works effectually upon the heart of that person, and gives him or her the desire to be saved.

Sometimes, it takes more than one encounter with the gospel for a non-Christian (but one of the elect) to respond positively and accept Jesus Christ as his or her Lord and Savior. God knows how many times an elect non-Christian has to be approached before they experience Christ and He is faithful to send a needed witness to that person as many times as necessary until the gospel is embraced and the decision is made to repent and commit themselves to Christ. This is what has already been referred to as "irresistible grace." God has the wisdom and the power to bring any person to the point where he or she wants to be saved, no matter how long the process takes.

This process of the Holy Spirit bearing down in wisdom, enlightenment, and grace upon a sinner to be saved is referred to as "conviction." In John 16:8 Jesus told the disciples how the Holy Spirit would soon come and convict the world about sin and righteousness and judgment. The Holy Spirit has shown throughout church history that He brings conviction upon individuals and upon entire communities. What God did in the Old Testament through the preaching of Jonah to the City of Nineveh was an incredible example of what the Holy Spirit would do throughout church history in bringing individuals and communities under conviction of sin and to the point of corporate repentance and faith. The entire city of Nineveh repented of their sins and humbled themselves before God when they heard Jonah's message. The fear of God and the fear of destruction came down upon them in such a powerful way that they turned away from their sins and embraced Jehovah God as their God. Paul explains in 2 Corinthians 7:8–11 how the Holy Spirit, through conviction, brings about godly sorrow that brings repentance, which leads to salvation and leaves no regret. In Luke 18:13–14, Jesus told the story of a tax collector who had responded to the spiritual and moral convictions brought upon him with great humility and repentance. While a Pharisee in the temple was bragging on himself to God, this tax collector stood in a distant corner of the same room with his head bowed and cried out, "God have mercy on me, the sinner." The tax collector proved to be one of the elect and the Pharisee (religious leader) proved to be non-elect. Mark 13:27 tells of the time coming when God will send His angels to gather the elect from all over the world.

Therefore, evangelism encompasses all of the outward communication processes of the gospel needed to bring an elect sinner or sinners to repentance and salvation. Behind the scenes, the Holy Spirit works upon the human spirit, heart, mind, soul, and body of an elect sinner in helping that person understand his or her sinfulness, lostness, depravity, and separation from God while the outward processes of evangelism are in progress. At the right time and in the right place, all of the circumstances come together for conversion, called the new birth in John 3.

There are many cases where the Holy Spirit works with a lost person without the use of outside people in direct evangelistic efforts. This is the sovereign choice of God to bring elect sinners to salvation simply through the deep convictions regarding sin, death, and hell, along with the revelation of Christ as Lord and Savior, wrought upon the heart of the targeted individual by the Holy Spirit. Some people have been converted just by reading through the Bible. Through particular Scriptures, the Holy Spirit enables them to grasp their own sin and lostness and to see Christ as the only Savior. They have a spiritual epiphany and are saved alone with just God present. Others have been brought to repentance and faith through the reading of a gospel tract or Christian book.

Others have received true spiritual visions of Jesus Christ, similar to the apostle Paul's experience on the Damascus Road, and have been saved. In the 1700s the evangelist George Whitefield was scheduled to preach outside in the town square of a New England community. One couple owned a farm one mile from town. The wife wanted to go into town and hear Whitefield preach, but her husband (the farmer) had no interest in spiritual things and stayed home.

As Rev. Whitefield began to preach his sermon to the large crowd gathered in the town square, the farmer who had stayed home, was leaning upon his gate a mile away. All of a sudden, the words of George Whitefield began reaching the ears of the farmer. This was due to Whitefield's exceptional voice qualities and the perfect weather conditions on that day. At the end of the sermon, the farmer committed his life to Jesus Christ. When his wife got home and wanted to tell her husband about the sermon, she found he had been converted right there at home. This farmer was not interested in spiritual things, but the irresistible grace of God reached out to him through the voice of George Whitefield a mile away and out of sight, and saved this man. God is sovereign and chooses the specific orchestrations He will use to bring any individual or community to Jesus Christ.

George Whitefield believed and preached the sovereignty of God in salvation as expressed through election and predestination. In fact, he would end many of his sermons with this statement, "You cannot get saved unless you are one of the elect." Then he would get on his horse and begin his ride toward the next town or city to preach. Many people were so shocked and humbled by this statement that they would get on their horses and chase him down and ask him this question, "How can we know if we are one of the elect." He would say, "If you are one of the elect, you will want to get saved." It is as simple as that.

Some people ask Calvinists (those who believe in the traditional and historical definitions of election and predestination) why they go out and witness (share the gospel) to the lost if their salvation is already guaranteed. They say, "Why bother, if God is going to save the elect anyway?" People who do not embrace election and predestination believe that the salvation of the lost depends upon them. They feel they must go out and share the gospel with as many lost sinners as possible or there is no hope for those people. The emphasis is on their duty and responsibility to share the gospel. This is noble, but puts tremendous pressure on those who do the witnessing. What if they fail to do an adequate job in communicating the gospel? Will their failure mean "hell" for those they talked with? If you are a sincere Christian, the idea of your poor communication skills resulting in someone spending eternity in hell, would make it hard to sleep at night. In fact it could produce nightmares. You would feel like you just had to convince every person (to whom you witnessed) to repent and accept Christ. If the decision is totally between you and the person you share with, you must do whatever it takes, no matter how unresponsive the target. This can result in the "witness" putting the wrong kinds of pressure on the person being witnessed to, so that pressure (not coming from the Holy Spirit) backfires and actually hardens the heart of the person.

On the other hand, those who embrace election and predestination believe that as they go out and share the gospel with as many lost people as possible, they will come across those who have been elected, and the elect will respond to the gospel. Their evangelism is simply an exercise in fishing for the elect. Did not Jesus tell the apostles in Matthew 4:19 that He would make them into fishers of men (women and children, too, of course)?

Those who share the gospel with everyone possible have the confidence that the elect will respond and be saved, and the non-elect will not. When they go to bed each night, after faithfully sharing the gospel with someone, they have the confidence that the Holy Spirit will do His sovereign work in the hearts of the elect and eventually bring them to Christ. Paul explained in 1 Corinthians 3:4–9 how some fishers of men plant the seeds of the gospel with their witnessing, others water those seeds with their witnessing, and others will be involved in the reaping of new born-again souls with their witnessing, but the growth of the seed and the manifestation of the new fruit (eternal life) is from God. Review these verses from 1 Corinthians 3:4–9:

For when one says, "I am of Paul," and another, "I am of Apollos," are you not mere men? What then is Apollos? And what is Paul? Servants through whom you believed, even as the Lord gave opportunity to each one. I planted, Apollos watered, but God was causing the growth. So then neither the one who plants nor the one who waters is anything, but God who causes the growth. Now he who plants and he who waters are one, but each will receive his own reward according to his own labor. For we are God's fellow workers. You are God's field, God's building.

Consider some amazing illustrations of God's sovereignty in the following "salvation stories." Many years ago I read a book called *God's Got Your Number*, by evangelist Ken Gaub. This is an exceptional book illustrating the sovereignty of God involved in the salvation of the elect. Rev. Gaub shares a personal experience he had with a suicidal woman. Read the testimony below and see if you are not overwhelmed with God's ability to orchestrate the right gospel witness at the perfect time with an elect sinner under deep conviction.

At the time, I was driving on 1–75 near Dayton, Ohio, with my wife and children. We turned off the highway for a rest and refreshment stop. My wife, Barbara, and children went into the restaurant. I suddenly felt the need to stretch my legs, so waved them off ahead saying I would join them later.

I bought a soft drink, and as I walked toward a Dairy Queen, feelings of self-pity enshrouded my mind. I loved the Lord and my ministry, but I felt drained, burdened. My cup was empty.

Suddenly, the impatient ringing of a telephone nearby jarred me out of my doldrums. It was coming from a phone booth at a service station on the corner. Was not anyone going to answer the phone? Noise from the traffic flowing through the busy intersection must have drowned out the sound because the service station attendant continued looking after his customers, oblivious to the incessant ringing.

"Why doesn't somebody answer that phone?" I muttered. I began reasoning. It may be important. What if it is an emergency? Curiosity overcame my indifference. I stepped inside the booth and picked up the phone.

"Hello," I said casually and took a big sip of my drink.

The operator said, "Long distance call for Ken Gaub." My eyes widened, and I almost choked on a chunk of ice. Swallowing hard, I said, "You're crazy!" Then, realizing I shouldn't speak to an operator like that, I added, "This cannot be! I was walking down the road, not bothering anyone, and the phone was ringing."

The operator interrupted, "Is Ken Gaub there? I have a long distance call for him."

It took a moment to gain control of my babbling, but I finally replied, "Yes, he is here." Searching for a possible explanation, I wondered if I could possibly be on Candid Camera!

Still shaken and perplexed, I asked, "How in the world did you reach me here? I was walking down the road, the pay phone started ringing, and I just answered it by chance. You cannot mean me."

Well, the operator asked, "Is Mr. Gaub there, or isn't he?"

"Yes, I am Ken Gaub," I said, finally convinced by the tone of her voice that the call was real. Then, I heard another voice say, "Yes, that is him, operator. That is Ken Gaub."

I listened dumbfounded to a strange voice identify herself. "I am Millie from Harrisburg, Pennsylvania. You don't know me, Mr. Gaub, but I am desperate. Please help me."

"What can I do for you?"

She began weeping. Finally, she regained control and continued, "I was about to commit suicide and had just finished writing a note, when I began to pray and tell God I really didn't want to do this. Then, I suddenly remembered seeing you on television and thought if I could just talk to you, you could help me. I knew that was impossible, because I didn't know how to reach you. I didn't know anyone who could help me find you. Then, some numbers came to my mind and I scribbled them down."

At this point she began weeping again and I prayed silently for wisdom to help her. She continued, "I looked at the numbers and thought, Wouldn't it be wonderful if I had a miracle from God and He has given me Ken's phone number? I decided to try calling it. I cannot believe I am talking to you. Are you in your office in California?"

I replied, "Lady, I don't have an office in California. My office is in Yakima, Washington."

A little surprised, she asked, "Oh really, then where are you?"

"Don't you know?" I responded.

"You made the call!" she explained.

"But I don't even know what area I am calling. I just dialed the number that I had on this paper. Ma'am, you will not believe this, but I am in a phone booth in Dayton, Ohio!"

"Really?" she exclaimed. "Well, what are you doing there?"

I kidded her gently, "Well, I am answering the phone. It was ringing as I walked by. So I answered it."

Knowing this encounter could only have been arranged by God, I began to counsel the woman. As she told me of her despair and frustration, the presence of the Holy Spirit flooded the phone booth, giving me words of wisdom beyond my ability. In a matter of moments, she prayed the sinner's prayer and met the One who would lead her out of her situation into a new life.

I walked away from that telephone booth with an electrifying sense of our heavenly Father's concern for each of His children. What were the astronomical odds of this happening? With all the millions of phones and innumerable combinations of numbers, only an all-knowing God could have caused that woman to call that number in that phone booth at that moment in time. Forgetting my drink and nearly bursting with exhilaration, I headed back to my family, wondering if they would believe my story. Maybe I'd better not tell this, I thought, but I couldn't contain it. "Barb, you will not believe this, but God knows where I am!" ["Call unto me and I will answer thee and show you great and mighty things, which thou knowest not." (Jeremiah 33:3, KJV)].[19]

Dennis Pollock with the Spirit of Grace Ministries researched and shared another incredible story of how God used the ministry of evangelism to orchestrate the salvation of a spiritually lost and perishing man on the Titanic through the faithful witness of a Christian named John Harper.

---

[19] Ken Gaub, *God's Got Your Number*, excerpt from http://www.cslewisinstitute.org/
From_the_Book_Gods_Got_Your_Number_FullArticle.
https://www.encyclopedia-titanica.org/titanic-victim/john-harper.html.

I have summarized the story below, but the full article can be found online at this URL: http://www.encyclopedia-titanica.org/titanic-victim/john-harper.html. This article has so much more of the fascinating details of John Harper's life, family, ministry, and even a photograph. I so hope you will take the time to find it and read it. Here is my summary:

A Scottish preacher on the Titanic named John Harper was thirty-nine years old the day the ship went down on April 14, 1912. John became a Christian when he was fourteen. During his eighteenth year he felt the Holy Spirit burdening him for the lost and calling him to a ministry of preaching and evangelism. He began preaching on the streets and continued this approach with such passion for several years until a Baptist church with twenty-five members took notice and called him as their pastor. The church grew rapidly under John's zeal for the next thirteen years, until he was called to a larger church in London that could seat nine hundred. This church also began to grow quickly and did not have enough room for all the people who wanted to attend. His pleading with God for the lost, through his prayer life, led to passionate preaching in the pulpit and personal soul winning.

The news of his effective ministry made its way across the Atlantic, and he was invited to preach at D. L. Moody's famous church in Chicago. The Holy Spirit used John so powerfully in these meetings that he ended up preaching there for three months before returning to London. Shortly after returning home, the Moody Church wrote to him and asked him to come back and preach another three months. He accepted their invitation and made his plans to sail back to America on the *Lusitania*, but his departure was delayed for a week and he ended up sailing on the *Titanic's* maiden voyage. There were seven hundred survivors who provided details of John Harper's evangelistic activities on the ship and how he pleaded with souls to be saved in the water as they all watched it sink. He was able to get his young daughter Nana safely on to a lifeboat, and she survived, but he refused to get on any of the lifeboats and pleaded with women and children and anyone not sure of their salvation to get on a boat first before any adult Christians. John felt it was just wrong for those who were saved to get on a lifeboat before any unsaved people or women and children. He even gave his lifejacket to another man.

When the ship slipped completely under the freezing waters, John did his best to stay afloat without a lifejacket, as he continued to plead with anyone the waters brought him into talking distance with, to believe in Christ and trust Him for his or her salvation. Over a year later, a young man reported how he met John in those freezing waters. He said that as people were screaming and dying, he saw John drift near to him. Then he heard John cry out to him, "Man, are you saved?" The young guy sadly told John that he was not saved. John Immediately told him, "Believe on the Lord Jesus Christ and you will be saved." Then the water carried John away from him, but a few minutes later God's providence brought John back near him again. Once again he heard John cry out to him, "Are you saved?" and once again he sadly told John he was not yet saved. So again John faithfully told him, "Believe on the Lord Jesus Christ and you will be saved." Shortly after that second encounter, John was overcome by the freezing water. As far as anyone knows, those were John Harper's last words. That young man continued floating on a piece of wood from the ship until he was picked up by a lifeboat and then rescued by the *Carpathia*. Later he testified, "There two miles above the ocean floor, I did believe on the Lord Jesus Christ for my salvation. I was John Harper's last convert."

John's story is such an incredible demonstration of God's providence in providing the message of salvation to those who could very quickly be dead and to those who survived by His grace, like this one young man. Only the supernatural love and mercy of our sovereign God could motivate a human being (like John Harper) to spend his last minutes in this life doing everything he could to help others get saved and not do everything he could to preserve his own life. And how awesome is it, how God orchestrated the people John came into contact with, to bring His elect to Christ?

John Harper and Family

The following excerpt from chapter four of J. I. Packer's book, *Evangelism and the Sovereignty of God*, does an excellent job of explaining why election and evangelism are divinely linked together.

Divine Sovereignty and Evangelism

Whatever we may believe about election, the fact remains that evangelism is necessary, because no man can be saved without the gospel. "There is no difference between the Jew and the Greek," proclaims Paul; "for the same Lord over all is rich unto all that call upon him. For whosoever shall call upon the name of the Lord (Jesus Christ) shall be saved." Yes; but nobody will be saved who does not call upon the name of the Lord, and certain things must happen before any man can do this. So Paul continues: "How then shall they call on him in whom they have not believed? and how shall they believe in him of whom they have not heard? and how shall they hear without a preacher?" [Rom x.12 ff.] They must be told of Christ before they can trust Him, and they must trust Him before they can be saved by Him. Salvation depends on faith, and faith on knowing the gospel. God's way of saving sinners is to bring them to faith through bringing them into contact with the gospel. In God's ordering of things, therefore, evangelism is a necessity if anyone is to be saved at all.

We must realize, therefore, that when God sends us to evangelize, He sends us to act as vital links in the chain of His purpose for the salvation of His elect. The fact that He has such a purpose, and that it is (so we believe) a sovereign purpose that cannot be thwarted, does not imply that, after all, our evangelizing is not needed for its fulfillment. In our Lord's parable, the way in which the wedding was furnished with guests was through the action of the king's servants, who went out as they were bidden into the highways and invited in all whom they found there. Hearing the invitation, the passersby came. [Mt xxii.1 ff.] It is in the same way, and through similar action by the servants of God, that the elect come into the salvation that the Redeemer has won for them.

Were it not for the sovereign grace of God, evangelism would be the most futile and useless enterprise that the world has ever seen and there would be no more complete waste of time under the sun than to preach the Christian gospel. Why is this? Because of the spiritual inability of man in sin.[20]

Moving on from the wisdom of J. I. Packer, let us consider some other illustrations of God's sovereignty in salvation.

More Illustrations of God's Sovereignty in Personal Stories of Salvation

One time a drunk boy came home and passed out on his bed. His mother found him there and tenderly caressed him. The father came into the room and asked her what she was doing. She said, "I am loving him while he is asleep. He won't let me love him when he is awake." This is a very accurate portrait of how God loves and watches over elect sinners when they are in the depth of their lostness and rebellion and resistance to their need for a personal relationship with the Lord. The Holy Spirit stays by the side of a lost but elect sinner and tenderly convicts and draws that sinner with unconditional and irresistible love and grace. Eventually the heart of that elect sinner is won over and his or her resistance melts into grateful submission to and faith in Jesus Christ as Lord and Savior.

I (present author sharing) spent many years doing fulltime evangelism, which consisted of sharing the gospel from house to house, preaching and sharing with prisoners in different county jails, and sharing in church revival meetings. During these years, I had many wonderful experiences, where I saw firsthand the work of the Holy Spirit in preparing the hearts and souls of elect sinners to come to Christ just at the right time in the right place.

[20] J. I. Packer, *Evangelism and The Sovereignty Of God* (Downers Grove, IL: InterVarsity Press, 1961, 2008), cf. www.ivpress.com.

One day I was knocking on doors on a particular street that I wanted to target with the gospel. As I left one home and began walking toward the next home, I had to pass a group of five young men in their twenties who were having a street party around one of their cars. They were drinking and cutting up just like I did before I met the Lord. I quickly decided that this would not be an appropriate time to try and discuss the seriousness of eternal life with people who were half drunk already. So I said hello to them as I passed their car and kept walking toward the next house. As I took the first step down the sidewalk of the next home toward their front door, the Holy Spirit impressed me, as much as I have ever been impressed about changing my direction in some activity, and convinced me to turn around and go back and at least attempt to share the gospel with these five young men.

As I reached their car, I asked if I might have the privilege of talking with them for a few minutes about where they would go when they died. They all laughed and said, "Sure, go ahead and preach it, brother." So with their permission, I began to share the truth with them. After a few minutes, two of them began to cut up again and make fun of me and what I was sharing. I tried to continue, but got nowhere. Finally, one of the other young men stopped me and admitted that his friends were not taking me seriously, but he acknowledged that he would like to hear what I had to share in a better environment. He then asked me to come back to his house in a couple of days and talk with him alone. I agreed and thanked the group for their time.

I ended up having to go out of town and did not get back to his house until a week later. I knocked on his door and when he opened the door and remembered who I was, he turned white as a sheet. He invited me in, and I asked him if everything was okay. He said things were terrible and explained what had happened, during the previous two days, to the two young men who had mocked me. Two days before, one of them was driving too fast on a motorcycle on a gravel road outside of our town, lost control, hit a telephone post, and died on the spot. The next day the other young man was driving his car to another city sixty miles away. He was also involved in an accident with another vehicle and was in an intensive care unit and not expected to live.

The young man sharing this with me said, "I want to get saved right now. How do I do it?" After making sure he understood everything he needed to know about repentance and faith in Christ, I led him in the sinner's prayer and he was born again. He rejoiced so much after receiving the Lord into his life and was so grateful that I had made the effort to come down his street with the good news.

HOW CAN I KNOW IF I AM ONE OF GOD'S ELECT?

I was so blessed and overwhelmed with the providential work of the Holy Spirit in leading this elect sinner to Christ. I had determined to pass by this group of partying young people the week before and the Lord would not let me. Proverbs 16:9 says that a man makes his plans, but the Lord directs his steps. The Lord took control of my will, changed my mind, and sent me back to this group of party goers. And the salvation of this one young man was the outcome. God worked in my life and he worked in this man's life and brought us together at the right time in the right place for God's will to be accomplished.

This experience also increased my fear of God. God had mercy upon all five of these young men, in giving them the opportunity to hear the gospel, with God's knowledge that a few days later, one would be dead and another close to death. God also allowed each one to exercise his will and reject the opportunity He was giving them to hear the truth and respond to it. Four of them said no to God and two of them perished shortly after. One of them, as one of the elect, was overcome with conviction and the fear of God, and responded by grace to the truth that set him free. God does not always deal with mockers so quickly and severely, but in this case, He did, and it was an eye opener for me.

On another day, I finished preaching to about forty men in our local county jail, and I asked the men to bow their heads for prayer. After praying for them, I then asked them as a group if any of them wanted to pray with me to receive Christ into their lives as their personal Lord and Savior. Three men raised their hands and I led them in the prayer. After we finished praying together, I approached each of these three men individually to rejoice with them, to see if I could answer any other questions or pray for them about any specific issues, and to encourage them to read the Bibles each day, that I had just given them. I also urged them to seek out baptism and participation in a church that would feed their souls, as soon as they were released.

As I approached one of the three, he just did not look like the type of guy that should be in jail. If he would have had a business suit on, he would have looked like a Fortune 500 business executive pictured in some issue of *Forbes Magazine*. He just had that kind of appearance and air about him. So I wanted to find out who he was, where he was from, and how in the world he got into this county jail in a small city in south Texas. He told me he was forty years old and from Houston, Texas. He had been arrested by the federal government for international drug trafficking and was on his way to do his time in a federal facility in central Texas. He said he had made thirty million dollars during the last ten years and that he had three homes, one in Houston and two in the Caribbean. He had been living the good life with lots of money. He also had a Christian wife, with whom he attended a Baptist church each week, whenever he was in town. He had heard the gospel many times during the last ten years, but it never reached him. He would walk out of the church service each time and get back to work as a drug trafficker.

I thought how ironic this situation was, and it made me wonder how many other people in similar lifestyles attend some kind of church each week with their hearts and minds never being penetrated with whatever truth they may have heard.

But here in a county jail, a five-hour drive away from his home and his wife in Houston, the Lord reached him and gave me the pleasure and privilege of leading him to Christ. The Holy Spirit finally brought that kind of effectual conviction of sin and the proper fear of God that motivated him to repent and commit his life to Jesus Christ. He was not really afraid of going to the prison he was headed for, because it was one of those country-club type facilitates for nonviolent criminals (so to speak). So he did not come to Christ out of a fear of where he would be spending the next several years of his life.

He came to Christ at this time because our sovereign God reached out and touched his heart and mind in just the way he needed to be touched as he listened to me share the Word of God. His appointed time had come and the Lord of all mercy and grace swept him into the kingdom of God. Again, this was such an encouraging experience for me to continue sharing the Word of God (the gospel) in every opportunity the Lord gave me.

On that particular day, I preached to forty men, all of whom needed Christ. Thirty-seven of them of listened and walked away from salvation of their own volition (I assumed none of them were Christians yet). Only three of the forty were rescued by the Lord and shown to be a part of that remnant chosen by grace before the foundations of the world.

Another time I went to see our county judge about the possibility of an early release of an inmate whom I was mentoring spiritually after he had come to Christ in one of the preaching times. The prisoner told me that he might get an early release if he had a sponsor. So I told the judge I would be willing to sponsor him (and assume responsibility for his faithfulness to the conditions of an early release). The judge told me he would agree to the early release if the inmate would be willing to meet with me once a week for at least six months to continue the mentoring process. The inmate agreed, the judged agreed, and he was released. I had a wonderful time of discipleship and prayer with this young man once a week for six months. He eventually found a job, was restored to his wife and family, and went on the good path for as long as I lived in that city.

As I walked out of the judge's office that day, a lady was standing there, and she said hello. I returned the greeting and then she asked who I was and what I did. As I explained who I was and the kind of ministries I was involved in, her smile brightened and she said she was a county social worker, and asked me if would be willing to meet a lady she was working with. She had been trying to help this woman for a long time, but with no success.

The lady's husband had left her a couple of years before, leaving her with three children at home. She was living in poverty with no indoor plumbing or electricity and she was having severe depression and mental problems. All I could say was that I would be glad to meet her and see if the Lord might open the door for me to help in any way possible.

This social worker met me at the lady's house one day, introduced me, and left so I could visit with her. She was truly in bad shape in every way you can imagine. Every aspect of her life (mental stability, family life, living conditions, and finances) was in total chaos. I asked her if she would like to meet once a week and begin praying about all of her needs. I explained to her that I had no power to help her, but the Lord Jesus did, if she would open her heart to him. She agreed to meet with me once a week and to allow me to visit with her about the Lord and spiritual things.

As we met, studied the Bible together, and prayed together over the next six months, she finally opened her heart to the Lord and accepted Christ as her Lord and Savior. It was not a quick decision, but it was a genuine decision after six months of consideration. When the Lord came into her life, her spirit immediately changed and she experienced that joy unspeakable and full of glory.

Her three teenage children begin to see the change in her even though their lives were in a total mess. Her oldest child was a high school junior who got pregnant out of wedlock during the first six months of my meetings with her mom. The two younger children were sons. The oldest one was in high school and the younger one was in the ninth grade (a junior high grade at that time). They were both on drugs. They were growing marijuana in their backyard and also using other drugs, which was not a cool thing in eyes of Texas law enforcement back then. Every time I showed up to meet with their mother, they ran out the back door and hid until I left. I never got the opportunity to talk with them personally. They just observed me working with their mother from afar and continued on with their life of sin. The daughter finally did begin to sit in on the Bible studies and prayer time. Eventually she accepted Christ and began growing spiritually, just as her baby grew in the womb.

During this initial six months of time with this family, my wife and I were able to take the mother and the daughter to a weekly women's Bible study that I had been invited to lead. I had grown up with these very dedicated Christian women in the community in a local church. These wonderful ladies took a real interest in this woman and her daughter and demonstrated their Christian love in many tangible ways. They paid to have electricity and indoor plumbing installed in the lady's home (a toilet and sink in an unfinished bathroom and a kitchen sink in their unfinished kitchen). For the first time in their lives, this family had the convenience of electricity and indoor plumbing—and this was in the last part of the twentieth century in America! This was a life-changing experience for all four of them.

These awesome ladies also hosted a baby shower right before the teenage mother gave birth to her child. She was overwhelmed by the generosity of these ladies who provided every single thing she would need as a new mother to care for her baby. This teenage mother went on to graduate from high school, secure a part time job, and attend college part time as a growing Christian. She worked at my favorite hamburger place in town, and every time I went into eat, she got the biggest smile on her face, which blessed my heart to no end.

To end this story, the mother's life was stabilized by the grace of God and the goodness of Christians. The daughter's life was stabilized, and she was able to begin raising her child as a Christian parent. And maybe most exciting of all, the two sons who had avoided me at all costs finally got over being scared of me and let me begin visiting with them. I would take them out to lunch on a regular basis and visit with them about the Lord. Because of the goodness of God that they saw poured out upon their mother and sister, they eventually came to Christ about two years after this whole process started with their family. I had the awesome privilege and pleasure of seeing these two young men baptized in the church that I belonged to at the time.

Two years later, they were both in different Bible colleges (one in state and one out of state) preparing for different kinds of ministries that they each felt called to. It was unbelievable to see these two young men, who would not even talk to me for almost two years, now in Bible colleges, wanting to serve the Lord and reach others for Christ. They were so able to relate to other struggling families that they would come across in the future and they were so ready to pour out the love of God in Christ to the people God would prepare for them to minister to. Romans 2:4 is so true as it states that it is the goodness of God that motivates people (the elect) to repentance.

As I look back on the experience with this family, I see the providence of God throughout. I see God's sovereign grace at every turn. I would have never met this lady to begin with, if the Lord had not led me into the jail ministry during those particular years of my life. The power of God had worked slowly but surely in the lives of each one in this family. This family was chosen before the foundations of the world to come to Christ out of their sad, depressed, chaotic, poverty-stricken, sin-filled lives. And now they glorify their creator and redeemer. God used His ordained means of evangelism to bring His elect into the family of God, and I had the extreme pleasure of seeing it all unfold and come to fruition.

I want to share one last story. In the same church mentioned above, where the two young men were baptized, I participated in the church's weekly visitation program. Each Thursday night, we met at the church, had prayer together, and went out on teams of two or three to visit anyone who had visited the church services for the first time or who wanted a follow-up visit or anyone who was a possible prospect for salvation, that we had learned about.

On one particular Thursday evening, my wife and I were assigned to go and visit a young couple with one young child, who had visited our Sunday morning service the week before. We arrived at the home and were invited in.

I began my normal processes of trying to get to know the couple a little bit, wanting to discover where they were spiritually at this point in their life. Eventually, I began sharing the gospel with them and from the point I started my presentation, a young man (sitting way over in one corner of the room by himself) began asking me questions about the points I was sharing. I did not understand who this man was or why he was there with this young couple. I continued to direct my conversation to the young couple who had visited the church. They were polite, but did not show any interest in the gospel. I could not figure out what had motivated them to visit our church. Try as I may to reach the hearts of the young couple, they just sat there looking at me out of their lostness, while this other young man in the corner kept asking me relevant questions.

Finally I got the point from the Holy Spirit, that I was not there (this night anyway) for the young couple, but for this stranger. I got up and moved a chair next to this fellow, and continued sharing with him. After about thirty minutes of further discussion, this man called on the Lord and was saved. After that night, I began meeting with this man once a week, discipling him in the faith. He was hungry for the Word of God and for the knowledge of how to serve the Lord. He was also baptized at our church. It is always so refreshing to see God save a lost person and turn him or her into a pure, holy child of God, desiring to please their heavenly Father.

During our first meeting at his own house, I asked him why he was at that young couple's home that night and who they were to him. He explained that the young woman was actually his wife and that she had left him and moved in with the other man. The young child was his and he was there that night to visit his child when I showed up, and he unexpectedly got the chance to hear the gospel for the first time. I was so saddened to hear of his family situation, but so happy to know God had worked through the circumstances to bring him to salvation.

We continued our weekly discipleship time together and eventually he agreed to go with me as I shared the gospel from house to house in different small towns. He was Hispanic and was so helpful in translating for me when we came across those who were not fluent in English (in the south Texas area). He was my partner in gospel work for almost two years until the Lord moved me on to another area of Texas, by which time he was thoroughly grounded in the Scriptures and very experienced in sharing his faith. As we both moved into new phases of our lives and service to the Lord, I was sad to lose my fellowship with him. But we both knew how our great God had orchestrated his salvation and made him an eternal part of the family of God, and we rejoiced in God's goodness. He gloried in being one of God's elect.

In the next chapter, we will consider how "biblical prophecy" springs from election and predestination.

12

The Foundation of Biblical Truth: Prophecy

Election and predestination are also the basis of or the foundation for biblical prophecy. Biblical prophecy simply involved the foretelling or prediction of things that would happen in the future that God wanted His chosen people to know beforehand, so they could plan and prepare accordingly. These declarations of specific things to come were communicated by men and women chosen by God to utter the prophecies, predictions, instructions, exhortations, and revelations under divine inspiration. The apostle Peter put it this way in 2 Peter 1:19–21:

> So we have the prophetic word made more sure, to which you do well to pay attention as to a lamp shining in a dark place, until the day dawns and the morning star arises in your hearts. But know this first of all, that no prophecy of Scripture is a matter of one's own interpretation, for no prophecy was ever made by an act of human will, but men moved by the Holy Spirit spoke from God.

In 1 Kings 8:56 Solomon explained how every one of God's promises (prophetic words) to Israel through Moses had come to pass: "Blessed be the Lord, who has given rest to His people Israel, according to all that He promised. Not one word has failed of all His good promise, which He promised through Moses His servant."

The biblical prophecies contain descriptions of a broad range of issues like global politics, natural disasters, the future of the nation of Israel, the coming of the Jewish Messiah and a Messianic kingdom, divine judgments, and the ultimate destiny of humanity and history.

Predictive prophecy in the Bible can be broken down into several groups of related prophecies sharing a central theme such as the following:

- **General:** These Bible prophecies deal with various places and people throughout history.
- **Divine Judgments:** These prophecies foretell God's specific judgments upon individuals, communities, and nations for their sin.
- **Eschatology:** These prophecies deal with the end times.
- **Millennialism:** These prophecies describe the thousand-year reign of Christ on earth.
- **Israel:** These prophecies are about the people and the nation of Israel.
- **Messianic**: These prophecies foretell the Messiah.

General Prophetic Facts

J. Barton Payne's *Encyclopedia of Biblical Prophecy* lists 1,239 prophecies in the Old Testament and 578 prophecies in the New Testament, for a total of 1,817. These encompass 8,352 verses. By Payne's count, the 1,817 prophecies involve 8,352 of the approximate 31,124 verses in the Bible. This means the number of prophetic verses amounts to about 27 percent of the total number of verses in the Bible. That would mean about one-fourth of the Bible is prophecy.[21]

Other sources claim that there are close to 2,500 prophecies throughout the Bible and that 2,000 of these have been fulfilled already. This would leave another 500 or so prophecies to be fulfilled before the end of history. The end of history or time, from a biblical perspective, is usually seen as coming at the end of the millennial kingdom when the Great White Throne Judgment takes place followed by the creation of the new heaven and new earth as addressed by the apostle John in Revelation 21:1: "Then I saw a new heaven and a new earth. For the first heaven and the first earth passed away and there is no longer any sea."

In Luke 24:25 the Lord Jesus rebuked the disciples when they had a hard time believing they were really seeing the resurrected Christ according to all the prophecies about His

---

[21] J. Barton Payne, *Encyclopedia of Biblical Prophecy: The Complete Guide to Scriptural Predictions and Their Fulfilment* (Baker Pub Group, 1980).

resurrection: "And He said to them, 'O foolish men and slow of heart to believe in all that the prophets have spoken!'"

In John 16:13 the Lord Jesus promised that the Holy Spirit would come to the disciples after His resurrection and reveal to them all that they needed to know about the future (from then to the end of time): "But when He, the Spirit of truth, comes, He will guide you into all the truth. For He will not speak on His own initiative, but whatever He hears, He will speak and He will disclose to you what is to come."

The point is that there is no way God could predict intimate details about the future without controlling the future. God knew everything that would ever happen, because He planned history to be fulfilled according to His will. He elected and predestined all the events necessary to bring the elect to salvation. Therefore, prophecy is based upon election and predestination. Prophecy was God's way of sharing the details He would bring about to save the elect.

The Prophecy of Isaiah Concerning Cyrus the King

One of the most amazing illustrations of this is the prophecy of Isaiah about a Persian King named Cyrus who would be born around 150 years after the prophecy was spoken by Isaiah. This prophecy is found in Isaiah 44 and 45. Isaiah prophesied during the reigns of Uzziah, Jotham, Ahaz, and Hezekiah. His prophetic ministry occurred in the latter portion of the eighth century BC (740–701 BC) one hundred and fifty years before Cyrus came to the throne!

The prophet Isaiah foretold Cyrus' birth, his name, and the projects that God had predetermined for him to accomplish of behalf of the Jewish people. The Bible records many people were foreordained to be born and carry out specific tasks for God during their lifetime, but only a few of these individuals were ever named before their birth. Cyrus the Great was one of those individuals (whom God announced 150 years ahead of time) who was predestined to play a vital role in God's awesome plan for Jewish redemption. Cyrus the Great is mentioned over twenty-two times in the Bible and his tomb in Iran can be visited today. Here is what Isaiah foretold about Cyrus 150 years before he was born. Think about the miraculous nature of this prophecy.

Thus says the Lord to Cyrus His anointed, whom I have taken by the right hand to subdue nations before him, and to loose the loins of kings and to open doors before him so that gates will not be shut. I will go before you and make the rough places smooth. I will shatter the doors of bronze and cut through their iron bars. I will give you the treasures of darkness and hidden wealth of secret places, so that you may know that it is I the Lord, the

God of Israel, who calls you by your name. For the sake of Jacob My servant and Israel My chosen one, I have also called you by your name. I have given you a title of honor though you have not known Me. I am the Lord and there is no other. Besides Me there is no God. I will gird you, though you have not known Me, that men may know from the rising to the setting of the sun that there is no one besides Me. I am the Lord and there is no other, the One forming light and creating darkness, causing wellbeing and creating calamity. I am the Lord who does all these. (Isaiah 45:1–7)

According to the Greek historian Herodotus (*The Histories* i.46),[22] Cyrus was the son of Cambyses I and the grandson of Astyages, King of the Medes. He was born in the province of Persis, in southwest Iran in 590 BC and died in battle in 530 BC. He founded the Archaemenian dynasty and the Persian Empire. He overthrew the three great empires of the Medes, Lydians, and Babylonians. Nine years after he came to the Persian throne in 559 BC, he conquered the Medes, thus unifying the kingdoms of the Medes and the Persians. He also united most of the ancient Middle East into a single state stretching from India to the Mediterranean Sea, which meant that he possessed the largest empire in the world at that time.

Isaiah referred to Cyrus as "Jehovah's Shepherd" and the "Lord's Anointed" who would be providentially appointed to facilitate the divine plan of restoring the Jews to their homeland. The prophecies tell how God would lead (150 years later) this monarch to "subdue nations" and "open doors" (an allusion to the Jews' release from Babylonian captivity). He would make "rough places smooth" referring to the Israelites return to their Palestinian homeland. Cyrus would ultimately be responsible for the rebuilding of Jerusalem and the reconstruction of the temple. The fulfillment of these very clear and specific predictions is set forth in 2 Chronicles 36:22–23 and Ezra chapters 1–6 below:

Now in the first year of Cyrus king of Persia—in order to fulfill the word of the Lord by the mouth of Jeremiah—the Lord stirred up the spirit of Cyrus king of Persia, so that he sent a proclamation throughout his kingdom, and also put it in writing, saying, "Thus says Cyrus king of Persia, 'The Lord, the God of heaven, has given me all the kingdoms of the earth, and He has appointed me to build Him a house in Jerusalem, which is in Judah. Whoever there is among you of all His people, may the Lord his God be with him, and let him go up!'" (2 Chronicles 36:22–23)

---

[22] Herodotus, *The Histories, Reissue Edition by Herodotus*, ed. John M. Marincola, trans. Aubrey De Selincourt (Penguin Group 1954, revised edition 1972, revised edition with new introductory matter and notes 1996, further revised edition 2003, translated copyright 1954, by Aubrey de Selincourt).

Now in the first year of Cyrus king of Persia, in order to fulfill the word of the Lord by the mouth of Jeremiah, the Lord stirred up the spirit of Cyrus king of Persia, so that he sent a proclamation throughout all his kingdom, and also put it in writing, saying: "Thus says Cyrus king of Persia, 'The Lord, the God of heaven, has given me all the kingdoms of the earth and He has appointed me to build Him a house in Jerusalem, which is in Judah. Whoever there is among you of all His people, may his God be with him! Let him go up to Jerusalem which is in Judah and rebuild the house of the Lord, the God of Israel. He is the God who is in Jerusalem. Every survivor, at whatever place he may live, let the men of that place support him with silver and gold, with goods and cattle, together with a freewill offering for the house of God which is in Jerusalem.'" Then the heads of fathers' households of Judah and Benjamin and the priests and the Levites arose, even everyone whose spirit God had stirred to go up and rebuild the house of the Lord which is in Jerusalem. All those about them encouraged them with articles of silver, with gold, with goods, with cattle and with valuables, aside from all that was given as a freewill offering. Also, King Cyrus brought out the articles of the house of the Lord, which Nebuchadnezzar had carried away from Jerusalem and put in the house of his gods and Cyrus, king of Persia, had them brought out by the hand of Mithredath the treasurer, and he counted them out to Sheshbazzar, the prince of Judah. Now this was their number: 30 gold dishes, 1,000 silver dishes, duplicates, 30 gold bowls, 410 silver bowls of a second kind and 1,000 other articles. All the articles of gold and silver numbered 5,400. Sheshbazzar brought them all up with the exiles who went up from Babylon to Jerusalem. (Ezra 1:4–10)

Now when the enemies of Judah and Benjamin heard that the people of the exile were building a temple to the Lord God of Israel, they approached Zerubbabel and the heads of fathers' households and said to them, "Let us build with you, for we, like you, seek your God and we have been sacrificing to Him since the days of Esarhaddon king of Assyria, who brought us up here." But Zerubbabel and Jeshua and the rest of the heads of fathers' households of Israel said to them, "You have nothing in common with us in building a house to our God, but we ourselves will together build to the Lord God of Israel, as King Cyrus, the king of Persia has commanded us." Then the people of the land discouraged the people of Judah and frightened them from building and hired counselors against them to frustrate their counsel all the days of Cyrus king of Persia, even until the reign of Darius king of Persia. (Ezra 4:1–5)

However, in the first year of Cyrus king of Babylon, King Cyrus issued a decree to rebuild this house of God. Also, the gold and silver utensils of the house of God, which Nebuchadnezzar had taken from the temple in Jerusalem, and brought them to the temple of Babylon—these King Cyrus took from the temple of Babylon and they were given to one whose name was Sheshbazzar, whom he had appointed governor. He said to him, "Take these utensils, go and deposit them in the temple in Jerusalem and let the house of God be rebuilt in its place." Then that Sheshbazzar came and laid the foundations of the house of God in Jerusalem and from then until now it has been under construction and it is not yet completed.' "Now if it pleases the king, let a search be conducted in the king's treasure house, which is there in Babylon, if it be that a decree was issued by King Cyrus to rebuild this house of God at Jerusalem and let the king send to us his decision concerning this matter." (Ezra 5:13–17)

Then King Darius issued a decree and search was made in the archives where the treasures were stored in Babylon. In Ecbatana in the fortress, which is in the province of Media, a scroll was found and there was written in it as follows: "Memorandum—In the first year of King Cyrus, Cyrus the king issued a decree: 'Concerning the house of God at Jerusalem, let the temple, the place where sacrifices are offered be rebuilt and let its foundations be retained, its height being 60 cubits and its width 60 cubits with three layers of huge stones and one layer of timbers. And let the cost be paid from the royal treasury. Also let the gold and silver utensils of the house of God, which Nebuchadnezzar took from the temple in Jerusalem and brought to Babylon, be returned and brought to their places in the temple in Jerusalem and you shall put them in the house of God.' "Now therefore, Tattenai, governor of the province beyond the River, Shethar-bozenai and your colleagues, the officials of the provinces beyond the River, keep away from there. Leave this work on the house of God alone. Let the governor of the Jews and the elders of the Jews rebuild this house of God on its site. Moreover, I issue a decree concerning what you are to do for these elders of Judah in the rebuilding of this house of God. The full cost is to be paid to these people from the royal treasury out of the taxes of the provinces beyond the River and that without delay. Whatever is needed, both young bulls, rams, and lambs for a burnt offering to the God of heaven, and wheat, salt, wine and anointing oil, as the priests in Jerusalem request, it is to be given to them daily without fail, that they may offer acceptable sacrifices to the God of heaven and pray for the life of the king and his sons. And I issued a decree that any man who violates this edict, a timber shall be drawn from his house and he shall be impaled on it and his house shall be made a refuse heap on account of this. May the God who has caused His name to dwell there overthrow any king or people who attempts to change it, so as to destroy this house of God in Jerusalem. I, Darius, have issued this decree, let it be carried out with all diligence!" Then Tattenai, the governor of the province beyond the River, Shethar-bozenai and their colleagues carried out the decree with all diligence, just as King Darius had sent. And the elders of the Jews were successful in building through the prophesying of Haggai the prophet and Zechariah the son of Iddo. And they finished building according to the command of the God of Israel and the decree of Cyrus, Darius, and Artaxerxes king of Persia. This temple was completed on the third day of the month Adar in the sixth year of the reign of King Darius. (Ezra 6:6–15)

The *Encyclopedia Britannica* acknowledges that in 538 BC Cyrus granted to the Jews, whom Nebuchadnezzar had relocated to Babylon, the freedom to return to Palestine and that he helped the Jews rebuild the city of Jerusalem and their sacred temple (www.britannica.com).

In his book, *The Outline of History*, H. G. Wells concedes that the Jews returned to Jerusalem and rebuilt their temple there under the auspices of Cyrus, the Persian Monarch (1931, p. 253).

Imagine the awe and sober introspection Cyrus must have experienced as he became aware of Isaiah's prophecy and realized he had been named in the Hebrew Holy Books almost 150 years before his birth and that he had been ordained by the God of the Israelites to become a mighty conquering king and perform a task for this God, whom he neither knew nor worshipped (until then). God protected and guided the events of his life, so that he could and would fulfill his destiny. Cyrus was one of the elect and predestinated to bring about the restoration of the Jews within his kingdom to their ancestral home of Israel and to help them rebuild the city of Jerusalem and their all-important sacred temple. Biblical prophecies cannot and will not fail, because they are guaranteed by the election and predestination of God Almighty.

13

Only Two Options: Mercy or Justice

From an eternal perspective, all people will either receive justice or mercy. If they receive Christ, they receive eternal mercy. If they do not receive Christ, they receive eternal justice. Justice simply means that they get precisely what they deserve in light of what they knew and in light of what they did. God will be unjust with no one! He will only deal with people according to what they deserve.

Dr. James Kennedy explained that there are three kinds of light shining in the world available to people made in the image of God. In his chart below, the three kinds of light are progressive, beginning with level one (Romans 1) at the bottom, moving up into level two (Romans 2), and then into level three (Romans 3) at the top. See chart on next page:

3 **Light of Christ**
Mercy {Based on Special Revelation}
{Romans 2:1-3, 15-16}

2 **Light of Conscience**
Justice {Based on Natural Revelation}
{Romans 2:1-3, 15-16}

1 **Light of Creation**

{Romans 1:18-20, Psalm 19:1-6}

Dr. Kennedy is saying that every person born into the world receives the light of creation (level 1) and conscience (level 2). At level one, Romans 1:18–20 and Psalm 19:1–6 explain how the attributes of God (even to the revelation of the Trinity, the Father, Son, and Holy Spirit) are clearly visible for everyone to see in the way the universe was created. This is the "light of creation." This is spelled out in the passages below:

For the wrath of God is revealed from heaven against all ungodliness and unrighteousness of men who suppress the truth in unrighteousness, because that which is known about God is evident within them, for God made it evident to them. For since the creation of the world His invisible attributes, His eternal power and divine nature, have been clearly seen, being understood through what has been made, so that they are without excuse. (Romans 1:18–20)

The heavens are telling of the glory of God and their expanse is declaring the work of His hands. Day to day pours forth speech and night to night reveals knowledge. There is no speech, nor are there words where their voice is not heard. Their line has gone out through all the earth and their utterances to the end of the world. In them He has placed a tent for the sun, which is as a bridegroom coming out of his chamber. It rejoices as a strong man to run his course. Its rising is from one end of the heavens and its circuit to the other end of them and there is nothing hidden from its heat. (Psalm 19:1–6)

As people consider the created universe, they will either embrace the light of God displayed in creation or they will reject that light (knowledge). The creation is so revealing about the reality of God, that no human being has an excuse for claiming there is no God. A person with this type of enlightenment (seen as a part of what is called "general or natural revelation") is accountable to God according to this knowledge. Therefore all people are accountable to God, because they all have this light from the creation.

Every person ever born into the world also has the "light of their conscience" as Paul explains in Romans 2. This is also seen as a part of "general or natural revelation." Observe the text in Romans 2:14–16:

For when Gentiles who do not have the Law do instinctively the things of the Law, these not having the Law are a law to themselves, in that they show the work of the Law written in their hearts, their conscience bearing witness and their thoughts alternately accusing or else defending them on the day, when according to my gospel, God will judge the secrets of men through Christ Jesus.

Paul is clearly teaching that our consciences reveal to us right and wrong, even though our inherited sinful depravity interferes with our ability (our will power) to do right in the eyes of God. Our standard can be right in our own eyes, but our sinful nature will cause us to violate what we know to be right. The conscience can say "do right" and yet we will "do wrong," especially when it comes to spiritual things pertaining to salvation. This type of enlightenment, springing from the conscience, makes people accountable to God (just as the light of creation does) so that once again we are without excuse.

Therefore every person has the "light of creation" and the "light of conscience," but if left to themselves, they will reject the knowledge of God emanating from the created order and from their own consciences. As they reject this light (the knowledge of God and the knowledge of right and wrong) they are left to themselves to do as they please, but they are without excuse before God. In following their own pursuits, they eventually reject any and all opportunities to believe in Christ and to receive Christ into their lives as their personal Lord and Savior. When they stand before God at the Great White Throne Judgment, without a Savior, they will not be able to blame God or anyone else for the condemnation of their sinfulness that will separate them eternally from God and all believers in heaven.

Their judgment and the degree of punishment they receive in hell (the Lake of Fire) will be based on how they lived up to the knowledge they had from the creation and from their consciences. What did they do with what they knew?

The third (3) level of light is the "light of Christ" revealed in Romans 3. This is referred to as "special revelation" as opposed to the "general or natural revelation" addressed on levels one and two above. As Paul demonstrates once again in Romans 3:21–26:

> But now apart from the Law the righteousness of God has been manifested, being witnessed by the Law and the Prophets, even the righteousness of God through faith in Jesus Christ for all those who believe. For there is no distinction. For all have sinned and fall short of the glory of God, being justified as a gift by His grace through the redemption, which is in Christ Jesus, whom God displayed publicly as a propitiation in His blood through faith. This was to demonstrate His righteousness, because in the forbearance of God He passed over the sins previously committed, for the demonstration, I say, of His righteousness at the present time, so that He would be just and the justifier of the one who has faith in Jesus.

The elect receive the light of creation (level 1) and the light of conscience (level 2), but they also receive as a free gift from God, the light of Christ (level 3). If left to themselves, they would naturally reject the light of creation and the light of conscience, as do the non-elect. But they are not left to themselves. They are pursued by the Father, Son, and Holy Spirit and brought to the point of repentance and sincere faith in Jesus Christ. God reveals Himself to elect sinners through the created order and He reveals the guilt in their consciences, as He brings deep conviction into their spirits. Elect sinners will experience the reality of God in body, soul, and spirit resulting in repentance, salvation, and eternal life through faith in Jesus Christ.

Again, from an eternal perspective, all people will either receive justice or mercy. The non-elect will receive perfect justice—no more and no less. The elect will receive unconditional, undeserved, and unmerited mercy and will glorify God for the rest of eternity. There is no condition in human experience that gives a person such a realization of freedom, being one of God's elect and knowing mercy!

14

God's Foreknowledge and Decree as It Relates to Salvation

This chapter illustrates how God's foreknowledge works through His eternal decree in the logistics of the salvation of the elect. The paragraph below is from an unknown source, but very enlightening:

There is in God, a necessary knowledge, including all possible causes and effects or results. This knowledge furnishes the material for the decree and is the perfect fountain out of which God drew the thoughts, which He desired to objectify. Out of this knowledge of all things possible He chose, by an act of His perfect will and led by wise considerations, what He wanted to bring to realization and thus formed His eternal purpose. The decree of God is, in turn, the foundation of His free knowledge. It is the knowledge of things as they are realized during the course of history. While the necessary knowledge of God logically precedes the decree, His free knowledge logically follows it.

To put things in perspective, consider the three lists below illustrating eternity and time.

Eternity Past	Time	Eternity Future
God chose to create.	Creation	Re-Creation
God chose to allow the fall of man.	Fall	Redemption
God chose to save a multitude of people out of the fallen race through Jesus Christ.	• Salvation • Judgment • Re-Creation	Glorification

With God's foreknowledge of the fall, God could have done one of three things:

1. Save everyone: This is what the Universalists believe.

The Universalists' idea is that Christ's death on the cross paid the sin debt of everyone; therefore, everyone will be saved and reconciled to God. Their two central beliefs are Universal Reconciliation and Theosis. Universal Reconciliation says that all people will eventually be reconciled to God without exception. The penalty for sin is not forever and there is no such thing as everlasting damnation to hell (of course this raises other issues that we will deal with in later chapters). Theosis is the belief that all souls will ultimately be conformed to the image of divine perfection in Christ.

2. Save anyone who chooses Christ.

Anyone can choose to be saved at any point in his or her life. It is totally up to the individual to make the decision to accept Jesus Christ. Everyone has the ability to make this "free will" decision and it is up to them to do so.

3. Save a definite number of depraved sinners who would never be saved on their own.

This is the belief of most people and groups who embrace the traditional understanding of election and predestination. They believe, as I do, that nobody could or would choose Christ on his or her own, because the choice is outside the nature of completely depraved sinners. We were all dead in our trespasses and sins and could not even see our need to be saved, much less make the righteous choice to be saved (on our own apart from irresistible grace). We would all blindly go to hell if God waited for us to make a decision on our own to be saved through Jesus Christ. Remember the claim in this book that a creature can only make choices according to its nature. For example, a horse could never choose to attend college. A pig could never choose to run for president of the United States. A snake could never choose to become a millionaire by the age of thirty. A dog could never decide to take voice lessons. Depraved sinners can never choose righteousness, because that decision is outside of their natures.

The Godhead chose and then decreed to create free moral creatures for His glory and pleasure. The apostle John wrote the following in Revelation 4:11: "Worthy are You, our Lord and our God, to receive glory and honor and power. For You created all things and because of Your will they existed and were created." The free moral creatures were to include angels and humans.

Hebrews 1 refers to the angels. Hebrews 1:7 says, "And of the angels He says, 'Who makes His angels winds and His ministers a flame of fire.'" Hebrews 1:14 says, "Are they not all ministering spirits, sent out to render service for the sake of those who will inherit salvation?"

Genesis 1 refers to human beings. Genesis 1:26–28 says,

> Then God said, "Let Us make man in Our image, according to Our likeness and let them rule over the fish of the sea and over the birds of the sky and over the cattle and over all the earth and over every creeping thing that creeps on the earth." God created man in His own image, in the image of God He created him, male and female He created them. God blessed them and God said to them, "Be fruitful and multiply and fill the earth and subdue it and rule over the fish of the sea and over the birds of the sky and over every living thing that moves on the earth."

How did God fashion human beings in His image? Below are a few suggestions (see also Genesis 1–3):

- **Rationality:** God created human beings like Himself (in His image) with the ability to think rationally.
- **Volitional Capacity:** Human beings were created like God with the ability to choose and make decisions.
- **Trinitarian:** God created Human beings in His image with three dimensions to their lives. The Godhead is made up of the Father, Son, and Holy Spirit. Each person has a spirit, a soul, and a physical body.
- **Morally Innocent:** God created human beings in His image with no moral

flaws, blemishes, or guilt in the original creation in the garden of Eden. He created Adam and Eve with complete innocence.

- **Communicative:** Human beings were created like God with the ability to intimately and effectively communicate with each other and with God.
- **Knowability:** God created human beings in His image, with the ability to know others and be known by others.
- **Completeness**: Human beings were created like God in a state of completion, meaning they lacked nothing in their original created state.

How were all people affected by the fall (the original transgression of Adam and Eve that brought sin and death into the world and into their three-dimensional lives)? What happened to Adam and Eve was passed on to all of us throughout history, except Jesus Christ.

- **Adam's rational nature (basis for thinking) became sinful.** He came under the influence of Satan and the power of sin in his spirit.
- **Adam's volition (ability to choose) became a slave to sin and an enemy of righteousness.**
- **Adam's trichotomous nature was marred.** His spirit died within him. His soul (mind, will, and emotions) became self-centered and self-serving. His body began dying even though the death process took 930 years (in his case).
- **Adam's innocence was lost.** He became guilty and accountable.
- **Adam's ability to communicate was marred.** Pure intimacy was lost. (Just ask Eve or any wife).
- **Adam's knowability was marred.** His transparency was lost.
- **Adam's completeness was lost.** He and Eve became spiritually empty and void of real meaning in life. People would never experience that sense of completeness again outside of being restored to God through Christ.

The Godhead chose to allow angels, Adam, and Eve to completely exercise their free moral agency, which resulted in rebellion within each group of created beings. Within the angelic realm, God did preserve the elect angels by His grace as seen in 1 Timothy 5:21 (NIV): "I charge you, in the sight of God and Christ Jesus and the elect angels, to keep these instructions without partiality, and to do nothing out of favoritism." And God allowed the non-elect angels to carry out their rebellion with Lucifer as seen in the following verses:

How you have fallen from heaven, morning star, son of the dawn! You have been cast down to the earth, you who once laid low the nations! You said in your heart, "I will ascend to the heavens. I will raise my throne above the stars of God. I will sit enthroned on the mount of assembly on the utmost heights of Mount Zaphon. I will ascend above the tops of the clouds. I will make myself like the Most High." But you are brought down to the realm of the dead, to the depths of the pit. (Isaiah 14:12–15, NIV)

The seventy returned with joy, saying, "Lord, even the demons are subject to us in Your name." And He said to them, "I was watching Satan fall from heaven like lightning. Behold, I have given you authority to tread on serpents and scorpions and over all the power of the enemy and nothing will injure you. Nevertheless, do not rejoice in this, that the spirits are subject to you, but rejoice that your names are recorded in heaven." (Luke 10:17–20)

And angels who did not keep their own domain, but abandoned their proper abode, He has kept in eternal bonds under darkness for the judgment of the great day, just as Sodom and Gomorrah and the cities around them, since they in the same way as these indulged in gross immorality and went after strange flesh, are exhibited as an example in undergoing the punishment of eternal fire. (Jude 6–7)

With human beings, God allowed Adam and Eve to make their free choice in the Garden of Eden and they chose to rebel (to sin) against the one and only limitation they had in Genesis chapter 2: "Do not eat the fruit off of the tree of good and evil." This is explained in Romans 5:12–19:

Therefore, just as through one man, sin entered into the world, and death through sin, and so death spread to all men, because all sinned. For until the Law sin was in the world, but sin is not imputed when there is no law. Nevertheless, death reigned from Adam until Moses, even over those who had not sinned in the likeness of the offense of Adam, who is a type of Him who was to come. For the free gift is not like the transgression. For if by the transgression of the one the many died, much more did the grace of God and the gift by the grace of the one Man, Jesus Christ, abound to the many. The gift is not like that which came through the one who sinned. For on the one hand the judgment arose from one transgression resulting in condemnation, but on the other hand the free gift arose from many transgressions resulting in justification. For if by the transgression of the one, death reigned through the one, much more those who receive the abundance of grace and of the gift of righteousness will reign in life through the One, Jesus Christ. So then as through one transgression there resulted condemnation to all men, even so through one act of righteousness there resulted justification of life to all men. For as through the one man's disobedience the many were made sinners, even so through the obedience of the One the many will be made righteous.

Consequently, the whole human race (in perpetuity), within the loins (DNA) of Adam, became sinful. Each person would still have his or her will (volition), but it would be fallen (marred) through Adam. Psalm 58:3 addresses this as it says, "The wicked are estranged from the womb. They go astray as soon as they be born, speaking lies" (King James Version). Human beings would no longer choose what was right. Consider what the apostle Paul wrote about our moral and spiritual predicament in Romans 3:10–18:

As it is written, "There is none righteous, not even one. There is none who understands. There is none who seeks for God. All have turned aside, together they have become useless. There is none who does good. There is not even one. Their throat is an open grave. With their tongues, they keep deceiving. The poison of asps is under their lips. Whose mouth is full of cursing and bitterness. Their feet are swift to shed blood. Destruction and misery are in their paths and the path of peace they have not known. There is no fear of God before their eyes."

Therefore the entire human race (through Adam) was in rebellion and separated from God, willfully choosing to sin and willfully rejecting righteousness. In eternal mercy, the Godhead chose to bring about the restoration (salvation from sin and the free gift of eternal life) of a multitude of individuals from the fallen race, according to His sovereign choice. His foreknowledge was based upon His choices and His decree (that brought it all about) was based upon His foreknowledge.

In the next chapter, we look at some of the eternal blessings God has given to His elect.

15 ✒

Our Spiritual Blessings in Christ

In Ephesians 1:1–14, the apostle Paul identifies many of the blessings the elect inherit through their relationship with Jesus Christ. Anyone who reads these verses has to be impressed with the excitement, the enthusiasm, and the hope Paul expresses toward our future with Christ. If you have believed upon the Lord Jesus Christ's sacrifice for you through His crucifixion, and have placed your everlasting destiny in his work upon that cross, then you consider yourself a Christ follower, and as a believer, you recognize that therefore, you are among the elect of God. No one can call upon the Name of Jesus Christ for salvation without having been drawn by the Holy Spirit (see John 6:44). Therefore, being among those God has chosen, you have inherited all the "spiritual blessings" that God has predestined for all of His people. Let's take a quick look at Paul's overview in Ephesians 1 and then take a brief look at a list of some of these blessings! This hope is the basis for much joy for all believers in Christ, as Ephesians 1:1–14 says:

> Paul, an apostle of Christ Jesus by the will of God, To the saints who are at Ephesus and who are faithful in Christ Jesus. Grace to you and peace from God our Father and the Lord Jesus Christ. Blessed be the God and Father of our Lord Jesus Christ, who has blessed us with every spiritual blessing in the heavenly places in Christ, just as He chose us in Him before the foundation of the world, that we would be holy and blameless before Him. In love He predestined us to adoption as sons through Jesus Christ to Himself, according to the kind intention of His will, to the praise of the glory of His grace, which He freely

bestowed on us in the Beloved. In Him we have redemption through His blood, the forgiveness of our trespasses, according to the riches of His grace which He lavished on us. In all wisdom and insight He made known to us the mystery of His will, according to His kind intention which He purposed in Him with a view to an administration suitable to the fullness of the times, that is, the summing up of all things in Christ, things in the heavens and things on the earth. In Him also we have obtained an inheritance, having been predestined according to His purpose who works all things after the counsel of His will, to the end that we who were the first to hope in Christ would be to the praise of His glory. In Him, you also, after listening to the message of truth, the gospel of your salvation—having also believed, you were sealed in Him with the Holy Spirit of promise, who is given as a pledge of our inheritance, with a view to the redemption of God's own possession, to the praise of His glory.

There is a simple outline seen in these verses that highlight the work of the Trinity (Godhead) in the salvation of the elect.

In verses 4–6, we see the selection of the elect by the Father.

In verses 7–12, we see the substitutionary sacrifice for the elect by the Son.

In verses 13–14, we see the sealing of the elect by the Holy Spirit.

From these verses, we can see some very crucial and key points about the work of the Trinity to bring us (the elect) to salvation:

- The cause of our salvation is seen in the phrase "he chose us."
- He chose us "before time began."
- We were passive in this choice (we were not even born yet).
- The goal was to make us "holy and blameless in his sight."
- The reason for the choice was "his good pleasure."
- The purpose of the choice was "for his praise."
- The process for the choice was how "he works all things after the counsel of his will."

If you have become a Christian and then learned about these truths of election and predestination, at some point you will wonder why God chose you. This is an extremely deep question, but has a very simple answer. Here is the answer. *He wanted you!* But why did He want you? He simply decided He wanted you and it gave Him eternal pleasure to choose you and to make you like His Son, Jesus Christ. You will give Him eternal praise and glory for His choosing you. In this life, such an insight should bring nothing but joy and peace!

The following is a simple list that cross-references at least thirty-three of the spiritual blessings that come to any and every believer in Jesus Christ, simply by believing upon the finished work of Christ upon the cross. As the great Apostle Paul said in Ephesians 2:8–9: "For by grace you have been saved through faith and that not of yourselves. It is the gift of God, not as a result of works, so that no one may boast."

In other words, your salvation is of God by His choice in eternity, and it is never by works! It is purely His gift to you. Along with that gift, as Dr. Lewis Sperry Chafer has outlined in his systematic theology, come (at least) the following thirty-three spiritual blessings. I have abbreviated these to a simple list with the scriptural references used by Dr. Chafer in his list. If you're unfamiliar with Dr. Chafer, he was a Presbyterian pastor and evangelist in the early part of the twentieth century and eventually, along with Dr. W. H. Griffith Thomas, a Reformed Anglican from England, founded the Dallas Theological Seminary and Graduate School of Theology in Dallas, Texas, in 1924. Here is Dr. Chafer's abbreviated list of our thirty-three spiritual blessings in Christ.

1. A Part in the Eternal Plan of God

Five words are used in the Scriptures to tell us how God has made us a part of His eternal plan. We were foreknown (Acts 2:23, I Peter 1:2, 20), predestined (Rom. 8:29), elected (I Thess. 1:4), chosen (John 15:16), and called (I Thess. 5:24).

2. Redeemed

We have been purchased by the shed blood of Christ out of the slave bond market of sin and now set free to serve the living God (Gal. 5:1, Rom. 3:24). One day also in the future we will have the redemption of our bodies and be given new glorious eternal bodies (Rom. 8:23).

3. Reconciled

In Christ, we have become a new creation, the old has gone and the new has come! "All this is from God, who reconciled us to Himself through Christ and gave us the ministry of reconciliation, not counting men's sins against them." (2 Cor. 5:17–19). It is Christ who has provided our eternal peace with God.

4. A Living Relationship with God (Propitiation)

God's wrath and anger toward sin has been satisfied in His Son, Jesus. I John 2:2 says, "He is the propitiation for our sins." Because of this, God in His justice is now free to move toward man and have a living relationship with man through His Son. As Chafer states, "to be in that relation to God in which His is propitious toward the specific sins of the child of God is a benefit of grace . . . more advantageous than heart or mind can comprehend."[23]

5. Forgiven

In the same sense that there is "now no condemnation to them which are in Christ Jesus" (Rom. 8:1), believers are forgiven all of their sins—past, present. and future. Colossians 2:13 states that "He forgave us all our sins, having cancelled the written code, with its regulations, that was against us and stood opposed to us; He took it away, nailing it to the cross." The slate has been wiped clean and now with a clear conscience "we can approach the throne of grace with confidence so that we may receive mercy and find grace to help us in our time of need" (Hebrews 4:16).

6. Placed "in Christ"

Over 170 times in the New Testament Paul makes reference to this glorious truth of being placed "in Him." We now are vitally joined to Christ "unto a new walk." This truth is the basis of all the other blessings we receive as we have been seated with Christ in the heavenlies and united with Him. In Him we are complete, "in Him" we now have access to all that Christ has access to, even God the Father Himself.

7. Free from the Law

Man does not have to perform to be accepted. He is already accepted in Christ. The performance standard of the Law, which man never met up to, is no longer a binding power; for man is now "free from the law" (Romans 8:2), because he is "dead to the law" (Romans 7:4) and "delivered from the law" (Romans 7:6, 6:14). Man is now under grace "doing" because of who he is and what God has done for him, not because he must, but because he desires to serve God. To be free from the law is to be free from a "works" orientation, a striving to someday make it. The law produced bondage, performance orientation, and legalistic guilt which man is now truly free from on a day-to-day relationship of grace.

8. Child of God

Ephesians 2:11 states that "formerly you were called uncircumcised," separated from Christ, excluded from citizenship in Israel and foreigners without hope and without God in the world. Now we have become children of God, legitimate and full heirs of that sonship. The Scriptures use several terms to explain this transformation: born again (John

---

[23] Lewis Sperry Chafer, *Systematic Theology* (Dallas Theological Seminary, 1948, 1976), vol. III, 238.

3:6), regenerated (Titus 3:5), quickened (Ephesians 5:21), Sons of God (2 Corinthians 6:18, Galatians 3:26), and a new creation (2 Corinthians 5:17)). As God's child, God no longer is our creator only, but now becomes our Father.

9. Adoption

"For He chose us in Him before the creation of the world to be holy and blameless in His sight. In love, He predestined us to be adopted as His sons through Jesus Christ in accordance with His pleasure and will." (Ephesians 1:4–5). Adoption here is different than adoption in the physical, earthly sense. We are already legitimate sons of God and adoption is the process where God treats us as adult sons and forgoes the childhood heirs of the grace of life and no period of irresponsible childhood is acknowledged. All believers are treated equally as full heirs of the grace of life as equal adult sons.

10. Acceptable to God

Ephesians 1:4 says, "We are made holy and blameless in His sight." I Peter 2:5 speaks of presenting gifts that are "acceptable to God by Jesus Christ." Because of our union with Christ, God sees Christ in us, and we are without condemnation, fully accepted, and without need to try to perform to gain acceptance. Because of this union with Christ, we are made righteous (John 20:31, 2 Corinthians 5:21), as righteous as Christ Himself, sanctified (1 Corinthians 6:11), perfected forever (Hebrews 10:14), made acceptable (Ephesians 1:6), and qualified (Colossians 1:12).

11. Justified

Justification is the divine act whereby God declares the fact that we are righteous and forgiven because of Christ's work in our lives. Justification is God's declaration that He now looks at us "just as if we had never sinned" (Romans 5:1, 4:5).

12. Brought Near

"Remembering that at one time you were separate from Christ, excluded from citizenship in Israel and foreigners to the covenants of the promise, without hope and without God in the world. But now in Christ Jesus you who were once far away have been brought near through the blood of Christ" (Ephesians 2:12–13). Because we have been brought near, our response as a believer is to keep the nearness through confessing sin and aligning ourselves with His will (James 4:8, Hebrews 10:22).

13. Delivered in the Power of Darkness

Colossians 1:14 states, "For He has rescued us from the dominion of darkness and brought us into the kingdom of the Son He loves in whom we have redemption, the forgiveness of sins." Throughout the Scripture we are told of Satan's binding power on men's minds (2 Corinthians 4:3–4), energies (Ephesians 2:1–2), and world (1 John 5:19). However, God rescues us out of Satan's domain and now tells us to wage a war against that domain (2 Corinthians 10:3–7) with new spiritual armor (Ephesians 6:10–12).

14. Entrance into a New Kingdom

Colossians 1:13 welcomes the believer "into the kingdom of the Son He loves . . . " I Thessalonians 2:12 proclaims "that ye walk worthy of God who has called you into His kingdom and glory." Second Peter 1:11 certifies that "you will receive a rich welcome into the eternal kingdom of our Lord and Savior Jesus Christ." We serve the King of Kings in a new kingdom in which we have been placed. What a privilege and challenge to further that kingdom!

15. On the rock, Christ Jesus

In Matthew 7:24–27 the parable states that everyone is building their lives upon some type of foundation. Only one foundation will last, all others are like sand and will collapse. The critical question of life is in regard to the foundation. First Corinthians 3:9–15 addresses the issue of the structure upon the foundation, but before we can even address that issue, we must clearly settle the question of our foundation; is it Jesus, the Rock?

16. A Gift from God the Father to Christ

Seven times in John 17 when Jesus is praying, it is stated that we are "those whom you gave me." We, as believers, are a gift to Jesus, as precious jewels, each valuable and unique, given by the Father.

17. Circumcised in Christ

"In Him you were also circumcised in the putting off of the sinful nature, not with a circumcision done by the hand of men, but with a circumcision done by Christ." (Colossians 2:11). "To stand before God as one whose sin nature or flesh has been judged and for whom a way of deliverance from the dominion of the flesh has been secured, is a position which grace has provided and is blessed indeed."[24]

[24] Lewis Sperry Chafer, *Systematic Theology*, 250–251.

18. Partakers of the Royal and Holy Priesthood

In Exodus 19:6, the nation of Israel was offered the privilege of being a holy nation and a kingdom of priests. However, they failed the conditional promise and the priesthood was restricted to one family. In the New Testament, we "are being built into a spiritual house to be a holy priesthood" (1 Peter 2:5) and each of us is "a chosen people, a royal priesthood, a holy nation, the people belonging to God" (1 Peter 2:9). Whereas Israel had a priesthood, the church is a priesthood.

19. A Chosen Generation, a Holy Nation, and a Peculiar People

We are a chosen generation in that we are the offspring of God (1 Peter 2:9). We are a holy nation in that we become a distinct grouping of people here on earth. We are a peculiar people in that we are not of this world, but our citizenship and home are in heaven—we belong to God!

20. Heavenly Citizenship

Philippians 3:20 states that "our citizenship is in heaven." Luke 10:20 tells us "our names are written in heaven" and in Hebrews 12:22 we are said to "come unto Mt. Zion and unto the city of the living God, the heavenly Jerusalem." Ephesians 2:19 adds, "Now you are no longer foreigners and aliens, but fellow citizen with God's people and members of God's household." Because we are citizens of heaven we become "strangers and pilgrims" (1 Peter 2:11) here on earth. Our job as citizens of heaven is to serve as "ambassadors" for Christ (2 Corinthians 5:20).

21. Of the Family and Household of God

Not only are we citizens of heaven, but we are now a part of the "household of God." Because of this, Galatians 6:10 tells us "as we have therefore opportunity, let us do good unto all men, especially unto them who are of the household of faith." 2 Timothy 2:19 tells us that "the Lord knoweth them that are His." Participation in God's household is an honor in proportion to the royalty and dignity of the hosting family—and that is God, Himself.

22. In the Fellowship of the Saints

Our "citizenship" pertains to our relationship to heaven, of the "household of God" pertains to our relationship with God, whereas the "fellowship of the saints" pertains to our relationship with other believers, before God that relationship as brothers and sisters in Christ carries responsibilities to "honor" each other, build each other up, and function as one (1 Corinthians 12). Four times in John 17 Jesus prayed that "we may be one" as He and His Father are one.

23. Heavenly Association

Because of our family ties and heavenly citizenship, we are linked in association with Christ which covers at least seven areas of common interest and undertaking. They are:

a. *Partners with Christ in life:* "Christ in you the hope of glory" (Colossians 1:27); "He that has the Son has life" (1 John 5:12).

b. *Partners in position:* "He has raised us up together and made us sit together in heavenly places in Christ Jesus" (Ephesians 2:6).

c. *Partners with Christ in service:* "God is faithful by whom you were called unto the fellowship of His Son Jesus Christ our Lord" (1 Corinthians 1:9), "For we are laborers together with God" (I Cor.3:9).

d. *Partners in suffering:* 2 Timothy 2:12; Philippians 1:29, 1 Peter 4:12–13; 1 Thessalonians 3:3.

e. *Partners in prayer:* John 14: 12–14.

f. *Partners in betrothal:* 2 Corinthians 11:2, Eph. 5:25–27.

g. *Partners in expectation:* Titus 2:13.[25]

24. Having Access to God

Perhaps no thought is more all-consuming than the reality of "let us come boldly unto the throne of grace, that we may obtain mercy and fine grace to help in time of need" (Hebrews 4:16). Believers boldly and confidently can come into the presence of the Almighty God, the King of all Kings and make requests and find mercy and grace to help in time of need. This privilege is available 24 hours a day, 365 days a year.

25. Within the "Much More" Care of God

God's love for unsaved man is infinite and perfect, yet the Scriptures speak of a "much more" attitude of God toward His children. "But God demonstrates His own love for us in this: while we were yet sinners, Christ died for us. Since we have now been justified by His blood, how much more shall we be saved from God's wrath through Him! For if, when we were God's enemies, we were reconciled to Him through the death of His Son, how

---

[25] Lewis Sperry Chafer, *Systematic Theology.*

much more having been reconciled, shall we be saved through His life!" The "much more" response of God makes us special objects of His love (Romans 5:8–10), grace (Ephesians. 4:7), power (Ephesians 1:19), and intercession (Romans 8:26, 34).

26. His Inheritance

Ephesians 1:18 says that as believers we are an inheritance of the Father and thus, "when Christ, who is our life, shall appear, then we shall also appear with Him in glory" (Colossians 3:23–24).

27. The Inheritance of the Saints

Not only are we an inheritance to the Father, but the Scriptures tell us that God and all He bestows is our inheritance. Peter writes of "an inheritance that can never perish, spoil, or fade—kept in heaven for you" (1 Peter 1:4). "Whatever you do, work at it with all your heart, as working for the Lord, nor for men, since you know that you will receive an inheritance from the Lord as a reward. It is the Lord Christ you are serving" (Colossians 3:23–24).

28. Light in the Lord

Ephesians 5:8 says that we "were once darkness but now are light in the Lord. Live as children of light." Not only are we to "walk in the light" (1 John 1:7), but the Scripture reveals that we have become light unto a dark world. Obviously, this speaks of the indwelling divine nature of the Spirit of God.

29. Vitally United to the Father, Son and the Holy Spirit

Chafer writes, "As perplexing as it is to the human mind, the Scriptures advance three distinct revelations regarding relationships between the Godhead and the believer and these relationships represent realities which find no comparisons in the sphere of human experience."

It is said that:

1. The believer is in God the Father (1 Thessalonians 1:1).
2. That God the Father is in the believer is in the Spirit (Romans 8:9).
3. And that the Spirit is in the believer (1 Corinthians 2:12).[26]

---

[26] Lewis Sperry Chafer, *Systematic Theology*, 262.

30. Blessed with the Earnest or Firstfruits of the Spirit:

The Holy Spirit actively indwells and works in a new believer's life and this working is described as an "earnest" (2 Corinthians 1:22, Ephesians 1:14) and "firstfruits" (Romans 8:23) of the Spirit. Five riches of the Holy Spirit are described as follows:

    a. Born of the Spirit (John 3:6).
    b. Baptized by the Spirit (1 Corinthians 12:13).
    c. Indwelt or anointed by the Spirit (John 7:39; Romans 5:5, 8:9; 2 Corinthians 1:21; Galatians 4:6; 1 John 2:27, 3:24).
    d. Sealed by the Spirit (2 Corinthians 1:22; Ephesians 4:30).
    e. Filled by the Spirit (Ephesians 5:18).

31. Glorified

At salvation God has given the promise of future glory. "For I reckon that the sufferings of this present time are not worthy to be compared with the glory which shall be revealed in us" (Romans 8:18). "When Christ who is our life shall appear, then shall we also appear with Him in glory" (Colossians 3:4). "Moreover, whom He did predestine, He also called and whom He called, them He also justified and whom He justified, them He also glorified" (Romans 8:30).

32. Complete in Him

While this truth may be a summary of all that has gone before, it is nonetheless a powerful truth of Scripture. Colossians 2:9–10 states, "For in Him dwells all the fullness of the Godhead bodily. And, you are complete in Him, which is the head of all principality and power." It is because of this incomprehensible truth that the Scriptures can assert in 2 Peter 1:3 that "His divine power has given us everything we need for life and godliness." Why? Because we are complete in Him!

33. Possessing Every Spiritual Blessing

Ephesians 1:3 so powerfully sums it up: "Blessed be the God and Father of our Lord Jesus Christ, who has blessed us with all spiritual blessings in heavenly places in Christ."

In the next chapter, we see the five unbreakable links of our salvation. If we are in one link, we are guaranteed to be in all of the links.

16 ✦

The Unbreakable Links of Our Salvation

A s we have seen from previous chapters, the doctrinal study we've been pursuing reveals some undeniable truths. By now, I hope you are convinced that the doctrines of grace presented here—especially those of election and predestination—are solid biblical truths. Now we turn to the doctrines of justification (which we have already studied extensively) and its link to the assurance of faith. There is an unbreakable chain in the broad scope of salvation. Once one is elected by God, He will see it through. Thus, salvation is clearly a *gift* from God, so that no one may boast in his or her works or claim to have contributed to his or her salvation. This unbreakable chain of events is demonstrated in the Scriptures repeatedly. No place is it more freeing for the believer or more convincing than in Romans 8:29–30:

> And we know that God causes all things to work together for good to those who love God, to those who are called according to His purpose. For those whom *He foreknew*, He also *predestined* to become conformed to the image of His Son, so that He would be the firstborn among many brethren. And these whom He predestined, *He also called* and these whom He called, *He also justified* and these whom He justified, *He also glorified* (emphasis mine).

Please study the following graphic of Romans 8:28–30!

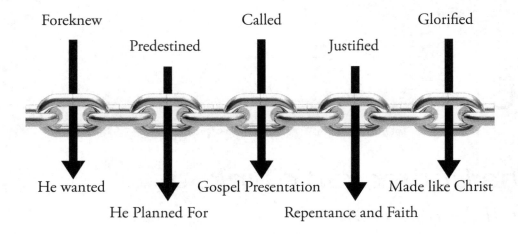

In the "**Foreknew**" link above God foreknew the individuals He wanted as His elect to become His throughout eternity. He chose them and His choice had nothing to do with any inherent inclinations, potential qualities, traits, or value in those individuals. We were all "bad apples" that He would redeem (literally "buy back") from the basket of fallen mankind and transform into creatures for His glory, conformed to the image of Christ. His choices were based on His foreknowledge of the ones He wanted, which led to the next link of "**Predestination**".

In the "**Predestined**" link above, God planned for the salvation of the elect by sending witnesses into all the world to preach the gospel. The last words of Jesus to His disciples (before His ascension to heaven) in Matthew 28 were to go into all the world and make disciples in all the nations. Here is how He said it:

And Jesus came up and spoke to them, saying, "All authority has been given to Me in heaven and on earth. Go therefore and make disciples of all the nations, baptizing them in the name of the Father and the Son and the Holy Spirit, teaching them to observe all that I commanded you and lo, I am with you always, even to the end of the age."

The words of Jesus in Matthew 28 are a fulfillment of the theoretical question in Romans 10:14: "How then will they call on Him in whom they have not believed? How will they believe in Him whom they have not heard? And how will they hear without a preacher?" The elect must hear the gospel, so they have the chance to respond to it, and inherit the salvation planned for them before the foundations of the world.

Jesus knows that in every generation, the world (under demonic influences) does as much evil to people as possible, in various ways and degrees. People are living in spiritual and moral darkness, similar to the physical conditions on earth during a total solar eclipse, when the moon completely covers the sun from our viewpoint on earth. Everything is dark. But the Holy Spirit is always at work, bringing the elect out of their spiritual darkness into the glorious light of the Son of God throughout all of the generations of history. 1 Peter 2:9 says it like this: "But you are a chosen race, a royal priesthood, a holy nation, a people for God's own possession, so that you may proclaim the excellencies of Him who has called you out of darkness into His marvelous light." Colossians 1:13 says it like this: "For He rescued us from the domain of darkness and transferred us to the kingdom of His beloved Son." And 2 Corinthians 4:6 says it like this: "For God, who commanded the light to shine out of darkness, hath shined in our hearts, to give the light of the knowledge of the glory of God in the face of Jesus Christ."

In the "**Called**" link of the diagram, evangelism is the process of calling the elect to salvation. Through evangelism, the gospel is presented throughout the world and at the right time, the elect respond to the call of the gospel and experience salvation. As Christians, we are commanded to preach (share) the gospel to the entire world. Those who obey this command pray as they share. As we pray and share, the Holy Spirit accomplishes the Father's will through the "word" that goes out of our mouths. Isaiah 55:11 promises this: "So will My word be which goes forth from My mouth. It will not return to Me empty, without accomplishing what I desire, and without succeeding in the matter for which I sent it."

The Holy Spirit will accomplish the Father's will through our prayers and through our witnessing. We do the work of evangelism by faith in God's sovereign power to quicken spiritually dead sinners that He chose before the creation of the universe. We do not have to resort to "human tactics or pressures" to bring the elect to faith in Christ. We use prayer and witnessing and we keep it up with targeted individuals as long as the Lord prompts us to do so.

In the "**Justified**" link of the diagram, an elect sinner will respond, by the grace of God, to the gospel message with genuine repentance and faith in Jesus Christ. From that time on, that "saved sinner" will begin the process of being conformed to the image of Christ. Spiritual growth and maturity will normally continue throughout the rest of that Christian's life.

In the "**Glorified**" link of the diagram, every Christian will receive a glorified body like the glorified body of Jesus Christ, at the time of the resurrection. They will spend the rest of eternity in a glorified state characterized by joy and worship and service.

In Romans 10:13 the Apostle Paul wrote those famous words, "Whosoever shall call upon the name of the Lord will be saved." In the next chapter, we ask, Who will call upon the name of the Lord?

17

Who Will Call upon the Name of the Lord?

In Romans 10:13 the Apostle Paul wrote that "whosoever shall call upon the name of the Lord will be saved." The question is, Who will call upon the name of the Lord? Those who *oppose* biblical election and predestination teach that anyone can call upon the name of the Lord for salvation at any time they wish. It is totally up to them and they have the free will to make that decision anytime.

Those who believe in the traditional and historical understanding of election and predestination, believe that no one will call upon the Lord for salvation in a genuine way, without the irresistible grace of God motivating them and providentially leading them to do so. Sinners left to themselves will continue to live in sin with "self" enthroned as Lord. Sinners pursued by the irresistible grace of God will eventually repent and call upon the name of the Lord Jesus for salvation in fulfillment of Romans 10:13.

God has to give special spiritual glasses to the elect (called faith glasses) that enable them to see beyond their own spiritual blindness, the blinding influences of the world, and Satan's blinding influences that normally keep sinners in ignorance and bondage as addressed in 2 Corinthians 4:3–4: "And even if our gospel is veiled, it is veiled to those who are perishing, in whose case the god of this world has blinded the minds of the unbelieving so that they might not see the light of the gospel of the glory of Christ, who is the image of God."

In Ephesians 4:7 the apostle Paul mentions how Christ gives sufficient grace to each elect person to believe, be saved, and live according to the will of God: "But to each one of us grace was given according to the measure of Christ's gift."

Many years ago some creative person thought up a good graphic to illustrate Romans 10:13 from the perspective of election and predestination. This person envisioned a sign over the gate leading into heaven, which said, "Whosoever shall call upon the name of the Lord shall be saved." As the saints of God die and approach this gate to enter heaven, they all read the sign. Then, as they pass through the gate and under the sign, they turn around and look at the back side of the sign, which reads, "Chosen before the foundations of the world" (Ephesians 1:4). This graphic (in a very simple way) illustrates how those who do call upon the name of the Lord (in a genuine way) are those who were chosen before the foundations of the world.

"Come, you who are blessed by my Father, take your inheritance, the kingdom prepared for you since the creation of the world" (Matthew 25:34, NIV).

You are now inside the kingdom of Heaven. Look up!

What did the Lord Jesus say about predestination and election? The following verses are from the NASB:

For many are called, but few are chosen. (Matthew 22:14)

For false christs and false prophets will arise and perform great signs and wonders, so as to lead astray, if possible, even the elect. (Matthew 24:24)

And He will send out his angels with a loud trumpet call, and they will gather his elect from the four winds, from one end of heaven to the other. (Matthew 24:31)

And will not God give justice to His elect who cry to him day and night? Will He delay long over them? (Luke 18:7)

For as the Father raises the dead and gives them life, so also the Son gives life to whom He will. (John 5:21)

All that the Father gives me will come to me and whoever comes to me I will never cast out. For I have come down from heaven, not to do my own will, but the will of him who sent me. And this is the will of Him who sent me, that I should lose nothing of all that He has given me, but raise it up on the last day. (John 6:37–39)

I am not speaking of all of you. I know whom I have chosen. But the Scripture will be fulfilled, "He who ate my bread has lifted his heel against me." (John 13:18)

You did not choose me, but I chose you and appointed you that you should go and bear fruit and that your fruit should abide, so that whatever you ask the Father in my name, He may give it to you. (John 15:16)

If you were of the world, the world would love you as its own, but because you are not of the world, but I chose you out of the world, therefore the world hates you. (John 15:19)

Again, it is the marvelous grace of God that makes our salvation possible. Our salvation is secure and everlasting into eternity future. This brings us great joy. One of the most exciting events we can look forward to is the final revelation in eternity, when God will demonstrate His glory and we will be able to enjoy Him forevermore. It is such a great salvation and comfort to know that those of us who believe will never be cast out!

I've heard it said that when we get to heaven, we will arrive and upon our first step on heavenly ground we all say, "Oh!" At that point, we will mercifully and fully "get it"! So great a salvation Christ bought for us at the cross! Rejoice, my brethren! Rejoice!

In the next chapter, let us look at the bottom line of all of what we've studied so far.

18 ❧

The Bottom Line: Salvation Is God's Action toward Us

Christ's death on the cross removed the penalty of Adam's sin from every person. As the innocent Lamb of God, His sacrificial death on the cross took care of the judicial punishment each of us should receive. Therefore, no one will ever go to hell for what Adam did. God's peace flag went up to sinners all over the world and the invitation to come to the salvation banquet was extended through the preaching of the gospel. On the night of Christ's birth, the angels sang, "Glory to God in the highest, and on earth, peace, good will toward men" (Luke 2:14, KJV). Ephesians 2:13–21 sums up the peace that God offers through Jesus Christ,

> But now in Christ Jesus you who formerly were far off have been brought near by the blood of Christ. For He Himself is our peace, who made both groups into one and broke down

the barrier of the dividing wall, by abolishing in His flesh the enmity, which is the Law of commandments contained in ordinances, so that in Himself He might make the two into one new man, thus establishing peace, and might reconcile them both in one body to God through the cross, by it having put to death the enmity. And He came and preached peace to you who were far away and peace to those who were near. For through Him we both have our access in one Spirit to the Father. So then you are no longer strangers and aliens, but you are fellow citizens with the saints, and are of God's household, having been built on the foundation of the apostles and prophets, Christ Jesus Himself being the corner stone, in whom the whole building, being fitted together, is growing into a holy temple in the Lord, in whom you also are being built together into a dwelling of God in the Spirit.

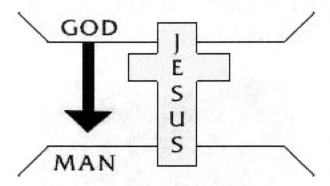

With Christ destroying the curse left upon humanity by Adam's sin, this leaves each person responsible and accountable only for his/her own sin.

Jeremiah 31:30 says, "But everyone will die for his own iniquity. Each man who eats the sour grapes, his teeth will be set on edge." The eternal question is, What will you do with Jesus Christ? Do you feel the Lord giving you the desire to be saved? If you are one of the elect, you will, at some point, want to be saved.

The Chinese Bamboo tree is a great illustration of how the Lord works in the hearts and minds of elect sinners to bring them to Christ and cause them to grow into Christlike maturity. Sometimes it happens quickly and sometimes it happens slowly like the Chinese Bamboo tree, but it will happen to each one of the elect.

A Chinese family will plant their Chinese bamboo tree seed and water and fertilize it during the entire first year, but nothing happens. During the second year, they continue to water and fertilize the seed, but still nothing happens. As the third year rolls around, the Chinese continue to water and fertilize the seed, and yet there is still no signs of growth. The same work and care continue during the fourth year, but still nothing happens. Finally in the fifth year, after watering and fertilizing, something spectacular happens. During the fifth year, in a period of about six weeks, the Chinese bamboo tree grows about ninety feet. This question always comes up. Did the Chinese bamboo tree grow ninety feet in six weeks, or did it grow ninety feet in five years? Obviously, it grew ninety feet in five years, because without the five years of water, fertilizer, cultivation, and protection, there would have been no Chinese bamboo tree.

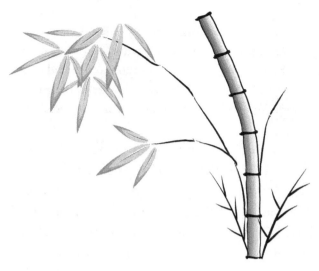

The life of an elect sinner can look much like a Chinese bamboo tree to Christians praying for and witnessing to any one person. It can take days, weeks, months, or years for one of the elect to have his or her eyes opened and feel the needed motivation to repent and commit his or her life to Jesus Christ. But it will happen and when it does, it seems to have happened literally overnight. In reality, it took all of those days, weeks, months, or years for God's sovereign will to providentially work into the life of that elect person. But when it happens everyone is amazed just as much or even more than a Chinese family watching their Chinese bamboo tree grow ninety feet in six weeks.

If you are a Christian praying for and witnessing to someone, do not give up. Galatians 6:9 gives us this challenge, "Let us not lose heart in doing good, for in due time we will reap if we do not grow weary." The famous George Müller, who took care of ten thousand orphans by faith in Bristol, England, was converted to Christ in his twenties and immediately began praying for the salvation of his twelve closest friends. When he died in his nineties, ten of those friends had been saved. Shortly after his death, the other two became Christians.

If you are not a Christian yet, but you feel the Lord drawing you to Himself, why resist any longer? Humble yourself today before God Almighty and admit your sinfulness to Him. Then surrender yourself into the loving arms of Jesus Christ. Ask the Lord Jesus to save you and come into your life as your person Lord and Savior. If you are ready, you can pray the prayer below and become a Christian today and manifest your eternal destiny as one of God's beloved elect.

A Sinner's Prayer

Heavenly Father, I realize now that I was born into this world as a sinner. I admit that I have broken Your moral and spiritual laws. I know that my sin nature and my sins have separated me from You. I am truly sorry and now I want to turn away from my sinful life to You. Please forgive me. I believe that Your Son, Jesus Christ, died for my sin, was resurrected from the dead, is alive, and hears my prayer. Right now, I ask You, Lord Jesus, to become the Lord of my life and to rule and reign in my heart from this day forward. Please send Your Holy Spirit into my life to live in and through me to help me obey You and to do Your will for the rest of my life. In Jesus's name I pray. Amen!

One of the friends I grew up with joined the Navy after high school. He was stationed on a Navy carrier ship that patrolled back and forth off the Vietnam coast during that conflict. He grew up, as I did, without knowing the Lord. During his time aboard ship, he became very depressed and eventually suicidal. The depression got so bad that he finally decided to commit suicide by jumping off of the top deck of his ship at night when no one was around to rescue him from the water after the 80-100 foot fall.

He was standing under a light on the side of the ship looking down, and as he put his hands and one foot on the rail to climb over and began to pull himself up to jump, the wind blew something up against his foot still on the deck. It distracted him enough that he decided to see what it was. He bent down and picked it up. It was a spiritual tract (a booklet) produced by the Billy Graham Evangelistic Association called "Steps to Peace with God." He was shocked that this piece of literature would blow up against his foot just as he was about to commit suicide. He decided to sit down and read it.

You can probably guess by now how this turned out. My friend decided that making peace with God was a superior choice to committing suicide. He called on the Lord and experienced a glorious salvation and deliverance from guilt and depression right there under that light on the ship. The light of the gospel conquered the darkness of sin, guilt, depression, and lostness. As my friend grew in the grace and knowledge of Jesus Christ and studied his Bible fervently, he came to realize how the Lord had sovereignly and mercifully rescued him that night on the ship and saved him from killing himself and going to hell. It took all of those days, weeks, months, and years for God's sovereign will to be providentially worked into his life, but when it happened, everyone was amazed. My friend became a spiritual Chinese bamboo tree and everyone that knew him got to watch him grow, what appeared to be ninety feet in six weeks. In reality, it was years of sovereign work and protection in the life of one of God's elect.

Years ago, I picked up another hitchhiker for the dual purpose of giving him a ride and sharing Christ with him. I knew I only had a short time to share whatever I could share, so I jumped right into it with as much tact as I could. Twenty minutes down the road, we reached the point where I had to turn off the road and he needed to continue down the same direction, so as I pulled over to let him out, I appealed to him to receive Christ. He politely declined, but thanked me for sharing with him. I took off, and he put out his thumb hoping to catch another ride as I drove off down a different highway.

Years later, a pastor friend of mine approached me in a restaurant and shared an amazing story with me. He had not had the opportunity to share this with me until now. He had been close behind me the day I had picked up that hitchhiker. (This is a great example of how people are always watching us, as well as the Lord.) Because he knew me, he said he had a good idea that I would try to share Christ with this stranger. So when I let the hitchhiker out of my car and drove off, he stopped and picked up the guy.

As he drove off with this hitchhiker, he began sharing the gospel with him. The hitchhiker was shocked and told my pastor friend that he had just escaped from another Christian trying to lead him to God. My pastor friend made the point to him that this was a very strong sign that God was pursuing him and that he should really consider what God wanted to do for him—to establish a personal and eternal relationship with him.

The hitchhiker finally got over his shock, relaxed, and sat back to let this pastor explain more of the gospel to him over the next thirty minutes together. By the time they reached the point where this guy wanted to get out, he had reached the point (by the grace of God) where he wanted to be saved and to receive Christ into his life as his personal Lord and Savior. Because the hitchhiker had not been ready with me, the Lord had sovereignly and providentially prepared a second spontaneous witness for this lost man who would complete the work of witnessing and have the pleasure of reaping the fruit for the kingdom of God.

Over the years, I have had the privilege of meeting two astronauts who were part of the Apollo teams. One of the astronauts was Charlie Duke, who was the lunar module pilot on Apollo 16 in 1972. He was the tenth person (and the youngest as of 2020) to walk on the moon. General Duke shares his story of how, after he retired from NASA and became very successful in business ventures, he experienced internal family problems that led he and his wife to a Bible study about the end times. Through this study, they both came to the Lord, and then became dedicated Christians who share their faith all over the world. You can read more about Mr. Duke's Christian testimony and about his experiences in space at his personal website at https://charlieduke.com

The other astronaut, Bob Steward, taught a Sunday morning Bible study in a church I belonged to at that time. He was on the STS-41-B *Challenger* (February 1984) and participated in two extravehicular activities to conduct first flight evaluations of the Manned Maneuvering Units. These EVAs represented man's first untethered operations from a spacecraft in flight. Upon completion of this mission he became the first Army officer awarded the Army Astronaut Badge.

One day he and his wife brought over to our home a gift for our newborn girl (our tenth child). As we visited, I asked him how he came to the Lord. He told us how one of his daughters began having serious problems for which he had no solutions. These problems eventually motivated him to visit with a local pastor who had the privilege of leading him to the Lord. Bob and his wife both became totally dedicated Christians and also share their faith on a worldwide basis.

Both of these astronauts are highly intelligent, driven, and successful people who have had out-of-this-world experiences that only a handful of people in history have ever experienced. Although they both professed they had always believed in God growing up, as young professional adults they had never come to know Jesus Christ personally. As many church attendees, they had somehow missed out on a personal relationship with God and Christ. It took the supernatural and providential work of the Holy Spirit to wake them up and show them the difference in an intellectual belief in God and a personal relationship with God and bring them to real faith in Christ. They were very satisfied with their careers and accomplishments. If God had not allowed things to happen in their lives and families to get their attention, they would have gone on the rest of their lives in their independence and self-sufficiency, died without Christ, and spent the rest of eternity in Hell.

Both of their testimonies genuinely illustrate for me the absolute necessity of election and predestination for any one person to ever be saved. God knows exactly how to touch and reach the most intelligent person or the most ignorant person in the world, the richest or poorest person in the world, the most highly educated or the most illiterate person in the world, the most religious person or the greatest pagan in the world, and the most immoral person or the most moral person in the world. God says in Jeremiah 32:27, that "He is the God of all flesh, and that nothing is too hard for Him."

As mentioned earlier, for four years, I had the great pleasure to work for Bibles for the World in Colorado Springs, Colorado. BFTW was founded by Rochunga[27] and Mawii Pudaite from the Hmar tribe in the state of Manipur in northeast India. Their tribe was a well-known, fierce, and feared head-hunting tribe until 1910 when God told a nineteen-year-old Welshman named Watkin Roberts to go to India, seek out this tribe, and share the gospel with them. The British government tried to prevent Watkin Roberts from going into this tribe's territory, believing they would cut off his head as soon as he got there.

---

[27] Rochunga Pudaite left this world to be with the Lord at a Colorado Springs hospital on October 10, 2015. He was six weeks short of his eighty-ninth birthday. His legacy lives on and the work of Bibles for the World live on through his beloved wife, Mawii, and their son, John Pudaite, and the many people involved with Bibles for the World.

But Watkin went anyway and eventually found himself surrounded by a group of fierce, tribal warriors with their blades in hand. God allowed him to communicate with the tribe, through an interpreter, that he had come to tell them about God who created the universe and everything in it, loved them, and wanted a relationship with them.

Because God had sent Watkin Roberts, God gave him favor with the fierce headhunters and they let him visit with their tribal leaders for a very short time before the British authorities found out he was there and made him leave India. Rather than return to Wales, he decided to move to Canada, where he became a chemist and invented and patented the pain reliever we know as Bufferin, as well as several other noteworthy pharmaceutical products. He used the money he earned from his patents to financially support the Hmar tribe in their evangelistic work and church planting efforts.

During his very short time there, through an interpreter, this young missionary (all alone in a faraway hostile environment) was able to communicate the biblical history of creation and the important truths in the Old and New Testaments, ending in the life, death, and resurrection of Christ for our salvation. God opened up the hearts of five of their tribal leaders (who were totally ignorant of all religions and were never Hindu) and they became Christians. One of these five men was the father of Dr. Rochunga Pudaite, founder of Bibles for the World.

The story of redemption in this isolated pagan, illiterate, head-hunting tribe in northeast India is one of the greatest stories in church history. You can learn more about this story by ordering the DVD about them from BFTW.org. The movie is called *Beyond the Next Mountain*. The story is in book form also with the same name. But I have to give you a little more of their story here and now.

Rochunga's father, one of those five original converts in 1910, became the chief tribal preacher and evangelist. He traveled back and forth throughout their tribal area sharing Christ with as many of the 150,000 Hmar tribal people as he could, but it was a challenge when their tribe had no written language. He could only share the biblical stories he had learned from Watkin Roberts and later on from others God brought into his life, but he was anointed by the Holy Spirit for this work and other tribal members responded to the gospel everywhere he went until 90 percent of the tribe had come to Christ. Their time had come. God had prepared their hearts. God had sent the needed messenger (the nineteen-year-old Watkin Roberts), and the Holy Spirit supernaturally brought the tribe into the kingdom of God.

As true Christians, so grateful to know the Lord and being led and exhorted by their tribal preacher, they needed the Word of God in their own language. Rochunga's father dreamed of having a Bible he could read and preach from. The Lord gave him the vision of his son, Rochunga, growing up, going to a Christian school somewhere, and using his education to develop a written language for their tribe, so he could then translate the Bible into their language. This was his vision, his dream, and his all-consuming prayer. Through his zealous prayers from 1910 until the late 1950s, his vision was fulfilled.

Rochunga attended a mission school all the way through high school, then higher studies at a college in Calcutta, another college in Scotland, and finally at Wheaton College in Illinois. During these extremely busy years of school, he was able to create a written language for his tribe, and by the time he finished his master's degree at Wheaton, he had completed his original translation of the New Testament from the Greek.

Imagine the unspeakable joy Rochunga's father had when he received his first copy of the New Testament (translated by his own son) delivered to him in northeast India (the state of Manipur) all the way from America. A few years later, Rochunga finished his translation of the Old Testament, and his dad (and his tribe) had the complete Bible in their Hmar language. Rochunga's dad faithfully studied and preached his Bible throughout his tribe and other areas, edifying Christians and evangelizing more lost souls, until he died in the 1980s at the age of 100.

Today, through the work of Rochunga and others who have assisted him, his tribe has established over eighty churches, a Bible college and seminary, over thirty Christian schools providing a Christ-centered education for first graders through high school, a Christian hospital, and has sent missionaries into other parts of India. The Hmar story, from Watkin Roberts getting saved in the Welsh Revival through today, is a supernatural demonstration of a loving God providentially drawing in His elect from the four corners of the earth. The *International Dictionary of Church History* says this about the Welsh Revival:

> The 1904–1905 Welsh Revival was the largest Christian revival in Wales during the twentieth century. While by no means the best known of revivals, it was one of the most dramatic in terms of its effect on the population, and triggered revivals in several other countries. The movement kept the churches of Wales filled for many years to come, seats being placed in the aisles in Mount Pleasant Baptist Church in Swansea for twenty years or so, for example. Meanwhile, the Awakening swept the rest of Britain, Scandinavia, parts of Europe, North America, the mission fields of India and the Orient, Africa and Latin America.[28]

In the next chapter, we shall see how the final unfolding of history has revealed the merciful destiny of God's elect.

---

[28] *New International Dictionary of the Christian Church*, (Zondervan, 1978).

19 ⁊◠◗⁑

The Final Unfolding of History: The Merciful Destiny of God's Elect

What if God, although willing to demonstrate His wrath and to make His power known, endured with much patience vessels of wrath prepared for destruction? And He did so to make known the riches of His glory upon vessels of mercy, which He prepared beforehand for glory, even us, whom He also called, not from among Jews only, but also from among Gentiles.
Romans 9:22–24

God had to allow history to unfold and finish its course, so that the elect would have the chance to be born. Some of the elect died in the womb or died before they reached the age of accountability, demonstrating that they had been chosen as part of the elect. The rest of the elect, after their birth, require the chance to grow and mature to the point they may understand their need to be saved, understand the gospel, and then respond to it. At the point of their salvation, the elect inherit the eternal life and the riches of God's glory He prepared for them as the objects of His mercy (remember the list of our thirty-three spiritual blessings previously listed).

This plan also necessitated the opportunity for the non-elect to be born and live out their lives, so they could fulfill their part in helping bring the elect into the world. Some elect are born of non-elect parents (either one or both). Some non-elect are born of elect parents (either one or both). The two groups have been interwoven together in the web of life throughout history, like a large group of diverse fish caught together in one net. At the end of time, God will send His angels to separate the elect from the non-elect, as described by Christ in three different gospels.

> But in those days, after that tribulation, the sun will be darkened and the moon will not give its light, and the stars will be falling from heaven, and the powers that are in the heavens will be shaken. Then they will see the Son of Man coming in clouds with great power and glory. And then He will send forth the angels and will gather together His elect from the four winds, from the farthest end of the earth to the farthest end of heaven. (Mark 13:24–27)

> But immediately after the tribulation of those days the sun will be darkened, and the moon will not give its light, and the stars will fall from the sky, and the powers of the heavens will be shaken. And then the sign of the Son of Man will appear in the sky, and then all the tribes of the earth will mourn, and they will see the Son of Man coming on the clouds of the sky with power and great glory. And He will send forth His angels with a great trumpet and they will gather together His elect from the four winds, from one end of the sky to the other. (Matthew 24:29–31)

> But when the Son of Man comes in His glory and all the angels with Him, then He will sit on His glorious throne. All the nations will be gathered before Him and He will separate them from one another, as the shepherd separates the sheep from the goats. He will put the sheep on His right and the goats on the left. Then the King will say to those on His right, "Come, you who are blessed of My Father, inherit the kingdom prepared for you from the foundation of the world." (Matthew 25:31–34)

Thus, that final unfolding of history will once again demonstrate God's mercy toward us, in that while we were yet sinners, Christ died to set us free! The angels themselves will gather all of us together in the fullness of time, which will be a time of joy unspeakable!

In the next chapter, we will see how election is the key, the secret, and the basis of genuine spiritual worship.

20 ✦

Election: The Key to Worship

The secret to genuine heartfelt worship is gratefulness. If you do not feel grateful, you will not worship. Election is the key, the secret, and the basis of feeling grateful. As you begin to understand that God made a personal choice to save you before anything was created, you will become exceptionally grateful. The more you meditate upon this, the more grateful you will become. The realization of the truth of your election can establish permanent gratefulness in your heart and spirit and can become the foundation of your sincere and genuine worship. One example of this is found in the experience of the ten lepers Jesus healed in Luke 17:11–19:

> While He was on the way to Jerusalem, He was passing between Samaria and Galilee. As He entered a village, ten leprous men who stood at a distance met Him and they raised their voices, saying, "Jesus, Master, have mercy on us!" When He saw them, He said to them, "Go and show yourselves to the priests." And as they were going, they were cleansed. Now one of them, when he saw that he had been healed, turned back, glorifying God with a loud voice and he fell on his face at His feet, giving thanks to Him. And he was a Samaritan. Then Jesus answered and said, "Were there not ten cleansed? But the nine—where are they? Was no one found who returned to give glory to God, except this foreigner?" And He said to him, "Stand up and go. Your faith has made you well."

The one leper (a Samaritan was half Jew and half Gentile) who came back to thank Jesus was filled with gratitude. He realized it was Jesus who healed him and recognized it was the sovereign power of God that Jesus applied to his body, equating Jesus with God. He was more interested in thanking and worshipping Jesus (acknowledging who Jesus was and what Jesus had done for him) than reporting to the priests. His gratefulness brought him into a state of genuine worship. Ten lepers got healed, but only one leper was saved (as far as we know). It appears the other nine lepers never came back to thank Jesus or acknowledge what He had done for them.

Another example of this is King Nebuchadnezzar. Because of Nebuchadnezzar's pride, the Lord drove him into the wilderness to live like an animal for seven years. At the end of seven years, the Lord restored the King's sanity and his kingdom. At that time, Nebuchadnezzar realized and confessed who God was and in the deepest gratitude, he worshipped God in truth and spirit. Daniel 4:34 says, "But at the end of that period, I, Nebuchadnezzar, raised my eyes toward heaven and my reason returned to me and I blessed the Most High and praised and honored Him who lives forever, for His dominion is an everlasting dominion, and His kingdom endures from generation to generation."

The writer of Hebrews explains below, how realizing that we (as the elect) have been made part of an eternal and unshakeable kingdom (the family of God), will produce genuine gratitude that results in reverential worship and awe. Hebrews 12:28 says, "Therefore, since we receive a kingdom which cannot be shaken, let us show gratitude by which we may offer to God an acceptable service with reverence and awe."

The apostle Paul explains in Colossians 2:6–7 (below), that after a person receives Christ as Lord and Savior, he or she should be overflowing with gratitude. This is especially true when he or she realizes that his or her salvation was planned before the creation of the universe. Christians who realize this will be firmly rooted and established in their relationship with Jesus Christ. Their gratefulness will overflow into a deep and abiding worship of God. Colossians 2:6–7 says, "Therefore as you have received Christ Jesus the Lord, so walk in Him, having been firmly rooted and now being built up in Him and established in your faith, just as you were instructed and overflowing with gratitude."

Paul also illustrates in 1 Thessalonians 5:16–18 how the grateful child of God will fulfill the will of God by doing three specific things: "always rejoicing, always praying, and always giving thanks to God." The child of God, who realizes he or she was chosen before the foundations of the world, will find it natural and easy to rejoice, pray, and give thanks to God. 1 Thessalonians 5:16–18 says, "Rejoice always! Pray without ceasing! In everything give thanks! For this is God's will for you in Christ Jesus."

Consider the manifestation of gratefulness in this Psalm that results in joyful worship (thanksgiving and praise) to (of) the Lord. Psalm 100:1–5 says,

Shout joyfully to the Lord, all the earth. Serve the Lord with gladness. Come before Him with joyful singing. Know that the Lord Himself is God. It is He who has made us and not we ourselves. We are His people and the sheep of His pasture. Enter His gates with thanksgiving and His courts with praise. Give thanks to Him, bless His name. For the Lord is good. His lovingkindness is everlasting and His faithfulness to all generations.

Grateful believers (especially the ones who know they were specifically elected into the family of God in eternity past as the sheep of His pasture) will sing and shout joyfully to the Lord. They will serve the Lord with gladness. They will enter His gates with thanksgiving. They will enter His courts with praise. They will bless His holy name for His everlasting faithfulness and lovingkindness.

In the next chapter, we will address some of the hard questions that tend to spring up from any discussion about election and predestination.

21 ᴔᲔ

Some of the Hard Questions about Election and Predestination

Every book dealing with difficult theological subjects, such as election and predestination, should include a Frequently Asked Questions section. The FAQ section here deals with what most consider the most difficult questions about these doctrines.

Question 1. Why are election and predestination absolutely necessary for anyone to be saved?

God created the world and human beings in a state of perfection with Adam and Eve born into a relationship with God that would last forever, if they simply obeyed one command. With their obedience to this one command, their children, grandchildren, and all of their descendants (all the way down to you and me) would have been born into a natural and eternal relationship with God and need no salvation. This was God's desire. He never wanted Adam and Eve to sin and bring humanity into a state of sin, depravity, suffering, and separation from Him.

God's original plan included everyone, but He wanted people to have true "free will." He wanted Adam and Eve to freely choose to love Him and honor His one command. Therefore, He allowed them to carry out their choices, knowing that if they sinned, it would affect all of their offspring until the end of history. But there was no other way to do it, if people were to have true "free will" and be responsible for their choices and actions.

Anything short of this would have meant that Adam and Eve needed to be created as some kind of human robot with degrees of mechanical obedience.

Once the transgression occurred, all of future humanity was separated from God. The need for redemption (salvation) and restoration was in place. People would still have their free will, but their free will was corrupted by their sinful nature. They would only be able to choose (use their free will) within the limitations of their sinful nature.

With the ability to only make choices based upon their innate sinfulness, people were (are) incapable of seeking out redemption and restoration with God. By nature, they run from God just as Adam did in the garden, the first time God came down to visit with him after he sinned. The human race has been running from God ever since Adam's first jog (game of hide and seek) in the Garden of Eden. This means no one would ever come to God on his or her own. The only way any person could ever be saved (redeemed and restored to God) was for God to initiate the relationship through His "irresistible grace."

Irresistible grace means that the Holy Spirit pours all of the energy and effort into a relationship that is needed, for as long as needed, to overcome all of the stubbornness, resistance, rebellion, and natural enmity found in the heart of man toward God. Without this "irresistible grace," every person would choose to go on his or her way freely and happily without God and Jesus Christ and plunge into hell without a second thought until after he or she got there (i.e., the rich man in Luke 16:19–31).

Beginning with the birth of Adam and Eve's first child (Cain), every person has been born into this world spiritually dead. We come into the world with physical life and with an eternal soul, but with no spiritual life. Our spiritual life is in a negative state (meaning "dead") and we have no ability to relate to God or connect with God.

Spiritually, we are like Lazarus in John 11, who was in the grave four days. Lazarus was completely dead physically. He had no physical powers or abilities. His body lay there completely helpless and in a state of decay. If left to himself, he would never be a part of this world again, but Jesus had other plans. The Lord stood outside his tomb, called to Lazarus by name, told him to rise up and come out of that tomb, and come out of his state of physical death. The irresistible power of Jesus's words caused Lazarus to get up, come out of that tomb, and resume his life here on earth.

Such is the case with all sinners in a state of complete spiritual death. We have no ability or power to rise up out of our spiritual grave and join Jesus and the family of God. Jesus has to call out to us by name with irresistible power (grace), give us the desire and strength to acknowledge our sins to God (repentance), and to ask the Lord to personally save us, forgive us, and leads us to restore us to God. Without this process, initiated by the Lord, it does not happen. If God had not chosen to pursue a certain number of specific sinners with His irresistible power (grace), no one would have ever been saved and restored spiritually to Him. We would have all gladly gone to hell (until we got there).

The Lord Jesus commanded that the gospel (how to be saved through faith in Him) be preached all over the world to every nation, tribe, language group, and ethnic group. As the gospel is preached, people have the opportunity to understand the need to be saved and how to be saved. As people exercise their corrupted free will, they naturally reject the truth, and continue on in their spiritual lostness. For the "elect," the Holy Spirit continues to pursue them until they are overcome by His irresistible power (grace) and they see their need, repent, and commit themselves to the Lordship of Jesus Christ. For everyone else, God simply lets them go their way and do as they please.

Question 2. Why didn't God choose everyone to be saved?

God could have chosen everyone. Some people believe He did, and they call their system of belief "universalism." But the Bible is very clear that not everyone born into this world will be saved and end up in heaven. Therefore, the question can legitimately be asked, "Why didn't God choose everyone to be saved and go to heaven?" The answer lies totally within God's sovereign rights as creator. Every creature belongs to God through rights of ownership. As owner of everything, God can do as He pleases with everything.

Within the Godhead (Father, Son, and Holy Spirit) decisions were made in eternity past (before the creation of anything) that some human beings would spend eternity in heaven (with the Godhead and the elect angels) and some would be left to themselves to do as they pleased, which eventually results in them dying in a state of unbelief and spending eternity with the devil and his fallen angels in the Lake of Fire. The reason(s) for God choosing certain ones to be saved and leaving others to their own devices lies completely within His own eternal knowledge and purposes. He has done as He wished. You and I simply don't have the wisdom or knowledge or ability to figure out His reason(s) and we don't have the power or right to challenge Him about His decisions. Romans 11:33–36 says,

> Oh, the depth of the riches both of the wisdom and knowledge of God! How unsearchable are His judgments and unfathomable His ways! For who has known the mind of the Lord, or who became His counselor? Or who has first given to Him that it might be paid back to him again? For from Him and through Him and to Him are all things. To Him be the glory forever. Amen. (Romans 11:33–36)

Question 3. Why did God choose you?

Within God's sovereign rights as creator and His perfect knowledge of the creation and created beings, He made a free choice of (for) you as one of the elect, before He created anything. There was absolutely nothing in you to make Him want you above any other person born into the world with an eternal soul. You were just as lost and depraved as any other sinner born into the world, but God made the decision to choose you. According to His own free and sovereign pleasure. God chose you to become a creature who would become what He wanted you to be, which was a human being conformed to the moral and spiritual image of Jesus Christ. He chose you to be a vessel to display His mercy, bearing the precious eternal qualities of His beloved Son. Through your union and oneness with Jesus Christ, you are equipped to glorify God throughout eternity. A great deal of your eternal joy and pleasure will be in praising and glorifying the Father, Son, and Holy Spirit.

Paul, an apostle of Christ Jesus by the will of God, To the saints who are at Ephesus and who are faithful in Christ Jesus: Grace to you and peace from God our Father and the Lord Jesus Christ. Blessed be the God and Father of our Lord Jesus Christ, who has blessed us with every spiritual blessing in the heavenly places in Christ, just as He chose us in Him before the foundation of the world, that we would be holy and blameless before Him. In love, He predestined us to adoption as sons through Jesus Christ to Himself, according to the kind intention of His will, to the praise of the glory of His grace, which He freely bestowed on us in the Beloved. In Him we have redemption through His blood, the forgiveness of our trespasses, according to the riches of His grace which He lavished on us. In all wisdom and insight, He made known to us the mystery of His will, according to His kind intention which He purposed in Him with a view to an administration suitable to the fullness of the times, that is, the summing up of all things in Christ, things in the heavens and things on the earth. In Him also we have obtained an inheritance, having been predestined according to His purpose who works all things after the counsel of His will, to the end that we who were the first to hope in Christ would be to the praise of His glory. In Him, you also, after listening to the message of truth, the gospel of your salvation—having also believed, you were sealed in Him with the Holy Spirit of promise, who is given as a pledge of our inheritance, with a view to the redemption of God's own possession, to the praise of His glory. (Ephesians 1:1–14)

Question 4. How many elect are there?

There is no way any human being could ever figure out or calculate how many elect there might be in Heaven by the end of history. Most people would probably agree that there will be millions and millions or even billions out of all the people who have lived from Adam and Eve through the end of the millennial kingdom. There are a few examples in the Bible of angels and people who were manifested to be a part of God's elect in various situations. These examples do not satisfy the question of how many elect there will be, when it is all said and done, but they are interesting to consider.

Angels

Based upon verses like Isaiah 14:1–17, Luke 10:18, Jude 6, and Revelation 12:3–9 there are elect angels and non-elect angels. From the biblical testimonies, God preserved two-thirds of the angels from rebelling with Lucifer, and allowed one-third of the angels to follow Lucifer. Lucifer and the angels who followed him were cast out of Heaven. Lucifer became the Devil (or Satan), and his fallen angels became demons. In this case, the elect were two-thirds and the non-elect were one-third.

Sodom and Gomorrah

Some sources estimate the population of these two cities at the time of their destruction in Genesis 19 as between six and twelve hundred people. The angel of the Lord escorted Lot, his wife, and his two daughters out of the area in safety. Four people made it out of the cities alive, but as you know, Lot's wife turned into a pillar of salt when she looked back to see what was happening. Therefore, only three people out of the possible six to twelve hundred residents stayed alive. If you refer to these as elect, as those who experienced salvation and protection from the destruction, then the percentage of elect to non-elect in these two cities was very low. Three out of 600 would equal one-half of one percent. Three out of twelve hundred would equal one quarter of one percent. If you consider the three other cities who were destroyed along with Sodom and Gomorrah, then percentages of elect go much, much lower.

Noah and The Ark

When God told Noah to build the ark so he and his family could be saved from the worldwide flood, Christian mathematicians and scientists estimate the population of the earth to be between two and five billion. Eight people got on the ark (Genesis 6:18–21; 1 Peter 3:20; 2 Peter 2:5) and were kept alive (as elect) to continue life after the effects of the flood were over. The rest of humanity perished as non-elect. The percentage of elect to non-elect in this scenario was very low.

City of Nineveh

Some sources estimate the population of Nineveh around 600,000 at the time Jonah was sent into the city to preach his message of coming destruction (forty more days and Nineveh would be destroyed). In this case, the entire population seems to have genuinely repented following the lead of their king. With their repentance came God's mercy, so that the city was not destroyed. Therefore, by the grace of God, every person alive in Nineveh at this time, ended up being one of the elect, which is one of the most awesome examples in the Bible of God's ability to save those He desires to save.

Parable of The Soils

In Luke 8:4–21, Jesus explained to the apostles what is called the Parable of the Soils. In this scenario, there were four kinds of soils that produced four different results. Only one type of soil produced fruit or a harvest. The other three produced nothing. Jesus then compared these four soils to the way people respond to the gospel when they hear it. Only one of the four produced fruit for the kingdom of God. The other three were barren. One way to interpret this parable would be that only one out of four people (on average) who hear the gospel respond in a way that demonstrates they really became believers (children of God through genuine faith in Christ). Only one out of four produced spiritual fruit in their lives that demonstrated they really did have a relationship with Jesus Christ. The other three, no matter what they confessed, were spiritually barren.

What about the Age of Accountability?

The age of accountability, or age of innocence, is an implied doctrine inferring that people, as they are growing up, reaches a certain age where they finally know right from wrong and are accountable for their sins (wrongdoing) from then on. That age would vary from person to person depending on how they are raised, the moral values they are taught, the moral values they see demonstrated, and the kind of spiritual influences they have. The better moral environment one has should in theory help children or teenagers reach the point where they really know right from wrong earlier.

Some people prefer to call it the "point of God consciousness," which can occur at practically any age and at which point a person becomes "accountable" for his sinfulness and responsible for choosing or rejecting God's viewpoint and plan of salvation.

Once a person reaches his or her unique age of accountability, he or she becomes responsible for his or her own actions and is in need of salvation. In Jewish tradition, a child becomes an adult around the age of thirteen. In reality, any one person could know right from wrong at an earlier age or a later age, but the Jews would at least let thirteen-year-olds know they would be held accountable for their attitudes and actions from then on (if not before). Only the Lord knows when that moral clock kicks in for each person. There are also those who may never reach this point of moral accountability because of brain damage or mental disability. But the teaching, primarily based on 2 Samuel 12:21–23, says that if a person dies before he or she reaches their unique age of accountability, he or she would go to heaven (as one of the elect), because he or she never had the chance to hear the gospel and accept Jesus Christ as his or her personal Lord and Savior. The point would also be made that he or she never had the spiritual understanding and ability to make a decision for the Lord.

The context of these verses goes back to when King David committed adultery with Bathsheba, with a resulting pregnancy. The prophet Nathan was sent by the Lord to inform David that because of his sin, the Lord would let the baby die. David responded to this with grieving, mourning, fasting, and praying for the child. But once the child died, David immediately stopped his mourning. David's servants were shocked. They said to King David, "What is this thing that you have done? While the child was alive, you fasted and wept, but when the child died, you arose and ate food."

David's response was, "While the child was still alive, I fasted and wept, for I said, 'Who knows, the LORD may be gracious to me, that the child may live.' But now he has died. Why should I fast? Can I bring him back again? I shall go to him, but he will not return to me."

David's response implies that those who do not have the ability to believe in Christ, either because of premature death, or ignorance due to age or mental impairment, are safe in the Lord. David said that he could go to the child (in heaven), but that he could not bring the child back to him (on earth). Also, and just as important, David seemed to be comforted over this. In other words, David seemed to be saying that he would see the child in heaven, though he could not bring him back from physical death.

Another biblical passage that hints at an age of accountability is Isaiah 7:15–16, which says: "He will eat curds and honey at the time He knows [enough] to refuse evil and choose good. For before the boy will know [enough] to refuse evil and choose good, the land whose two kings you dread will be forsaken."

One more biblical passage that hints at an age of accountability is Deuteronomy 1:39: "Moreover, your little ones who you said would become a prey, and your sons, who this day have no knowledge of good or evil, shall enter there, and I will give it to them and they shall possess it."

For many, even the limited passages above, are sufficient to establish the principle that those who die without having the ability to perceive the issues of the gospel are covered by the blood of Christ (revealing them as part of the elect) and are saved. Children or young people who have reached that point of God consciousness are, from then on, held accountable to the justice of God.

I have to share a joke about the age of accountability as an illustration that I hope you will enjoy. The college I graduated from in south Texas is now a part of the Texas A&M University system. It was called Texas A&I at the time I graduated, but since then it has been taken over by the behemoth Texas A&M system. Texas A&M, the state's first public institution of higher education, was opened on Oct. 4, 1876, as the Agricultural and Mechanical College of Texas, and at that time the "A" and "M" initials were used to abbreviate the name components. Students at Texas A&M are referred to as Aggies.

In the early 1900s, Texas A&M students were referred to as "Farmers." The term *Aggie* began to be used in the 1920s, and in 1949, when the yearbook changed its name from *The Longhorn* to *Aggieland*, Aggie became the official student body nickname. Many people who attend other universities enjoy making fun of Texas Aggies with the implication that Aggies are inferior students. I have no idea how the tradition got started, but it continues to this day. People enjoy making fun of Aggies with every kind of joke under the sun. Maybe it is jealousy or maybe something happened way back when, with one or more students doing something stupid or illogical that beckoned humorous criticism, but I don't have a clue. This joke goes like this:

Question: Do you know why all Aggies go to heaven?
Response: No! Why do they?
Answer: They never reach the age of accountability!

Of course, the best explanation for the questions of the age of accountability, as well as what about those who've never heard the gospel (like those little children in the heart of the Congo), is the trustworthiness of God Himself. If God is the God that the Judeo-Christian Scriptures present to us, as we believe it does, then He is a perfect God who makes perfect decisions in every situation. If God always makes perfect decisions, then we can be rest assured that no matter what one's circumstances are, He will know his or her heart and whether or not he or she is among His elect—so He will make a perfect decision regarding his or her eternal destiny! I hope this offers peace to all of us who might be concerned for the eternal welfare of others! Another providential benefit of understanding who God is, as well as His doctrines of election and predestination, is the benefit of realizing the peace that passes all understanding—resting in His perfect will!

In the next chapter, we will examine illustrations of the decrees of election and predestination from literature.

22 🦢

Analogies and Illustrations of the Decrees of Election and Predestination

No analogy or illustration will be perfect when trying to express two of God's deepest truths. The following examples are offered solely for the purpose of stimulating your imagination.

Romeo and Juliet

We are all familiar with the famous tragedy *Romeo and Juliet*, by William Shakespeare, about two young smitten lovers whose deaths ultimately reconcile their feuding families. Everyone can't wait for that special moment when Romeo kisses Juliet. In the play, Romeo (within his own mind and will and with all of his heart) wanted to kiss Juliet, but we also know that Shakespeare wrote the play. Similarly in life, people do what they want, but God wrote the play of life. Fiction writers play a god-like role in the story that emerges from their minds and pens.

A Great Ship on Its Way to Heaven

One analogy of election and predestination could be a great ship symbolically sailing on its way to heaven. The ship (the church) is the body of Christ. Jesus is the captain and pilot of this ship, which in reality, is His spiritual body. The elect are chosen and predestinated to be passengers on this ship. They gain access to this ship the moment they genuinely accept Jesus Christ as their personal Lord and Savior, but their ticket (passage) was paid for before the creation of the universe. Election tells us who will be on the ship, and predestination tells us how the elect will eventually end up on the ship, about the ship's destination, and what God has prepared for those who have entered it. The Holy Spirit stands on the ship's bow and calls out to everyone to come aboard the heaven bound ship through faith in Jesus Christ, but only the elect respond to the invitation. Everyone else turns a deaf ear and walks on by.

An Ocean Liner Leaves New York Bound for Liverpool

An ocean liner leaves New York bound for Liverpool. Its destination has been determined by proper authorities. Nothing can change it. On board the liner are scores of passengers. These passengers are not in chains, neither are their activities determined for them by decree. They are completely free to move about as they will. They eat, sleep, play, lounge about on the deck, read, talk, and interact together as they please, but all the while the great liner is carrying them steadily onward toward a predetermined port. Both freedom and sovereignty are present here and they do not contradict. So it is, I believe, with man's freedom and the sovereignty of God. The mighty liner of God's sovereign design keeps its steady course over the sea of history.[29]

A Great Airliner on its Flight from Earth to Heaven

Another analogy of election and predestation could be a great airliner on its flight from earth to heaven. The airplane is Jesus Christ—the vessel of our salvation. The passengers are those who have been elected (chosen) before the creation of the world to be saved. Predestation represents all the logistics involved in the flight itself. There is only one flight from earth to heaven. There are many people going through the airport to catch flights to many other places, but there is only one flight to heaven. The elect passengers have been given free tickets (paid for by the blood of Christ) for the one flight to heaven on the good ship Jesus Christ. Predestation has provided each of the passengers with tickets (conversion and regeneration), their assigned seats on the airplane (all the details of life on earth), the fellowship of those sitting close to them, the amenities provided on the flight (provisions for life), safety during the turbulences (trials and tribulations of life), and the time of arrival (death and entry into heaven).

---

[29] A.W. Tozer, *Knowledge of the Holy* (San Francisco: HarperOne [original publication, *The Knowledge of the Holy: The Attributes of God: Their Meaning in the Christian Life*, 1961]), 1978.

The Hard-to-Control Daughter

In his sermon on the doctrine of predestination, Mark Driscoll gives an analogy from his personal experience that he thinks help illustrate how the Calvinist interpretation of election or predestination works. He describes a situation where his young daughter would often run from him toward 40 mph traffic in a busy road outside their house, unaware of the danger of her actions, as he was loading their car. He would repeatedly tell her that she shouldn't do that and warn her of the consequences of her actions. And then one time she began to run full speed toward the busy road and Mark chased her, screaming, "Ashley, stop!" to no avail.

Ultimately, she ran into the traffic lane only to be yanked out of the way, just in time by Mark, as a large truck whizzed by. He maintains this analogy faithfully represents the doctrine of election. His chasing his daughter and screaming for her to turn back represents the genuine call of God to the sinner to repent. However, as sinners do not always respond, God must often coercively pull the elect back to Himself to save them.

A Ranching Analogy

A rancher owns a select number of cattle that roam on an open range. At roundup time, the rancher graciously cuts out his cattle from the rest of the cattle roaming the open range. They were his cattle before, but he simply rounds them up at the appointed time. God chose to save some in eternity, and those whom He chose to save in eternity, He graciously cuts out from the rest of mankind at the time of gathering the elect from the four corners of the earth.

A Man Randomly Handing Out Money

A man decides to randomly hand out money to five people in a crowd of twenty. Would the fifteen people who did not receive money be upset? Probably so. Do they have a right to be upset? No, they do not. Why? Because the man did not owe anyone money. He simply decided to be gracious to some.

Two Ropes

During his days as guest lecturer at Calvin Seminary, R. B. Kuiper once used the following illustration of God's sovereignty and human responsibility:

I liken them to two ropes going through two holes in the ceiling and over a pulley above. If I wish to support myself by them, I must cling to them both. If I cling only to one and not the other, I go down. I read the many teachings of the Bible regarding God's election, predestination, His chosen, and so on. I read also the many teachings regarding "whosoever will, may come" and urging people to exercise their responsibility as human beings. These seeming contradictions cannot be reconciled by the puny human mind. With childlike faith, I cling to both ropes, fully confident that in eternity I will see that both strands of truth are, after all, of one piece.

The Testimony of the Vietnamese–American Immigrant

The movie *The Beautiful Country* (2004)[30] is about a boy in Vietnam whose father had been an American GI. Because he was of mixed race, no one in Vietnam accepted him, and he was miserable. His mother wanted him to escape to America to find his father. But the boy thought, *How could I ever find him?* Then his mother showed him a copy of their marriage certificate. This was the proof he needed. He went through a terrible ordeal trying to make it to America, and all along the way, he would pull out that wrinkled marriage certificate to inspire him to keep going. You and I have a similar certificate, the Holy Bible. If you question whether or not you are predestined, I simply urge you to take out your Scriptures. Read the promises therein. Do you believe them? Do you believe that Jesus is God's Son and that He died for your sins? If so, then you are part of that divine destiny. May God bless you in that awesome destiny.

A Train Ride Guaranteed by the Ticket

The book *Subjects of Sovereignty* by Andrew Telford, pastor of Berachah Church in Philadelphia, gives this illustration of predestination. Last night I was in Washington, DC. Yesterday afternoon I went down to the ticket office in the railroad station. I put down my clergy ticket and for $5.90, the clerk handed me a strip of paper, two halves divided by perforated lines. On one line of one-half of the ticket, she had stamped, "From North Philadelphia to Washington," and on the other ticket half, "From North Philadelphia to Washington."

Now turn to the word "predestination" in reference to the railroad ticket. "Pre," which means *beforehand*, and implies that the railroad corporation decided that for $5.90, they would carry a man from Philadelphia to the destination—Washington, DC. The railroad company, beforehand, guarantees the delivery of the man to a certain destination. They have taken the responsibility of delivering the individual to the destination. This had been thought of, planned, and worked out, beforehand.

---

[30] Michael Walther at Outreach Web Properties, 5550 Tech Center Drive, Colorado Springs, CO, 80919.

That is the illustration of the meaning of the important word "predestination." It means precisely what the word itself declares.

In the next chapter, we will study an insightful and enlightening sermon by Octavius Winslow called "Practical Predestination".

23

Practical Predestination

I am indebted to the work of the Reformed Baptist English minister, Octavius Winslow for this chapter. It is a reprint of his excellent sermon called "Practical Predestination." Octavius Winslow was born in August of 1808 and died in March 1878. He was a prominent nineteenth-century evangelical preacher in England and America. For most of his ministry, he was a Baptist minister and was a contemporary of Charles Spurgeon and J. C. Ryle. He eventually seceded to the Anglican church in the last decade of life. He is remembered as "The Pilgrim's Companion," as a direct descendant of John Winslow and Mary Chilton, who braved the Atlantic to travel to America on the Mayflower in 1620. Tradition has it that Mary was the first female of the little group to set foot in the New World. In 1624 she married John Winslow, brother to Edward Winslow (1595–1655), a celebrated Pilgrim leader. On April 2, 1834, Winslow married Miss Hannah Ann Ring, the only daughter of Roland Z. Ring. They would go on to have ten children. Over the years, Octavius pastored five different churches in England and America. During these years, he wrote more than a hundred books and pamphlets (many transcribed from sermons he preached), in which he promoted an experimental knowledge of "the precious truths of God." If you are interested, several of his books and sermons have been reprinted in recent years and are available online.[31] In his time, Winslow was a popular speaker for special occasions, such as the meeting held for the opening of Charles Spurgeon's Metropolitan Tabernacle in 1861.

---

[31] https://www.gracegems.org/6/practical_predestination.htm.

Winslow's Sermon

"For whom He did foreknow, He also did predestinate to be conformed to the image of His Son, that he might be the first born among many brethren" (Romans 8:29). Guided by the latter clause of the preceding verse, we were led to advert to the settled purpose and plan of God as it related to the conversion of His people. The passage under present consideration carries forward the same argument another step, and shows that the doctrine thus clearly enunciated is not a crude and speculative dogma of the schools, which some suppose, but is a truth of distinct revelation, divine in its origin, experimental in its nature, and sanctifying and comforting in its effects. Let us then, divesting our minds of all prejudice, address ourselves to its consideration, in prayerful reliance upon the teaching of the Spirit and with the earnest simplicity of children desiring to come to a knowledge of the truth, and to stand complete in all the will of God.

"Whom He did foreknow": In this place, the word "foreknow" assumes a particular and explicit meaning. In its wider and more general application it must be regarded as referring not simply to the divine prescience, but more especially to the divine prearrangement. For God to foreknow is, in the strict meaning of the phrase, for God to foreordain. There are no guesses, conjectures, or contingencies with God as to the future. Not only does He know all, but He has fixed, appointed, and ordered "all things after the counsel of his own will" In this view there exists not a creature, and there transpires not an event, which was not as real and palpable to the divine mind from eternity as it is at the present moment. Indeed, it would seem that there were no future with God. An eternal being, there can be nothing prospective in His looking on all things. There must be an eternity of perception, and constitution, and presence; and the mightiest feature of His character—that which conveys to a finite mind the most vivid conception of His grandeur and greatness—is the simultaneousness of all succession, variety, and events to His eye. "He is of one mind and who can turn him?"

But the word "foreknow" as it occurs in the text adds to this yet another, a more definite and to the saints, a more precious signification. The foreknowledge here spoken of, it will be observed, is limited to a particular class of people who are said to be "conformed to the image of God's Son." Now this cannot, with truth, be predicated of all creatures. The term, therefore, assumes a particular and impressive signification. It includes the everlasting love of God to, and His most free choice of, His people, to be His special and peculiar treasure. We find some examples of this—"God has not cast away his people which he foreknew" (Romans 11:2). Here the word is expressive of the two ideas of love and choice. Again, "Who verily was foreordained (Greek: foreknown) before the foundation of the world" (1 Peter 1:20). "Him, being delivered by the determinate counsel and foreknowledge of God" (Acts 2:23). Clearly, then, we are justified in interpreting the phrase as expressive of God's special choice of, and His intelligent love to, His church—His own peculiar people. It is a foreknowledge of choice, of love, of eternal grace and faithfulness.

"He also did predestinate." This word admits of but one natural signification. Predestination, in its lowest sense, is understood to mean the exclusive agency of God in producing every event. But it includes more than this: it takes in God's predeterminate appointment and fore-arrangement of a thing beforehand, according to His divine and supreme will. The Greek is so rendered—"For to do whatever your hand and your counsel determined before to be done" (Acts 4:28). Again, "Having predestinated us unto the adoption of children by Jesus Christ to himself, according to the good pleasure of his will" (Ephesians 1:5). It is here affirmed of God, that the same prearrangement and predetermination that men in general are agreed to ascribe to Him in the government of matter, extends equally, and with yet stronger force, to the concerns of His moral administration. It would seem impossible to form any correct idea of God, disassociated from the idea of predestination. As a divine wrote, "The sole basis of predestination is the practical belief that God is eternal and infinite in and over all. And the sole aim of its assertion should be, as the sole legitimate effect of that assertion is, to settle down the wavering and rebel soul from the vague, skeptical, and superstitious inapplicability's of chance as to this world's history, unto the living, overwhelming, and humbling practicality of conviction, that, just because God sees all things, provides all things, and has power over all things, therefore man must act as if he believed this to be true. The first and the last conviction of every honest inquirer must be, that God is, and is Lord over all—and the whole of Scripture bears testimony to the fact of His infinitude."

And yet how marvelously difficult it is to win the mind to a full, unwavering acquiescence in a truth which, in a different application, is received with unquestioning readiness! And what is there in the application of this law of the divine government to the world of matter, which is not equally reasonable and fit in its application to the world of mind? If it is necessary and proper in the material, why should it not be equally or more so in the spiritual empire? If God is allowed the full exercise of a sovereignty in the one, why should He be excluded from an unlimited sovereignty in the other? Surely it were even more worthy of Him that He should prearrange, predetermine, and supremely rule in the concerns of a world over which His more dignified and glorious empire extends, than that in the inferior world of matter He should fix a constellation in the heavens, guide the gyrations of a bird in the air, direct the falling of an autumn leaf in the pathless desert, or convey the seed, borne upon the wind, to the spot where it should fall. Surely if no fortuitous ordering is admitted in the one case, on infinitely stronger grounds it should be excluded from the other. Upon no other basis could divine foreknowledge and providence take their stand than upon this. Disconnected from the will and purpose of God, there could be nothing certain as to the future, and consequently there could be nothing certainly foreknown.

And were not providence to regulate and control people, things, and events—every dispensation, in fact—by the same preconstructed plan, it would follow that God would be exposed to a thousand unforeseen contingencies, or else that He acts ignorantly or contrary to His will.

But it is not so much our province to establish the truth of this doctrine and explain its reasonableness and the harmony of its relations, as to trace its sanctifying tendency and effect. Predestination must be a divine verity, since it stands essentially connected with our conformity to the divine image. . . . "Predestinated to be conformed to the image of his Son." Addressing ourselves to this deeply interesting and important branch of our subject, let us first contemplate the believer's model.

"The image of his Son." . . . No standard short of this will meet the case. How conspicuous appears the wisdom and how glorious the goodness of God in this—that in making us holy, the model or standard of that holiness should be Deity itself! God would make us holy and in doing so, He would make us like Himself. But with what pen—dipped though it were in heaven's brightest hues—can we portray the image of Jesus? The perfection of our Lord was the perfection of holiness. His Deity, essential holiness—His humanity without sin, the impersonation of holiness, all that He was, said, and did, was as flashes of holiness emanating from the fountain of essential purity, and kindling their dazzling and undying radiance around each step He trod. How lowly, too, His character! How holy the thoughts He breathed, how pure the words He spoke, how humble the spirit He exemplified, how tender and sympathizing the outgoings of His compassion and love to man. He is "the chief among ten thousand, the altogether lovely."

Such is the believer's model. To this he is predestinated to be conformed. And is not this predestination in its highest form? Would it seem possible for God to have preordained us to a greater blessing, to have chosen us to a higher distinction? In choosing us in Christ before the foundation of the world, that we should be holy, He has advanced us to the loftiest degree of honor and happiness to which a creature can be promoted—assimilation to His own moral image. And this forms the highest ambition of the believer. To transcribe those beauteous lineaments which, in such perfect harmony and beautiful expression, blended and shone in the life of Jesus, is the great study of all His true disciples. But in what does this conformity consist?

The first feature is a conformity of nature. And this is reciprocal. The Son of God, by an act of divine power, became human. The saints of God, by an act of sovereign grace, partake "of the divine nature," as 2 Peter 1:4 says. This harmony of nature forms the basis of all conformity. Thus grafted into Christ, we grow up into Him in all holy resemblance. The meekness, the holiness, the patience, the self-denial, the zeal, the love, traceable in us—though faint and imperfect—are transfers of Christ's beauteous and faultless lineaments to our renewed soul. Thus, the mind that was in Him is in some measure in us. And in our moral conflict, battling as we do with sin, Satan, and the world, we come to know a little of fellowship with His sufferings and conformity to His death.

We are here supplied with a test of Christian character. It is an anxious question with many professors of Christ, "How may I arrive at a correct conclusion that I am among the predestinated of God—that I am included in His purpose of grace and love—that I have a saving interest in the Lord's salvation?" The passage under consideration supplies the answer—conformity to the image of God's Son. Nothing short of this can justify the belief that we are saved. No evidence less strong can authenticate the fact of our predestination. The determination of God to save men is not so fixed as to save no matter what their character may be. Christ's work is a salvation from sin, not in sin . . ."According as he has chosen us in him before the foundation of the world, that we should be holy" (Ephesians 1:4). In other words, that we should be conformed to the divine image. That we should be like Christ in His divine nature, in the purity of His human nature, in the humility He exemplified, in the self-denial He practiced, and in the heavenly life He lived. In a word, in all that this expressive sentence comprehends—"conformed to the image of his Son."

As we grow day by day more holy, more spiritually minded, more closely resembling Jesus, we are placing the truth of our predestination to eternal life in a clearer, stronger light, and consequently the fact of our salvation beyond a misgiving and a doubt. In view of this precious truth, what spiritual heart will not breathe the prayer from Townshend,

O Lord! I cannot be satisfied merely to profess and call myself Yours. I want more of the power of vital religion in my soul. I pant for Your image. My deepest grief springs from the discovery of the little real resemblance which I bear to a model so peerless, so divine— that I exemplify so little of Your patience in suffering; Your meekness in opposition; Your forgiving spirit in injury; Your gentleness in reproving; Your firmness in temptation; Your singleness of eye in all that I do. Oh, transfer Yourself wholly to me. What were this world, yes, what were heaven itself, without You? A universe of creatures, the fondest, the holiest, could not be Your substitute to my yearning, longing soul, O Lord! Come and occupy Your own place in my heart. Awaken it to Your love. Sweep its chords with Your gentle hand, and it shall breathe sweet music to Your dear name.

I love You, Savior, for my soul craves joy! I need You, without hope I cannot live! I look for You, my nature pants to give its every power a rapture and employ, and there are things which I would sincerely destroy within my bosom, things that make me grieve; Sin, and her child, Distrust, that often weave about my spirit darkness and annoy: and none but You can these dissolve in light; and so I long for You, as those who stay in the deep waters, long for dawning day! Nor would I only have my being bright, but peaceful, too, so ask You if I might my head on Your dear bosom lean always."

"That he might be the firstborn among many brethren." . . . The Son of God sustains to us the relation of the Elder Brother. He is emphatically the "Firstborn." In another place we read, "Forasmuch then as the children are partakers of flesh and blood, he also likewise took part of the same." He is the "Brother born for adversity." Our relation to Him as our Brother is evidenced by our conformity to Him as our model. We have no valid claim to relationship which springs not from a resemblance to His image. The features may be indistinctly visible, yet one line of holiness, one true lineament, drawn upon the heart by the Holy Spirit, proves our fraternal relationship to Him, the "Firstborn."

And how large the brotherhood—"many brethren"! What the relative proportion of the church is to the world—how many will be saved—is a question speculative and profitless. But this we know, the number will be vast, countless. The one family of God is composed of "many brethren." They are not all of the same judgment in all matters, but they are all of the same spirit. The unity of the family of God is not ecclesiastical, nor geographical. It is spiritual and essential. It is the "unity of the Spirit." Begotten of one Father, in the nature of the Elder Brother, and through the regenerating grace of the one Spirit, all the saints of God constitute one church, one family, one brotherhood—essentially and indivisibly one. Nor is this relationship difficult to recognize.

Consider the following illustration: Two brethren in the Lord of widely different sections of the church, and of much dissonance of sentiment on some points of truth, meet and converse together. With the Word of God in hand, each is surprised that the other does not read it as he reads it and interpret it as he interprets it. But they drop the points of difference and take up the points of agreement. They speak of Christ—the Christ who loves them both, and whom they both love. They talk of the one Master whom they serve and of their common labors, infirmities, trials, temptations, discouragements, failures, and successes. They talk of the heaven where they are journeying and of their Father's house, in which they will dwell together forever. They kneel in prayer; they cast themselves before the cross; the oil of gladness anoints them; their hearts are broken, their spirits are humbled, their souls are blended; they rise and feel more deeply and more strongly than ever that they both belong to the same family, are both of the "many brethren" of whom the Son of God is the "Firstborn," the elder brother. Oh, blessed unity! What perfect harmony of creed, what strict conformity of ritual, what sameness of denominational relation, is for a moment to be compared with this? Have you, my reader, this evidence that you belong to the "many brethren?"

It is our purpose to conclude by briefly showing how encouraging the doctrine of predestination is to the soul in sincere and earnest seeking of Christ, and by tracing some of the peculiar blessings which flow from it to the saints of God. There is a class of individuals, unhappily a large one, over whose spiritual feelings the doctrine of divine predestination would seem to have cast a deep and settled gloom. We refer to those who are apt to regard this truth with deep antipathy, if not with absolute horror, as constituting in their view, one of the most formidable and insurmountable obstacles to their salvation. But the validity of this objection we by no means admit. There can be nothing in the Bible adverse to the salvation of a sinner. The doctrine of predestination is a revealed doctrine of the Bible. Therefore, predestination cannot be opposed to the salvation of the sinner. So far from this being true, we don't hesitate most strongly and emphatically to affirm that we know of no doctrine of God's Word more replete with encouragement to the awakened, sin-burdened, Christ-seeking soul than this.

What stronger evidence can we have of our election of God than the Spirit's work in the heart? Are you really in earnest for the salvation of your soul? Do you feel the plague of sin? Are you sensible of the condemnation of the law? Do you come under the denomination of the "weary and heavy laden"? If so, then the fact that you are a subject of divine drawings—that you have a felt conviction of your sinfulness—and that you are seeking for a place of refuge, affords the strongest ground for believing that you are one of those whom God has predestinated to eternal life. The very work thus begun is the Spirit's first outline of the divine image upon your soul—that very image to which the saints are predestinated to be conformed.

But while we thus vindicate this doctrine as being inimical to the salvation of the anxious soul, we must, with all distinctness and earnestness declare that in this stage of your Christian course, you have primarily and mainly to do with another and a different doctrine. We refer to the doctrine of the atonement. If you could look into the book of the divine decrees, and read your name inscribed upon its pages, it would not impart the joy and peace which one believing view of Christ crucified will convey. It is not essential to your salvation that you believe in election, but it is essential to your salvation that you believe in the Lord Jesus Christ. In your case, as an individual debating the momentous question, "how a sinner may be justified before God," your first business is with Christ, and Christ exclusively. You are to feel that you are a lost sinner, not that you are an elect saint. The doctrine which meets the present phase of your spiritual condition is not the doctrine of predestination, but the doctrine of an atoning Savior. The truth to which you are to give the first consideration, and the most simple and unquestioning credence is, that "Christ died for the ungodly," that He came into the world to save sinners, that He came to call, not the righteous, but sinners to repentance, and that in all respects, He is in the great business of our salvation. He stands before us in the relation of a Savior, while we stand before Him in the character of a sinner. The mental conflict into which you have been brought touching this doctrine, is but a subtle and dexterous stroke of the enemy to divert your thoughts from Christ. Your soul is at this moment in what may be termed a transitional state. A crisis in your history has been reached. How momentous the result! Shall we portray your present feelings? You are sensible of your sinfulness, are oppressed by its guilt, and are in dread of its condemnation. You have no peace of mind, no joy of heart, no hope of heaven. Life with you has lost its charm, society its attractions, and pleasure its sweetness. A somber hue paints every object and insipidity marks every engagement. Where this marvelous revolution, this essential and wondrous change? We answer, it is the Spirit of God moving upon your soul. And what truth, do you think, meets the case? Predestination? Election? Oh, no! These are hidden links in the great chain of your salvation, upon which in your present state, you are not called to lay your hand in grasping that chain.

But there are other and intermediate links, visible, near, and within your reach. Take hold of them, and you are saved:

"This is a faithful saying, and worthy of all acceptation, that Christ Jesus came into the world to save sinners."

"God so loved the world, that he gave his only begotten Son, that whosoever believes in him should not perish, but have everlasting life."

"The blood of Jesus Christ his Son cleanses us from all sin."

"Come unto me, all you that labor and are heavy laden and I will give you rest."

"Him that comes unto me I will in no wise cast out."

"Whosoever will, let him take of the water of life freely."

"Being justified freely by his grace through the redemption that is in Christ Jesus."

"Ho, every one that thirsts, come you to the waters."

"In whom we have redemption through his blood, the forgiveness of sins, according to the riches of his grace."

"By grace are you saved, through faith and that not of yourselves. It is the gift of God."

"Wherefore he is able also to save them to the uttermost that come unto God by him."

"Believe on the Lord Jesus Christ, and you shall be saved."

Grasp, in simple faith, each or any one of these golden links and from that moment for you there is no condemnation. But what is the real difficulty? It is not predestination.

Travel into the inmost recesses of your heart and ascertain. May there not be some defect in your actual conviction of sin? Were you thoroughly convinced of your lost and ruined condition as a sinner, would you cavil and demur at any one revealed doctrine of Scripture? Would this, of all doctrines, prove a real stumbling block in your way? Would the question of election give you a moment's serious thought? Would it interpose a true and valid objection to your coming to Christ to be saved by Him? To illustrate the idea, suppose you were roused from sleep in the dead hour of night by the approach of flames kindling fiercely around you. One avenue of escape presented itself. Would you pause for an instant upon its threshold to debate the question of your predestinated safety? Would you not at once decide the question in your favor, by an instant retreat from the devouring element, through the only door that proffered you deliverance? Most assuredly. To a matter so momentous as your salvation apply the same reasoning. Were it not folly, yes, insanity itself, to hesitate for a moment to consider whether you are predestinated to escape the wrath to come, when, if you do not escape, that wrath will assuredly overwhelm you? One refuge alone presents itself. One avenue only invites your escape. Let no other doctrine, but faith in the Lord Jesus Christ, occupy your thoughts at this juncture of your religious course. Diverging from this path, you will be plunged into a sea of perplexities, you know not how inextricable, which may land you, you know not where. For they who have reasoned high of providence, foreknowledge, will, and fate, fixed fate, freewill, foreknowledge absolute, have found no end in wandering mazes lost.

O let one object fix your eye and one theme fill your mind—Christ and His salvation. Absorbed in the contemplation and study of these two points, you may safely defer all further inquiry to another and a more advanced stage of your Christian course. Remember that the fact of your predestination, the certainty of your election, can only be inferred from your conversion. We must hold you firmly to this truth. It is the subtle and fatal reasoning of Satan, a species of atheistically fatalism, to argue, "If I am elected, I shall be saved whether I am regenerated or not." The path to eternal woe is paved with arguments like this. Men have cajoled their souls with such vain excuses until they have found themselves beyond the region of hope!

But we must rise to the fountain by pursuing the stream. Conversion and not predestination, is the end of the chain we are to grasp. We must ascend from ourselves to God, and not descend from God to ourselves, in settling this great question. We must judge of God's objective purpose of love concerning us, by His subjective work of grace within us. One of the martyr Reformers has wisely remarked,

"We need not go about to trouble ourselves with curious questions of the predestination of God, but let us rather endeavor ourselves that we may be in Christ. For, when we are in Him, then are we well, and then we may be sure that we are ordained to everlasting life. When you find these three things in your hearts, repentance, faith, and a desire to leave sin, then you may be sure your names are written in the book, and you may be sure also, that you are elected and predestinated to eternal life. If you are desiring to know whether you are chosen to everlasting life, you may not begin with God, for God is too high, you cannot comprehend Him. Begin with Christ, and learn to know Christ, and wherefore He came; namely, that He came to save sinners, and made Himself subject to the law, and a fulfiller of the law, to deliver us from the wrath and danger thereof. If you know Christ, then you may know further of your election." And illustrating his idea by his own personal experience, he says, "If I believe in Christ alone for salvation, I am certainly interested in Christ and interested in Christ I could not be, if I were not chosen and elected of God."

In conclusion, we earnestly entreat you to lay aside all fruitless speculations, and to give yourself to prayer. Let reason bow to faith, and faith shut you up to Christ, and Christ be all in all to you. Once more we solemnly affirm that, conversion, and not predestination, is the doctrine with which, in your present state of inquiry, you have to do. Beware that you come not short of true conversion—a changed heart, and a renewed mind, so that you become "a new creature in Christ Jesus." And if as a poor lost sinner—you repair to the Savior, all vile, guilty, unworthy, and weak as you are, He will receive you, and shelter you within the bosom that bled on the cross, to provide an atonement and an asylum for the very chief of sinners. Intermeddle not, therefore, with a state which you can only ascertain to be yours by the Spirit's work upon your heart. Your election will be known by your interest in Christ and your interest in Christ by the sanctification of the Spirit. Here is a chain of salvation. The beginning of it is from the Father, the dispensation of it through the Son, and the application of it by the Spirit. In looking after the comfort of election, you must look inward to the work of the Spirit in your heart, then outward to the work of Christ on the cross, then upward to the heart of the Father in heaven. Oh, let your prayer be "God be merciful to me a sinner," until that prayer is answered in the assurance of full pardon sealed upon your conscience by the Holy Spirit. Thus, knocking at mercy's door, the heart of God will fly open, and admit you to all the hidden treasures of its love.

We can but group some of the great blessings which flow from this truth to the saints of God. The doctrine of predestination is well calculated to confirm and strengthen the true believer in the fact and certainty of his salvation through Christ. Feeling, as he does, the plague of his own heart, experiencing the preciousness of the Savior, looking up through the cross to God as his Father, exulting in a hope that makes not ashamed, and remembering that God the Eternal Spirit only renews those who are chosen by God the Father, and are redeemed by God the Son, this doctrine is found to be most comforting and confirming to his faith. The faintest lineaments of resemblance to God, and the feeblest breathing of the Spirit of adoption he discovers in his soul, is to him an indisputable evidence of his predestination to divine sonship and holiness.

Another blessing accruing from the doctrine is the sweet and holy submission into which it brings the mind under all afflictive dispensations. Each step of his pilgrimage, and each incident of his history, the believer sees appointed in the everlasting covenant of grace. He recognizes the discipline of the covenant to be as much a part of the original plan as any positive mercy that it contains. That all the hairs of his head are numbered, that affliction springs not out of the earth, and therefore is not the result of accident or chance, but is in harmony with God's purposes of love and, thus ordained and permitted, must work together for good. Not the least blessing resulting from this truth (2 Thessalonians 2:13) is its tendency to promote personal godliness. The believer feels that God has "chosen us to salvation through sanctification and belief of the truth" and that He has "chosen us that we should be holy and without blame before him in love" (Ephesians 1:4), that we are "his workmanship, created in Christ Jesus unto good works, which God has before ordained that we should walk in them" (Ephesians 2:10). Thus, the believer desires to "give all diligence to make his calling and election sure" or undoubted, by walking in all the ordinances and commandments of the Lord blameless and standing complete in all the will of God.

And what doctrine is more emptying, humbling, and therefore sanctifying, than this? It lays the axe at the root of all human boasting. In the light of this truth, the most holy believer sees that there is no difference between him and the vilest sinner that crawls the earth, but what the mere grace of God has made. Such are some of the many blessings flowing to the Christian from this truth. The radiance which it reflects upon the entire history of the child of God, and the calm repose which it diffuses over the mind in all the perplexing, painful, and mysterious events of that history, can only be understood by those whose hearts have fully received the doctrine of predestination. Whatever betides him, inexplicable in its character, enshrouded in the deepest gloom, as may be the circumstance—the believer in this truth can "stand still" and calmly surveying the scene, exclaim: "This also comes forth from the Lord of Hosts, who is wonderful in counsel, and excellent in working. He who works all things after the counsel of His own will has done it, and I am satisfied that it is well done."

In conclusion, saints of God, have close relations and intimate dealings with your Elder Brother. Repose in Him your confidence, yield to Him your affections, consecrate to Him your service. He regards you with ineffable delight. With all your interests, He is identified and with all your sorrows, He sympathizes. He may, like Joseph, at times speak roughly to His brethren, in the trying dispensations of His providence; yet, like Joseph, He veils beneath that apparent harshness a brother's deep and yearning love. Seek a closer resemblance to His image, to which, ever remember that you are predestinated to be conformed. In order to this—study His beauty, His precepts, His example, that with "open face, beholding as in a glass the glory of the Lord, you may be changed into the same image, from glory to glory, even as by the Spirit of the Lord."

In the next chapter, we will review some of the Biblical witnesses to election and pre-destination in the Old Testament.

24

The Witnesses to Election in the Old Testament

We continue our survey of illustrations of election and predestination in literature with a look at some of the original witnesses to God's glorious plan in the Old Testament.

Abraham

As God planned the creation of the Jewish race in the Old Testament, He chose a single individual, out of all of humanity, to use in establishing this new race of people. This selected individual would become the first Jew. God's choice was a man named Abram living in Mesopotamia. Abram's father was Terah who was the tenth generational descendant of Noah. Terah had three sons named Abram, Nahor, and Haran. Out of these three sons, God picked (chose) Abram to be the very first Jew.

Genesis 11–25 describes how God appeared to Abram and told him to leave his country and his father's house for a land that He would show him. God promised to make Abram into a great nation, to bless him, to make his name great, and to bless those who blessed him and curse those who cursed him. God gave grace to Abram to obey and follow the command given to him. At age seventy-five, Abram took his wife Sarai, his nephew, Lot, and the wealth and people in his household and traveled to Shechem in Canaan.

Through this experience, God established His unconditional covenant with Abram and his descendants, which would lead to the nation of Israel and to the promised Messiah, Jesus Christ. As Abram, by grace, followed God's revelation and exercised faith in God as his Lord, God changed his name to Abraham. His new name represented the separation from his old life to his new role as God's child, friend, and father of the new chosen race, the Jews or Israelites. The important point here is how Abraham did not choose God, but God chose Abraham, revealed Himself to Abraham, and gave Abraham the needed grace that empowered him to believe and follow God's revealed will. Abraham and his son Isaac and his grandson Jacob are all excellent examples of election. They were chosen by God to have a personal relationship with Him, and they were empowered by grace to believe, obey, and fulfill His will.

Moses

Moses is one of the most fascinating characters in biblical history and a powerful illustration of both personal election to salvation and election to a specific role in history. He was born near the end of the Jews' time in Egypt as slaves. He was born to Jewish parents, but providentially raised in the palace of Pharaoh. He was endowed with great intelligence and impressive physical traits. Acts 7:20–22 states: "It was at this time that Moses was born and he was lovely in the sight of God and he was nurtured three months in his father's home. And after he had been set outside, Pharaoh's daughter took him away and nurtured him as her own son. Moses was educated in all the learning of the Egyptians and he was a man of power in words and deeds." Unknown to himself, Moses was being providentially prepared to lead his people out of Egyptian bondage, and later to serve as mediator in establishing the special covenant between God and Israel.

When Moses was a young adult, the Holy Spirit awakened Moses's conscience to his Jewish roots and to the suffering of his people in harsh slavery under the same Pharaoh he lived with in luxury. At the age of forty, Moses interceded on behalf of an Israelite being oppressed by a task master, and he killed the oppressor. In fear of retaliation from Pharaoh, he fled from Egypt and spent the next forty years in the wilderness. Then God appeared to Moses in a burning bush and spoke to him from the fire. God told Moses that he had been chosen to lead the Israelites out of slavery in Egypt and into the promised land. Moses was, of course, afraid and shocked by this and tried to claim incompetence, but God would have none of it and confirmed to him that he was the chosen vessel for this project. The task was even harder than Moses could have ever imagined, but by the power and miracles of God, the process was successful, and the Israelites came out of Egypt as a freed people.

You have probably read of these experiences in Exodus, Leviticus, Numbers, and Deuteronomy. In these books of the Bible, it becomes very clear how God planned the birth and life of Moses to fit into the deliverance of Israel from Egypt. Moses did not choose God, but God chose Moses before the foundations of the world to become an Israelite, a true child of God, and the anointed leader of the descendants of Abraham into freedom.

Rahab

The story of Rahab is found in the first six chapters of Joshua. The following article is called "Unlikely and Unworthy, yet Chosen by God." Following the short article is a comment by me.

"There once was a woman named Rahab, who lived in the great walled city of Jericho. She was a prostitute, and did well for herself, living in a prominent house on the edge of the city, right along the wall. Rahab's home was the perfect stop for many visitors from far-away lands. As many men came and went, Rahab heard numerous stories from the outside world. One of these was of the great and mighty God of the Israelites. Their God had parted the Red Sea for His people, delivering them out of slavery in Egypt. This God had also empowered His people to bring down the Amorites, completely destroying their land. As Rahab heard more and more, she found herself in awe of this God's power and might. Her desire was to know this God of the Israelites, for His people were surely safe from all harm.

One day while Rahab was stationed at her window, possibly looking for men to invite in, she noticed two odd-looking fellows. They were not dressed like the locals and seemed a bit uneasy. Intrigued, she called to the men, inviting them in. They kindly accepted Rahab's offer and entered her home. She soon learned that these men were Israelite spies. Their God was leading them to soon take down the city of Jericho and they were sent ahead to prepare. Somehow, the king heard that spies had entered Rahab's home. The king sent men to call on Rahab, instructing her to bring them out. Instead, she hid the spies and helped them. She told the king that they had left before sunset when the city's gates were about to close. Once the king's men departed, the spies prepared to escape the city, but Rahab made them wait.

She knew very little about these men and what was to become of her city, Jericho. But she did know that they belonged to a powerful God. She believed that this God could save her and her family, because of His unmatched might. She begged the spies to guarantee the safety of herself and her family in exchange for the kindness she showed them. They agreed, as long as she did not inform the king that their people were planning an attack. Rahab gathered her family in her house in the days that followed and prepared for the Israelites' descent on Jericho. When God led the Israelites to the city and brought down the walls, the spies returned for Rahab and her family. While every other person in the city was slain and their possessions burned, the Israelites spared Rahab and her family. It was because of Rahab's simple faith in the great God she had heard of that she was able to receive protection from harm and hope for a future.

Rahab went on to join the Israelite people who rescued her and began worshipping their God and adopting their customs. She married an Israelite man named Salmon and gave birth to a son named Boaz, both of which [sic] are in the lineage of Jesus Christ. This detail makes her a woman of utmost importance in the Bible. Her great acts of faith—welcoming spies and trusting in their God—are noted several times in Scripture. Rahab's decision to put her hope in God and believe in His power are what secured her future and earned her a place of honor in the sight of God."[32]

The author shares a few notes on Rahab:

God began to work in the heart and mind of Rahab from the very first time she heard of God's work on behalf of Israel. She began to fear and be in awe of Jehovah—the God of Israel. By grace, she began to be drawn to the one true God in conviction and faith. The Holy Spirit enabled her (in contradiction to every other person in her city) to act courageously in protecting the Jewish spies and securing their blessing upon her and her family as God turned Jericho over to Israel. Rahab's actions manifested her destiny as one of God's elect who was also grafted into the linage of Jesus Christ. Her transformation from a pagan prostitute to a genuine child of God is a glorious example of the Lord's sovereign power to save anyone He has chosen. Rahab is mentioned in Matthew 1:5 as one of the ancestors of Jesus. She married Salmon of the tribe of Judah and was the mother of Boaz. Amazingly she was ancestress to King David, all the kings of Judah, and the Lord Jesus. She is also mentioned as an example of a person of faith in Hebrews 11:31 and a person who demonstrated her faith with good works in James 2:25.

Gideon

The story of Gideon is found in Judges 6–8. The name Gideon means "he who casts down." Gideon was the son of Joash the Abiezrite from the town of Ophrah. He was Israel's fifth judge. During Gideon's time, a large army of Midianites and other small nations had gathered against Israel. The Lord approached Gideon and told him he would be made strong, so that he could save Israel from the Midianites. After asking God to confirm that He would really help Gideon do this, through the two fleece tests, Gideon raised an army

---

[32] Hayley Hudson, "Unlikely and Unworthy, Yet Chosen by God," https://sites.google.com/site/unlikely-women/rahab-s-story.

of thirty-two thousand. The Lord told Gideon that He would not get the glory with so many volunteer soldiers involved and that He would show Gideon how to whittle down the group to the point it would be obvious who provided the victory over Midian. Eventually the army was reduced to three hundred men.

God did this so that the people of Israel would not boast to Him that they saved themselves by their own strength. At night, Gideon and his three hundred men lit torches, blew trumpets, and shouted. Then they stood by and watched as God caused the enemy to panic and began fighting and killing each other. God orchestrated the entire event. Midian never recovered from this defeat and there was peace for forty years during Gideon's lifetime. Gideon lived to be an old man and was buried near his father in the town of Ophrah. His victory over the Midianites was remembered for many generations as the "Day of Midian" (Isaiah 9:4).

The point of mentioning Gideon in this book is to show how God chose Gideon as His "elect representative" to lead the charge against the Midianites. Gideon did not choose this for himself. Gideon was minding his own business, hiding grain from the Midianites and just trying to survive, when God approached him. Gideon did not want the assignment or feel qualified for the task, but God did what it took to convince him and motivate him to cooperate. Gideon received grace to believe and to follow God's revealed will, which resulted in God being glorified and Israel being liberated.

Samuel

Samuel was the son of Elkanah and Hannah and was born at Ramathaim-zophim in the hill country of Ephraim. In fulfillment of a vow made by his mother, Samuel was brought to the Tabernacle at Shiloh as a young child to serve God for the rest of his life. He succeeded Eli as the high priest and judge of Israel. When the Philistines destroyed Shiloh, Israel's religious center, Samuel returned to Ramah to live. Samuel made annual circuits through many cities of Israel, judging the people, exhorting them to stop worshipping idols, and using his influence to hold the tribes together. He served very effectively as a judge and a prophet.

At the time, Israel was under Philistine domination, constant threats from the Ammonites, and disunion among its own tribes. As Samuel grew old, the people lacked respect for Samuel's corrupt sons, Joel and Abijah, whom he appointed to judge Israel in his stead. The elders urged Samuel to find a strong national leader to become king. Under God's guidance, Samuel anointed Saul, son of Kish of the tribe of Benjamin, as Israel's very first King.

Samuel later broke with Saul, because Saul disobeyed divine orders twice. Directed by the Lord, Samuel then proclaimed that Saul was rejected as king of Israel and that his dynasty would not continue on the throne. God supernaturally led Samuel to David, selecting him and secretly anointing him king of Israel. Samuel's last days were tense, because of the conflict between Saul and David. The Bible makes a brief reference to his death and burial at Ramah. Samuel was considered one of the greatest of the judges, but was also numbered among the prophets. He was not a warrior, but like Moses, he was a genuine, honest, and sincere leader who rallied the spirit of his people in the midst of oppression, keeping alive their hope and faith.

The Scriptures make it clear how God sovereignly orchestrated Samuel's birth and life through the providential workings in the life of his mother Hannah. Hannah's husband Elkanah had another wife named Peninnah in addition to Hannah (1 Samuel 1). Peninnah bore children for Elkanah, whereas God kept Hannah from conceiving. Peninnah taunted Hannah, because she could not conceive. Hannah was continually grieved in this situation, which caused her to pray and seek the Lord with all of her heart, for God's blessing upon her. Her grief finally reached a pinnacle, which caused her to pray to the Lord that if He would bless her with a son, she would dedicate the boy's entire life to God's service. God then answered her prayer and she conceived and gave birth to Samuel. The Hebrew name *Samuel* can mean either "name of God" or "God has heard" or "asked of God." Hannah chose this name, because "God specifically heard her prayer" and her son Samuel was literally "asked of God."

After Hannah finished nursing Samuel, she took her young child to Eli at the tabernacle to live and serve God for the rest of his life. God began to speak directly to young Samuel and to reveal Himself to Samuel. God confirmed his life's purpose as a judge and prophet to Israel. Samuel was an elect child of God (for all of eternity) and he was elected by God to lead and guide Israel during its formative years as a nation. Samuel's life and activities are recorded in 1st & 2nd Samuel. God even allowed Samuel to come back in spiritual form (after Samuel's death) to alert King Saul about Saul's own pending death the very next day after their conversation.

King David

David is another interesting character in the Old Testament. He rose from a lowly shepherd boy to become one of the most popular monarchs the world has ever known. David was born in the city of Bethlehem in Judea and he was the youngest son of a man named Jesse who had eight sons. David was also the grandson of Boaz and Ruth. Through God's sovereignty and providence, David became the second king of Israel and the first of the royal line that governed Judah and Israel until the exile. He wrote many of the psalms and the

Lord Jesus Christ comes from the "Davidic Line" also referred to as the "House of David" and known in Hebrew as "Malkhut Beit David" (דוד תיב תוכלמ)—"Royal House of David."

David was King Saul's most successful warrior, but his successes against the Philistines (including the killing of Goliath) caused the king's jealousy, and David was forced to live on the run for many years. After Saul's death, David became king over Judah in Hebron at the age of thirty, and seven years later was recognized as the king over all Israel. He made Jerusalem the political and religious capitol of his kingdom and built a palace for himself on its highest hill called "Zion." He brought the Ark of the Covenant there and kept it under a tent. He united the many tribes of Israel and extended his territory from Egypt to the Euphrates. The later part of his reign was troubled by the revolts of his sons Absalom and Adonijah.

David chose Solomon, his son by Bathsheba, to succeed him as king. Aside from his great military victories, David is remembered for his deep worship of God as expressed in the psalms he wrote and for his desire to build a great temple, worthy of God's glory. God told him he would not be the one to build the temple (because of all the blood he shed in war), so David accumulated all the resources he could for the building project, which his son Solomon used to complete the temple.

First Samuel 16 reveals how God chose David as the second king of Israel to replace King Saul. God told Samuel to go to Bethlehem and anoint David as King, which Samuel did. It appears David was in his late teens at the time, but had a heart fully committed to God. Goliath disdained David because of his youth and his appearance. By grace—David was a young man after God's own heart. He sought the Lord and fully trusted in the Lord. During all of those years, as he was waiting upon God's promise that he would become king, he experienced many trials and tribulations trying to survive on the run from King Saul (who wanted to kill him). But God's Word finally came to pass and David was recognized as King over Judah. Seven years later he was recognized as King over all of Israel and he reigned for a total of forty years. There are fifty-three New Testament verses that refer to David or the House of David by name. Once again, we see that God chose David rather than David choosing God.

God worked in David's life from his early years and gave him a very sensitive heart toward spiritual and moral things. It is believed that David spent much time meditating upon God and His greatness and His goodness, as displayed in creation and salvation, as he watched over his father's sheep among the hills and pastures of Judea. David fulfilled God's purposes and glorified God throughout his life, even with his failures that the Bible explains in detail.

The Prophet Jeremiah

Jeremiah 1:1 explains that Jeremiah was a priest, the son of Hilkiah, the high priest who found the Book of the Law (2 Kings 22:8). Verses two and three tell us that his calling as a prophet was in the thirteenth year of King Josiah's reign (627 BC), and that his ministry continued to the eleventh year of King Zedekiah, when the kingdom of Judah was destroyed by the Babylonians (586 BC)—a period of just over forty years. Verse 5 explains how God chose Jeremiah for his prophetic ministry long before he was ever born. Jeremiah 1:5 states, "Before I formed you in the womb I knew you, before you were born I set you apart. I appointed you as a prophet to the nations." (New International Version)

After the counsel of His own Will, God chose and ordained Jeremiah as a prophet to speak His revealed Word to the small kingdom of Judah and to some of the surrounding nations. These divine choices were made by the sovereign Lord, before Jeremiah was conceived in his mother's womb, as a part of God's eternal decree and plan. What was true of Jeremiah is true of you. Before He formed you in the womb, He knew you in His eternal mind. Before you were ever conceived or born, He set you apart as one of His chosen children. You were ordained to be one of those holy and beloved elect—in Christ Jesus. Give praise to His holy name. In the next chapter, we will continue our survey of examples of God's electing power and the evidence for predestination with a look now at some of the witnesses of His Works from the New Testament.

25 ✒

The Witnesses to Election in the New Testament

We continue our survey of examples of God's electing power and the evidence for predestination with a look now at some of the witnesses of His Works from the New Testament.

The Twelve Apostles

The New Testament list the names of the twelve original apostles in Matthew 10:2–4, Mark 3:14–19, and Luke 6:13–16. Here is the list from Matthew 10:2–4: "Now the names of the twelve apostles are these: The first, Simon, who is called Peter and Andrew his brother, and James the son of Zebedee and John his brother, Philip and Bartholomew, Thomas, and Matthew the tax collector, James the son of Alphaeus and Thaddaeus, Simon the Zealot, and Judas Iscariot, the one who betrayed Him."

The Lord Jesus Christ specifically chose these twelve men from among a larger group of His early followers to become His closest disciples and to continue His ministry after He went back into heaven. These men were commissioned and empowered to take (carry and proclaim) the gospel message of salvation to the world. You can read about their charge from Jesus Christ in Matthew 28:16–2 and Mark 16:15. These men, who became the pioneering leaders of the New Testament church, were not perfect. They each had their own idiosyncrasies and had to grow in the grace and knowledge of their Lord and Savior.

Not one of the original twelve apostles was a Jewish Rabbi or Old Testament scholar. They came from ordinary backgrounds and did not possess any extraordinary skills that made them well known or powerful people in society (although Matthew was known as an official tax collector for the Roman government). Jesus chose each one of them individually to become (by His grace and power) the believers and spiritual messengers He wanted them to be. They all fulfilled His will, even Judas who betrayed Him.

Each of these men who were called to be apostles were sovereignly chosen by the Lord Jesus Christ before time began. They were in the heart and mind of God before the creation of the world. What is true of them is also true of you. If you are a born-again Christian, you were chosen and called by Jesus Christ before the universe was created. At the right time, just as He called each apostle at the beginning of His three-year ministry, He called you to follow Him and to declare His gospel message to a lost and dying world. Have you responded to His call? Are you faithfully declaring His message of love and grace to each person He brings into your life?

The Apostle Paul

The famous apostle Paul in the New Testament is one of the best illustrations of election and predestination you can find anywhere. Through God's providence, Paul was born as a Jew named Saul of Taurus, grew up in a very conservative Jewish family, and became one of the leading religious leaders of the early first century. He knew the Old Testament as well as anyone in his day and became involved with the group known as the Pharisees. As a Pharisee, Paul believed Jesus was a false prophet and His followers (Christians) had been led astray into apostasy. Paul also believed it was his job to cleanse the land of Christians by driving them out of Israel, putting them into prison, or executing them as heretics. Acts 8:3 records that he went from house to house and dragged believers off to prison.

One day Paul set off for Damascus in pursuit of more "misguided" Christian troublemakers. However, the Lord Jesus had other plans for Saul of Tarsus that had been ordained from eternity past. Acts 9 gives us the following information about the conversion of Saul of Tarsus to the Apostle Paul. As he neared Damascus on his journey, suddenly a light from heaven flashed around him. Jesus revealed Himself to Paul in such a direct and personal manner that there can be no doubt, in the spirit and mind of Paul, as to the truth of Jesus Christ being the Son of God.

He told Saul. "I am Jesus whom you are persecuting" (Acts 9:5). Paul encountered the living Christ on the road to Damascus and was literally blinded from the brilliant light—but his life was forever changed. After three days, Jesus sent a man named Ananias to restore Paul's sight. When Ananias hesitated because of Paul's destructive reputation, Jesus made it clear that Saul (Paul) was now God's servant. The Lord said to Ananias, "Go! This man is My chosen instrument to carry My name before the Gentiles and their kings and before the people of Israel" (Acts 9:15).

Paul shared his salvation experience with a crowd in Acts 22:1–16 (NIV):

Brethren and fathers, hear my defense which I now offer to you. And when they heard that he was addressing them in the Hebrew dialect, they became even more quiet and he said, "I am a Jew, born in Tarsus of Cilicia, but brought up in this city, educated under Gamaliel, strictly according to the law of our fathers, being zealous for God just as you all are today. I persecuted this Way to the death, binding and putting both men and women into prisons, as also the high priest and all the Council of the elders can testify. From them I also received letters to the brethren and started off for Damascus in order to bring even those who were there to Jerusalem as prisoners to be punished. But it happened that as I was on my way, approaching Damascus about noontime, a very bright light suddenly flashed from heaven all around me and I fell to the ground and heard a voice saying to me, "Saul, Saul, why are you persecuting Me?" And I answered, "Who are You, Lord?" And He said to me, "I am Jesus the Nazarene, whom you are persecuting." And those who were with me saw the light, to be sure, but did not understand the voice of the One who was speaking to me. And I said, "What shall I do, Lord?" And the Lord said to me, "Get up and go on into Damascus and there you will be told of all that has been appointed for you to do." But since I could not see because of the brightness of that light, I was led by the hand by those who were with me and came into Damascus. A certain Ananias, a man who was devout by the standard of the Law and well-spoken of by all the Jews who lived there, came to me and standing near said to me, "Brother Saul, receive your sight!" And at that very time I looked up at him. And he said, "The God of our fathers has appointed you to know His will and to see the Righteous One and to hear an utterance from His mouth. For you will be a witness for Him to all men of what you have seen and heard. Now why do you delay? Get up and be baptized, and wash away your sins, calling on His name."

The Lord Jesus told Paul that certain things had been appointed for him to do. Ananias told Paul that he had been appointed by God to know His will, to personally see the "Righteous One" (the resurrected Lord Jesus), and to personally hear Jesus talk to him. Ananias also told Paul that one reason he had been chosen and appointed as a representative of Christ was so that he would take the gospel to many Gentile nations. The choosing, the appointment, the personal revelation, and the job assignment of Paul was all from God. Saul of Tarsus was minding his own business and trying to do what he thought he was called to do, when Jesus Christ interrupted his life and sent him the opposite direction.

Paul also shared his personal testimony with King Agrippa in Acts 26:1–31 with some additional commentary about his calling and experiences. This version of his testimony is below for you to review:

Agrippa said to Paul, "You are permitted to speak for yourself." Then Paul stretched out his hand and proceeded to make his defense:

"In regard to all the things of which I am accused by the Jews, I consider myself fortunate, King Agrippa, that I am about to make my defense before you today, especially because you are an expert in all customs and questions among the Jews. Therefore, I beg you to listen to me patiently.

"So then, all Jews know my manner of life from my youth up, which from the beginning was spent among my own nation and at Jerusalem, since they have known about me for a long time, if they are willing to testify, that I lived as a Pharisee according to the strictest sect of our religion. And now I am standing trial for the hope of the promise made by God to our fathers, the promise to which our twelve tribes hope to attain, as they earnestly serve God night and day. And for this hope, O King, I am being accused by Jews. Why is it considered incredible among you people if God does raise the dead?

"So then, I thought to myself that I had to do many things hostile to the name of Jesus of Nazareth. And this is just what I did in Jerusalem. Not only did I lock up many of the saints in prisons, having received authority from the chief priests, but also when they were being put to death I cast my vote against them. And as I punished them often in all the synagogues, I tried to force them to blaspheme and being furiously enraged at them, I kept pursuing them even to foreign cities.

"While so engaged, as I was journeying to Damascus with the authority and commission of the chief priests, at midday, O King, I saw on the way a light from heaven, brighter than the sun, shining all around me and those who were journeying with me. And when we had all fallen to the ground, I heard a voice saying to me in the Hebrew dialect, 'Saul, Saul, why are you persecuting Me? It is hard for you to kick against the goads.' And I said, 'Who are You, Lord?' And the Lord said, 'I am Jesus whom you are persecuting. But get up and stand on your feet. For this purpose, I have appeared to you to appoint you a minister and a witness not only to the things which you have seen, but also to the things in which I will appear to you, rescuing you from the Jewish people and from the Gentiles to whom I am sending you, to open their eyes so that they may turn from darkness to light and from the dominion of Satan to God, that they may receive forgiveness of sins and an inheritance among those who have been sanctified by faith in Me.'

"So, King Agrippa, I did not prove disobedient to the heavenly vision, but kept declaring both to those of Damascus first and also at Jerusalem and then throughout all the region of Judea and even to the Gentiles, that they should repent and turn to God, performing deeds appropriate to repentance. For this reason, some Jews seized me in the temple and tried to put me to death. So, having obtained help from God, I stand to this day testifying both to small and great, stating nothing but what the Prophets and Moses said was going to take place, that the Christ was to suffer and that by reason of His resurrection from the dead He would be the first to proclaim light both to the Jewish people and to the Gentiles."

While Paul was saying this in his defense, Festus said in a loud voice, "Paul, you are out of your mind! Your great learning is driving you mad." But Paul said, "I am not out of my mind, most excellent Festus, but I utter words of sober truth. For the king knows about these matters, and I speak to him also with confidence, since I am persuaded that none of these things escape his notice, for this has not been done in a corner. King Agrippa, do you believe the Prophets? I know that you do." Agrippa replied to Paul, "In a short time you will persuade me to become a Christian." And Paul said, "I would wish to God, that whether in a short or long time, not only you, but also all who hear me this day might become such as I am, except for these chains."

The king stood up and the governor and Bernice and those who were sitting with them and when they had gone aside, they began talking to one another, saying, "This man is not doing anything worthy of death or imprisonment." And Agrippa said to Festus, "This man might have been set free if he had not appealed to Caesar."

In Galatians 1, Paul gives another excellent overview of being chosen by God for both personal salvation and ministry. Galatians 1:11–24:

For I would have you know brethren, that the gospel which was preached by me is not according to man. For I neither received it from man, nor was I taught it, but I received it through a revelation of Jesus Christ. For you have heard of my former manner of life in Judaism, how I used to persecute the church of God beyond measure and tried to destroy it, and I was advancing in Judaism beyond many of my contemporaries among my countrymen, being more extremely zealous for my ancestral traditions. But when God, who had set me apart even from my mother's womb and called me through His grace, was pleased to reveal His Son in me so that I might preach Him among the Gentiles, I did not immediately consult with flesh and blood, nor did I go up to Jerusalem to those who were apostles before me, but I went away to Arabia and returned once more to Damascus. Then three years later I went up to Jerusalem to become acquainted with Cephas and stayed with him fifteen days. But I did not see any other of the apostles except James, the Lord's brother. (Now in what I am writing to you, I assure you before God that I am not lying.) Then I went into the regions of Syria and Cilicia. I was still unknown by sight to the churches of Judea which were in Christ, but only they kept hearing, "He who once persecuted us is now preaching the faith which he once tried to destroy." And they were glorifying God because of me.

Paul made it very clear, through his testimony and his writings, that God chose him to be saved and chose him to be an ambassador for Christ in this world, proclaiming the gospel message to all those he would be sent to from dungeons to palaces and everything in between. By the grace of God, he was faithful to his appointment and calling.

Most of us do not encounter Jesus in the dramatic fashion Paul did, but we are chosen and called just the same. The Lord Jesus simply meets us on our road of life, reveals Himself to us, forgives us, and sends us on our way as a child of God and His ambassador in this world, just like the apostle Paul (2 Corinthians 5:20).

In the next chapter, we will consider several lesser known or seldom studied doctrines, which owe their relevance in our biblical theology to the presence of the doctrines of election and predestination.

26 🙟

The Witness of Other Biblical Doctrines to Election

Several lesser known or seldom studied doctrines owe their relevance in our biblical theology to the presence of the doctrines of election and predestination. These decrees of God provide the backbone for some other clear biblical truths that make up the larger superstructure of the Christian life. We will unpack these ideas further in this chapter.

Adoption

In the late 1990s an American couple (friends of mine) decided to adopt a Russian baby or child from Siberia. They had to pay an established price to the Russian government and the adoption agency, then they chose a female baby and began working with the adoption agency to finalize the process. They had to travel to Siberia two or three times during the process, but finally brought their adopted baby girl back to their home in the Pacific Northwest. The baby was now their child, was called by their name, and would grow up in their home as a US citizen. She now had all the privileges and obligations as each of the other family members. During this process, this young baby had no idea what was going on, what was happening to her, or how it would affect (for good) the rest of her life, and possessed no previous claim on her adopted parents' benevolence or assets.

The decision to adopt this baby girl was an unconditional choice made by my friends. No one could tell them they had to adopt any baby or child. No one could tell them they *had to adopt* a certain baby or child, but they were free to make the choice for the child they wanted. That is exactly what they did.

In the same way, before God created the universe or any people who would need salvation, He made a choice to adopt certain lost and hell-bound sinners into His eternal family. He made the choice of those He wanted. Jesus Christ paid the price on the cross for the sin natures and sins of these chosen ones. The Holy Spirit has worked throughout history to bring these chosen sinners into the family of God through the spiritual adoption process (conviction of sin, repentance, faith in Jesus Christ, and the new birth described in John 3). The elect are adopted by God, but they are also born into His family. We, as the elect, are twofold the children of God forever. With this wonderful story of adoption in mind, consider the following verses:

> There was the true Light which, coming into the world, enlightens every man. He was in the world and the world was made through Him and the world did not know Him. He came to His own and those who were His own did not receive Him. But as many as received Him, to them He gave the right to become children of God, even to those who believe in His name who were born, not of blood nor of the will of the flesh nor of the will of man, but of God. (John 1:9–13)

> You did not choose Me, but I chose you and appointed you that you would go and bear fruit and that your fruit would remain, so that whatever you ask of the Father in My name He may give to you. (John 15:16)

> For all who are being led by the Spirit of God, these are sons of God. For you have not received a spirit of slavery leading to fear again, but you have received a spirit of adoption as sons by which we cry out, "Abba! Father!" The Spirit Himself testifies with our spirit that we are children of God and if children, heirs also, heirs of God and fellow heirs with Christ, if indeed we suffer with Him so that we may also be glorified with Him." (Romans 8:14–17) [Remember that "Abba" is a term of endearment and closeness, similar to "daddy." We are not just God's adopted children, but we are children born into His family with all the intimacy that involves.]

> For you are all sons of God through faith in Christ Jesus. (Galatians 3:26)

Blessed be the God and Father of our Lord Jesus Christ, who has blessed us with every spiritual blessing in the heavenly places in Christ, just as He chose us in Him before the foundation of the world, that we would be holy and blameless before Him. In love, He predestined us to adoption as sons through Jesus Christ to Himself, according to the kind intention of His will, to the praise of the glory of His grace, which He freely bestowed on us in the Beloved. In Him we have redemption through His blood, the forgiveness of our trespasses, according to the riches of His grace which He lavished on us. (Ephesians 1:3–8)

Linchpin

A linchpin is something that holds the various elements of a complicated structure together. Here is an illustrative sentence: "The monarchy was the linchpin of the nation's traditions and society." Another example of a linchpin is a pin inserted through the end of an axletree (shaft between wheels: a shaft that runs underneath the body of a vehicle such as a cart or carriage and connects a pair of wheels) to keep the wheel on. Election is the "linchpin" that holds together the complicated structure of God's decree, prophecy, history, evangelism, salvation, and the security of the believer. Everything that happens during history, happens for the sake of the elect and for the glory of God. Election is the "pin" inserted through the end of the axletree of God's decree, prophecy, history, evangelism, salvation, and the security of the believer. Ephesians 1:11–12 says, "In him we were also chosen, having been predestined according to the plan of him who works out everything in conformity with the purpose of his will, in order that we, who were the first to put our hope in Christ, might be for the praise of his glory."

Integrant

Dictionary.com defines an "integrant" as an adjective as something that makes up or is a part of a whole (constituent). As a noun, it means an "integrant part" or a "solid, rigid sheet of building material composed of several layers of the same or of different materials." "Integrant" comes from the Latin word *integrāre* meaning "to integrate." It is also related to the mathematical word "integer."

Each elect born-again Christian is a "spiritual integrant." He or she makes up or is a part of the whole body of Christ chosen before the foundations of the world. Each born-again child of God is a "spiritual integrant" part of the family of God. The Holy Spirit harmoniously "integrated" each individual elect person into the world, at the right time and at the right place, to become a part of the universal church according to the will of God the Father, in a way that would allow them to fulfill their part in history.

Therefore I, the prisoner of the Lord, implore you to walk in a manner worthy of the calling with which you have been called, with all humility and gentleness with patience, showing tolerance for one another in love, being diligent to preserve the unity of the Spirit in the bond of peace. There is one body and one Spirit, just as also you were called in one hope of your calling, one Lord, one faith, one baptism, one God and Father of all who is over all and through all and in all. But to each one of us grace was given according to the measure of Christ's gift. Therefore, it says, 'When He ascended on high, He led captive a host of captives, and He gave gifts to men.' (Now this expression, 'He ascended,' what does it mean except that He also had descended into the lower parts of the earth? He who descended is Himself also He who ascended far above all the heavens, so that He might fill all things.) And He gave some as apostles and some as prophets and some as evangelists and some as pastors and teachers, for the equipping of the saints for the work of service, to the building up of the body of Christ—until we all attain to the unity of the faith and of the knowledge of the Son of God, to a mature man to the measure of the stature which belongs to the fullness of Christ. As a result, we are no longer to be children, tossed here and there by waves and carried about by every wind of doctrine, by the trickery of men, by craftiness in deceitful scheming—but speaking the truth in love, we are to grow up in all aspects into Him who is the head, even Christ, from whom the whole body, being fitted and held together by what every joint supplies, according to the proper working of each individual part, causes the growth of the body for the building up of itself in love. (Ephesians 4:1–16)

Coaptation

Dictionary.reference.com explains "coaptation" as a joining or adjustment of parts to one another, such as the coaptation of a broken bone. Webster's says, "the adaptation or adjustment of things, parts, or people to each other." In our day, the term "assimilation" would be similar, as in immigrants "assimilating" or "coapting" to another culture. The World English Dictionary defines it as the joining or reuniting of two surfaces and that it comes from the Latin *coaptatio*, which means a meticulous and precise joining together.

The Latin *co* means "together" and *aptāre* means "to fit." The sovereignty and omniscience of God works together, according to His perfect will, in bringing all of the elect into the eternal family of God. The Holy Spirit meticulously and precisely weaves together all the elements and circumstances needed to bring each "elect person" to salvation and to place each "elect person" into the human family at just the right time in history (His-Story) to complete His plan and will. Everyone fits together perfectly into God's puzzle of salvation.

History as "His-Story"

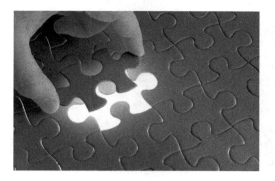

God's plan of salvation for your life comes together like the perfect puzzle. Ephesians 1:7–14 explains how God worked throughout His-Story to orchestrate every circumstance needed to make sure your birth took place at the right time in the right place to the right parents so you would grow up where and when He wanted, to experience anything and everything in your life that would eventually lead you into an eternal relationship with the Lord Jesus Christ. If you went back and added, removed, or changed one piece of your life puzzle, things would not have happened the way they needed to. Not only is all of history *His-Story* but your life is *His-Story*.

> In Him we have redemption through His blood, the forgiveness of our trespasses, according to the riches of His grace which He lavished on us. In all wisdom and insight, He made known to us the mystery of His will, according to His kind intention, which He purposed in Him with a view to an administration suitable to the fullness of the times, that is the summing up of all things in Christ, things in the heavens and things on the earth. In Him, we have also obtained an inheritance, having been predestined according to His purpose who works all things after the counsel of His will, to the end that we who were the first to hope in Christ would be to the praise of His glory. In Him—you also, after listening to the message of truth, the gospel of your salvation—having also believed, you were sealed in Him with the Holy Spirit of promise, who is given as a pledge of our inheritance, with a view to the redemption of God's own possession, to the praise of His glory.

Mishpocha

Mishpocha is originally a Hebrew term which refers to an entire family network comprising of relatives by blood and marriage and sometimes including close friends. According to Dictionary.com, this word can also refer to a clan. Mishpocha entered English in the mid-1800s and comes from the Yiddish and Hebrew words for "family" or "clan."

The elect (chosen ones of God) are a spiritual *Mishpocha*, referring to the entire family network of God's born-again children all around the world and throughout the centuries who are related by the blood of Christ. The following verses, from the Old and New Testament, illustrate the intimacy between God and His chosen people and between God's chosen people with each other, which make up the spiritual *Mishpocha*. The word *Mishpo-cha* is not specifically seen in these verses, but the concept is observed in these verses. Each verse is quoted from the NASB.

For you are a holy people [person] to the Lord your God. The Lord your God has chosen you to be a people [person] for His own possession out of all the peoples who are on the face of the earth. (Deuteronomy 7:6)

Yet they are Your people, even Your inheritance, whom You have brought out by Your great power and Your outstretched arm. (Deuteronomy 9:29)

For the Lord will not abandon His people on account of His great name, because the Lord has been pleased to make you a people [person] for Himself. (1 Samuel 12:22)

Blessed is the nation [person] whose God is the Lord, the people [person] whom He has chosen for His own inheritance. (Psalm 33:12)

How blessed is the one whom You choose and bring near to You, to dwell in Your courts. We will be satisfied with the goodness of Your house, Your holy temple. (Psalm 65:4)

Know that the Lord Himself is God. It is He who has made us and not we ourselves. We are His people and the sheep of His pasture. (Psalm 100:3)

I will give them [him or her] a heart to know Me, for I am the Lord and they [he or she] will be My people [person] and I will be their God, for they will return to Me with their whole heart. (Jeremiah 24:7)

But as many as received Him, to them He gave the right to become children of God, even to those who believe in His name who were born, not of blood nor of the will of the flesh nor of the will of man, but of God. (John 1:12–13)

All [each one] that the Father gives Me will come to Me, and the one who comes to Me I will certainly not cast out. (John 6:37)

This is the will of Him who sent Me, that of all that He has given Me I lose nothing [not one], but raise it up on the last day. (John 6:39)

No one can come to Me unless the Father who sent Me draws him; and I will raise him up on the last day. (John 6:44)

For this reason I have said to you, that no one can come to Me unless it has been granted him from the Father. (John 6:65)

I am the good shepherd and I know My own and My own know Me, even as the Father knows Me and I know the Father and I lay down My life for the sheep. I have other sheep, which are not of this fold. I must bring them also, and they will hear My voice, and they will become one flock with one shepherd. (John 10:14–16)

But you do not believe, because you are not of My sheep. My sheep hear My voice and I know them and they follow Me and I give eternal life to them and they will never perish and no one will snatch them out of My hand. My Father, who has given them to Me, is greater than all and no one is able to snatch them out of the Father's hand. I and the Father are one. (John 10:26–30)

No longer do I call you slaves, for the slave does not know what his master is doing, but I have called you friends, for all things that I have heard from My Father I have made known to you. You did not choose Me, but I chose you and appointed you that you would go and bear fruit and that your fruit would remain, so that whatever you ask of the Father in My name He may give to you. This I command you, that you love one another. If the world hates you, you know that it has hated Me before it hated you. If you were of the world, the world would love its own, but because you are not of the world. I chose you out of the world and because of this the world hates you. (John 15:15–19)

I have manifested Your name to the men [those men, women, and children] whom You gave Me out of the world. They were Yours and You gave them to Me and they have kept Your word. Now they have come to know that everything You have given Me is from You. For the words which You gave Me I have given to them and they received them and truly understood that I came forth from You, and they believed that You sent Me. I ask on their behalf. I do not ask on behalf of the world, but of those whom You have given Me. For they are Yours and all things that are Mine are Yours and Yours are Mine and I have been glorified in them. (John 17:6–10)

For the promise is for you and your children and for all who are far off, as many as the Lord our God will call to Himself. (Acts 2:39)

By now I hope that you as a reader of Scripture, as a believer in Jesus Christ, and as one for whom Christ has provided multiple spiritual blessings, are comforted by this great web of belief, this grand superstructure of doctrine laid upon doctrine—all resting on the unquestionable truth of God's grace in His election and predestination of His saints. May it bring you even more comfort as we now turn to the witness of Church history and the great cloud of witnesses to God's glory who've gone before us.

27

Early Church Fathers Who Affirmed Election and Predestination

Many prominent Christians of the Early Church through the middle of the eighteenth century bear witness from many prominent Christian thinkers of the validity and critical nature of the decrees of election and predestination as we have seen from our earlier studies in the Scriptures and the lives of Jesus and His apostles.

Here we start our journey with a look at men of God, from the first few centuries, who believed in the traditional understanding of election and predestination and bear witness to these truths in ways that support the previous contentions of this book. These truths are foundational to the Christian faith and provide hope and comfort to every believer in Christ Jesus. The men are listed in chronological order based on the year of their birth.

The Apostle Paul (5–67 AD)

The apostle Paul, originally Saul of Tarsus, was from the city of Tarsus in the Roman province of Cilicia. He wrote in Galatians 1:13-14 that he was a "Hebrew born of Hebrews," a Pharisee, and one who advanced in Judaism beyond many of his peers. He zealously persecuted the early followers of Jesus and violently tried to destroy the newly forming Christian church until his conversion to Christ on the road from Jerusalem to Damascus. Soon after that he became known as the apostle Paul. After his conversion to Christ, he began to preach that Jesus of Nazareth was the Messiah and the Son of God. God called him to take the gospel to the Gentiles. Paul wrote thirteen of the twenty-seven New Testament books. Paul authored the books of Romans, I and II Corinthians, Galatians, Ephesians, Philippians, Colossians, I and II Thessalonians, I and II Timothy, Titus and Philemon. Although open to discussion, many have good reason to believe he also wrote Hebrews as it contains many Pauline distinctives. Tradition says Paul was beheaded in Rome during the reign of Nero in the mid-60s AD at "Tre Fontane Abbey."

One of Paul's most well-known statements on election and predestination is found in Ephesians 1:1–14 (NASB):

Paul, an apostle of Christ Jesus by the will of God, To the saints who are at Ephesus and who are faithful in Christ Jesus: Grace to you and peace from God our Father and the Lord Jesus Christ. Blessed be the God and Father of our Lord Jesus Christ, who has blessed us with every spiritual blessing in the heavenly places in Christ, just as He chose us in Him before the foundation of the world, that we would be holy and blameless before Him. In love, He predestined us to adoption as sons through Jesus Christ to Himself, according to the kind intention of His will, to the praise of the glory of His grace, which He freely bestowed on us in the Beloved. In Him we have redemption through His blood, the forgiveness of our trespasses, according to the riches of His grace which He lavished on us. In all wisdom and insight, He made known to us the mystery of His will, according to His kind intention which He purposed in Him with a view to an administration suitable to the fullness of the times, that is, the summing up of all things in Christ, things in the heavens and things on the earth. In Him also we have obtained an inheritance, having been predestined according to His purpose who works all things after the counsel of His will, to the end that we who were the first to hope in Christ would be to the praise of His glory. In Him, you also, after listening to the message of truth, the gospel of your salvation—having also believed, you were sealed in Him with the Holy Spirit of promise, who is given as a pledge of our inheritance, with a view to the redemption of God's own possession, to the praise of His glory.

Ignatius (35–110 AD)

Ignatius was one of the five Apostolic Fathers, the earliest authoritative group of the Church Fathers who followed the original apostles and disciples in leading the early church. He was the third Bishop of Antioch and was a direct student of the apostle John. He became a Christian at a young age. On his way to Rome, he wrote six letters to the churches in the region and one to a fellow bishop, which have been preserved as an example of very early Christian theology. According to Christian legend, he was sentenced to die at the Colosseum. One of his statements on predestination was, "To the predestined ones before all ages, that is, before the world began, united and elect in a true passion, by the eternal will of the Father."[33]

Irenaeus (130–202 AD)

Irenaeus was a disciple of Polycarp, who was a disciple of the apostle John. He was first a presbyter (an elder) under Pothinus, Bishop of Lyons, in France and when Pothinus died (who suffered martyrdom about AD 178) he succeeded him as bishop of that place. He also became a martyr. He wrote five books against the heresies of the Valentinians and Gnostics, which remain to this day, and from which we gather his sense concerning the decrees of God. He spoke of a certain number of persons chosen to eternal life, and of God's giving up others to, and leaving them in, their unbelief. He refers to the stability and immovableness of the decree of election when he calls it *turris electionis* (the tower of election).

In his book *Against the Heresies* Irenaeus wrote, "But He Himself in Himself, after a fashion which we can neither describe nor conceive, predestinating all things, formed them as He pleased, bestowing harmony on all things, and assigning them their own place, and the beginning of their creation."[34]

Clement of Alexandria (150–215 AD)

As presbyter of the church in Alexandria, Clement has been recognized as one of Christianity's greatest scholars. He was versed in the Old and New Testaments, apocryphal and Gnostic writings, Greek literature, and philosophy. Clement succeeded Pantaenus as head of the catechetical school at Alexandria, where he taught, among others, Origen and Alexander of Jerusalem. One of the oldest known Christian hymns was written by him called "Shepherd of Tender Youth."

Regarding predestination, Clement said the following:

Therefore, in substance and idea, in origin, in pre-eminence, we say that the ancient and Catholic (Universal) Church is alone, collecting as it does into the unity of the one faith—which results from the peculiar Testaments, or rather the one Testament in different times

---

[33] Michael Horton, *Put Amazing Back into Grace—Embracing the Heart of the Gospel* (Baker Books, 2011), 238.

[34] St. Irenaeus of Lyons, *Against the Heresies* (book 2), (Paulist Press, 2012).

by the will of the one God, through one Lord—those already ordained, whom God predestinated, knowing before the foundation of the world that they would be righteous.[35]

Quintus Florens Tertullian (160–225 AD)

As a prolific Christian author from Carthage in the Roman province of Africa, Tertullian was the first Christian author to produce an important study of Latin Christian literature. He was also an early Christian apologist and a polemicist against heresy. Tertullian has been called "the father of Latin Christianity" and "the founder of Western theology." He is perhaps most famous for being the oldest extant Latin writer to use the term "Trinity" (Latin, *trinitas*) and for giving the oldest extant formal exposition of a Trinitarian theology. He addresses the Christian after this manner,

> "But thine order and thy magistracy and the name of thy court is the church of Christ. Thou art his, *conscriptus* in libris vitae, written in the books of life." In referring to heretics he said, "Theirs were wits of spiritual wickedness, with whom we and the brethren wrestle, the necessary articles of faith merit our contemplation (*ut electi manifestentur, ut reprobi detegantur*) that the elect may be manifested, that the reprobate may be detected."[36]

Cyprian (200–258 AD)

As the Bishop of Carthage in North Africa and important early Christian writer, many of Cyprian's Latin works are extant. He received a classical education and after converting to Christianity, he became a bishop in 249, and eventually died a martyr in Carthage. Here is one short statement by Cyprian: "This is therefore the predestination, which we faithfully and humbly preach."[37]

Augustine of Hippo (354–430 AD)

Augustine of Hippo (better known as St. Augustine) was born in North Africa to a pagan father and a Christian mother. A product of a mixed marriage, he loved his mother

---

[35] *Encyclopedia of Christian Theology*, vol. 3: P-Z, ed. Jean-Yves Lacoste (Taylor & Francis, 2005). The *Encyclopedia of Christian Theology*, translated from the French *Dictionnaire Critique de Théologie 2nd Edition*, features over 530 entries, contributed by 250 scholars from fifteen different countries.

[36] McClintock, John. Strong, James. Entry for "Tertullian(us), Quintus Septimius Florens." Cyclopedia of Biblical, Theological and Ecclesiastical Literature (New York: Harper & Brothers), 1870. https://www.studylight.org/encyclopedias/tce/t/tertullianus-quintus-septimius-florens.html.

[37] *Catalogue of the Libri Canonici of the Old and New Testaments*. The writings of Cyprian, both treatises and letters, are also indicated with the number of lines contained in each. Siegmar Döpp and Wilhelm Geerlings, *Dictionary of Early Christian Literature*, pp. 148–153. Lewis Ayres, Frances Young, and Andrew Louth, *Cambridge History of Early Christian Literature*, pp. 152–160.

deeply, which may partially explain his later conversion to Christianity. He was educated at Carthage in North Africa, but quickly gave into lust and temptation. At the age of eighteen he took a mistress and together they had one son. It was at this time that Augustine was attracted to the heretical teachings of a man called Mani (216–276), who believed that one God could not be responsible for both good and evil, so there had to be two gods—but in 387, under the influence of men like St. Jerome and his mother, he became a Christian.

In 399, Augustine was elected Bishop of Hippo, one of the intellectual centers of the time where numerous theological issues were debated. Augustine spent more than thirty years combating heresy, writing commentaries, and interpretations of Christian theology. He wrote the first autobiography in western history, *The Confessions.* His most important work, however, is *The City of God*, a massive book written between 413 and 426. *The City of God* was written to show that it was God's plan that Rome would fall, and that Christianity was the salvation of mankind. According to St. Augustine, history has direction and meaning, which is the unfolding of God's grand plan. People could not overcome their sins on their own. Moral and spiritual regeneration came only from God's grace and it was God who determined who would be saved.[38]

Augustine described election based on Romans 5:5 in the quote below:

> He chooses us, not because we believe, but that we may believe—lest we should say that we first chose him. The human will is so divinely helped in the pursuit of righteousness, that he [the believer] receives the Holy Spirit, by whom there is formed in his mind a delight in and a love of that supreme and unchangeable good, which is God. By this gift to him of the down payment, as it were, of the free gift, he [the believer] conceives a burning desire to cleave to his Maker. A man's free will, indeed, does not help at all except to sin, if he does not know the way of truth. And even after he begins to know his duty and proper aim, unless he also takes delight in and feels a love for it, he neither does his duty, nor sets about it, nor lives rightly. Now, in order that such a course may engage our affections, God's love is shed abroad in our hearts, not through the free will which arises from ourselves, but through the Holy Spirit, who is given to us [Rom 5: 5].[39]

Summing Up the Early Church's Response to the Decrees of Election and Predestination

From the first century, Christian leaders like the apostle Paul and Ignatius all the way into the fifth century with the brilliant works of St. Augustine, the early church was replete

---

[38] Mary T. Clark, RS, *Augustine of Hippo: Selected Writings* (Paulist Press, 1988).

[39] Peter Brown, Augustine of Hippo (Berkeley: University of California Press, 1967) and The Westminster Dictionary of Church History, ed. Jerald C. Brauer (Philadelphia: Westminster Press, 1971, 72–74).

with articulate commentary affirming the doctrines of election and predestination as biblical thinking. There was no hesitation from any of these major leaders of the early church in proclaiming the truths of these two foundational doctrines.

Now let us move forward into the Middle Ages, often thought of as a dark period, but one where theology was vigorously taught and the doctrines we're discussing were not ignored.

28 ✣

Church Fathers of the Middle Ages Who Affirmed the Decrees

The church in the early Middle Ages (from about 500 AD to 1,500 AD—generally speaking) was characterized by the maturation of the Roman Catholic Church. The Roman Catholic Church became organized into an elaborate hierarchy with the Pope as the supreme head in western Europe. The church was the only universal institution in Europe. The Pope in Rome ended up with supreme power in western Europe. The Patriarch of Constantinople (in modern day Istanbul, Turkey) was the church leader in eastern Europe. In western Europe, the Catholic Church controlled vast amounts of wealth and was the largest landowner in Europe. The people paid the "tithe" (a tenth of their income) to the church year by year. Church leaders controlled education and learning. Church leaders serving at the top of the hierarchy were also advisors to kings and emperors. The Pope claimed and used the power to excommunicate secular rulers, if there were unresolvable conflicts with these rulers. Through this maneuver, the Pope thought he could free the citizens under these rulers from their oaths of obedience to their rulers and keep their loyalties to the church. Obviously, this could create much tension and stress, especially when the church's network of parishes reached into every town and village in western Europe. The kings and rulers of these centuries would ignore the church's will at their own risk.

Therefore, the medieval church played a far greater role in Medieval Europe than the church does today. In Medieval Europe, the church dominated everybody's life. Just about everyone believed that God and heaven and hell existed, and they were taught that the only way they could get to heaven was through the rituals/sacraments of the Roman Catholic Church. The established church had what seemed like total control over the people. The cathedrals were huge and sometimes larger than the royal palaces. Their grand and glorious size would make them visible to the common people from miles around, which would reaffirm in their minds the absolute power of the Roman Catholic Church across Europe. The established church viewed itself as Christ's kingdom on earth, and as such, believed it shared in Christ's power.

For medieval Christians, the Bible was what we call the Vulgate. The Vulgate was a Latin translation of the Old Testament, which Christians called the Jewish Scriptures along with the New Testament. Later on, the Protestant Reformers were able to persuade many that the Bible was actually neglected during the Middle Ages, even though many copies of the Bible were made and the Bible was a very familiar book. Martin Luther said that the Bible "had come to lie forgotten in the dust under the bench" (see Luther [1539] 1915: vol. 1, 7; cf. 2 Kings 22:8). The common person was totally dependent on the professional clergy to tell them what the Bible said and what it meant. The majority of the population could not read and a small percentage could read, but not write. The only way to be considered "literate" at the time was to be able to read Latin. Literacy in other languages didn't count. The monasteries were the home of most of what was considered the educated populace, but even there, where certain scribes were engaged in copyist work, they were trained in a very mechanistic form of writing. Their use of continuous script, without word breaks, reveals a very mechanical, letter by letter, approach to copying. Petrucci (Petrucci 1995)[40] believes that such works were copies for the sake of copying, rather than works for proper reading, and that some of the scribes selected for this work were actually the less intellectually able, who were trained in it as a mechanical skill. The term "writing" was used by medieval authors, whether they were actually carrying out the process of putting the words to parchment themselves, or simply dictating. The scribes of this type were more like modern typists.

Therefore, even though the Bible had its place in European society during these centuries, this period of European history (following the centuries referred to as the time of the Early Church Fathers) has been called the Dark Age or Dark Ages because very few intellectual writings were produced during this period and because of the practical illiteracy of the populace. *A Companion to Britain in the Later Middle Ages* makes the argument that

---

[40] http://medievalwriting.50megs.com/literacy/writing.htm.

literacy in Europe began to increase starting in 1100 AD, after which all the kings were literate in Latin and French, although there was again a difference between reading and writing. By 1500, he estimates the literacy among males still did not exceed 10–25 percent.

In the publication *World History Medieval to Early Modern Times* by Berstein, Stanley and Richard Sheck, (Austin, Texas: Holt Publishing, 2006), the Dark Ages are summed up as follows:

> When Rome fell, western European civilization hit a wall and stumbled backward into a period now known as the Dark Ages. This affected the lives of many Europeans in ways like this:
>
> * limited or no trade
> * many people were illiterate
> * little if any advances in technology
> * people fled cities and went back to farm life
> * roads were destroyed
> * very little communication
> * reliance on local leaders

These were just some of the effects on Europe after Rome fell. Through all this darkness there were still bits of spiritual light. The churches remained, and the feudal system was started. Some people compare the loss of classical culture during the Dark Ages by comparing the life of a medieval peasant to that of a Roman pleb. "Plebs" was the general body of Roman citizens, distinct from the privileged class of the patricians. A member of the plebs was known as a plebeian (Latin: plebeius). With this background information in mind, let us look at some of the "spiritual stars" of the Middle Ages and their perspectives on election and predestination.

Gottschalk (803–869 AD)

Gottschalk of Orbais was born in Saxony (Germany) and died near Reims, France. He was a Benedictine monk, poet, and theologian whose teachings on predestination shook the Roman Catholic Church in the ninth century. He was a student of Augustine's writings. Holding that Christ's salvation was limited and that His power of redemption extended only to the elect, Gottschalk taught that the elect went to eternal glory and the reprobate went to damnation. A work by Gottschalk called *De praedestinatione* ("Of Predestination") was discovered in Bern, Switzerland in 1930. For his teachings on predestination, he was condemned as a heretic at the Catholic Council of Quierzy in 853. He never recanted, and died while imprisoned in a monastery.

Thomas Aquinas (1225–1274 AD)

Thomas Aquinas was an Italian Dominican priest and influential philosopher and theologian. Thomas came from one of the noblest families of the kingdom of Naples. His parents held the titles Count of Aquino and Countess of Teano. He is best known for the works *Summa Theologiae* and *Summa Contra Gentiles*. As one of the thirty-five doctors of the Catholic Church, he is considered one of the church's greatest theologians and philosophers. Here is one quote from Thomas's *Summa Theologiae*:

> The reason for the predestination of some and reprobation of others (*praedestinationis aliquorum, et reprobationis aliorum*) must be sought for in the divine goodness. . . . God wills to manifest His goodness in those whom He predestines, by means of the mercy with which He spares them. And in respect of others whom He reprobates, by means of the justice with which He punishes them. This is the reason why God chooses some (*quosdam eligit*) and reprobates others (*quosdam reprobat*). Yet why He chooses some for glory and reprobates others has no reason except the divine will (*non habet rationem nisi divinam volun*tatem). . . . Clearly predestination is like the plan, existing in God's mind, for the ordering of some persons to salvation. The carrying out of this is passively as it were in the persons predestined, though actively in God. When considered executively in this way, predestination is spoken of as a *calling* and a *glorifying*, thus St. Paul says, "Whom He predestinated, them also He called and glorified."[41]

John Wycliffe, The Morningstar of the Reformation (1320–1384)

John Wycliffe was an English philosopher, theologian, lay preacher, translator, reformer, and university teacher at Oxford in England. Wycliffe was an early dissident in the Roman Catholic Church during the fourteenth century. His followers were known as Lollards and preached biblical reforms within the church. The Lollard movement was a precursor to the Protestant Reformation. For this reason, Wycliffe is sometimes called The Morning Star of the Reformation. Wycliffe advocated the translation of the Bible into the common language of the people. He completed his own translation (now known as Wycliffe's Bible) directly from the Latin Vulgate into vernacular English between 1382 and 1384.

Wycliffe's writings described the Church of Christ as consisting only of those who have been predestined to enjoy heaven. Non-elect men and women may indeed be part of the visible church, but that does not automatically qualify them as members of the true

---

[41] St. Thomas Aquinas, *Summa Theologiae*, vol. 1 (1a.23.5) (EYRE & SPOTTISWOODE, 1964).

or invisible church. His biblical starting point for promoting predestination was Romans 8:28–30. In commenting on this passage of Scripture he wrote,

> This predestination is the principle gift of God, most freely given, since no one can merit his own predestination. Since it cannot be present without being present at the first moment of existence of the predestinate, it follows what is commonly said of grace that this is the principle grace. It can never be lost, since it is the basis of glory and bliss, which equally cannot be lost. Therefore, such predestination is a divine decree rather than the personal choice of any man.[42]

John Wycliffe died from a stroke on the last day of 1384. The religious authorities never excommunicated him, because they feared public opinion. The people loved John and his fame was international. He was buried in consecrated soil. About thirty years later, the Council of Constance revenged itself on his criticism by condemning his teachings and ordering his bones to be dug up and burned.

John Huss (1369–1415 AD)

John Huss was born as a peasant in Husinec, Bohemia (from which his name is derived). He studied theology at the University of Prague. He was ordained a priest in 1400, and in 1402 was appointed preacher of the Bethlehem Chapel, a foundation dedicated to preaching in the Czech language. He was influenced by the writings of John Wycliffe and translated Wycliffe's *Triologus* into Czech. In his sermons, Huss attacked the abuses of the clergy, thus earning the hostility of many priests and leaders of the Catholic Church.

He denied the infallibility of the pope and asserted the ultimate authority of Scripture over the church. Eventually, the pope excommunicated Huss. His writings were condemned, and he was sentenced to be burned at the stake, where he died heroically. Through his death, he became a national hero. He was declared a martyr by the University of Prague and the modern Czech Protestant church claims to continue his tradition. He is considered one of the forerunners of the Protestant Reformation. He was condemned by the Council of Constance (1414–1418) for many doctrinal points, but the following relate to his beliefs about election and predestination:

- One and only is the holy universal Church, *which is the aggregate of the predestined.*

---

[42] George M. Ella, http://gonewfocus.co.uk/articles/app/category/biography/article/john-wycliffe-star-of-the-reformation.pdf, accessed October 16, 2006.

- The foreknown are not parts of the Church, since no part of it finally will fall away from it, because *the charity of predestination which binds it will not fall away*.
- The foreknown, although at one time he is in grace according to the present justice, yet is never a part of the holy Church and *the predestined always remains a member of the Church*, although at times he may fall away from additional grace, but not from the grace of predestination.
- Assuming the *Church as the convocation of the predestinated*, whether they were in grace or not according to the present justice, in that way the Church is an article of faith.
- *The grace of predestination is a chain* by which the body of the Church and any member of it are joined insolubly to Christ the Head.

Mark Galli writes of Huss in the *Christian History Magazine*,

Early in his monastic career, Martin Luther, rummaging through the stacks of a library, happened upon a volume of sermons by John Huss, the Bohemian who had been condemned as a heretic. "I was overwhelmed with astonishment," Luther later wrote. "I could not understand for what cause they had burnt so great a man, who explained the Scriptures with so much gravity and skill."[43]

Only two centuries after Huss was burned, in 1517, Luther was striking a similar blow to the corruption of doctrine and practice in the Catholic Church when he posted his *Ninety-Five Theses* to the door of the Wittenburg Church. It is to that high Reformation era we now turn.

---

[43] Mark Galli, "Jan Hus: Incendiary Preacher of Prague," *Christian History*, issue 68, 2000.

29 ᗢ

Church Fathers of the Protestant Reformation Who Affirmed the Decrees

This chapter is focused on spiritual leaders during the Protestant Reformation who affirmed the decrees of election and predestination.

Wolfgang Capito (1478–1541)

Wolfgang Capito was a German religious reformer born of humble parentage at Haguenau in Alsace. He was educated for the medical profession, but also studied law and applied himself so earnestly to theology that he received a doctorate. He joined the Benedictines and taught for some time at Freiburg. He acted for three years as pastor in Bruchsal and was then called to the cathedral church of Basel (1515). It was here he made the acquaintance of Zwingli and began to correspond with Luther.

In 1519 he moved to Mainz at the request of Albrecht, archbishop of that city, who soon made him his chancellor. In 1523, he settled at Strasbourg, where he remained till his death in November 1541. He had found it increasingly difficult to reconcile the new religion with the old and from 1524 was one of the leaders of the Reformed faith in Strasbourg. Capito held that there were two classes of men, elect and rejected, or vessels of mercy whom God had determined from eternity to eternity for blessedness and vessels of wrath whom He had prepared for destruction. The only basis for this contrast was the free, eternal, and unchangeable decree of God. The former had implanted within them from birth a seed of piety, a religious and moral inclination to the good, whereas the others carried within them the seed of vice. He denied all freedom of the will: "Freedom of the will is the worst plague of true religion."[44]

Martin Luther (1483–1546)

Martin Luther was a former German monk and Catholic priest, who became a famous professor of theology and leading figure in the sixteenth-century Protestant Reformation. He strongly disputed the claim that freedom from God's punishment for sin could be purchased with money (buying indulgences). He confronted indulgence salesman Johann Tetzel with his *Ninety-Five Theses* on All Hallow's Eve, October 31, 1517. He refused to retract all of his writings at the demand of Pope Leo X in 1520 and the Holy Roman Emperor Charles V at the Diet of Worms in 1521. This resulted in his excommunication by the pope and condemnation as an outlaw by the Emperor. Luther wrote,

> "The human doctrine of free will and of our spiritual powers is futile. The matter (salvation) does not depend on our will, but on God's will and election. Since salvation is totally of God's doing, the doctrine of election comforts those who believe. We can say, I belong to God! I have been chosen by God. I am one of his sheep!" Amen and Amen![45]

Martin Luther, the great German reformer, called the doctrine of predestination the "core ecclesia." Core being the Latin for "heart," and ecclesia being the Latin for "the church." In effect what Luther was saying was that the doctrine of predestination is the heart of the church. Luther wrote:

> In chapters nine, ten and eleven of Romans the apostle teaches about the eternal predestination of God. He tells how it originally comes about that a person will believe or not, will become rid of his sins or not. He does so in order that our becoming pious be taken entirely out of our own hands and placed into the hands of God. And indeed, it is supremely necessary that this be done, for . . . if the matter depended on us, surely not a single person would be saved. Since, however. . . His predestination cannot fail and no one can defeat His purpose, our hope against sin remains.[46] That is what reason can neither grasp nor en-

[44] J. Heberle, "Capitos Verhältnis zum Anabaptismus," in Zeitschrift für historische Theologie (1857), 296–306 ff.

[45] Drew Blankman, *Martin Luther: Righteous Faith* (Downers Grove, Illinois: InterVarsity Press, 2002), 60.

[46] Martin Luther, "Commentary on Romans," chapter 8. This translation was made by Bro. Andrew

dure and what has offended all these men of outstanding talent who have been so received for so many centuries. Here they demand that God should act according to human justice, and do what seems right to them or else cease to be God.[47]

Ulrich Zwingli (1484–1531)

Ulrich Zwingli was a leader of the Protestant Reformation in German-speaking Switzerland. Zwingli arrived at his spiritual conclusions by studying the Scriptures as a Christian humanist scholar. Because of his studies, Zwingli took the Swiss Reformation in a different direction than Luther in Germany by insisting that Scripture provided a workable model for public life, an emphasis that would be carried forward by John Calvin in Geneva. Zwingli was killed in battle at Kappel, while trying to defend Zurich against an attack by an alliance of Swiss Catholic forces. One of his comments on election was, "God's free election does not follow faith, but faith follows election. For those who have been elected from eternity have undoubtedly been elected before faith. Therefore, those who because of their age have not faith, should not be rashly condemned by us. For although they do not as yet have it, yet God's election is hidden from us. If before Him they are elect, we judge rashly about things unknown to us."[48]

Zwingli described the Church as the elect:

Of the Church, therefore we thus think that the word "Church" in the Scriptures is to be taken in various meanings. It is used for the elect, who have been predestined by God's will to eternal life. Of this church, Paul speaks when he says that it has neither wrinkle or spot (Ephesians 5:27). This is known to God alone, for according to the word of Solomon (Proverbs 15:11), He alone knows the hearts of the children of men. Nevertheless, those who are members of this church, since they have faith, know that they themselves are elect and are members of this first church, but are ignorant about members other than themselves. For thus it is written in Acts 13:48: "And as many as were ordained to eternal life believed." Therefore, those that believe are ordained to eternal life. But no one, save he who believes, knows who truly believe. He is already certain that he is elect of God. For, according to the apostle's word (2 Corinthians 1:22), he has the seal of the Spirit, by

Thornton OSB, for the Saint Anselm College Humanities Program in 1983 by Saint Anselm Abbey. This translation may be used freely with proper attribution.

[47] Martin Luther's *The Bondage of the Will: A New Translation of De Servo Arbitrio (1525), Martin Luther's Reply to Erasmus of Rotterdam. Trans. J. I. Packer and O. R. Johnston, The Sovereignty of God*, sections 9–27. *(Old Tappan, New Jersey: Fleming H. Revell Co.), 1957.*

[48] Ulrich Zwingli, *On Providence and Other Essays*, edited by William John Hinke for Samuel Macauley Jackson (Durham, NC: American Society of Church History, reprinted 1983, with permission of the ASCH).

which, pledged and sealed, he knows that he has become truly free, a son of the family, and not a slave. For the Spirit cannot deceive. If He tells us that God is our Father and we confidently and fearlessly call Him Father, untroubled because we shall enter upon the eternal inheritance, then it is certain that God's Spirit has been shed abroad in our hearts. It is therefore settled that he is elect who has this security and certainty, for they who believe are ordained to eternal life. Yet many are elect who as yet have no faith. For the mother of Jesus [Mary], John, and Paul, did not believe while infants and yet they were elect, even before the foundation of the world. But this they knew not, either through faith or revelation. Were not Matthew, Zacchaeus, the thief on the cross, and Mary Magdalene elect before the foundation of the world? Nevertheless, they were ignorant of this until they were illumined by the Spirit and drawn to Christ by the Father. From these facts, it follows that this first church is known to God alone and they only who have firm and unwavering faith know that they are members of this church. ("An Account of the Faith of Huldereich Zwingli Submitted to the Roman Emperor Charles," July 3, 1530).[49]

Thomas Cranmer (1489–1556)

As the Archbishop of Canterbury, Thomas Cranmer became increasingly Calvinistic throughout the 1540s. He was one of the leaders of the English Reformation and Archbishop of Canterbury during the reigns of Henry VIII, Edward VI, and for a short time, Mary I. A few of his words on election and predestination follow:

Predestination to life, is the everlasting purpose of God, whereby (before the foundations of the world were laid) He hath constantly decreed by His counsel secret to us, to deliver from curse and damnation, those whom He hath chosen in Christ out of mankind. As the godly consideration of predestination and our election in Christ, is full of sweet, pleasant and unspeakable comfort to godly persons, so for curious and carnal persons to have continually before their eyes the sentence of God's predestination, is a most dangerous downfall.[50]

Guillaume Farel (1489–1565)

Guillaume Farel was a French reformer born of a noble family near Gap in Dauphine in 1489. As an ardent friend and coworker of Calvin, he was an energetic pioneer in the Reformation in France and was involved in introducing it in Geneva, Switzerland. He persuaded Calvin to settle there. He was a systematic thinker who well-articulated doctrines

---

[49] *The Latin Works and Correspondence of Huldreich Zwingli*, vol. 2, trans. S. M. Macauley (Philadelphia: Heidelberg Press, 1922), 42–56.
[50] Article 17 of "The 39 Articles of the Church of England," Thomas Cramner, English reformer.

of the trinity, baptism, predestination, and communion. Farel worked to train missionary preachers who spread the Protestant cause to other countries and especially to France. Along with the other Reformers, he understood salvation to be by grace alone and affirmed a doctrine of particular election (the teaching that some people are chosen by God for salvation).[51]

Martin Bucer (1491–1551)

As a protestant reformer based in Strasbourg, France, Martin Bucer influenced Lutheran, Calvinist, and Anglican doctrines and practices. Bucer was originally a member of the Dominican Order, but after meeting and being influenced by Martin Luther in 1518, he arranged for his monastic vows to be annulled. He then began to work for the Reformation. Bucer wrote the following about election and predestination:

> The Greek word *proorismos* means literally "predetermination," though the common rendering is 'predestination'. St. Paul, in fact, uses the verb *proorizein* to signify two things: first, the election of the saints and their separation from the remaining polluted mass of lost mankind (what Scripture denotes by the word *hibdîl*, which is used by the Lord when he speaks of the election of his own people out of the rest of the nations) and secondly, the election of the saints before they are even born. Now the apostle's objective in this passage (in Romans 8) is to teach us that God destined us for salvation before we were born, let alone before we had performed any good works. From this fact, God proceeds to demonstrate that His purpose for our salvation is fixed and unshakeable and cannot be frustrated by any of His creatures, because God adopted it on His own initiative and out of His own kindness, which cannot change and not out of any regard for our merit, which always fluctuates so wretchedly. Hence foreknowledge, predetermination and election are at this point one and the same thing, so to speak. For God chose us in Christ before the foundations of the world were laid, having predetermined (*proorisas*) us to adoption as sons.[52]

William Tyndale (1494–1536)

William Tyndale was the sixteenth-century religious reformer and scholar who translated the Bible into the early modern English of his day. Forbidden to work in England, Tyndale translated and printed his English New Testament and half of the Old Testament between 1525 and 1535 in Germany and the Low Countries. He worked from the Greek and Hebrew original texts when knowledge of those languages in England was rare. His

---

[51] Stephane Simonnin, "Guillaume Farel (1489-1565)," *Western Theological Seminary* (2013).
[52] Martin Bucer, *Concerning the True Care of Souls* (Banner of Truth, reprint edition 2009).

pocket-sized Bible translations were smuggled into England and then ruthlessly sought out by the Church, confiscated, and destroyed. Condemned as a heretic, Tyndale was strangled and then burned at the stake outside Brussels in 1536. Much of Tyndale's work eventually found its way to the King James Version (or Authorized Version) of the Bible published in 1611, which through the work of fifty-four independent scholars, is based primarily on Tyndale's translation. One of his comments on election was,

> Before the foundation of the world God made a plan for man's salvation. The covenant was made. God the Father would elect those to adopt as His children. God the Son would shed His blood to make this possible. God the Holy Spirit would apply the covenant to those God chose to be His children, who then cease to be children of the devil. Election means the chosen have God for their Father and are His children and part of God's family.[53]

Wolfgang Musculus 1497–1563)

Wolfgang Musculus was born in the German-speaking village of Duss (Moselle) and grew up as a lover of music and the knowledge of languages. His great musical skills made him known all over Europe and the oral tradition of his songs are still heard today in the temples of the Reformation. He became a highly reputed exegete and theologian who taught theology in Bern and produced commentaries on books of the Bible and his Loci Communes in 1560. He emphasized a general covenant between God and creation and a special covenant between God and the elect, with Christ as the Mediator of the Special Covenant. He was so concerned with the historical effecting of God's salvation that he placed the atonement prior to Christology in his Loci.[54]

Nicholas Ridley (1500–1555)

As the Edwardian Bishop of London, Nicholas Ridley was executed in October 1555, during Mary Tudor's reign. As an active publicist, he composed in prison a treatise that promoted the Reformed view of Holy Communion. Ridley's work was published in Emden (1555) and in Strasbourg (1556). In 1556, A *Brief Declaration* found its way to Geneva where a community of English exiles had it translated into Latin (Conrad Badius then issued a version in French). The translation became a Calvinist manifesto with a transnational readership. Ridley was burned at the stake, as one of the Oxford Martyrs, during the Marian Persecutions.[55]

---

[53] Steven Lawson, *The Daring Mission of William Tyndale* (Sanford, FL: Reformation Trust), 2014.

[54] Wolfgang Musculus (1560), *Loci communes in usus S. Theologiae Candidatorum parati* (reprint by Pranava Books, 2018).

[55] Nicholas Ridley, *A Brief Declaration of the Lord's Supper* (London: Forgotten Books, 2016).

George M. Ella gives the following insights into Ridley's belief in election and predestination in his online article at: http://go-newfocus.co.uk/articles/app/category/biography/article/nicholas-ridley:

> By Ridley's day, Rome had given up the ancient and Biblical doctrine of grace and when the Reformer was called before his papist persecutors, one of the first doctrines they condemned was his belief in election and predestination as witnessed in the work formerly called Ponet's Catechism, published in 1553. Ridley was charged with authoring the work but instead of merely denying this to save his life, Ridley said that he had read and used it and consented to its teaching. Alexander Nowel extended the catechism for the Elizabethan Church and since then it has been referred to as Nowel's Catechism.5 Toplady calls the catechism's teaching, (sponsored by the same committee who produced the Anglican Articles of Religion), 'the highest Calvinism'. He finds all his favourite doctrines in it, including Justification from Eternity which choice doctrine Toplady shared with his friends the Particular Baptists.

Peter Martyr Vermigli (1500–1562)

Peter Martyr Vermigli was an Italian theologian of the Reformation period who converted from Roman Catholicism to Protestantism. He was a very influential figure in the early development of Reformed theology and in the English Reformation. Born in Florence, he entered the Canons Regular of the Saint Augustine religious order and was influenced by reading Protestant theologians such as Martin Bucer and Ulrich Zwingli. To avoid persecution, he fled Catholic Italy for the Reformed safe haven of Switzerland. Thomas Cranmer invited him to assist in the nascent English Reformation and he was appointed to a professorship at Oxford University.

Vermigli was forced to leave England on the ascension of Queen Mary I. He lived his final days teaching theology in Zurich. Here is a taste of his theology:

> This word predestination will signify nothing else than the eternal ordinance of God regarding His creatures (*Dei de creaturis suis aeternam dispositionem*), relating to a certain use. The Scriptures do not often use the word predestination in this sense except with reference to the elect alone. Although in Acts 4 we read 'they assembled together to do whatever your hand and purpose predestined to happen' (Acts 4:28). If these words refer to the death of Christ and the redemption of mankind, they do not pass beyond the bounds of election to salvation. If they include those who gathered together against the Lord, they also include the reprobate. Let us make our judgments based on how the Scriptures most often use the term predestination.[56]

---

[56] Peter Martyr Vermigli, *Predestination and Justification,* vol. 8, trans. by Frank A. James (Kirksville, MO:

Heinrich Bullinger (1504–1575)

Heinrich Bullinger was the Swiss reformer who became the successor of Huldrych Zwingli as head of the Zurich church and pastor at Grossmünster. A much less controversial figure than John Calvin or Martin Luther, his importance has long been underestimated. Recent research shows that he was one of the most influential theologians of the Protestant Reformation in the sixteenth century. Bullinger underscores God's sovereign grace through these comments:

We are saved solely through the goodness and mercy of God." The ineffable mercy and divine grace of the eternal God are proven, first, in that God offers this covenant not in any way because of the merits of humans, but rather out of the sheer goodness which is God's nature. I do not know whether humans are capable of conceiving this mystery fully or conveying how praiseworthy it is.[57]

John Calvin (1509–1564)

John Calvin was the leading French theologian and pastor during the Protestant Reformation. He was a principal figure in the development of the system of Christian theology later called Calvinism. Originally trained as a lawyer, after his conversion, he read the works of Martin Luther, and soon thereafter broke from the Roman Catholic Church, around 1530.

After religious tensions provoked a violent uprising against Protestants in France, Calvin fled to Basel, Switzerland, where he published the first edition of his seminal work "The Institutes of the Christian Religion" in 1536.

Our Hope:

I have no other hope or refuge than His predestination upon which my entire salvation is grounded. The foundation and first cause, both of our calling and of all the benefits which we receive from God, is here declared to be His eternal election. If the reason is asked, why God has called us to enjoy the gospel, why He daily bestows upon us so many blessings, why He opens to us the gate of heaven—the answer will be constantly found in this principle, that He hath chosen us before the foundation of the world. The very time when the election took place proves it to be free. For what could we have deserved, or what merit did

Sixteenth Century Essays and Studies, 2003), 16.
[57] Heinrich Bullinger, *"Of the Ceremonial Laws of God," Decades*, **2:169–175**. Found on: https://deovivendiperchristum.wordpress.com/2013/10/05/heinrich-bullinger-1504-1575-on-the-covenant-of-grace-2/.

we possess, before the world was made? How childish is the attempt to meet this argument by the following sophism! 'We were chosen because we were worthy, and because God foresaw that we would be worthy.' We were all lost in Adam; and therefore, had not God, through His own election, rescued us from perishing, there was nothing to be foreseen. The same argument is used in the Epistle to the Romans, where, speaking of Jacob and Esau, he says, "For the children being not yet born, neither having done any good or evil, that the purpose of God according to election might stand, not of works, but of him that calleth" (Romans 9:11). But though they had not yet acted, might a sophist of the Sorbonne reply, God foresaw that they would act. This objection has no force when applied to the depraved natures of men, in whom nothing can be seen but materials for destruction.

In Christ:

This is the second proof that the election is free. For if we are chosen in Christ, it is not of ourselves. It is not from a perception of anything that we deserve, but because our heavenly Father has introduced us, through the privilege of adoption, into the body of Christ. In short, the name of Christ excludes all merit and everything which men have of their own, for when he says that we are chosen in Christ, it follows that in ourselves we are unworthy.

That We Should Be Holy:

This is the immediate, but not the chief design. For there is no absurdity in supposing that the same thing may gain two objects. The design of building is, that there should be a house. This is the immediate design, but the convenience of dwelling in it is the ultimate design. It was necessary to mention this in passing, for we shall immediately find that Paul mentions another design, the glory of God. But there is no contradiction here, for the glory of God is the highest end, to which our sanctification is subordinate.

Holiness and Purity:

This leads us to conclude, that holiness, purity, and every excellence that is found among men are the fruit of election, so that once more Paul expressly puts aside every consideration of merit. If God had foreseen in us anything worthy of election, it would have been stated in language the very opposite of what is here employed, and which plainly means that all our holiness and purity of life flow from the election of God. How comes it then that some men are religious and live in the fear of God, while others give themselves up without reserve to all manner of wickedness? If Paul may be believed, the only reason is, that the latter retain their natural disposition, and the former have been chosen to holiness. The cause, certainly, is not later than the effect.

Election:

Election, therefore, does not depend on the righteousness of works, of which Paul here declares that it is the cause. We learn also from these words, that election gives no occasion to licentiousness or to the blasphemy of wicked men who say, 'Let us live in any manner we please; for, if we have been elected, we cannot perish.' Paul tells them plainly, that they have no right to separate holiness of life from the grace of election; for "whom he did predestinate, them he also called, and whom he called, them he also justified."[58]

One interesting side note is that Calvin was only eight years old in France when Luther nailed his *Ninety-Five Theses* to the door of his church in Wittenberg, Germany.

In his book *The Institutes of Religion*, Calvin wrote:

Paul begins here to extend as it were his hand to restrain the audacity of humans, in case they should clamor against God's judgments. We cannot by our own faculties examine the secrets of God, but we are admitted into a certain and clear knowledge of them by the grace of the Holy Spirit. And just as we ought to follow the guidance of the Spirit, so where He leaves us, we ought to stop there and fix our standing. If anyone will seek to know more than what God has revealed, he shall be overwhelmed with the immeasurable brightness of inaccessible light. But we must bear in mind the distinction between the secret counsel of God and His will made known in Scripture. For though the whole doctrine of Scripture surpasses in its height the mind of man, yet an access to it is not closed against the faithful, who reverently follow the Spirit; but with regard to God's hidden counsel, the depth and height of it cannot be reached. Those who try to overturn that prime article of our faith, God's eternal predestination, demonstrate their malice no less than their ignorance.

In view of his approaching death, John's doctor and friends told him that he must slow down the pace and stress of his ministry. He then replied, "What! Would you have the Lord find me idle when he comes?" He preached his very last sermon on February 6, 1564, and had to be carried to and from the pulpit. As a part of this last sermon, he made this statement: "I, John Calvin, servant of the Word of God in the Church of Geneva, have no other hope or refuge than His predestination, on which my entire salvation is grounded."[59]

---

[58] *The Institutes of the Christian Religion*, volume 1, edited by John T. McNeill, translated by Ford Lewis Battles, Library of Christian Classics edition (Philadelphia: The Westminster Press, 1960, 2006).
[59] John Calvin, *The Institutes of the Christian Religion*, chapter 21, section 1 (Grand Rapids, MI: Christian Classics Ethereal Library). Public Domain.

John Bradford (1510–1555)

John Bradford was the English Reformer and martyr best remembered for his utterance "There, but for the grace of God, goes John Bradford," which has survived in its common version, "There, but for the grace of God, go I." He spoke these words while imprisoned in the Tower of London when he saw criminals being led toward their execution. Bradford was in the Tower of London for alleged crimes against Mary Tudor for his Protestant faith. Bradford was burned at the stake on July 1, 1555. During his time in prison, he continued to write religious works and preach to all who would listen. At one point, he was put in a cell with three other Reformers, Archbishop Thomas Cranmer, Bishop Nicholas Ridley (who had ordained him), and Hugh Latimer. Their prison time was spent in careful study of the New Testament. All of them were martyred.

The following testimony about Bradford comes through Foxe's *Book of Martyrs* from a Mr. Sampson twenty-seven years after Bradford's conversion to Christ. Mr. Sampson was a friend, fellow student of Bradford's at the Inner Temple, and was the human means under divine providence whereby Bradford genuinely embraced the Law and Gospel:

> I did know when and partly how it pleased God by effectual calling, to turn his heart unto the true knowledge and obedience of the most holy Gospel of Christ our Savior, of which God did give him such an heavenly hold and lively feeling, that as he did then know that many sins were forgiven him, so surely he declared by deeds that he 'love much.' For, where he had both gifts and calling to have employed himself in civil and worldly affairs profitably, such was his love of Christ and zeal to promoting of his glorious gospel, that he changed not only the course of his former life, as the woman did (Luke vii.), but even his former duty, as Paul did change his former profession and study. Touching the first, after that God touched his heart with that holy and effectual calling, he sold his chains, rings, brooches and jewels of gold, which before he used to wear and did bestow the price of this his former vanity in the necessary relief of Christ's poor members, which he could hear of or find lying sick or pining in poverty. Touching the second, he declared his great zeal and love to promote the glory of the Lord Jesus, whose goodness and saving health he had tasted, that, with marvelous favor to further the kingdom of God by the ministry of his holy word, he gave himself wholly to the study of the holy Scriptures. The which his purpose to accomplish the better, he departed from the Tempt at London, where the temporal law is studied, and went to the University of Cambridge, to learn, by God's law, how to further the building of the Lord's temple.[60]

---

[60] John Day, *Fox's Book of Martyrs,* chapter 16, "Persecutions in England during the Reign of Queen Mary," first published in English in 1563.

John Knox (1513–1572)

John Knox was the famous Scottish clergyman and leader of the Protestant Reformation who brought reformation to the church in Scotland. He was educated at the University of St. Andrews and was ordained to the Catholic priesthood in 1536. Influenced by early church Reformers such as George Wishart, he joined the movement to reform the Scottish church.

John Knox first publicly professed the Protestant faith near the end of 1545. Knox helped overthrow Roman Catholicism in Scotland and helped establish Presbyterian polity in Scotland. In that regard, Knox is considered the founder of the Presbyterian denominations which have millions of members worldwide. In 1558, while Knox was living in Geneva, he was asked by friends back in England to write a response to a book circulating back there titled *Careless by Necessity* (a work by an Anabaptist that denied the doctrine of predestination). Knox agreed to this request from England and wrote *On Predestination in Answer to the Cavillations*. (An answer to the cavillations of an adversary respecting the doctrine of predestination: M.D.LX 1856, by John Knox [Printed for the Bannatyne Club, 1856]). He probably finished the work while in Dieppe, while he waited for official permission to reenter England. This writing ended up being the longest of Knox's works. The title of this book, reveals the heart of the fiery Scottish Reformer, as do his quotes below. Knox was independently named as its author when permission was granted for it to be printed in Geneva on Nov. 13, 1559. The quotes below show Knox in his most expressive self:

P. 25: "But yet I say, that the doctrine of God's eternal predestination is so necessary to the church of God, that, without the same, can faith neither be truly taught, neither surely established; man can never be brought to true humility and knowledge of himself; neither yet can he be ravished in admiration of God's eternal goodness, and so moved to praise him as appertaineth."

P. 28: "And therefore we say, that such as attribute anything to themselves in the grace of their election, have not learned to give God the honour which to Him appertaineth, because they do not freely confess what maketh them to differ from others."

P. 29: "Such as desire this Article to be buried in silence, and would that men should teach and believe that the grace of God's election is common to all, but that one receiveth it and another receiveth it not, proceedeth either from their obedience or disobedience; such deceive themselves and are unthankful and injurious to God."

P. 65: "If these things do displease you, remember first, that they are the voices of the Holy Ghost and secondly, call to mind the condition of mankind (compared with that sovereign Majesty) be but worms creeping upon the earth, and therefore, we cannot climb up to heaven and so reason or plead with the Almighty."

P. 73: "If Predestination proceedeth from God's purpose and will as the apostle affirmeth that it doth, then the purpose and will of God being eternal, cannot be moved by our works or faith being temporal."

P. 76: "Now seeing that good works spring forth from election, how can any man be so foolish as to affirm that they are the cause of the same?"

P. 76: "Now if man hath nothing but that which he receiveth of grace, of free gift, of favour and mercy, what odious pride and horrible unthankfulness is this, that man shall imagine that for his faith and for his works, God did elect and did predestinate him to that dignity! Even as if two or three beggars, chosen from the number of many, were, of the liberal mercy of a Prince, promoted to honour, should after brag and boast that their good service was the cause that the Prince did choose them."

P. 78: "Let the whole Scriptures be read and diligently marked, and no sentence (rightly understood) shall be found, that affirmeth God to have chosen us in respect of our works, or because He foresaw that we should be faithful, holy and just. But to the contrary, many places shall we find (yes, even so many as intreat of that matter) that plainly affirm that we are freely chosen according to the purpose of His good will, and that in Christ Jesus."

P. 85: "We presume not to define what number God shall save and how many He shall justly condemn: but with reverence we refer judgement to Him who is the universal Creator, whose goodness and wisdom is such that He can do nothing but wisely and whose judgement is so perfect, that His works are exempted from the judgement of all creatures."

P. 96: "We affirm and most constantly do believe, that in Christ Jesus, the eternal Son of the eternal Father, were we elected before all time. This you (the Anabaptists) cannot abide, and therefore you seek all means to obscure the glory of Him to whom the Father hath given all power in heaven and in earth."

P. 100: "Acceptation of persons is when an unworthy person is preferred to a worthy, either by corrupt affection of those that do prefer him, either yet for some quality or external beauty that appeareth in man . . . For as God respecteth not the person of man, so respecteth He nothing that is or can be within man as the chief cause of his election. For what can God foresee, consider or know, to be in man that good is, which floweth not from His free mercy and goodness, as it is written, 'We are not sufficient of ourselves to think anything that good is, but all our sufficiency is of God, who worketh in us to do and to perform'."

P. 113: "We plainly affirm, that man, when he sinned, did neither look to God's will, God's counsel, nor eternal purpose; but did altogether consent to the will of the devil, which did manifestly gainsay God's revealed will."

P. 114: "We say not that God's ordinance is the cause of reprobation, but we affirm that the just causes of reprobation are hid in the eternal counsel of God, and known to His godly wisdom alone."

P. 121: "Ye (the Anabaptists) be proud contemners of the free grace of God offered to man in Christ Jesus. For with the Pelagians and Papists ye are become teachers of free will, and defenders of your own righteousness."

P. 136: "But justly leaving the reprobate to themselves, and to Satan their father, they willingly follow, without all violence or compulsion on God's part, iniquity and sin, and so finally the way of perdition, to which they are naturally inclined. But if yet that any will affirm that therefore God's foreknowledge doth but idly behold what they will do, and that in His eternal purpose, counsel and will, He will one thing and they will another, so that their will prevail against His, he shall not escape the crime of horrible blasphemy."

P. 141: "Neither yet therefore doth it follow that His foreknowledge, prescience, will or power, doth take away the free will of His creatures, but in all wisdom and justice (however the contrary appears to our corrupted judgements) He uses them as best pleases His wisdom to bring to pass in time that which before all time He had decreed."

P. 144: "Violence is done to the will of the creature when it willeth one thing and yet by force, by tyranny or by a greater power it is compelled to do the things which it would not . . . Do we say that God did (or doeth) any such violence to His creatures? Did He compel Satan to tempt the woman when his will was contrary thereto? Did the will of Adam resist the temptation of the woman, and did he so hate and abhor to eat of that fruit, that it behooved God to compel his will repugnant thereto to eat of it, and so to break the commandments? Or did he not rather willingly hear and obey the voice of his wife?"

P. 157: "True it is that we be elected in Christ Jesus to be holy and to walk in good works which God hath prepared. But every reasonable man knoweth what difference there is betwixt the cause and the effect. Election, in which I include the free grace and favour of God, is the fountain from which springeth faith, and faith is the mother of all good works. But what foolishness were it therefore to reason: 'My works are the cause of my faith, and my faith is the cause of my election'?"

P. 164: "We do not imagine the faithful members of Christ's body to be stocks and stones insensible, without will or study of godliness, but we affirm that it is God that worketh in us the good will and good thought, for of ourselves we are not sufficient to think one good thought."

P. 177: "That we be apt to discern that we have a will, to do this or that, this is a natural gift: but that we can choose, desire and do nothing but that which is evil, that cometh from the corruption of sin."

P. 205: "We say not, we teach not, nor believe, that Christ Jesus doeth only offer medicine and prescribe a diet as a common physician, leaving the using and observation of it to our will and power. But we affirm that in the hearts of His elect, He worketh faith, He openeth their eyes, He cureth their leprosy, He removeth and overcometh their disobedience—yea, by violence—He pulleth them forth from the bondage of Satan and so sanctifieth them by the power of His Holy Spirit, that they abide in His truth, according as He hath prayed for them and so continue His vessels of glory forever."

P. 210: "Do we not continually affirm, that as God of His great mercy hath called us to the dignity of His children, so hath He sanctified us, and appointed us to walk in pureness and holiness all the days of our life; that we shall continually fight against the lust and inordinate affections that remain in this our corrupt nature; that if we find not the Spirit of Christ working in us, that then we can never be assured of our election."

P. 300: "Impossible it is that Christ's death shall lack its effect, which is the life of those that of His Father are committed to His charge, of whom impossible it is that any shall perish. For the number of the brethren must be complete. Neither doth it follow that exhortations and admonitions be superfluous and vain, for they are means which the wisdom of God knoweth to be most necessary to stir up our dull senses, which always be ready to lie in a certain security."

P. 387: "The Word falling into the heart of the elect doth mollify and illuminate, but falling into the heart of the reprobate, it doth harden and more execrate the same, by reason of the quality and incurable corruption of the person."

P. 405: "The omnipotence of God and the freedom of His will we must constantly maintain: but we cannot admit that our God be variable, inconstant, subject to ignorance, neither yet that His godly will depend on the will and disposition of man. For that were not to leave God's will free, but to bring it under the bondage of His creatures."

P. 407: "If God willeth all men to be saved and to come to the knowledge of the truth, and yet many do perish in ignorance, and shall be condemned as Christ Jesus doth pronounce: then must it either follow that God's will is mutable and so He is inconstant and not at all times like Himself, or else He is not omnipotent."

P. 410: "The apostle in these words, 'God willeth all men to be saved and to come to the knowledge of the truth' (1 Tim. 2:4), speaketh not of every man and of every particular person, but of all men in general, that is to say, of men of all estates, all conditions, all realms, all ages. For as in Christ Jesus there is neither Jew nor Gentile, man nor woman, freeman nor servant, but all are one in Him, so can estate, no condition of man, no realm, no age, be proved so wicked and corrupt, but out of the like hath God called some to the participation of His light. . . . For God willeth you (the church) to pray for your persecutors, that their eyes may be opened and they converted to the living God: who, no doubt, will save some of all estates, of all conditions, and vocations of men."

P. 418: "The Apostle Peter saith, 'The Lord that hath promised is not slow, but He is longsuffering toward us, while He will none to perish, but all to come to repentance'

(2 Peter 3:9). The Apostle here meaneth not that all without exception shall be received to life by true repentance, but that the cause why God so long deferreth (as it were) the extreme judgement, is that the elect number of God's children may be complete (as answer was given to those that cried under the altar to be revenged of the tyrannies that dwell on the earth) of these elect children God will none to perish."

Girolamo Zanchi (1516–1590)

Girolamo Zanchi (or Jerome Zanchius) was an Italian Protestant Reformation clergyman and educator. As one of the most learned theologians of the second half of the sixteenth century, he was not considered to be an original thinker, but he was regarded an excellent teacher. He considered himself a Calvinist. Zanchi was a voluminous writer whose works include *Confession of the Christian Religion* and *Observation on the Divine Attributes*. He may be known best for his book *The Doctrine of Absolute Predestination*, which is still in publication today. Here are a few of his thoughts on Effectual Redemption:

And although there were more Israelites which were besieged of the enemies then Jews, yet not they but only these were delivered. So though there be much more reprobate than Elect, yet the deliverance made by Christ did not appertain to the reprobate, but to the elect only. So that the Prophet truly admiring spake thus: For Christ, according to the purpose of his Father, for the Elect only that is, for those who according to the eternal election should believe in Him, was born, suffered and died, and rose again, and makes intercession at the right hand of his Father. Christ according to the purpose, of both His Father's and His own will, neither prayed nor suffered but for the Elect only, which is proved fully by many places of Scripture.[61]

Zanchi wrote of a minister's responsibility,

An ambassador is to deliver the whole message with which he is charged. He is to omit no part of it, but must declare the mind of the sovereign he represents, fully and without reserve. . . Let the minister of Christ weigh this well."

The whole circle of arts have a kind of mutual bond and connection, and by a sort of reciprocal relationship, are held together and interwoven with each other. Much the same may be said of this important doctrine of predestination. It is the bond which connects and

---

[61] Girolamo Zanchi, *The Doctrine of Absolute Predestination Stated and Asserted* (Palala Press, 2018), 335–336, 344.

keeps together the whole Christian system, which without this, is like a system of sand, ever ready to fall to pieces. It is the cement which holds the fabric together. Nay, it is the very soul which animates the whole frame. It is so blended and interwoven with the entire scheme of Gospel doctrine that when the former is excluded, the latter bleeds to death.[62]

Theodore Beza (1519–1605)

Theodore Beza was a French Protestant Christian theologian and scholar who played an important role in the Reformation. He was a member of the Monarchomach movement who opposed absolute monarchy. He was a disciple of John Calvin and lived most of his life in Switzerland. Here are a few of his words on election:

> This election or predestination to everlasting life, being considered in the will of God, that is to say, this selfsame determination or purpose to Elect, is the first cause and origination of the salvation of God's children. It is not grounded, as some say, because God did foresee their faith or good works. Rather the cause is found in His own good will, from whence afterward the Election, the faith and the good works spring forth. Therefore, when Scripture reconfirms the children of God in full and perfect hope, it does not stray in alleging the testimonies of the second causes, that is to say, in the fruits of faith, or the second causes themselves, as calling by the Gospel and faith in Christ Himself, who ascended on high, and who is our Head, in whom we are adopted according to that eternal purpose which God hath determined only in Himself.[63]

---

[62] Jay P. Green Sr. The Doctrine of Absolute Predestination, stated and asserted by Jerome Zanchius (1516–1590) (Sovereign Grace Publishers Inc., 2001). "Hieronymus Zanchius," thus Anglicized to "Jerome Zanchi/Zanchius," was an Italian Protestant Reformation clergyman and educator.

[63] *Theodore Beza* "On Double Predestination," chapter 1, ed. Rand Winburn, https://www.iconbusters.com/iconbusters/htm/beliefs/Theodore%20Beza%20On%20Double%20Predestination.pdf
Also see: Theodore Beza's "Table of Predestination," from *The Treasure of Trueth* (London, 1576). Source: Philip Benedict, *Christ's Churches Purely Reformed: A Social History of Calvinism* (New Haven: Yale University Press, 2002), 106.

30 ✤

Puritan Era Leaders Who Affirmed the Doctrines

The period referred to as the Puritan movement in England began during the reign of Elizabeth I from 1558 to 1603. During this time, those Christians who came to be known as Puritans (also called Precisionists) were in conflict with those leading the Church of England. Church of England leaders used various methods to restrict the Puritan movement. The movement in England was initially influenced by several of the reforming movements on the European continent like Erasmian, Lutheran, and Reformed. At the same time, the practices of the Church of England continued in its similarities to the Roman Catholic Church. Under the reign of Henry's son, Edward VI, evangelical initiatives began to show up. The English Reformation began to manifest Calvinistic qualities and some of the leading Reformed spiritual leaders from other countries sought refuge in England including John Laski from Poland, Peter Martyr Vermigli from Italy, and Martin Bucer from Germany. The spirit of the Puritan movement was very successful in the northern English colonies in the New World as it became the foundation for the civil society of New England, which we know has had lasting effects on American life ever since. During this time, Thomas Cranmer (the Archbishop of Canterbury who lived from 1489 to 1556) was one of the well-known leaders of the Church of England. He supported the annulment of Henry's marriage to Catherine of Aragon and the separation of the official English Church from the Church in Rome. He went on to promote church reforms in the

Book of Common Prayer (a complete liturgy for the English Church). He affected changes in communion, pastoral celibacy, the use of images in churches, and the veneration of saints. Cranmer also gave refuge to several key European Reformers who had migrated to England. After Mary I came to the throne (reigning from 1553 to 1558), with her continued loyalties to the Roman Catholic Church, Cranmer was eventually put on trial for heresy and treason and executed. He died as a martyr for the principles of the English Reformation and his death was reported in *Foxe's Book of Martyrs*. Many great things developed spiritually from the Puritans and the following men, who were a part of that group and carried on the convictions regarding the doctrines of election and predestination.[64]

William Perkins (1558–1602)

William Perkins was an influential Anglican clergyman and Cambridge theologian who received both a BA and MA. He was one of the foremost leaders of the Puritan movement in the Church of England during the Elizabethan era, although he did not accept all of the ecclesiastical practices of the Church of England. He was sympathetic to the nonconformist Puritans and even faced disciplinary action for his support. He wrote over forty works, many of which were published posthumously. In addition to writing, he also served as a fellow at Christ's College and as a lecturer at St. Andrew's Church in Cambridge. Perkins was a firm proponent of Reformed theology, particularly the supralapsarian theology of Theodore Beza (who promoted a balanced combination of Reformed theology and Puritan piety) and John Calvin. In addition, he was a staunch defender of Protestant precepts, specifically the five *solae* with a particular emphasis on *solus Christus* and *sola Scriptura*. The five *solas* are five Latin phrases popularized during the Protestant Reformation that emphasized the distinctions between the early Reformers and the Roman Catholic Church. The word *sola* is the Latin word for "only" and was used in relation to five key teachings that defined the biblical convictions of Protestants. They are:

1. *Sola scriptura*: "Scripture alone"
2. *Sola fide*: "faith alone"
3. *Sola gratia*: "grace alone"
4. *Solo Christo*: "Christ alone"
5. *Soli Deo gloria*: "to the glory of God alone"

---

[64] The highlights above, giving the a brief summary of this period of time, come from a number of sources including: *Heal, Felicity (2005); Reformation in Britain and Ireland, Oxford University Press, Kendall, R. T. (1970); Calvin and English Calvinism; Lathbury, Thomas (1853); and History of the Convocation of the Church of England*.

Perkins worked hard to explain the tenets of election and predestination in a way that anyone could understand them. He experienced an untimely death from kidney stones in 1602 at age forty-four. Perkins has often been called The Father of Puritanism.

By the time of his death, Perkins' writings in England were outselling those of Calvin, Beza, and Bullinger combined. At least fifty editions of Perkins's works were printed in Switzerland and in various parts of Germany. His writings were also translated into Spanish, French, Italian, Irish, Welsh, Hungarian, and Czech. Nearly one hundred Cambridge men who led early migrations to New England, including William Brewster of Plymouth, Thomas Hooker of Connecticut, John Winthrop of Massachusetts Bay, and Roger Williams of Rhode Island, grew up in Perkins's shadow. Richard Mather was converted while reading Perkins. Jonathan Edwards was fond of reading Perkins more than a century later.

Dr. Joel R. Beeke wrote of Mr. Perkins that . . .

He was primarily concerned with the conversion of souls and subsequent growth in godliness and Perkins believed that a biblical realization of God's sovereign grace in predestination was vital for spiritual comfort and assurance. He believed how predestination worked out experimentally in the souls of believers and was inseparable from sovereign predestination in Christ. Far from being harsh and cold, sovereign predestination was the foundation upon which experimental faith could be built. It was the hope, expectation, and guarantee of salvation for the true believer. Perkins denied that God creates anyone to damnation, but rather He creates the reprobate to manifest His justice and glory in their deserved damnation. God decreed damnation, not as damnation, but as an execution of His justice. Sin, therefore, is not an effect, but a consequence of the decree of reprobation. Sin, however, is the meriting cause of actual damnation." Perkins asserted that "though Adam's fall allows no one to make any claim on God, the holy God wills to take His elect out of the mass of mankind for His own everlasting love and glory. The elect become vessels of God's mercy solely out of God's will and without regard to their good or evil. They are ordained to salvation and heavenly glory.[65]

Andrew Willet (1562–1621)

Andrew Willet was an English clergyman, controversialist, and a prolific writer who is well known for his antipapal works. His views were Calvinist, conforming, and non-separatist. He earned his BA in 1581, MA in 1584, BD in 1591, and DD 1601. Willet published his major work called the *Synopsis Papismi* in 1594 and completed the *Tetrastylon* in 1596. He and his wife had eighteen children. The following paragraph by Dr. Willet

---

[65] Irvonwy Morgan, *Puritan Spirituality* [xliv] [44] (London: Epworth Press, 1973), 24, https://www.apuritansmind.com/puritan-favorites/william-perkins/perkins-on-predestination-and-preaching/.

on Romans 2:4 is from his book, *Hexapla: That is, A Six-fold Commentary upon the Most Divine Epistle of the Holy Apostle. St. Paul to the Romans*:

> It will be here objected, that seeing the long sufferance of God calls all unto repentance, and whom He would have repent, He would have saved. It seems then, that none are rejected or reprobate, whom the Lord so invites and calls unto repentance. Such as are effectually called unto repentance by God's patience and longsuffering, are indeed elected, for the elect only are effectually called to repentance, but such as abuse God's patience and are impenitent still, may not withstanding be in the state of reprobation. For though the same means be offered unto them to bring them to repentance, yet they have not the grace. The decree then concerning the rejecting of such impenitent persons and the offer of such means, as might lead them unto repentance may very well stand together, because it is of their own hardness of heart that the means offered are not effectual. And thus, also another objection may be answered, that if it be God's will that such should come to repentance, whether the malice of man therein can resist the will of God, for if it were God's absolute will and good pleasure, that such should come unto repentance, no man could resist it. God is able to change and turn the most impenitent and hard heart, if it pleased Him. But here we must distinguish between effectual calling, which always takes place and none can hinder it, and calling not effectual, yet sufficient if men did not put in a bar by their own hardness of heart. God's absolute will then, is not resisted, when men come not to repentance. For His will is to leave such to themselves by His just judgment and not to give them of His effectual grace. Now hereof no other reason can be given, why God does not give His effectual grace to all, but His good pleasure, as our Blessed Savior says in Matthew 11:26. "It is so Father, because thy good pleasure is such."[66]

John Davenant (1572–1641)

John Davenant was educated at Queen's College in Cambridge, England. He was made Professor of Divinity in 1609, and in 1614, he was elected President of Queens College. In 1618, he was chosen by James I, with three other theologians, to assist in the work of the Calvinistic Synod of Dort in Holland. In 1621, he became Bishop of Salisbury and wrote various books including *A Treatise on Justification, God's Love to Mankind, An Exhortation to Brotherly Love,* and a *Dissertation on the Death of Christ.* John Davenant had strong Calvinistic leanings and loved the doctrines of grace. In his words: "I know that no man can embrace Arminianism in the doctrines of predestination and grace without deserting the Articles agreed upon by the Church of England. And regarding the point of perseverance,

---

[66] *Hexapla: That is, A Six-fold Commentary upon the Most Divine Epistle of the Holy Apostle, St. Paul to the Romans* (printed by Cantrell Legge, printer for the University of Cambridge, 1611), 104–105.

but he would have to vary from the received opinions of the best approved doctors in the English Church."[67]

Bishop Joseph Hall (1574–1656)

Bishop Joseph Hall was known as an English bishop, satirist, and moralist. His peers knew him as a devotional writer and a high-profile controversialist of the early 1640s. In church politics, he leaned toward a middle way. Hall was involved as a mediator, taking an active part in the Arminian and Calvinist controversy in the English Church, and trying to get other clergy to accept Dort. In his work *Via Media, The Way of Peace* (1619), he did everything he could to persuade Calvinists and Armenians to accept a compromise.

In 1627, he became Bishop of Exeter. In spite of his Calvinistic opinions, he maintained that to acknowledge the errors, which had arisen in the Catholic Church, did not necessarily imply disbelief in her catholicity, and that the Church of England having repudiated these errors should not deny the claims of the Roman Catholic Church on that account. His points on God's predestination were:

1. Whatsoever God, who is the God of truth, hath engaged himself by promise to do, the same He undoubtedly hath willed, and will accordingly perform.
2. There is no son of Adam to whom God hath not promised that, if he shall believe in Christ, repent, and persevere, he shall be saved.
3. This general and undoubted will of God must be equally proclaimed to all men through the world, without exception, and ought to be so received and believed as it is by Him published and revealed.
4. All men, within the pale of the church especially, have from the mercy of God such common helps toward this belief and salvation, as that the neglect thereof makes any of them justly guilty of their own condemnation.
5. Besides the general will of God, He hath eternally willed and decreed to give a special and effectual grace to those that are predestinate according to the good pleasure of His will, whereby they do actually believe, obey, and persevere, that they may be saved: so as the same God, that would have all men to be saved if they believe and be not wanting to His Spirit, hath decreed to work powerfully in some whom He hath particularly chosen, that they shall believe, and not be wanting to His Spirit in whatsoever shall be necessary for their salvation.

---

[67] C. Sydney Carter, *English Church in Seventeenth Century* (London, 1909), 18.

6. It is not the prevision of faith, or any other grace or act of man, whereupon this decree of God is grounded; but the mere and gracious good will and pleasure of God, from all eternity appointing to save those whom He hath chosen in Christ, as the head and foundation of the elect.

7. This decree of God's election is absolute, and unchangeable, and from everlastings. God doth not either actually damn or appoint any soul to damnation, without the consideration and respect of sin.[68]

John Diodati (1576–1649)

John Diodati was born in Geneva to an Italian Protestant refugee family. His father, Carlo Diodati, was declared a heretic by Rome in 1568, but had already fled to Geneva for safety the year before. John became a part of the third generation of Reformation theologians in Geneva, following Calvin and Theodore Beza. One of his students was the celebrated Francis Turretin whose own Institutes became a standard work of Reformed theology for two hundred years. John became a student in Calvin's Academy before serving there as a professor, first as a Hebrew teacher, and then succeeding Beza as professor of theology. He remained in that position for the rest of his life. He also served as pastor in the church in Geneva and he became well-known as the man who first provided Italians with a translation of the Bible in 1607, which became the standard version of the Bible for Italian Protestants until the twentieth century. Diodati was involved in major doctrinal disputes in the first decades of the seventeenth century. He was the Genevese representative at the famous Synod of Dort (1618–1619), which counteracted the growing influence of the teaching of Jacobus Arminius (1560–1609), who had also been a student in the Genevan Academy under Beza before going to Leyden to study under Gomarus. Later, Diodati was involved in the dispute over the teaching of Moses Amyraut (1596–1664) in France, opposing the "hypothetical redemption" which became known as "Amyraldianism." Diodati's "twenty-five theses" on the doctrine of the Scriptures was first published in 1596 when he was only twenty years old.[69]

His theses about the Holy Scriptures are in harmony with the same doctrinal flavors of his predecessors in Geneva, Calvin and Beza, and with his successor, Turretin. Many feel he deserves to be remembered as a champion of Reformed and Protestant theology.

---

[68] Joseph Hall's devotional pamphlet, "The Great Mysteries of Godliness," 1650.

[69] Andrea Ferrari, *John Diodati's Doctrine of Holy Scripture (Reformed Historical-Theological Studies)*, (Reformation Heritage Books, 2006).

Richard Sibbes (1577–1635)

Richard Sibbes (or Sibbs) was an English theologian known as a skilled biblical exegete and as a representative with William Perkins and John Preston of what has been called "mainline" Puritanism. Sibbes adhered to Calvinist covenant theology, shaped by the English theologians Perkins, Preston, William Ames, and Thomas Taylor. Sibbes believed the Second Coming was necessary to complete the work that Christ had begun. He also promoted religious tolerance.

Sibbes' greatest contribution to the literature on the doctrine of election came in his exposition of Galatians 2:20: "I have been crucified with Christ; and it is no longer I who live, but Christ lives in me; and the life which I now live in the flesh I live by faith in the Son of God, who loved me and gave Himself up for me" (NASB).

He held a high view of the election of God, but also a high view of promoting the gospel. In his exposition he wrote:

> Why doth Christ by the ministry persuade all in the church to believe in Christ, and to believe in forgiveness of sins, if Christ did not die for them all? I answer, that in the church He calls all, that He may cull out His own. The minister speaks promiscuously both to the elect and those that are not, because God will not rob His own children of the benefit, though they are mingled with others to whom the blessed things do not belong; as it is with the rain, it rains as well upon the rocks and the sea, and upon the barren heath as upon the good ground.[70]

Sibbes' preaching had great balance. He offered the gospel freely to all, trusting that God would call out His elect in a perfect way.

Thomas Adams (1583–1653)

Thomas Adams was an English Calvinist Episcopalian in terms of his church government and as a preacher he was known to have been called *The Shakespeare of the Puritans* by Robert Southey. It was claimed that John Bunyan read his works. Much of the information about Adams comes from title pages and dedications in his works, summarized very nicely at: http://www.reformedchurchpublications.org/works_of_thomas_adams_in_3_volumes.htm. He earned his BA from the University of Cambridge in 1601 and MA in 1606. From 1614 to 1618 he was the Vicar of Wingrave, Buckinghamshire. From 1618 to 1623 he held the preachership of St. Gregory and during the same period preached occasionally

---

[70] Richard Sibbes, *Salvation Applied,* vol. 5 of *The Works of Richard Sibbes,* ed. Alexander Grosart (1862–64; repr. Edinburgh: Banner of Truth Trust, 2001), 388.

at St. Paul's cross and Whitehall. He was "observant chaplain" to Henry Montagu, first Earl of Manchester, Lord Chief Justice of England. J. I. Packer wrote that Adams's sermons were evangelically eloquent and biblically faithful. It was said that his doctrine was unambiguously Calvinistic, but with a pastoral, rather than a speculative or controversial orientation. Spurgeon said that Adam's Commentary on the Second Epistle of Peter was the best Puritan commentary (printed under James Sherman's editorship). Spurgeon claimed, "It was full of quaintness, holy wit, bright thought, and deep instruction. We know of no richer and racier reading."[71]

John Cotton (1585–1652)

John Cotton was a Clergyman in England and in the American colonies, who by most accounts, was the preeminent minister and theologian of the Massachusetts Bay Colony. In 1635, he was responsible for establishing the first public school in America called the Boston Latin School, modeled on the Free Grammar School in Boston, England, which taught Greek and Latin. Five of the fifty-six signers of the Declaration of Independence were students of the Boston school (John Hancock, William Hooper, Samuel Adams, Benjamin Franklin, and Robert Treat Paine). The building of *Boston Latin School* predated Harvard College by a year. It was supported by public funds, and began without a formal building, holding classes in the home of headmaster Philemon Pormort. Harvard was founded in 1636 by general vote of the Massachusetts Bay Colony and was often referred to as *The School of the Prophets* for its focus on theology. The college awarded its first professorship in divinity in 1721, making it the oldest endowment in America. In later years, the college would become Harvard University.

As a Puritan pastor, Cotton wanted to do away with the ceremony and vestments associated with the established Anglican Church and preach in a simpler, more consensual manner. He wanted to reform the English Church rather than leave it. Along with John Wilson, as the second pastor of the first church established in Boston, he generated more conversions in his first six months than had been made during the entire previous year. He continued to preach in the Boston church until his death. He is considered to be the one who gave the name Congregationalism to this form of church polity. While orthodox on his doctrines of predestination, Cotton is said to have been a "hypothetical Universalist" (see *Conformity and Orthodoxy in the English Church*, c. 1560–1660, edited by Peter Lake and Michael Questier, p. 86). Cotton's orthodoxy is witnessed to by the fact that he was invited to attend the Westminster Assembly. The question of Cotton's hypothetical universalism notwithstanding, he has adopted the reading of 1 John 2:2 which is reminiscent of Calvin and Zanchius.

---

[71] http://www.solid-ground-books.com/detail_679.asp?flag=1.

Gisbertus Voetius (1589–1676)

Gisbertus Voetius was born of a Dutch Reformed minister in the town of Heusden in the Netherlands. He was an ecclesiastical politician, a minister, a dogmatician, and an academic. He was industrious and possessed a photographic memory.

Voetius hated Arminianism and defended the strictest forms of Calvinism. He viewed Arminianism as a wholesale attack on the very heart of the gospel, the Reformed faith, and fundamentally a return to Roman Catholicism and its doctrine of salvation by works.

At the Utrecht school of higher education, he taught theology, logic, physics, metaphysics, and the Semitic languages of Hebrew, Arabic, and Syraic. In addition to this massive load of teaching, he also became the pastor of the church in Utrecht, and the street where he lived bears his name to this day. He was a prolific writer in many different fields even though many of those who have read his writings complain that they were almost impossibly boring and difficult to read. To complete all this work, he rose at 4:00 a.m. to begin his studies for the day and prepare for his many lectures. Voetius was a godly and virtuous man and one of the first books he wrote was titled *Proof of the Power of Godliness*. His thesis in this book was that, while Arminianism is destructive of Christian morality, the orthodox faith gives attestation to itself in a godly and upright life. The book was a testimony to the writings of a man who lived what he believed. He was firmly convinced and showed it in his own life, that the Reformed faith, when embraced wholeheartedly, led to Christian virtue and purity.[72]

John Spilsbury (1593–1668)

John Spilsbury was an English cobbler (someone who repairs shoes.) and Particular Baptist minister who set up a Calvinist Baptist church in London in 1638. The earliest Baptists, as well as General Baptists, established their churches by agreement to a confession of faith. Spilsbury considered this as necessary for the wellbeing of the church. He declared that saving faith must be manifest in the hearty approval and assertion of a body of propositional truths. No church, and thus no baptism, could exist apart from submission to orthodox evangelicalism embodied in a confession of faith. Spilsbury would join with the other Particular Baptist churches in London in publishing and signing the First London Confession. Spilsbury also published a personal confession consisting of ten articles. The first three articles address the nature of God, total depravity, and election and predestination. An excerpt from these articles follows from Tom Nettles's book *The Baptists: Key People Involved in Forming A Baptist Identity (Beginnings in Britain)*:

---

[72] Herman Bavinck, Reformed Ethics: Created, Fallen, and Converted Humanity (Baker Academic, 2019).

I do believe that there is only one God, who is distinguished in three persons; God the Father, God the Son, and God the Holy Ghost; yet but one in nature, or essence, without divisions, and incommunicable, who made the world, and all things therein, by the word of His power, & governs them by His wise providence.

I believe that God made man in His own image, an upright and perfect creature, consisting of soul and body: which body God framed of the earth, and breathed into the same the breath of life, and man became a living soul. To whom God gave a law, upon his keeping of which depends all his happiness, and upon the contrary attended his misery, which took effect; for he breaking that law, he fell under the curse, and wrath of God lay upon him and all his posterity. By which fall man lost the knowledge of God, and utterly disabled himself of all ability ever to recover the same again.

I believe God out of the counsel of His will, did, before He made the world, elect and choose some certain number of His foreseen fallen creatures, and appointed them to eternal life in His Son, for the glory of His grace: which number so elected shall be saved, come to glory, & the rest left in sin to glorify His justice.[73]

Hanserd Knollys (1599–1691)

Hanserd Knollys was an English minister who studied at the University of Cambridge before he was ordained as a minister of the Church of England by the Bishop of Peterborough in 1629. He experienced a change of heart after becoming acquainted with several Puritans. He preached three and even four times on Sundays, besides sermons on saints' days and at funerals. But scruples and doubts agitated his mind and he finally reached the conviction that his position in the Church of England was not in accordance with the New Testament. He renounced his ordination, resolving not to preach any more until he had "received a clear call and commission from Christ to preach the gospel."

In 1871, the Baptist historian J. M. Cramp reported that during Knollys' silence he underwent much mental distress, which was removed by the instrumentality of Mr. Wheelwright, one of the Puritan ministers. He then recommenced preaching. Knollys' said, "I began to preach the doctrine of free grace, according to the tenor of the new and everlasting covenant, for three or four years together, whereby very many sinners were converted, and many believers were established in the faith." After experiencing persecution in England, he migrated to New England and then to Germany before returning to England to finish his life preaching and teaching in his home country. He published a Grammar of the Latin, Greek, and Hebrew languages. He died at the age of ninety-three. The Hanserd

---

[73] Tom Nettles, *The Baptists: Key People Involved in Forming a Baptist Identity (Beginnings in Britain)* (Ross-shire, Scotland: Christian Focus, 2005), 390.

Knollys Society was founded and named after him in 1845 for the republication of the works of early Baptist authors.[74]

Henry Jessey (1601–1663)

Henry Jessey was a Puritan Chaplain, Independent Baptist Pastor, Millenarian Politician and Prophet. Jessey evolved from an Independent pastor to a pastor with Baptist convictions, while serving the JLJ church in London from 1637–1650 ((JLJ is the first initial of its first three pastors, Henry Jacob (1562-1624), John Lathrop (1584-1653), and Henry Jessey.). He played a role in the emerging "Particular Baptist" movement as well as in various transformations and transitions of the JLJ church. Jessey worked with Oliver Cromwell and the Fifth Monarchists to complete a new translation of the Bible and worked politically to advance the cause of Jewish readmission into England.

Poor Jews in Jerusalem were in a very distressed state and all supplies from their richer brethren in other countries, upon whom they depended for subsistence, had been cut off. So Rev. Jessey raised a collection for their relief and he sent them £300, with letters strongly persuading them to embrace Christianity.

Note: Particular Baptists emerged from a "separatist" congregation that Henry Jacob gathered in London in 1616. In 1633, several members left the "JLJ church" and formed a congregation that baptized only believers. By 1638 the original "JLJ church" was also baptizing believers only. By 1644 there were seven Particular Baptist churches in London. As a Particular Baptist, Jessey believed God's power effects everything He desires, and therefore the elect (chosen before the foundations of the world) will be the ones redeemed.[75]

John Arrowsmith (1602–1659)

Dr. Arrowsmith was a member of the Westminster Assembly and preached to the Long Parliament on a number of occasions. He wrote the following regarding election:

Election having once pitched upon a man, it will find him out and call him home, wherever he be. Election called Zacchaeus out of accursed Jericho; Abraham out of idolatrous Ur of the Chaldees; Nicodemus and Paul out from the Pharisees; Dionysius and Damaris out of superstitious Athens. In whatsoever dunghills God's elect are hid, election will find them out and bring them home!"[76]

---

[74] Cramp's article on Knollys can be found at: http://baptisthistoryhomepage.com/knollys.hanserd.html.

[75] Jason G. Duesing, *Henry Jessey: Puritan Chaplain, Independent and Baptist Pastor, Millenarian Politician and Prophet* (Mountain Home, AR: BorderStone Press LLC, 2016).

[76] John Arrowsmith, DD, *Armilla Catechetica*, or *A Chain of Theological Principles* (printed by John Field, printer to the University of Cambridge, 1659).

Roger Williams 1603–1684)

Roger Williams is known as the founder of the first Baptist church in America. Williams was born in London and raised in the Episcopal Church, of which he was made a rector. Becoming dissatisfied with the ritual and ceremony of his church, he became a Puritan. He came to America and preached in Boston and Plymouth, Massachusetts, where he taught complete religious freedom. He was driven from Salem, Massachusetts, because of his spiritual convictions.[77]

He went south to Narragansett Bay, where he did missionary work among the Indians. It was there that he founded the settlement of Providence, Rhode Island. At this time, he became a Baptist and was baptized by immersion for the first time since his conversion. He served as governor of the new colony from 1654 to 1657. Under his leadership, Rhode Island was the first colony in the New World to establish complete religious liberty for all men. Williams identified with what is known as Particular Baptists like John Bunyan (1600s), William Carey (early 1800s), and Charles Spurgeon (late 1800s). Particular Baptists are Baptists who believe in a Calvinist or Reformed interpretation of salvation. The Particular Baptists arose in England in the 1600s and took their name from the doctrine of particular redemption (redemption by election and predestination).

John Clarke (1609–1676)

John Clarke was a medical doctor, Baptist minister, cofounder of the colony of Rhode Island and Providence Plantations, author of its influential charter, and a leading advocate of religious freedom in the Americas. Under the influence of Mark Lucar, who came from the Particular Baptists of London, Clarke initiated baptism by immersion of believers only as the manner of entrance into the church in what became the second Baptist church founded in America. Clarke was called a Puritan of the Puritans and dedicated himself to eliminating the king's ability to direct the church. Church historian, Dr. Tom Nettles says that certain comments from Clarke's confession of faith show him to be a decided Calvinist. A number of people have called him the Father of American Baptists. Here is one of John Clarke's quotes from Tom Nettles:

Election is the decree of God, of his free love, grace, and mercy, choosing some men to faith, holiness and eternal life, for the praise of his glorious mercy; I Thes. i. 4, II Thes. ii. 13, Rom. viii. 29, 30. The cause which moved the Lord to elect them who are chosen, was

---

[77] Ruckman, "Roger Williams, 1603–1684, First Baptist Church," https://believersweb.org/view.cfm?ID=146, posted on: March 17, 2003.

none other but his mere good will and pleasure, Luke xii, 32.[2].[78]

John Owen (1616–1683)

John Owen was a Puritan by upbringing. He became an English Nonconformist church leader, theologian, and academic administrator at the University of Oxford. John Owen was called the Prince of the English Divines. He was regarded as a genius with learning second only to Calvin and indisputably the leading proponent of high Calvinism in England in the late seventeenth century. He entered Queen's College, Oxford, at the age of twelve and studied the classics, mathematics, philosophy, theology, Hebrew, and rabbinical writings. Throughout his teen years, young Owen studied eighteen to twenty hours per day.

In 1644, Owen married Mary Rooke and the couple had eleven children, but ten of them died in infancy. The one daughter who survived to adulthood got married, but died of consumption shortly thereafter. Oliver Cromwell liked Owen and took him as his chaplain on his expeditions both to Ireland and Scotland (1649–1651). Owen's fame was at its height from 1651 to 1660 when he played a prominent part in the religious, political, and academic life of the nation. He was active in preaching and writing until his death. He declined invitations to the ministry in Boston (1663) and the presidency of Harvard (1670). Of his more than eighty works, one of his main compositions on election and predestination was called *The Display of Arminianism* (1642). Here is an extract from John Owen's *The Death of Death in the Death of Christ*:

> To which I may add this dilemma to our Universalists. God imposed His wrath due unto, and Christ underwent the pains of hell for:
>
> 1. Either all the sins of all men,
> 2. Or all the sins of some men,
> 3. Or some sins of all men.
>
> If the last, some sins of all men, then have all men some sins to answer for and so shall no man be saved. For if God entered into judgment with us, though it were with all mankind for one sin, no flesh should be justified in his sight. . . . "If the LORD should mark iniquities, who should stand?" (Ps. cxxx.2 [sic.][Psalm 130:2]) We might all go to cast all that we have 'to the moles and to the bats, to go into the clefts of the rocks, and into the tops of the ragged rocks, for fear of the Lord, and for the glory of his majesty." [Isa. ii. 20, 21]

---

[78] https://graceonlinelibrary.org/church-history/baptists/the-rise-demise-of-calvinism-among-southern-baptists-by-tom-nettles/.

If the second, that is it which we affirm, that Christ in their stead and room suffered for all the sins of all the elect in the world. If the first, why then, are not all freed from the punishment of all their sins? You will say, "Because of their unbelief, they will not believe." But this unbelief, is it a sin or not? If not, why should they be punished for it? If it be, then Christ underwent the punishment due to it, or not. If so then why must that hinder them more than their other sins, for which He died from partaking of the fruit of his death? If He did not, then did He not die for all their sins. Let them choose which part they will.[79]

William Kiffin (1616–1701)

William Kiffin was a seventeenth century English Baptist minister (Particular Baptist) who also became rich as a successful business man in the wool trade with Holland and other countries. He carried on his business affairs with so much skill that in a few years he was among the wealthiest men in London and known by all classes of society throughout the kingdom as one of the greatest of English merchant-princes.

The English monarch Charles II once asked Kiffin for a loan of £40,000. Instead, Kiffin decided to give a gift of £10,000 to Charles. He estimated this saved him £30,000! More significantly, Kiffin would use his influence with the king to plead for and obtain religious toleration for his fellow dissenters. After he was born in London in 1616, the Black Plague swept over his native city in 1625, depriving him of both parents and leaving him with six plague sores. The plague sores were considered incurable. Through the influence of two separate sermons preached by Mr. Davenport and Mr. Coleman in London, Mr. Kiffin received Christ as his personal Lord and Savior.

After joining a Congregational church, he felt called to the ministry and in 1638, he joined the Baptist church where Rev. John Spilsbury was pastor. From this church, another group went forth in 1640 that formed still another church. This new organization met in Devonshire Square and elected Mr. Kiffin as their pastor. He kept this position for sixty-one years. He was the only man to sign both the First London Confession of Faith of 1644 and the Second London Confession of Faith of 1689.

The First London Confession of Faith (1644) became the religious statement for the newly organized London Particular Baptists. It was a pro-Calvinist statement of doctrine and one of the first published documents of its type in England. This document predates the Westminster Confession of Faith (1646). The second edition was issued as the London Confession of Faith (1649). The Particular Baptists embraced the Calvinistic perspective of predestination (Particular Atonement meaning salvation for the particular elect). This is one theory for the possible origin of the name.

[79] Vol X, p 173, *The Works of John Owen.*

Particular Baptists congregations could be Independent or Congregational in their church government, administration, and leadership styles. Particular Baptists congregations were known for their very strict administration of their congregations. During the period known as the Interregnum (1649–1660),[80] the Particular Baptists with their strong Calvinist message, attained large memberships throughout Great Britain and Ireland. By 1644, there were some forty-seven congregations outside of London. Many Particular Baptists also sought religious freedom in the New World where they were able to multiply and grow in the new English colonies.[81]

Thomas Manton (1620–1677)

Thomas Manton was an English Puritan clergyman. Although Manton is not well known now, in his day he was held in as much esteem as men like John Owen. He was most known for his skilled expository preaching and was a favorite of John Charles Ryle (who championed his republication in the mid-nineteenth century) and Charles Spurgeon. When speaking of Manton, Ryle said he was "a man who could neither say, nor do, nor write anything without being observed." Spurgeon said his works contained "a mighty mountain of sound theology" and his sermons were "second to none" to his contemporaries." Spurgeon went on to say, "Manton is not brilliant, but he is always clever. He is not oratorical, but he is powerful. He is not striking, but he is deep."

Manton's finest work was probably his *Exposition of James*. Rev. Manton said,

His justice cannot be impeached, because He infuseth no evil, enforceth to no evil, only ordaineth what shall be. His goodness cannot be impeached for suffering things which He can turn to such advantage for His own glory and the creature's good. And therefore, as the sun shineth upon a dunghill without having his beams polluted by it, so God's ordination taketh in the sin of the creatures without any blemish to itself. God's decrees are immanent

---

[80] Cromwell's military successes at Drogheda in Ireland (1649), Dunbar in Scotland (1650) and Worcester in England (1651) forced Charles I's son, Charles, into foreign exile despite being accepted and crowned King in Scotland. From 1649 to 1660, England was therefore a republic during a period known as the Interregnum ("between reigns"). The country's rulers tried to redefine and establish a workable constitution without a monarchy. Throughout the Interregnum, Cromwell's relationship with Parliament was a troubled one, with tensions over the nature of the constitution and the issue of supremacy, control of the armed forces and debate over religious toleration. In 1653 Parliament was dissolved, and under the Instrument of Government, Oliver Cromwell became Lord Protector, later refusing the offer of the throne. Further disputes with the House of Commons followed and at one stage Cromwell resorted to regional rule by a number of the army's Major Generals. After Cromwell's death in 1658, and the failure of his son Richard's short-lived Protectorate, the army under General Monk invited Charles I's son to become King as Charles II (Interregnum (1649–1660), The Royal Family), www.royal.uk/interregnum-1649–1660.

[81] This summary of William Kiffin's life, work, and ministry is found at http://particularbaptist.com/history/particular_williamkiffin.html.

in Himself, working nothing that is evil in the creatures. Other things might be said, but I would not perplex the matter.[82]

Thomas Watson (1620–1686)

Thomas Watson was an English Nonconformist, Puritan preacher, and author. He wrote the following about being elected and called:

Whom he predestinated, them he also called. Election is the foundation cause of our effectual calling. It is not because some are more worthy to partake of the heavenly calling than others, for we were "all in our blood" (Ezekiel 16:6). What worthiness is in us? What worthiness was there in Mary Magdelene, out of whom seven devils were cast? What worthiness was in the Corinthians, when God began to call them by the gospel? They were fornicators, effeminate, idolaters, "such were some of you, but you are washed." Before being effectually called by God, we were not only without strength, but His "enemies" (Colossians 1:21). So, the foundation of our effectual calling is election. 2 Timothy 1:9: "It is God who saved us and chose us to live a holy life. He did this not because we deserved it, but because that was His plan long before the world began—to show His love and kindness to us through Christ Jesus."[83]

Francis Turretin (1623–1687)

Francis Turretin was a Swiss-Italian Reformed scholastic theologian known as a zealous opponent of the theology of the Academy of Saumur (embodied by Moise Amyraut and called Amyraldianism). As an earnest defender of the Calvinistic orthodoxy represented by the Synod of Dort and as one of the authors of the Helvetic Consensus, he defended the formulation of predestination from the Synod of Dort and the verbal inspiration of the Bible.

Ought predestination to be publicly taught and preached?

We affirm. . . . Wearied with the contentions arising from this doctrine in almost every age, they [other teachers and preachers] think that it is best for the peace of the church and the tranquility of conscience to let these questions alone (since by them scruples are suggested and doubts generated, which are calculated to weaken the faith of the weak and

[82] James Darling, *The Complete Works of Thomas Manton,* vol. 3 (Cyclopaedia Bibliographica, 1854), 1953–1954.

[83] Thomas Watson, A Body of Divinity: Contained in Sermons upon the Westminster Assembly's Catechism. Copyright 2009, (Zeeland, MI: Reformed Church Publications, 2009), www.reformedchurchpublications. org.

to drive men to desperation or into carnal security). But this opinion is more honest than true and cannot be readily received by those who have known the richest fruits of consolation and sanctification to redound to believers from this doctrine properly understood. Hence we think that this doctrine should be neither wholly suppressed from a preposterous modesty nor curiously pried into by a rash presumption. . . . we maintain (with the orthodox) that predestination can be taught with profit, provided this is done soberly from the word of God. . . . Christ and the apostles frequently taught it (as appears from the Gospel, Matthew 11:20, 25; 13:11; 25:34; Luke 10:20; 12:32; John 8:47; 15:16 and in other places, and from the epistles of Paul (the whole of Rom. 9 and Rom. 8:29, 30; Eph. 1:4, 5; 2 Tim. 1:9; 1 Thess. 5:9; 2 Thess. 2:13). Nor otherwise do Peter, James and John express themselves who speak repeatedly of this mystery whenever occasion offered. Now if it was proper for them to teach it, why is it not proper for us to learn it?

Why should God teach what would have been better (*arrifton*) unspoken (*ameinon*)? Why did He wish to proclaim those things which it would be better not to know? Do we wish to be more prudent than God or to prescribe rules to Him? . . . . It is one of the foundational gospel doctrines of our faith. It cannot be ignored without great injury to the church and to believers. For it is the fountain of our gratitude to God, the root of humility, the most firm anchor of our confidence in all temptations, the fulcrum of the sweetest consolation, and the most powerful spur (*incitamentum*) to piety and holiness. . . . If some abuse this doctrine either to licentiousness or to desperation, this happens not per se from the doctrine itself, but accidentally, from the vice of men who most wickedly wrest it to their own destruction. Indeed there is no doctrine from which more powerful incitements to piety can be drawn and richer streams of confidence and consolation flow (as will be seen in the proper place). . . .

The mystery of predestination is too sublime to be comprehended by us as to the why (to *diod*) (as he is rash who would attempt to find out or to assign the reasons and the causes of it). But this does not hinder it from being taught in Scripture as to the fact (to *hoti*) and from being firmly held by us. To things therefore must be distinguished here: the one, what God has revealed in His Word; the other, what He has concealed. The former we cannot despise (unless rashly). "The secret things," says Scripture, "belong unto God: but those things which are revealed belong unto us and to our children" (Dr. 29:29). To neglect things revealed argues ingratitude, but to search into things concealed argues pride. "We must not therefore deny what is plain, because we cannot comprehend what is hidden," as Augustine expresses it (On the Gift of Perseverance). . . .The election of some necessarily implies the passing and rejecting of others: "Many are called," said Christ, "but few chosen" (Matthew 20:16) and Paul, 'The election hath obtained, and the rest were blinded' (Romans 11:7). Hence, Paul uses the verb "heilto" to designate election, which implies the separation of some from others: "God from the beginning heilto, i.e., hath taken out and separated you to salvation through sanctification of the Spirit and belief in the truth" (2 Thess. 2:13).[84]

Turretin wrote the following about predestination:

Predestination should be taught, because it is one of the primary Gospel doctrines, and foundations of faith. It cannot be ignored without great injury to the Church and to believers, since it is the fount of our gratitude to God, the root of humility, the foundation and most firm anchor of confidence in all temptations, the fulcrum of the sweetest consolation, and the most powerful spur to piety and holiness. If some abuse this doctrine, either to licentiousness or to desperation, this happens not per se from the doctrine itself, but accidentally from the vice of men who most wickedly wrest it to their own destruction. Indeed, there is no doctrine from which more powerful incentives to piety can be drawn and richer streams of confidence and consolation flow. Again, predestination should be taught, because Christ and the apostles frequently taught it. Nor otherwise do Peter, James and John express themselves, who speak repeatedly of this mystery whenever occasion offered. Now if it was proper for them to teach, why is it not for us to learn? Why should God teach what would have been better to be unspoken? Why did He wish to proclaim those things which it would be better not to know? Do we wish to be more prudent than God or to prescribe rules to Him?[85]

Stephen Charnock (1628–1680)

Stephen Charnock was an English Puritan Presbyterian clergyman born in London and converted to the Christian faith while studying at Emmanuel College in Cambridge. He began his spiritual journey as a Puritan divine and eventually gained a position as senior proctor at New College, Oxford. He moved on to Ireland where he became a chaplain to Henry Cromwell, governor of Ireland. In Dublin, he began a regular ministry of preaching to other believers from different classes of society and various denominations. He became well known for his preaching and edifying skills in the pulpit. Charnock began a co-pastorship at Crosby Hall back in London in 1675 and this was his last official place of ministry

[84] *Institutes of Elenctic Theology* (translated by George Musgrave Giger, edited by James T. Dennison, Jr. 1992)

[85] Francis Turretin, *Institutes of Elenic Theology*, 685, Question 6 (P&R Publishing). (Initially published in 1679–1685, Francis work was the fruit of thirty years of teaching at the Academy of Geneva. It became one of the most important works of 17th century Reformed dogmatics. Composed of three volumes, this set of Turretin's *Institutes of Elenctic Theology* is the first edition to be published in the English language. As an ##"elenctic" theology—which affirms and demonstrates the truth in refutation of false doctrine—the Institutes contrasts Reformed understandings of Christian doctrine with conflicting theological perspectives, particularly Roman Catholic, Arminian, and Socinian.)

before his death in 1680. The numerous writings attributed to him were transcribed after his death. (**Note:** A Puritan divine was a member of a religious reform movement known as Puritanism that arose within the Church of England in the late sixteenth century. They believed the Church of England was too similar to the Roman Catholic Church and should eliminate ceremonies and practices not rooted in the Bible.)

Charnock's theological reputation rests mostly upon his "Discourses upon the Existence and Attributes of God," which were a series of lectures delivered to the members of his congregation at Crosby Hall. Here are a few of his thoughts about Ephesians 1:22:

> God hath given all things into His (Jesus) hand, all creatures to rule them, all treasures to bestow them, and all power to protect his people. He hath given Him the world of men and angels to govern and the world of His elect to redeem. He hath put all things under His feet and made Him the head over all things for the church.[86]

John Bunyan (1628–1688)

John Bunyan was the very well-known English Christian writer and preacher who is best known for his book, *The Pilgrim's Progress*. He became a nonconformist and member of an independent church. Although he has been described both as a Baptist and as a Congregationalist, he preferred to be described simply as a Christian.

Regarding the subject of our study, Bunyan wrote,

> I believe that election is free and permanent, being founded in grace and the unchangeable will of God . . . I believe that we are predestinated to be conformed to the image of his Son (Rom 8:29, 30) . . . I believe that without Christ Jesus there is neither election, grace, nor salvation (Eph. 1:3–14) . . . I believe that no man can know his election, but by his calling. Election does not foretell or prevent the means which are appointed of God to bring us to Christ, to grace and to glory (2 Pet. 1:6–11). I believe that in effectual calling the Holy Ghost must accompany the work of the Gospel and that with mighty power. Calling is the fruit of electing love (I Thess. 1:4–10), an effectual awakening about the evil of sin and especially of unbelief and great awakenings about the world to come and the glory of unseen things.[87]

---

[86] *The Complete Works of Stephen Charnock*, vol. 4, "The Misery of Unbelievers," John 3:36 (Banner of Truth Trust).

[87] John Bunyan, *Miscellaneous Works,* vol. 4, *A Confession of Faith*, edited by T. L. Underwood (Clarendon Press, first edition, 1990).

Benjamin Keach (1640–1704)

Benjamin Keach was the Particular Baptist preacher in London whose name was given to *Keach's Catechism*. He was baptized at the age of fifteen and began preaching at eighteen. He first pastored a congregation at Winslow, before moving in 1668 to the church at Horse-lie-down, Southwark where he remained for thirty-six years as pastor. This church eventually became the New Park Street Church. Then it moved to the Metropolitan Tabernacle under the leadership of Charles Spurgeon.

Keach wrote between 40 and 60 works and was the most prolific author among seventeenth century Baptists. His best-known work is *Parables and Metaphors of Scripture*. He wrote a work titled *The Child's Instructor*, which immediately brought him under persecution. He was fined and pilloried in 1664. ("Pilloried" means he was locked to a wooden framework on a post, with holes for his head and hands, to be exposed to public scorn as punishment.)

During the 1660s he continued to face many hardships and persecutions because of his preaching and publishing. At one time, between 1660 and 1668 (referred to as the era of great persecution), Keach was grabbed by a troop of cavalrymen while he was preaching. Four of them were so enraged with him that they swore they would trample him to death with their horses. They tied him up and forced him to lie on the ground. Just as they were about to spur their horses down upon him, their commanding officer arrived and stopped them. Without this officer's help, Keach would have probably been killed. Instead, he was imprisoned, but eventually released again.

As mentioned above, he is credited with the writing of a catechism commonly known as *Keach's Catechism*, even though it may have been compiled by William Collins. Keach is also known to have promoted the introduction of hymn singing in the Baptist churches. His church (Horsleydown) was probably the first church in England to sing hymns, as opposed to psalms and paraphrases. Keach's hymnbook, published in 1691, provoked heated debate in the 1692 Assembly of Particular Baptists. By the time the church at Horsleydown was established, Keach had become a Calvinist. Shortly after arriving in London he quickly became acquainted with prominent Calvinistic Baptist pastors like William Kiffin, Hanserd Knollys, and John Norcott.

He wrote the following (from one of his final major works published in 1704): "If God doth not meet a sinner or move toward a sinner by His Spirit, the sinner can never meet Him. Can that which is dead move itself? Sinners are dead or without a principle of divine life (naturally). When life is infused, the soul must be influenced by the Holy Spirit."[88]

---

[88] Benjamin Keach, *Gospel Mysteries Unveiled*, chapter 3 (Gale ECCO, Print Editions, 2010), 57.

Matthew Henry (1662–1714)

Matthew Henry was an English Presbyterian minister and commentator on the Bible. His father Philip possessed enough private means to give his son a good education. Matthew gave up his original legal studies for theology. He pastored in Chester and Hackney. In 1714 he died suddenly of apoplexy at the Queen's Aid House in Nantwich while on a journey from Chester to London. Matthew Henry's six-volume *Exposition of the Old and New Testaments* (1708–1710) or Complete Commentary, provides an exhaustive verse by verse study of the Bible. He covers the entire Old Testament and the Gospels and Acts in the New Testament. After his death, the work was finished (Romans through Revelation) by thirteen other nonconformist ministers, partly based upon notes taken by Henry's hearers, and edited by George Burder and John Hughes in 1811. In his commentary, he addresses TULIP (the five points of Calvinism) and shows he was a Five Point Calvinist who also believed in man's responsibility, soul-winning, and the free offer of the gospel to all, so that God could draw the elect to Himself. The evangelist George Whitefield (1714–1770) was born the year Matthew Henry died and was deeply touched by his commentary. He read it throughout his ministry. A recent study by an American scholar, David Crump, has shown that Henry's "in depth, practical, Calvinistic and biblical exposition" formed the backdrop for many of Whitefield's sermons. Whitefield read Matthew Henry's commentary through four times during his lifetime, while at the same time preaching an estimated 18,000 sermons, an average of five hundred a year or ten a week. Spurgeon advised his Bible students to read the entire multi-volume Matthew Henry commentary set in the twelve months after they graduated from his Pastor's College. Here are a few of Matthew Henry's words on the effectual calling of the Holy Spirit from his Westminster Shorter Catechism:

"Effectual calling is a work of God's Spirit whereby, convincing us of our sins and misery, enlightening our minds in the knowledge of Christ, and renewing our wills He doth persuade and enable us to embrace Jesus Christ, freely offered to us in the gospel."[89]

Cotton Mather (1663–1728)

Cotton Mather was an influential preacher in a large Boston church and a scientist. As a Calvinist in one of New England's first Puritan churches, he accepted the doctrines of Original Sin, Total Depravity, Predestination, and Eternal Damnation. He believed through Christ's death on the cross, God bestowed eternal grace to some chosen men, who from thenceforth were called the elect. During the last part of the 1600's he was consumed

---

[89] Matthew Henry, "Westminster Shorter Catechism Project: A Scripture Catechism in the Method of the Assemblies" (Andesite Press, 2015), 71.

with the desire to do charitable works. As a child and then as a Christian, medicine had a great appeal for him along with theology, because it combined the intellectual lure of the natural sciences and the moral appeal of doing good for fellow human beings. At one time, he thought a speech impediment might hinder him from entering the ministry, but he overcame his speech problem and never practiced medicine, even though he had gained a great knowledge of the subject.

His efforts to promote public health in the Boston area ushered in the beginnings of modern preventive medicine. Mather learned about successful smallpox inoculations in Europe and proposed its use to New England physicians when a smallpox epidemic threatened Boston. This won him the title of "a conscientious busy body" among the local physicians who did not like a preacher meddling in their profession. He was able to convince one physician named Zabdiel Boylson to try the smallpox inoculation technique. When it was successful it resulted in the acceptance of the smallpox inoculation in America.[90]

---

[90] Cotton Mather, *Free-grace, Maintained and Improved,* or *The General Offer of the Gospel* (printed in Boston by B. Green in 1706).

31 ✦

Eighteenth-Century Church Leaders through the American Revolution Who Affirmed the Decrees

This chapter is dedicated to great spiritual leaders from the 1700s who believed, taught, and wrote about election and predestination and had very positive effects upon civil society.

Hermann Boerhaave (1668–1738)

Hermann Boerhaave was the son of a Dutch Reformed (Dutch Calvinism) minister, who was expected to also become a minister like his father. Hermann eventually chose to become a botanist, as well as a physician, after becoming fascinated with chemistry. He is considered to be the founder of clinical teaching and of the modern academic hospital. One of his notable achievements was to demonstrate the connection of symptoms to lesions. He was also the first to isolate the chemical urea from urine. His motto was *Simplex sigillum veri* (simplicity is the sign of truth). From 1950 to 1970, Boerhaave's image was printed on Dutch twenty-guilder banknotes. The Leiden University Medical Centre organizes medical trainings called Boerhaave Courses. His reputation so increased the fame of the University of Leiden, especially as a school of medicine, that it became popular with visitors from every part of Europe. All the princes of Europe sent him pupils, who described him as a skillful professor, an indefatigable teacher, and an affectionate guardian.

When Peter the Great went to Holland in 1716, he also took lessons from Boerhaave. Linnaeus traveled to see him, as did Voltaire. A Chinese mandarin sent him a letter addressed to "the illustrious Boerhaave, physician in Europe," which did reach him in due time. The operating theatre of the University of Leiden, in which he once worked as an anatomist, is now at the center of a museum named after him (the Boerhaave Museum). The near-Earth minor planet (8176) 1991 WA in the Apollo group is nicknamed Boerhaave in his honor. He first described what is now known as the Boerhaave Syndrome, which involves tearing of the esophagus, usually a consequence of vigorous vomiting. In 1724, he described the case of Baron Jan von Wassenaer, a Dutch admiral who died of this condition, following a gluttonous feast and subsequent regurgitation.

In his *Biography of Boerhaave,* Samuel Johnson described Boerhaave's Christian life like this:

But his knowledge, however uncommon, holds, in his character, but the second place; his virtue was yet much more uncommon than his learning. He was an admirable example of temperance, fortitude, humility, and devotion. His piety, and a religious sense of his dependence on God, was the basis of all his virtues, and the principle of his whole conduct. He was too sensible of his weakness to ascribe anything to himself, or to conceive that he could subdue passion, or withstand temptation, by his own natural power; he attributed every good thought, and every laudable action, to the father of goodness. Being once asked by a friend, who had often admired his patience under great provocations, whether he knew what it was to be angry, and by what means he had so entirely suppressed that impetuous and ungovernable passion, he answered, with the utmost frankness and sincerity, that he was naturally quick of resentment, but that he had, by daily prayer and meditation, at length attained to this mastery over himself.

As soon as he arose in the morning, throughout his whole life, his daily practice was to retire for an hour to private prayer and meditation. He often told his friends that this gave him spirit and vigor in the business of the day, and this he, therefore commended, as the best rule of life. For nothing he knew could support the soul, in all distresses, but a confidence in the supreme being. Nor can a steady and rational magnanimity flow from any other source than a consciousness of the divine favor.

He asserted on all occasions, the divine authority and sacred efficacy of the Holy Scriptures and maintained that they alone taught the way of salvation, and that they only could give peace of mind. The excellency of the Christian religion was the frequent subject of his conversation. A strict obedience to the doctrine and a diligent imitation of the example of our blessed savior, he often declared to be the foundation of true tranquility. He recommended to his friends a careful observation of the precept of Moses, concerning the love of God and man. He worshipped God as He is in himself, without attempting to inquire into His nature. He desired only to think of God and what God knows of himself. There he stopped, lest, by indulging his own ideas, he should form a deity from his own imagination and sin by falling down before him. To the will of God, he paid an absolute submission, without endeavoring to discover the reason of His determinations and this he accounted the first and most inviolable duty of a Christian. When he heard of a criminal condemned to die, he used to think—Who can tell whether this man is not better than I or if I am better, it is not to be ascribed to myself, but to the goodness of God.

So far was this man from being made impious by philosophy or vain by knowledge or by virtue, that he ascribed all his abilities to the bounty, and all his goodness to the grace of God. May his example extend its influence to his admirers and followers! May those who study his writings imitate his life and those who endeavor after his knowledge, aspire likewise to his piety![91]

Isaac Watts (1674–1748)

Isaac Watts was the famous English hymn writer, pastor, theologian, and logician. He is recognized as the Father of English Hymnody and credited with some 750 hymns. Many of his hymns remain in use today, and have been translated into many languages. Watts was the oldest of nine siblings, the children of a Huguenot mother and a father bold enough to be jailed twice for his religious convictions. The elder Watts belonged to the Dissenters or the Nonconformists (the English brand of Puritanism).

Isaac was educated by his father and taught, from the youngest age, Latin, Hebrew, and Greek. He received his higher education from a Nonconformist Academy. Upon graduating from the Academy at age twenty, he returned home where he began writing hymns. His hymns were very Calvinistic in nature. One of his most hailed accomplishments was rewriting the Psalms of David in rhyming English verse. One of the best examples is His well-known "Joy to the World."

Kristen Johnson reported the following in her book called *Isaac Watts: His Life and Hymnody*:

Watts was officially introduced in America in 1729, when Benjamin Franklin reprinted *The Psalms of David*. In the 1740s with the Great Awakening, George Whitefield's lively preaching style needed to be supplemented with something other than the dissonant sounds of the dry metric Psalms. Watts, along with a few other English hymnists, proved to be the perfect remedy. Whitefield played a great role in introducing hymn-singing to New England, and consequently quickened an interest in hymn-singing, and increased the popularity of Watts' work.[92]

---

[91] Rina Knoeff in her work called *Herman Boerhaave* (1668–1738): Calvinist Chemist and Physician reported that he was a fully engaged Calvinist throughout his life.

[92] From *Isaac Watts: His Life and Hymnody*, by Kristen Johnson, 2000. Originally written for the course Eighteenth-Century American Theology, Hillsdale College, October 9, 2000.

The American Puritan pastor Jonathan Edwards commented in 1742 that his Northampton congregation sang Watts' hymns, almost to the exclusion of psalms. Watts and Edwards had a mutual respect for one another, and each made the other's work well-known in his own land through printing, and through allowing the other's work in his pulpit. For Watts, this meant reading Edwards's "A Faithful Narrative of the Surprising Work of God" to his congregation and overseeing its printing in England. For Edwards, this meant introducing Watts' hymnody into regular worship services at his Northampton church, thus popularizing Watts' work in New England.

Thomas Boston (1676–1732)

Thomas Boston was a Scottish church leader and schoolmaster. His parents were both Covenanters. He was educated at Edinburgh and licensed in 1697 by the presbytery of Chirnside. In 1699, he became minister of the small parish of Simprin, where there were only ninety examinable persons. Previously, he was a schoolmaster in Glencairn. In 1704, while visiting a member of his flock, he found a book brought into Scotland by a common-wealth soldier called *The Marrow of Modern Divinity* by Edward Fisher published in 1645. This was a compendium of the opinions of leading Reformation thinkers on the doctrines of grace and the offer of the gospel. Rev. Boston later published an edition of this book with his own notes. Here is an excerpt from his edition on the "effectual calling":

Effectual calling is the first entrance of a soul into the state of grace, the first step by which God's eternal purpose of love descends unto sinners, and we again ascend toward the glory to which we are chosen. And upon the matter, it is the same with conversion and regeneration. . . . It is neither the piety, parts, nor seriousness of those who are employed to carry the gospel call to sinners, I Cor. iii. 7. Indeed, if moral persuasion were sufficient to bring sinners back to God, men that have the art of persuading, and can speak movingly and seriously could not fail to have vast numbers of converts. But that work is not so brought about, Luke xvi. ult. Hence said Abraham to the rich man in hell, "If they hear not Moses and the prophets, neither will they be persuaded though one rose from the dead." Never did these, conjunctly or severally, appear in any, as in any, as in Christ, who "spake as never man spake." But behold the issue, John xii. 37, 38. But though he had done so many miracles before them, yet they believed not on him: that the saying Esaias the prophet might be fulfilled, which he spake, "Lord, who hath believed our report? and to whom hath the arm of the Lord been revealed?". . . Neither is it one that uses his own free will better than another does. . . .

Romans 9:6. "It is not of him that willeth, nor of him that runneth, but of God that sheweth mercy." For every man will be unwilling till the power from another quarter make him willing, John vi. 44. If it were so, one man should make himself to differ from another in that grand point. But hear what the Apostle Paul says, 1 Cor. 4:7. "Who maketh thee to differ from another?" Men are dead in trespasses and sins, and such cannot difference themselves . . . . We may say in this case, "Not by might, nor by power, but by the Spirit of the Lord." It is the Spirit of the Lord, accompanying the call of the word, that makes it effectual, John 6:63. Hence days of the plentiful effusion of the Spirit are good days for the take of souls, and contrarywise, when the Spirit is restrained, Psalm. cx.

Therefore, Isaiah resolves the question thus, "Who hath believed our report? and to whom is the arm of the Lord revealed?" The report may reach the ears, but it is the arm of the Lord that must open the heart. . .[93]

Clearly, Dr. Boston held that it is God's work that saves a man, and not his own.

John Gill (1697–1771)

John Gill was an English Baptist pastor, biblical scholar, and theologian who held to a firm Calvinistic theology of redemption. Born in Kettering, Northamptonshire, he attended Kettering Grammar School where he mastered the Latin classics and learned Greek by age eleven. He continued self-study in everything from logic to Hebrew and his love for Hebrew remained throughout his life. Rev. Gill summarized his convictions on election in this way:

Eternal predestination in this sense, is no other than eternal providence, of which actual providence in time is the execution. To deny this, is to deny the providence of God and His government of the world, which none but Deists and Atheists will do. It is to think and speak unworthy of God, as not being the all-knowing and all-wise and sovereign ruler of the world. Prophecy or foretelling things to come could not be without a predestination of them. There are so many instances in Scripture such as the stay of the Israelites in Egypt and their departure from thence, the seventy years captivity of the Jews in Babylon and their return at the end of that time, the exact coming of the Messiah at such a certain time, with many others. And some seemingly the most casual and contingent, as the birth of persons by name a hundred or hundreds of years before they were born, as Josiah and Cyrus and a man's carrying a pitcher of water at such a time, to such a place (1 Kings 13:2; Isa. 44:28; 45:1; Luke 22:10, 13). How could these things be foretold with certainty, unless it was determined and appointed, they should be?

---

[93] *The Whole Works of the Late Reverend and Learned Mr. Thomas Boston, Minister of the Gospel at Etterick,* vol. 7, by Thomas Boston, Arkose Press (October 21, 2015).

There is nothing that comes by chance to God, nothing done without His knowledge, nor without His will or permission and nothing without His determination. Everything, even the most minute thing, respecting His creatures and what is done in this world in all periods and ages of time, is by His appointment.

For the proof of which see the following passages (KJV):

To everything there is a season, and a time to every purpose under the heaven; a time to be born and a time to die, and a time fixed by the purpose of God for each of these. (Ecclesiastes 3:1–2)

Seeing his days are determined, the number of his months are with thee, thou hast appointed his bounds that he cannot pass. (Job 14:5)

He performeth the thing that is appointed for me, and many such things are with him. (Job 23:14)

And he doth according to his will in the army of heaven, and among the inhabitants of the earth, and none can stay his hand, or say unto him, what dost thou? (Daniel 4:35)

Being predestinated according to the purpose of him who worketh all things after the counsel of his own will. (Ephesians 1:11)

Known unto God are all his works from the beginning of the world. (Acts 15:18

And He hath determined the times before appointed, and the bounds of their habitation. (Acts 17:26)

Are not two sparrows sold for a farthing and one of them shall not fall to the ground without your Father; but the very hairs of your head are all numbered. (Matthew 10:29–30)[94]

Daniel Bernoulli (1700–1782)

Daniel Bernoulli was a Swiss mathematician, physicist, and one of the many prominent mathematicians in the Bernoulli family. He is particularly remembered for his applications of mathematics to mechanics, especially fluid mechanics, and for his pioneering work in probability and statistics. He contributed significantly to the fields of hydrodynamics and mathematical physics. Bernoulli's Principle is critical in aerodynamics applications. Bernoulli's work is still studied at length by many schools of science throughout the world. He adopted the Calvinist faith which had forced his grandparents to flee from Antwerp to avoid religious persecution.[95]

---

[94] John Gill, *The Doctrines of God's Everlasting Love to His Elect and Their Eternal Union with Christ* (published by BiblioBazaar, May 2010), 57.

[95] "The Religious Affiliation of Physicist, Mathematician and Hydrodynamics Scientist Daniel Bernoulli" from J. J. O'Connor and E. F. Robertson. "Johann Bernoulli" article on website of the School of Mathematics and Statistics, University of St Andrews, Scotland. Information can be found at: www.history.mcs.st andrews.ac.uk/
history/Mathematicians/Bernoulli_Johann.html, access September 26, 2005.

Jonathan Edwards (1703–1758)

Jonathan Edwards was an evangelical pastor and theologian, who is widely acknowledged to be America's most important and original philosophical theologian and one of America's greatest intellectuals. He liked to study for thirteen hours a day. Edwards's theological work is broad in scope, but he was rooted in Reformed theology from the Puritan heritage. Edwards played a vital part in shaping the First Great Awakening in the American colonies.

Edwards oversaw some of the first revivals from 1733–1735 at his church in Northampton, Massachusetts. He delivered his famous sermon titled "Sinners in the Hands of an Angry God," which caused a revival to break out among his church members. He authored many books like *The End For Which God Created the World, The Life of David Brainerd,* which helped to inspire thousands of missionaries throughout the eighteenth and nineteenth centuries and *Religious Affections,* which many Christians still read today. Edwards died from a smallpox inoculation shortly after beginning his presidency at the College of New Jersey (which later became Princeton). A long line of godly and highly accomplished descendants came from Edwards and his wife, Sarah. They produced scores of clergymen, thirteen presidents of institutions of higher learning, sixty-five professors, and many other persons of notable achievements. Edwards and his wife were also the grandparents of Aaron Burr, third vice president of the United States. Here a few of Edwards's comments on election, predestination, and the sovereignty of God:

> From childhood up, my mind had been full of objections against the doctrine of God's sovereignty. It used to appear like a horrible doctrine to me. But I remember the time very well, when I seemed to be convinced, and fully satisfied as to this sovereignty of God. But I never could give an account of how or by what means I was thus convinced, not in the least imagining at the time, nor a long time after, that there was any extraordinary influence of God's Spirit in it, but only that now I saw further and my reason apprehended the justice and reasonableness of it. However, my mind rested in it and it put an end to all those cavils and objections. And there has been a wonderful alteration in my mind, in respect to the doctrine of God's sovereignty from that day to this, so that I scarce ever have found so much as the rising of an objection against it. The doctrine has very often appeared exceeding pleasant, bright, and sweet. Absolute sovereignty is what I love to ascribe to God.
>
> Whether God has decreed all things that ever came to pass or not, all that own the being of God, own that He knows all things beforehand. Now, it is self-evident, that if He knows all things beforehand, He either doth approve of them or He doth not approve of them.

That is, He is either willing they should be or He is not willing they should be. But to will that they should be, is to decree them.[96]

"While it behooved God to create man pure and without sin, it was of His 'good pleasure' and 'mere and arbitrary grace' for Him to grant any person the faith necessary to incline him or her toward holiness, and that God might deny this grace without any disparagement to any of His character."[97]

Edwards described God's Sovereignty as follows:

The Sovereignty of God is the stumbling block on which thousands fall and perish and if we go contending with God about His sovereignty it will be our eternal ruin. It is absolutely necessary that we should submit to God as an absolute sovereign and the sovereign of our souls, as one who may have mercy on whom He will have mercy and harden whom He will.[98]

John Brine (1703–1765)

John Brine was an English Particular Baptist minister who took a principle lead in the public activities and dialogue that concerned the Particular Baptist denomination. Although he left orders that no special funeral sermon should be preached for him, his friend, Dr. John Gill did take that occasion to preach a sermon to his own congregation from 1 Corinthians 15:10: "By the grace of God I am what I am." John Brine was a strong Calvinist in his theology. The following comments are taken from his *Various Treatises*, specifically the section called "On the Depravity of Human Nature."[99]

1. Pride in men, as it is a sin, so it is extreme folly. For we have lost all that which was the true glory of our nature and are become the subjects of such base and sordid lusts, as render us most abominable and hateful.
2. Salvation must be unconditional and free, because as the human mind is thus debased, it is incapable of performing duty in order to the reception of divine benefits.

---

[96] *The Works of Jonathan Edwards*, (Philadelphia, PA: Banner of Truth Trust): vol. 2:525.

[97] From the "Public Lecture" Edwards preached in Boston on July 7, 1731; afterward published under the title, "God Glorified—in Man's Dependence."

[98] Jonathan Edwards, "A Divine and Supernatural Light, Immediately Imparted to the Soul by the Spirit of God" (1734), Sermon Chapbook Series (Minneapolis: Curiosmith Bookshop, 2012), www.curiosmith.com.

[99] See http://www.edintone.com/baptists/john-brine.

3. It is astonishing goodness in God favorably to regard men.

4. He is at full liberty to bestow the special blessings of His grace on whom He pleases, since none can prevent divine goodness by acts of holy obedience.

5. It betrays self-ignorance in those who extol human wisdom and power.

6. If we imagine that we have a natural capacity of doing good, it is an evidence that we are in state of unregeneracy.

Leonhard Euler (1707–1783)

Leonhard Euler was a Swiss mathematician and physicist, who made important discoveries in infinitesimal calculus and graph theory. He also introduced much of the modern mathematical terminology and notation, particularly for mathematical analysis, such as the notion of a mathematical function. He is also renowned for his work in mechanics, fluid dynamics, optics, and astronomy. Euler spent most of his adult life in St. Petersburg, Russia, and in Berlin, Prussia. He is considered to be the preeminent mathematician of the eighteenth century and one of the greatest mathematicians ever to have lived. His collected works fill sixty to eighty quarto volumes. A statement attributed to Pierre-Simon Laplace expresses Euler's influence on mathematics: "Read Euler, read Euler, he is the master of us all."

According to one website condensed from E. T. Bell's *Men of Mathematics,*

Euler was a committed Christian and, apparently, a biblical literalist. Having been born into a Calvinist family, Euler retained his firm Calvinist beliefs throughout life, holding daily prayer and worship in his home and sometimes preaching. His father, Paul, was a minister in the church, as was his grandfather. Euler's father wanted him to also follow him into the church ministry. However, being a good Calvinist he realized that one could serve God through mathematics as well as theology and seeing his son's ability in and passion for mathematics, he allowed him to pursue mathematics. Euler always kept his interest in theology as well as mathematics. He believed that mathematics gave him insight into God's good creation.[100]

Steve Bishop is the compiler of *A Bibliography for a Christian Approach to Mathematics* and the author of several articles on the relationship between faith and math and he reports this about Leonhard Euler:

---

[100] https://godandmath.com/2012/01/15/christian-mathematicians-euler/. Also see E.T. Bell, *Men of Mathematics* (Touchstone Book 1937).

Euler was one of the first inventors of the number game Sudoku (though he called it "Latin Squares"). He introduced the letter *e* to represent the base of natural logs, *f(x)* to denote functions, and made countless contributions to number theory and graph theory, most notably he showed that the Koinisberg bridge problem was unsolvable. His name is associated with angles, approximation, circles, cycle, criterion, graphs, operators, polynomials, pseudo primes . . .

George Whitefield (1714–1770)

George Whitefield was the English Anglican preacher who helped spread the First Great Awakening in Britain and throughout the North American colonies. He was probably the most well-known preacher in Britain and America in the eighteenth century. As he traveled through all of the American colonies and drew great crowds and media coverage, he became one of the most widely recognized public figures in colonial America. Mr. Whitefield expressed his views on election and predestination like this:

> Whatever men's reasoning may suggest, if the children of God fairly examine their own experiences—if they do God justice, they must acknowledge that they did not choose God, but that God chose them. And if He chose them at all, it must be from eternity, and that too without anything foreseen in them. Unless they acknowledge this, man's salvation must be in part owing to the free will of man; and if so, . . . Christ Jesus might have died, and never seen the travail of His soul in the salvation of one of His creatures. But I would be tender on this point, and leave persons to be taught it of God. I am of the martyr Bradford's mind. Let a man go to the grammar school of faith and repentance, before he goes to the university of election and predestination.[101]

> I hope we shall catch fire from each other, and that there will be a holy emulation amongst us, who shall most debase man and exalt the Lord Jesus. Nothing but the doctrines of the Reformation can do this. All others leave freewill in man and make him, in part at least, a Savior to himself. My soul, come not thou near the secret of those who teach such things . . . I know Christ is all in all. Man is nothing: he hath a free will to go to hell, but none to go to heaven, till God worketh in him to do of His good pleasure.[102]

> Oh, the excellency of the doctrine of election and of the saint's final perseverance! I am persuaded, till a man comes to believe and feel these important truths, he cannot come to himself, but when convinced of these and assured of their application to his own heart, he then walks by faith indeed! . . . Love, not fear, constrains him to obedience.[103]

[101] *George Whitefield's Journals* (London: Banner of Truth, 1960): 491. Quoted in *George Whitefield, Vol. 1* by Arnold Dallimore (Carlisle, PA.: Banner of Truth Trust, 1977): 570.
[102] George Whitefield, "*Works*" (Carlisle, PA: Banner of Truth Trust, 1967): 89–90.
[103] George Whitefield, "*Works*," op cit., 101.

David Brainerd (1718–1747)

David Brainerd was born in Haddam, Connecticut and he was the sixth child of ten children. He had prominent Puritan figures in his lineage such as Rev. Samuel Whiting. A convinced Calvinist, Brainerd became a Presbyterian missionary to the indigenous Indians in New England. Brainerd was a missionary to Indian tribes in New York, Pennsylvania, and New Jersey. The real fruit of Brainerd's labors became evident in the summer of 1745 when revival broke out among the Indians. Many of the Indians would be in tears as they listened to him preach. After speaking for a short time to them about their souls and salvation, tears would flow among them producing many sobs and many groans. They would be in such great distress for their souls that some could neither leave the meeting nor stand up on their feet. They would lie on the ground crying out in anguish to God for mercy. One of the Indians, who had intended to murder someone, said to his chief, "The paleface is a praying man. The Great Spirit is with him . . . and he brings a wondrous sweet message." His gravestone simply says, "A faithful and laborious missionary to the Stockbridge, Delaware and Susquehanna tribes of Indians."

In her book *From Jerusalem to Irian Jaya: A Biographical History of Christian Missions*, Ruth A. Tucker shares the following about David Brainerd.

> One of the most intriguing missionaries to the American Indians, and perhaps of all time, is David Brainerd, an heir of New England Puritanism and product of the Great Awakening. Brainerd was a zealot. Bringing the gospel to scattered wandering tribes of Indians was his single mission. He spent his life for that cause. At the age of twenty-nine, after a mere five years of missionary work, he died as a result of his strenuous labors. Brainerd's place in history is based largely on the tremendous inspiration his personal life has had on others. His journal, diary, and biography, published by Jonathan Edwards, are classics of Christian literature, and missionaries through the centuries, including William Carey and Henry Martyn, have been deeply influenced by his life.[104]

Brainerd was a Christian for only eight of his twenty-nine years on this earth, and he was a missionary to the Indians for only five of those eight years, but what a fruitful eight years it was though the power of God working in an individual totally offered up to Him. Here are just a few of his beloved quotes from his diary:

> There is a God in heaven who overrules all things for the best and this is the comfort of my soul. We are a long time in learning that all our strength and salvation is in God.

---

[104] Ruth A. Tucker, *A Biographical History of Christian Missions* (Grand Rapids, MI: Zondervan 1983), 80–84.

Oh! how amazing it is that people can talk so much about men's power and goodness, when if God did not hold us back every moment, we should be devils incarnate! God plans all perfect combinations.

The all-seeing eye of God beheld our deplorable state; infinite pity touched the heart of the Father of mercies; and infinite wisdom laid the plan of our recovery.[105]

John C. Ryland (1723–1792)

John C. Ryland was a preacher and pioneer Baptist converted under Benjamin Beddome during days of revival. According to his colleague and biographer William Newman (1773–1835), Ryland was "a star of the first magnitude." He took over a well-established Independent church (College Lane, Northampton) and increased its membership sevenfold. Like Whitefield and Wesley, he pioneered open-air preaching in public recreation areas. Ryland was concerned that the full gospel should be preached to all, including the condemning terrors of the Law. He preached an evangelical gospel of grace, compared to his critics, who preached a legal gospel of duties in order to appropriate salvation. At the time of a devastating eighteenth century eruption of Mount Aetna, which buried great cities, Ryland (as a Calvinist himself) proclaimed the following to his startled congregation.[106]

> Some high Calvinists neglect the unconverted, but Paul left no case untouched. He spoke properly and suitably to Felix, as well as to Timothy. Some neglect to preach the law and tell their hearers to accept Christ. O sinners, beware if Christ says, depart into a thousand Aetnas, bursting up for ever and ever. Your souls are now within an inch of damnation. I am clear of your blood. If you are condemned, I'll look you in the face at judgment and say, "Lord, I told that man—I told those boys and girls, on the 29th of August, 1790—I warned them—they would not believe—and now they stand shivering before the bar!"[107]

Robert Hall testified that after hearing Ryland preach, it was as if he had experienced a veritable earthquake himself. The evangelical giants of the Great Awakening, such as Harris, Hervey, Toplady, and Whitefield looked upon Ryland as one in the Spirit with them. Ryland was also famous for this saying, "No sermon is of any value, which has not the three Rs in it: ruin by the fall, redemption by Christ, and regenerated by the Spirit."[108]

[105] David Brainerd, *The Diary & Journal of David Brainerd*, vol 2, Banner of Truth, 2007, 78–182.

[106] Naylor, Peter, "John Collett Ryland (1723-1792," in *British Particular Baptists*, vol. 1, ed. Michael Haykin (Springfield, MO: Particular Baptist Press,1998).

[107] Peter Naylor, "John Collett Ryland (1723-1792)," in *British Particular Baptists*, vol. 1, ed. Michael Haykin (Springfield, Missouri: Particular Baptist Press 1998).

[108] *Biographia Evangelica*, "The Writings of George M. Ella, John Collet Ryland (1723–1792) and the Restructuring of Baptist History," http://evangelica.de/articles/john-collet-ryland-1723-1792-and-the-restructuring-of-baptist-history.

Also worth considering is a hymn that Ryland wrote about the sovereignty of God in creation, history, and personal salvation.

Sovereign Ruler of the Skies (John Ryland, 1777)

1. Sovereign Ruler of the skies,

Ever gracious, ever wise!

All my times are in Thy hand,

All events at Thy command.

2. His decree, who formed the earth,

Fixed my first and second birth;

Parents, native place and time,

All appointed were by Him.[109]

Isaac Backus (1724–1806)

Isaac Backus was a leading Baptist preacher during the American Revolution who campaigned against state-established churches in New England. Backus was influenced by the Great Awakening and the works of Jonathan Edwards and George Whitefield. He was converted in 1741. For five years, he was a member of a Separatist Congregationalist church before becoming a preacher in 1746. He was ordained in 1748 and became a Baptist in 1751 when he became pastor of the Middleborough Baptist Church in Middleborough, Massachusetts. In 1764, he was one of the original trustees for the chartering of what became known as Brown University, which was the first Baptist school of higher learning.

Here is one paragraph from a piece Rev. Backus wrote *The Doctrine of Particular Election and Final Perseverance Explained and Vindicated*:

If Christ died with a design to save all men, why are not all saved? Can the devil cheat him of a great part of his purchase? Or can men defeat his merciful designs? No, say many, he died for all, and he will finally save all. Others go farther and conclude that a God of

---

[109] *A Selection of Hymns for Public Worship—William Gadsby*, 1965, no. 64, also found at https://founders. org/2016/06/14/hymns-and-the-doctrine-of-election.

infinite goodness could not give existence to any creature that shall be miserable without end, but that he will finally deliver every child of Adam from hell, though many of
them will be tormented therein for ages of ages. But how is their deceit here discovered?
Fallen angels were as really the creatures of God as fallen men, yet no salvation was ever
revealed for them, but they are reserved in everlasting chains under darkness unto the
judgment of the great day. And this is a clear evidence against ungodly men who turn
grace into lasciviousness, Jude 4, 6. God was so far from ever proclaiming atonement to all
men, without any exception, that He said, "The soul that doth ought presumptuously, the
same reproached the Lord and that soul shall be cut off from among his people." And for
such presumption, Korah and his company perished most terribly, Num. xv, 30; xvi, 1–3,
31–34. And teachers who privily brought damnable heresies into the Christian Church
were presumptuous and selfwilled under the name of liberty. They despised government
and perished in the gainsaying of Core, 2 Pet. ii, 1, 10, 19; Jude 11. For if the inability of
debtors and criminals could release them from the authority of the laws, until rulers would
give them power to bring the government to their own terms, how would all dominion be
despised! These filthy dreamers have now filled the world with Babylonian confusion, Jude
8. The Jews called it heresy in Paul to believe in and obey Jesus as a lawgiver above Moses,
Acts xxiv, 14 and this is the first place where the word heresy is used in the Bible, and if
we observe what is said in the last chapter in it of every man who shall add to or take from
its words, must we not conclude that all men who do so and violently impose their inven-
tions upon others are guilty of heresy? The head of the Church of Rome assumed God's
place in the Church, and exalted himself above God, who never could violate his promise
or his oath or entice any into sin, and how justly are all those given up to strong delusion
who practice either of these evils? 2 Thess. ii, 3–12; Heb. vi, 18; James i, 13–15. And how
happy should we soon be if these iniquities were excluded from our land?[110]

John Newton (1725–1807)

John Newton was a British sailor and then an Anglican clergyman. He started his
career at sea at the age of eleven. He became involved with the slave trade for a few years
and was himself enslaved for a period of time. After experiencing a Christian conversion,
he became a minister, hymn writer, and later a prominent supporter of the abolition of
slavery, working with William Wilberforce to eradicate the practice from Great Britain.

Almost as notable as his contribution to abolition, Newton was the author of many
hymns, including perhaps the most well-known non-Christmas hymn in history: "Amazing Grace." He also wrote "Glorious Things of Thee are Spoken" and "How Sweet the

---

[110] Rev. Backus, *The Doctrine of Particular Election and Final Perseverance Explained and Vindicated* (printed
and sold by Samuel Hall, at no. 53, Cornhill, 1789).

Name of Jesus Sounds." His mother was a Nonconformist Christian. In a letter to a friend who believed the doctrine of election to be "absurd, shocking, & unjust," Newton wrote the following paragraphs, which are an amazing revelation into the heart of that former reprobate ship captain and slave trader who surrendered to what he called the invincible grace of God and later wrote one of the greatest hymns in church history, "Amazing Grace." This letter is one of many in a collection of his letters called "Cardiphonia," which contains about three hundred pages. None of these letters were originally intended for publication.

Letter IV.—Predestination—Divine sovereignty—Man made willing by the power of God. November 17, 1775.

My dear friend,

My present part is but to repeat what I have elsewhere expressed, only with some variety and enlargement. You yourself well state the situation of our debate, when you say, "Nor in truth do you offer any arguments to convince me, nor does it seem very consistent on your grounds so to do. And if this important change is to be brought about by the intervention of some extraordinary impulse of the Holy Spirit, and cannot be brought about without it—I do not see anything further that I have to do, than to keep my mind as much unbiased as I can, and to wait and pray for it." I think my letter from London was to the purpose of these your own words, though you seemed dissatisfied with it.

However, to take some notice of your queries as they offer themselves:

The first which occurs is complicated. The substance I think is, whether such belief and aims as you possess, will stand you in no stead unless you likewise believe grace irresistible, predestination absolute, faith in supernatural impulses, etc.? You may have observed, I have several times waived speaking about predestination or election, not that I am ashamed of the doctrine; because if it is indeed absurd, shocking, and unjust, the blame will not deservedly fall upon me, for I did not invent it—but upon the Scriptures, where I am sure it is laid down in as plain terms, as that God created the heavens and the earth. I own that I cannot but wonder, that people professing any reverence for the Bible should so openly and strongly declare their abhorrence of what the Bible so expressly teaches; namely, that there is a sovereign choice of people by the grace and good pleasure of God, where by nature there is no difference; and that all things respecting the salvation of these people is infallibly secured by a divine predestination.

I do not offer this as a rational doctrine, (though it be highly so to me,) but it is scriptural—or else the Scripture is a mere nose of wax, and without any plain meaning. What ingenuity is needful to interpret many passages in a sense more favorable to our natural prejudice against God's sovereignty! Matthew 11:25, 26, and 13:10–17; Mark 13:20–22; John 17; John 10:26; Romans 8:28–30, and 9:13–24, and 11:7; Ephesians 1:4, 5; 1 Peter 1:2.

If I were fond of disputing, as I am not—I think I could put a close reasoner hard to it, to maintain the truth of Scripture prophecies, or the belief of a particular providence—unless he would admit a divine predestination of causes and events as the ground of his arguments. However, as I said, I have chosen to waive the point; because, however true and necessary in itself—the knowledge and comprehension of the Scriptural doctrine of election, is not necessary to the being a true Christian, though I can hardly conceive he can be an established consistent believer without it.

Your two sheets may lead me to write as many quires, if I do not check myself. I now come to the two queries you propose, the solution of which you think will clearly mark the difference of our sentiments. The substance of them is:

I. Whether I think any sinner ever perished in his sins (to whom the gospel has been preached) because God refused to supply him with such a proportion of his assistance as was absolutely necessary to his believing and repenting, or without his having previously rejected the incitements of his Holy Spirit? A full answer to this would require a sheet. But briefly, I believe, that all mankind being corrupt and guilty before God, He might, without impeachment to his justice, have left them all to perish, as we are assured He did the fallen angels. But He has pleased to show mercy, and mercy must be free. If the sinner has any claim to it, so far it is justice, not mercy. He who is to be our judge assures us, that few find the gate that leads to life, while many throng the road to destruction. Your question seems to imply, that you think God either did make salvation equally open to all, or that it would have been more becoming his goodness to have done so.

But He is the potter, we are the clay; His ways and thoughts are above ours—as the heavens are higher than the earth. The Judge of all the earth will do right. He has appointed a day, when He will manifest, to the conviction of all—that He has done right. Until then, I hold it best to take things upon His Word, and not too harshly determine what it befits Jehovah to do. Instead of saying what I think, let it suffice to remind you of what Paul thought. Romans 9:15–21. But further, I say, that unless mercy were afforded to those who are saved, in a way peculiar to themselves, and what is not afforded to those who perish—I believe no one soul could be saved.

For I believe fallen man, universally considered as such, is as incapable of doing the least thing toward his salvation, until enlivened by the grace of God—as a dead body is of restoring itself to life. Whatever difference takes place between men in this respect is of grace, that is—of God, undeserved. Yes, His first approaches to our hearts are undesired too; for, until He seeks us—we cannot, we will not seek him. Psalm 110:3. It is in the day of His power, and not before—that His people are made willing.

But I believe where the gospel is preached, those who do perish—do willfully resist the light, and choose and cleave to darkness, and stifle the convictions which the truths of God, when His true gospel is indeed preached, will, in one degree or other, force upon their minds. The cares of this world, the deceitfulness of riches, the love of other things, the violence of sinful appetites, their prejudices, pride, and self-righteousness—either prevent the reception, or choke the growth of the good seed! Thus, their own sin and obstinacy is the proper cause of their destruction; they will not come to Christ—that they may have life. At the same time, it is true that they cannot, unless they are supernaturally drawn of God. John 5:40; 6:44.

They will not, and they cannot come. Both are equally true, and they are consistent. For a man's cannot is not a natural—but a moral inability: not an impossibility in the nature of things, as it is for me to walk upon the water, or to fly in the air; but such an inability, as, instead of extenuating, does exceedingly enhance and aggravate his guilt! He is so blinded by Satan, so alienated from God by nature and wicked works, so given up to sin, so averse from that way of salvation, which is contrary to his pride and natural wisdom—that he will not embrace it or seek after it; and therefore he cannot, until the grace of God powerfully enlightens his mind, and overcomes his obstacles.

But this brings me to your second query.

II. Do I think that God, in the ordinary course of His providence, grants this assistance in an irresistible manner, or effects faith and conversion—without the sinner's own hearty consent and concurrence? I rather chose to term grace invincible—than irresistible. For it is too often resisted even by those who believe; but, because it is invincible, it triumphs over all resistance—when He is pleased to bestow it.

For the rest, I believe no sinner is converted without his own hearty will and concurrence. But he is not willing—until he is divinely made so. Why does he at all refuse? Because he is insensible of his state; because he knows not the evil of sin, the strictness of the law, the majesty of God whom he has offended, nor the total apostasy of his heart; because he is blind to eternity, and ignorant of the excellency of Christ; because he is comparatively whole, and sees not his need of this great Physician; because he relies upon his own wisdom, power, and supposed righteousness. Now in this state of things, when God comes with a purpose of mercy—he begins by convincing the person of sin, judgment, and righteousness; he causes him to feel and know that he is a lost, condemned, helpless creature, and then reveals to him the necessity, sufficiency, and willingness of Christ to save those who are ready to perish, without money or price, without doings or deservings.

Then he sees saving faith to be very different from a rational assent, finds that nothing but the power of God can produce a well-grounded hope in the heart of a convinced sinner; therefore looks to Jesus, who is the author and finisher of faith, to enable him to believe. For this he waits on what we call the means of grace; he prays, he reads the Word, he thirsts for God, as the deer pants for the water brooks; and though perhaps for a while—he is distressed with many doubts and fears, he is encouraged to wait on, because Jesus has said, "Him that comes unto me—I will never cast out." The obstinacy of the will remains while the understanding is dark—and ceases when the understanding is enlightened.

Suppose a man walking in the dark, where there are pits and precipices of which he is not aware. You are sensible of his danger, and call after him; but he thinks he knows better than you, refuses your advice, and is perhaps angry with you for your importunity. He sees no danger, therefore will not be persuaded that there is any; but if you go with a light, get before him, and show him plainly, that if he takes another step he falls into a deep precipice, then he will stop of his own accord, blame himself for not minding you before, and be ready to comply with your further directions. In either case man's will acts with equal freedom; the difference of his conduct arises from conviction. Something like this is the case of our spiritual concerns. Sinners are called and warned by the Word; but they are wise in their own eyes, and take but little notice—until the Lord gives them light, which He is not bound to give to any, and therefore cannot be bound to give to all. They who have it, have reason to be thankful, and subscribe to the apostle's words, "By grace are you saved, through faith; and that not of yourselves, it is the gift of God."

I am not yet half done with my reply—but send this as a specimen of my willingness to clear my sentiments to you as far as I can. Unless it should please God to make what I offer satisfactory, I well know beforehand what objections and answers will occur to you; for these points have been often debated; and after a course of twenty-seven years, in which religion (Christianity) has been the chief object of my thoughts and inquiries, I am not entirely a stranger to what can be offered on either side. What I write, I write simply and in love; beseeching him, who alone can set a seal to his own truth—to guide you and bless you. This letter has been more than a week in hand: I have been called from it I suppose ten times, frequently in the middle of a period or a line. My leisure time, which before was small, is now reduced almost to a nothing. But I am desirous to keep up my correspondence with you, because I feel an affectionate interest in you, and because it pleased God to put it into your heart to apply to me. You cannot think how your first letter struck me: it was so unexpected, and seemed so improbable that you should open your mind to me. I immediately conceived a hope that it would prove for good. Nor am I yet discouraged.

When you have leisure and inclination, write back. I shall be always glad to hear from you, and I will proceed in answering what I have already by me, as fast as I can. But I have many letters now waiting for answers, which must be attended to.

I recommend you to the blessing and care of the Great Shepherd and remain,
Your sincere friend and servant.
John Newton[111]

---

[111] An editor named Josiah Bull is responsible for making these letters available online at the URL below if you would like to read more of his letters: http://gracegems.org/Newton/additional_letters_of_newton.htm.

John Gano (1727–1804)

The following summation of John Gano's life comes from *The Life of John Gano, 1727–1804* by Terry Wolever and published by the Particular Baptist Press.

John Gano's father was a descendant of Huguenots, his mother came from a family of English Baptists, and John was raised as a Presbyterian. After a powerful conversion experience and a period of intense study, Gano became a Calvinistic Baptist. He left the family farm to study at Princeton University (then the College of New Jersey), but left before graduating. He was eventually ordained as pastor of the Scotch Plains, New Jersey, Baptist Church in 1754.

In 1760, he became the founding pastor of what became two years later the First Baptist Church in the City of New York. Gano served as pastor of the New York Church until 1787, but he made long itinerant trips doing evangelism throughout the thirteen colonies. He made the statement that "he had a right to proclaim free grace wherever he went."[112]

During the American Revolution, Gano served as a soldier and a chaplain for the Continental Army, and was chosen by General Washington to say a prayer marking the official end of the American Revolutionary War in 1783. After the war, he returned to his congregation in New York. In 1787 he moved to Kentucky where he lived until his death in 1804. He is buried in the Daughters of the Revolutionary War section of the Frankfort Cemetery in Frankfort, Kentucky, just beyond Daniel Boone's grave. Before his death, Gano wrote and published an autobiography of his life. Gano's descendants include the noted billionaire Howard Robard Hughes Jr. (whose mother was Allene Gano Hughes), Rev. Stephen Gano, Admiral Roy Alexander Gano, Confederate States of America General Richard Montgomery Gano, and Union General Stephen Gano Burbridge.

Gano wrote the letter below to circulate throughout the Philadelphia Association and its affiliate churches:

We trust, you will unite your efforts with ours, to the same good purpose and that our thanksgivings for the present peace, harmony, and increase of our churches, our prayers for their further growth, with a more powerful effusion of the Divine Spirit and grace upon them, will be mutually offered up. May the consideration of our effectual calling prove an incentive thereunto! Which is the subject now to be considered, as in the tenth chapter of our confession of faith. . . . This is an act of sovereign grace, which flows from the everlasting love of God, and is such an irresistible impression made by the Holy Spirit upon a human soul, as to effect a blessed change. We are to consider who are the called. They are such as God hath chosen and predestinated both to grace and glory, elected and set apart in Christ,

---

[112] *Biographical Memoirs of the Late Reverend John Gano* by Southwick and Hardcastle.

as redeemed by his blood. The changes produced are from darkness to light, from bondage to liberty, from alienation and estrangedness to Christ to a state of nearness and fellowship with him and his saints. . . . This is a holy calling, and is effectual to produce the exercise of holiness in the heart, even as the saints are created in Christ Jesus unto good works.[113]

Abraham Booth (1734–1806)

Abraham Booth was a dissenting minister and author born at Blackwell, near Alfreton, Derbyshire in 1734. As the oldest child in a large family, he helped on the farm until he was sixteen, when he was able to get some further elementary education. At the age of twenty-four, he married Elizabeth Bowmar, a farmer's daughter, and then opened a school at Sutton-in-Ashfield, Nottinghamshire. During his early years, the preaching of some Baptists drew him into Christ, and in 1755 he was baptized by immersion. He also began preaching in the midland counties. In 1760, when the Baptists began to organize into churches, Booth became superintendent of the Kirby-Woodhouse congregation, but declined to be their pastor. Until this time he had been a strenuous advocate of the Arminian doctrines and at the age of twenty, he even wrote a poem against "Absolute Predestination."

Later on, he changed his views in favor of the Calvinistic doctrines held by the Particular Baptists, and seceded accordingly. Shortly after that, he began preaching on Sundays for Particular Baptist groups at Sutton-in-Ashfield, Chesterfield, and in other midland towns and villages. He continued his work of overseeing the school through the weekdays, as it was his only source of income. During this period, he composed his work called *The Reign of Grace* in 1768. This book shows how he was introduced to the doctrines of grace in 1768 and how the doctrines completely transformed his faith. They stirred up such a burning love for Christ and His Word that he was prompted to write his book and explain his new convictions.

In his book, Booth examines the very nature of divine grace and how it operates in every part of our salvation, dealing with its sovereignty in such subjects as our election, calling, adoption, sanctification, and perseverance, which lead us eventually to eternal glory. He sought to humble the pride of man and show that grace, when rightly understood and embraced, leads to a life of love and holiness. His burning desire was to glorify God. In this volume, Booth is on fire for God, and he longs for us to be on fire for God. The Scottish theologian John Murray regarded Booth's work as "one of the most eloquent and moving expositions of the subject of divine grace in the English language."[114]

---

[113] Rev. John Gano, Circular Letter," *Effectual Calling* (New York City: Philadelphia Baptist Association, First Baptist Church), 1784.
[114] Abraham Booth, *The Reign of Grace: From Its Rise to Its Consummation* (Nabu Press, January 4, 2010).

Augustus Montague Toplady (1740–1778)

Augustus Montague Toplady was an Anglican minister and hymn writer, a major Calvinist opponent of John Wesley, and best remembered as the author of the hymn "Rock of Ages," along with three of his other hymns, "A Debtor to Mercy Alone," "Deathless Principle, Arise" and "Object of My First Desire." One of Toplady's best quotes on predestination follows:

> The doctrine of predestination, though written as it were with a sunbeam in the volume of revelation, and which is to be found in the archives of every sound Protestant Reformed church, is certainly offensive to the pride of the human heart. Hence—we find, though our clergy solemnly and unequivocally aver before God at their ordination, that it is a doctrine "full of sweet, pleasant, and unspeakable comfort," yet no sooner do they enter upon the sacred office, but the greater part of them do all in their power to depreciate and to annul it altogether. Let us hear this preacher's opinion why it ought not to be suppressed, nor mutilated. Treating upon the publishing of this doctrine, he asks: "Why shouldn't this doctrine be preached and insisted upon in public, as a doctrine which is of express revelation and a doctrine that makes wholly for the glory of God, which conduces in a most peculiar manner to the conversion, comfort, and sanctification of the elect and leaves even the ungodly without excuse."[115]

John Rippon (1751–1836)

John Rippon was born in Devonshire, England in 1751. He was sixteen years old was he felt divine grace compelling him to follow Jesus Christ. At seventeen he entered the Briston Baptist College. At twenty-one he became the successor of the great Dr. Gill, in London. His personality was bold and witty, and his preaching was lively and affectionate in connecting with his congregation. His church administration was marked by great prudence and he became very popular. His church complex was enlarged and the community over which he presided was "one of the wealthiest" according to Spurgeon.

Dr. Rippon was a great friend of missions and his church gave large sums to the home and foreign Baptist missionary societies. He helped create and edited the *Baptist Annual Register* to give Baptists in Europe and America a vehicle through which they might address each other. Dr. Rippon is best known for his publication, *A Selection of Hymns from the Best Authors, Intended to Be an Appendix to Dr. Watts Psalms and Hymns,* which was reprinted twenty-seven times and for a long time, along with the hymns of Dr. Watts, was used in Baptist churches. Mr. Spurgeon says that his *Selection of Hymns* was an estate to him. He

---

[115] Augustus Toplady, *The Complete Works* (Harrisonburg: Sprinkle Publications, 1987).

was a friend to America in the revolutionary struggle. His pastored the church for over sixty years, which eventually became the Metropolitan Tabernacle, that C. H. Spurgeon later pastored. According to author Ken R. Manley (*Redeeming Love Proclaim: John Rippon and the Baptists*) Dr. Rippon was a leading exponent of the new moderate Calvinism, which brought new life to many Baptists.

His many writings expressed the denomination's growing maturity and mutual awareness of Baptists in Britain and America. The importance of John Rippon's contribution to Nonconformity, especially to the Particular Baptists in both Britain and America, is found in how he represented a combination of the best elements of both old and new traditions.

Andrew Fuller (1754–1815)

Andrew Fuller was an English Baptist theologian and missionary advocate who was deeply challenged with religious questions in his childhood. When he was sixteen, he joined the Baptist church in Soham and even though he had no special training for the ministry, his powers of exposition and exhortation gained him the opportunity of preaching to his church during a vacancy. Then he was called to be their pastor in the spring of 1775. He remained at Soham for several years until he accepted a call from the church at Kettering, Northamptonshire. In 1782, he moved to Kettering where he remained till his death.

Fuller was a very capable preacher and theological author. He was one of the founders of the Baptist Missionary Society, its first secretary, and its best promoter. Fuller received the degree of DD from Princeton College and from Yale College in the United States. He died at the age of sixty-one. He claimed to be a genuine Calvinist.

A conversation between Fuller and a certain clergyman is recorded by Dr. Ryland in his *Memoirs of Fuller.* When asked about the different shades of Calvinism, Fuller said:

There are three which we commonly describe, namely "the high Calvinists," "the moderate Calvinists," and "the strict Calvinists." The first are, if I may so speak, more Calvinistic than Calvin himself. In other words, they border on Antinomianism. The second group, or moderates, he goes on to describe as "half-Arminian" or as they are called with us "Baxterians" (referring to one of the main proponents of such Calvinism, Richard Baxter). The third class is those who really hold the system of John Calvin. I do not believe everything that Calvin taught, nor anything because he taught it, but I reckon strict Calvinism to be my own system.[116]

---

[116] A. H. Kirby, "Andrew Fuller—Evangelical Calvinist," in *Baptist Quarterly,* vol. XV, no. 5 (Jan. 1954): 195–202.

32 ✦

Nineteenth-Century Church Leaders from the Second Great Awakening through the Century's End Who Affirmed the Decrees

The history of the church from the middle of the eighteenth century through the present day has been an intellectual battle ground for the church. We note from the witness of many prominent Christian thinkers of the past two centuries; however, that despite the many attacks from Enlightenment thinkers through the modernist controversies and the new postmodernism, within the circles of Christian thinkers, the validity and critical nature of the decrees of election and predestination continue to be preached as biblical truth and foundational doctrines for the hope that is within all believers.

Here we will take a look at a number of quotes from prominent believers from the Second Great Awakening bearing witness to these truths that support the previous contentions of this book, that these truths are foundational to the Christian faith and provide hope and comfort to every believer in Christ Jesus.

John Leland (1754–1841)

John Leland was a pivotal American figure while serving as a faithful minister of the gospel and a firm supporter of religious liberty. His influence in our country's development was crucial, with many historians crediting him with "Freedom of Religion" as guaranteed by the First Amendment. From Grafton, Massachusetts, he was brought under conviction of sin and a call to the ministry at the age of eighteen and experienced a hope in Christ. He was baptized and began to preach in public in his twentieth year. He was married in his twenty-second year. During the sixty-seven years of his ministry, he labored with his own hands and never solicited money for himself. He went forth entirely undirected and unsupported by missionary societies or funds and preached four to fourteen times a week.

He preached from Massachusetts to South Carolina (fifteen years in Virginia from 1776 to 1791). He traveled more than a hundred thousand miles on foot and horseback and baptized 1,535 persons on a credible profession of faith. He faithfully preached the word undiluted with the doctrines and commandments of men. He was an earnest advocate of civil and religious liberty. He personally knew more than a thousand Baptist preachers, heard more than three hundred of them preach, and entertained more than two hundred of them at his house. He wrote about thirty pamphlets and many hymns including, "The Day is Past and Gone" and "Christians, If Your Hearts Be Warm, Ice and Snow Can Do No Harm." Here are a few of his words about his inability to come to Christ apart from sovereign grace:

> I found that I could no more believe, come to Christ, and give up my whole heart to Him, than I could create a world. Unless I was drawn by the Father, all the exertions of my natural powers of body and mind could not bring me to the Son. Unless I was born, not of blood, nor of the will of the flesh, nor of the will of man, but of God, and saved by grace, I must sink into hell.[117]

Richard Furman (1755–1825)

Richard Furman was a Baptist minister and educator born in New York and educated at home. He mastered both Latin and Greek and his discipline for self-education was recognized when Rhode Island College (later Brown University) awarded him a master's (1792) and Doctor of Divinity Degree (1800). He abandoned his Anglican upbringing and embraced the evangelistic Calvinism of Separate Baptists. He was ordained on May 10, 1774, and served as pastor of High Hills Baptist Church (1774–1787) and Charleston Baptist Church (1787–1825). Furman volunteered to fight during the Revolutionary War, but Governor John Rutledge persuaded him to plead the patriot cause among the Loyalists

---

[117] Elder Cushing Biggs Hassell, *History of the Church of God, From the Creation to A.D. 1885: Including Especially the History of the Kehukee Primitive Baptist Association*, revised and completed by Elder Sylvester Hassell (Gilbert Beebee & Sons, first edition, 1886).

in western South Carolina instead. Furman's success came to the attention of Lord Cornwallis, who, after capturing Charleston in 1780, apparently offered a £1,000 reward for Furman's capture.

As a champion of religious liberty, Furman met with a group of dissenters at High Hills in 1776 and their planning helped set the stage for disestablishment of the Church of England in South Carolina two years later. In 1790, as a delegate to the South Carolina constitutional convention, Furman supported extending the right of incorporation to all denominations. Furman's actions generally reflected the era's notion that religious liberty prohibited denominational favoritism, but not necessarily church-state interaction. Furman preached a sermon before Congress in 1781. He greatly influenced the development of the Baptist denomination, although his fellow Baptists sometimes disagreed with his preference for centralized church governance. He also helped found and served as the first president of the South Carolina Baptist Convention (1821–1825), which was the first statewide Baptist organization in America.

Furman also helped establish an educational fund to train Baptist ministers and also called for a national theological institution, which led to the creation of Columbian College (now George Washington University). Other institutions that resulted from his influence were Furman University, the Southern Baptist Theological Seminary, and Mercer University.[118]

Fisher Ames (1758–1808)

Fisher Ames began the study of Latin at the age of six and at the age of twelve, he was sent to Harvard College. After graduating in 1774, he began work as a teacher. While teaching school Ames also studied law. He was admitted to the bar and commenced practice in Dedham in 1781. His father, Dr. Nathaniel Ames was the author of the Ames almanac, which was the inspiration for the Poor Richard's Almanacs. In 1788, he served in the Massachusetts House of Representatives. He became a member of the Massachusetts convention that ratified the United States Constitution that same year. When referring to his religious affiliation, he identified himself as a Calvinist.[119]

William Wilberforce (1759–1833)

William Wilberforce was the famous English politician, philanthropist, and a leader of the movement to abolish the slave trade. In 1785, he had a conversion experience and

---

[118] A. Rogers, *Richard Furman: Life and Legacy*, (Mercer University Press, December 1, 2001).
[119] *Works of Fisher Ames: With a Selection from His Speeches and Correspondence,"* edited by Seth Ames (New York: DaCapo Press, 1965).

became an evangelical Christian, which resulted in major changes to his lifestyle and a lifelong concern for moral and political reforms. He became one of the leading English abolitionists. He headed the parliamentary campaign against the British slave trade for twenty-six years until the passage of the Slave Trade Act of 1807. Wilberforce was convinced of the importance of Christianity, morality, and education in society. In later years, Wilberforce supported the campaign for the complete abolition of slavery and continued his involvement after 1826, when he resigned from Parliament because of his failing health. That campaign led to The Slavery Abolition Act 1833, which abolished slavery in most of the British Empire.

Wilberforce died just three days after hearing that the passage of the Act was assured. He was buried in Westminster Abbey, close to his friend William Pitt. Throughout his Christian life, Wilberforce drew spiritual and intellectual strength from the Bible and the Puritans such as Richard Baxter, John Owen, and Jonathan Edwards and built his evangelical faith on a mildly Calvinist foundation. Philip Doddridge's *Rise and Progress of Religion in the Soul* continued to shape his spirituality, daily self-examination, extended times of prayer, regular communions and fasting, morning and evening devotions, and times of solitude. He also paid careful attention to God's providential provision in his life, the needs of others, and his own mortality.

In 1797 Wilberforce wrote a best-selling book called *A Practical View of the Prevailing Religious System . . . Contrasted with Real Christianity.* He once wrote to a relative, "My grand objection to the religious system still held by many who declare themselves orthodox churchmen . . . is that it tends to render Christianity so much a system of prohibitions rather than of privilege and hopes . . . and religion is made to wear a forbidding and gloomy air."[120]

William Plumer (1759–1850)

William Plumer was an American lawyer and Baptist lay preacher from Epping, New Hampshire. Born in 1759 in Newburyport, Massachusetts, he represented New Hampshire as a Federalist in the United States Senate from June 17, 1802 to March 4, 1807. Plumer later became a Democratic-Republican and served as a governor of New Hampshire from 1812–1813 and 1816–1819. He wrote the following about predestination:

The Lord Jesus Christ and His apostles all preached predestination, declaring to their hearers "all the counsel of God" (Acts 20.27; Romans 9–11; Ephesians 1; 1 Peter 1:18–21;Jude

---

[120] William Wilberforce, *Practical View of the Prevailing Religious System of Professed Christians, in the Higher and Middle Classes in This Country, Contrasted with Real Christianity* (Adamant Media Corporation, 2005).

4; John 17:12; 10:26–29; 6:64–65). What shall we then do? If the doctrine so offends men, shall we give it up? Are we to make peace with human wickedness by observing a profound silence on this topic? Nay, let us rather imitate Christ, who often preached it.[121]

William Carey (1761–1834)

William Carey was an English Baptist missionary and a Particular Baptist minister, known as the Father of Modern Missions. Carey was one of the founders of the Baptist Missionary Society. As a missionary in the Danish colony in Serampore, India, he translated the Bible into Bengali, Sanskrit, and numerous other languages and dialects. As a Calvinist and Baptist, he believed in Providence unashamedly and always based his belief in the necessity of missions on this idea:

> It has been said that we ought not to force our way, but to wait for the openings, and leadings of Providence. But it might with equal propriety be answered in this case, neither ought we to neglect embracing those openings in providence which daily present themselves to us. What openings of providence do we wait for? Where a command exists, nothing can be necessary to render it binding, but a removal of those obstacles which render obedience impossible and these are removed already. Natural impossibility can never be pleaded so long as facts exist to prove the contrary.[122]

Christmas Evans (1766–1838)

Christmas Evans was one of the great Welsh preachers born on Christmas day 1766 in Wales. As well as being a persistent and tireless evangelist, Evans was also an orthodox Calvinist. He greatly admired the ministries and preaching of John Owen and John Gill. Writing to a young minister, he urged, "Preach the gospel of the grace of God, intelligibly, affectionately, and without shame—all the contents of the great book from predestination to glorification."[123]

Jesse Mercer (1769–1841)

Jesse Mercer was a Baptist pastor, an editor, and an extremely effective spokesman for his denomination who was very prominent in the debates over Calvinism among the Southern preachers and pastors of his day. Calvinism played a key role in shaping the reli-

---

[121] William S. Plumer, *Jehovah-Jireh: A Treatise of Providence* (BiblioBazaar Publishing, 2013).

[122] William Carey, *Enquiry*, op. cit., 10–11, an 87-page manuscript published in 1792, which had an introduction and five chapters.

[123] *Reformation Today Magazine*, no. 29, (Jan.–Feb. 1976), 24, archived at https://reformation-today.org/wp-content/uploads/2016/09/RT_029.pdf).

gious mindset of the South among Baptists who debated the relationship between divine sovereignty and human responsibility, especially as it related to missions, education, and social reform. These debates led to the formation of two distinct Baptist groups referred to as "Primitive" and "Missionary." The Missionary group ultimately became the Southern Baptists. Jesse Mercer played a leading role within these debates, as he promoted the first form of the Georgia Baptist Convention. His Calvinistic theology governed his actions and life. He emphasized missions, theological training for pastors, and cooperation between churches in fulfilling the Great Commission. Mercer seemed to follow John Gill's model of Calvinism. For Mercer, the doctrine of election manifested the sovereignty of God in salvation. Here is a nice summation of Mercer's understanding of predestination:

These angels and men, thus predestinated and foreordained, are particularly and unchangeably designed. Their number is so certain and definite, that it cannot be either increased or diminished. This perseverance of the saints depends not upon their own free will, but upon the immutability of the decree of election, flowing from the free and unchangeable love of God the Father, upon the efficacy of the merit and intercession of Jesus Christ.[124]

Leonard Woods (1774–1854)

Leonard Woods was an American theologian widely known for upholding orthodox Calvinism. Woods graduated from Harvard in 1796 and was ordained pastor of the Congregational Church in West Newbury, MA in 1798. He was the first professor of Andover Theological Seminary and between 1808 and 1846 and he occupied the seminary's chair of Christian theology. He helped establish several societies including the American Tract Society, the American Education Society, the Temperance Society, and the American Board of Commissioners for Foreign Missions. He published six major works. The following paragraph is from one of Wood's lectures on the extent of the atonement:

Another point of inquiry is, whether there is any important sense, in which Christ died for His chosen people in distinction from others. The parties in the controversy generally agree that there is. He died for His peculiar people with a gracious and unalterable design actually to save them—not however to save them unconditionally, that is, whether they repent and believe or not, but to save them in the manner or on the conditions or terms stated in the gospel—their compliance with those terms being secured by His purpose, as a part of the free and full salvation which He gives. In this respect then there is a marked

[124] Anthony L. Chute, *A Piety Above the Common Standard: Jesse Mercer and Evangelistic Calvinism* (Mercer University Press, 2005), 66.

HOW CAN I KNOW IF I AM ONE OF GOD'S ELECT?

distinction. He died for those who were given Him of the Father—He laid down His life for the sheep with an ultimate design or destination which related to no others.[125]

Thomas Chalmers (1780–1847)

Thomas Chalmers was a Scottish minister, professor of theology, political economist, and a leader of the Church of Scotland and of the Free Church of Scotland. He has been called "Scotland's greatest nineteenth-century churchman." Below is a quote from one of his sermons:

All this, carries along with it so complete a dethronement of God—it is bringing His creation under the dominion of so many nameless and undeterminable contingencies—it is taking the world and the current of its history so entirely out of the hands of Him who formed it—it is withal so opposite to what obtains in every other field of observation, where, instead of the lawlessness of chance, we shall find that the more we attend, the more we perceive of a certain necessary and established order—that from these and other considerations which might be stated, the doctrine in question, in addition to the testimonies which we find for it in the Bible, is at this moment receiving a very general support from the speculations of infidel as well as Christian philosophers. Assenting, as we do, to this doctrine, we state it as our conviction, that God could point the finger of His omniscience to every one individual amongst us, and tell what shall be the fate of each, and the place of each, and the state of suffering or enjoyment of each, at any one period of futurity however distant. Well does He know those of us who are vessels of wrath fitted for destruction, and those of us whom He has predestinated to be conformed to the image of His dear Son, and to be rendered meet for the inheritance.[126]

William B. Johnson (1782–1862)

William B. Johnson was educated at home in South Carolina by his mother and private tutors. His mother was a Particular Baptist, believing that only the elect would be saved. As a child he met President George Washington and Dr. Richard Furman (pastor of the First Baptist Church Charleston) who made a great impression on him. He received a degree in 1804 from Brown University. He had originally planned to become a lawyer, but was converted during a Baptist revival in 1804, and then devoted the rest of his life to Christian

---

[125] Leonard Woods, "*Lectures*" in *The Works of Leonard Woods*, Lecture LXXXI. "Is the Atonement General or Particular?," point 11 (Boston: John P. Jewett & Company, 1851), 490–521.
[126] *Congregational Sermons: Vol. II*, Sermon VIII, Select works of Thomas Chalmers, DD (New York: R. Carter & Bros, 1850), comprising his miscellanies, lectures on Romans, astronomical, commercial, congregational, and posthumous sermons.

ministries. He and his wife had eight children who reached maturity. One was Francis C. Johnson who became a Southern Baptist missionary to China in 1846. After serving as president of the General Missionary (or Triennial) Baptist Convention from 1841–1844, Johnson went on to become the first president of the newly formed Southern Baptist Convention, serving in this position from 1845–1851. He was considered one of the major architects of the Southern Baptist Convention, which has become the largest Protestant body in the United States. Johnson Female University, founded in 1848 as Johnson Female Seminary, was named for him because of his support for female education. The largest and best-known work of Johnson, published in 1846, was titled *The Gospel Developed through the Government and Order of the Churches of Jesus Christ.*

This book reveals Johnson's concepts of the nature, officers, ordinances, authority, and duties of the Church of Jesus Christ is its local expressions. In the introduction to the book he identifies the sovereignty of God, as a foundational principle of the gospel of Christ, "The sovereignty of God in the provision and application of the plan of salvation" (p. 16). His definition of "church" in the first chapter highlights its universal nature (the whole body of the redeemed from Adam to the last believer) and summarizes his definition by saying, "This body consists of all that the Father hath given to Christ and this is his church" (p. 21).[127]

Luther Rice (1783–1836)

Luther Rice was an appointed Congregational missionary to India. Similar to his contemporary, Adoniram Judson, Rice became a convinced Baptist after leaving America. On March 15, 1813, five months after his baptism in Calcutta, Rice set sail back to America to raise support for his mission efforts among Baptists. Though he intended to return to India as soon as possible, it never happened. The rest of his life was spent in what was supposed to have been a short-term project of promoting missions among Baptists in America. He died at the age of fifty-three. He was successful in promoting the formation of a unified Baptist missionary-sending body, which culminated in the establishment of the Southern Baptist Convention. He also used funds raised for missions to establish The Columbian College, which is now The George Washington University in Washington, DC. He was an acknowledged believer in the doctrine of divine sovereignty. Rice saw God as working all things after the counsel of his own will. He believed that those who are recognized as the heirs of eternal life, have been called according to God's eternal purpose, which He

---

[127] W. B. Johnson, *The Gospel Developed through the Government and Order of the Churches of Jesus Christ* (1846) in *Polity* (Center for Church Reform, 2001), 243–44, https://www.9marks.org/wp-content/uploads/2015/07/Polity.pdf.

purposed in Christ Jesus, before the world began. Rice referred to this doctrine (so revealed and fully taught in the Scriptures), as furnishing deep humility and grateful praise in his own experience. Referring to this subject in a letter to a friend, he observes,

> You are aware that this is not only an item in my creed, but enters into the very ground-work of the hope of immortality and glory, that has become established in my bosom and constitutes the basis of the submission and joyfulness found in my religious experience. Why should it not be the very joy of our bosoms, that He has foreordained whatsoever to come to pass? What can real benevolence desire, but that everything should "come to pass" in the wisest and best manner, to the wisest and best ultimate end? Could not an infinitely wise and good God ordain everything to come to pass in this very way and to this very end? Such too, being the fact, is it not evidently the duty and happiness of everyone to give up himself in absolute submission to the will of God and to be pleased that all things are at the disposal and under the control of this infinitely wise and good Being.[128]

Asahel Nettleton (1783–1844)

Asahel Nettleton was an American theologian and pastor from Connecticut, who was highly influential during the Second Great Awakening, and credited with thirty thousand conversions during his ministry. He attended Yale College from 1805 until his graduation in 1809 and was ordained to the ministry in 1811. His theology was distinctly reformed, and he believed that salvation was a work of God alone.

Nettleton operated in stark contrast to many modern evangelists. He would often move into a community for several weeks or months to study the spiritual condition of the people before attempting any revival work. His preaching was seen as largely doctrinal, but always practical. He was blessed to fill the pulpits of churches where there was no pastor present. This allowed him to engage in an effective pastoral care for the people. He also refused to preach in any community where he had not been invited and he would some-times refuse to preach in a church if he believed the request was not sincere. He rejected the idea that he was the cause of any revival, and shunned those who looked to him rather than God, to bring revival to their community. Bennet Tyler and Andre Bonar wrote the follow-ing about the spiritual effects of the revivals where Nettleton was the primary instrument:

---

[128] This quote is adapted from chapter 16 of the James Taylor's memoir of Rev. Luther Rice, *One of the First American Missionaries to the East,* originally published in 1841. Taylor later became the first secretary of the Foreign Mission Board of the SBC. His memoir of Rice was reprinted by Broadman Press in 1937). Also see http://www.gracesermons.com/robbeeee/lutherrice.html.

He reestablished Calvinism and his Calvinism was thoroughly evangelical and had a great impact upon society. The fruits of these revivals were permanent. They were not temporary excitements. Prominent contemporary church historian Timothy Smith surmised the following: "Could Thomas Paine, the free-thinking pamphleteer of the American and French Revolutions, have visited the U.S. in the final decade of Nettleton's life, he would have been amazed to find that the nation conceived in rational liberty was in the grip of the power of evangelical faith. The emancipating glory of the great awakenings had made Christian liberty, Christian equality and Christian fraternity the passion of the land. The treasured gospel passed into the hands of the baptized many. Common grace, not common sense, was the keynote of the age. Religious doctrines which Paine, in his book, *The Age of Reason*, had discarded as the 'tattered vestment' of the past, became the wedding garment of many."[129]

Adoniram Judson (1788–1850)

Courtney Anderson wrote, "When Adoniram Judson entered Burma in July 1813, it was a hostile and utterly unreached place. William Carey had told Judson in India a few months earlier not to go there. It probably would have been considered a closed country today—with anarchic despotism, fierce war with Siam, enemy raids, constant rebellion, and no religious toleration. All the previous missionaries had died or left."[130]

Adoniram Judson experienced the death of many of his children, wives, and fellow missionaries. Judson even heard about the death of his father while Judson was in a Burma prison, because of his ministry. Yet by the grace of God, he was able to translate the Bible into the Burmese language and create a Burmese dictionary and there were the hundreds of genuine converts. "The largest Christian force in Burma is the Burma Baptist Convention, which owes its origin to the pioneering activity of the American Baptist missionary Adoniram Judson"[131]

Today, Patrick Johnstone estimates the Myanmar (Burma's new name) Baptist Convention to be thirty-seven hundred congregations with 617,781 members and 1,900,000 affiliates—the fruit of Judson's seed (Patrick Johnstone, *"Operation World,"* p. 462) who trace their origin to this man's labors of love demonstrated through his evangelical ministries. This is what Judson gave his life for, even though it personally cost him tremendously. One of his last sentences was, "How few there are who . . . die so hard!" He recognized the

---

[129] Timothy L. Smith, *Revivalism and Social Reform in Mid-nineteenth Century America* (New York: Abingdon Press, 1957), 7.
[130] Courtney Anderson, *To the Golden Shore: The Life of Adoniram Judson* (Grand Rapids: Zondervan, 1956), 134.
[131] David Barrett, ed., *World Christian Encyclopedia* (New York: Oxford University Press, 1982), 202.

importance of having a complete Burmese Bible that would not have to be revised within a few years. He translated from the original Greek and Hebrew, not from a translation. Judson developed a serious lung infection and doctors prescribed a sea voyage as a cure. On April 12, 1850, Adoniram Judson died at age sixty-one on board ship in the Bay of Bengal and was buried at sea. He had spent thirty-seven years in missionary service in Burma with only one visit back home in America. Here are selected quotes about Judson's beliefs in election and predestination: "Judson was a Calvinist, but did not wear his Calvinism on his sleeve."[132] "When we come to the doctrines of grace we find that he believed them implicitly rather than by explicit exposition."[133] "His father, who was a Congregationalist pastor in Massachusetts, had studied with Jonathan Edwards's student Joseph Bellamy, and Adoniram inherited a deep belief in the sovereignty of God. The great importance this has for my purpose here is to stress that this deep confidence in God's overarching providence through all calamity and misery sustained him to the end. He said, 'If I had not felt certain that every additional trial was ordered by infinite love and mercy, I could not have survived my accumulated sufferings.'"[134]

John Leadley Dagg (1794–1884)

John Leadley Dagg lived to be over ninety years old and became one of the most profound thinkers in American Baptist life. He had to overcome a limited education, near blindness, and a physical disability to become a great pastor in Philadelphia. He later became an educator both in Alabama and as president of Mercer University in Georgia. He was a convinced evangelical Calvinist who wrote a popular English prose.

His magnum opus called *Manual of Theology* (1857) was the first comprehensive systematic theology written by a Baptist in America and it was very influential with Baptists in the South. The following paragraphs are from his *Manual of Theology*:

The doctrine of election encounters strong opposition in the hearts of men and it is therefore necessary to examine thoroughly its claim to our belief. As it relates to an act of the divine mind, no proof of its truth can be equal to the testimony of the Scriptures. Let us receive their teachings on the subject without hesitation or distrust and let us require every preconceived opinion of ours and all our carnal reasonings, to bow before the authority of God's holy word.

[132] Erroll Hulse, *Adoniram Judson and the Missionary Call* (Leeds: Reformation Today Trust, 1996), 48.
[133] Thomas J. Nettles, *By His Grace and for His Glory* (Grand Rapids: Baker Book House, 1986), 148–154.
[134] Quoted in *Giants of the Missionary Trail* (Chicago: Scripture Press Foundation, 1954), 73.

The Scriptures clearly teach, that God has an elect or chosen people. "Who shall lay anything to the charge of God's elect." Elect according to the foreknowledge of God "shall not God avenge his own elect." "Ye are a chosen generation." "God hath chosen you to salvation." "According as He hath chosen us in Christ." Whatever may have been our prejudices against the doctrine of election as held and taught by some ministers of religion, it is undeniable, that, in some sense, the doctrine is found in the Bible. We cannot reject it without rejecting that inspired book. We are bound by the authority of God, to receive the doctrine and nothing remains, but that we should make an honest effort to understand it, just as it is taught in the sacred volume.[135]

Charles Hodge (1797–1878)

Charles Hodge was a leading Presbyterian theologian and principal of Princeton Theological Seminary between 1851 and 1878. He was a leading exponent of the Princeton theology, which was an orthodox Calvinist theological tradition in America begun during the nineteenth century. He defended adamantly the authority of the Bible as the Word of God. Many of his ideas were adopted in the twentieth century by Fundamentalists and Evangelicals. He began writing early in his theological career and continued publishing until his death. His *Commentary on the Epistle to the Romans* published in 1835 is considered to be his greatest exegetical work. His magnum opus is the three-volume *Systematic Theology* (1871–1873).

As a conservative, he spent his life defending Reformed theology as set forth in the Westminster Confession of Faith and Larger and Westminster Shorter Catechisms. He loved to say that Princeton had never originated a new idea, which simply meant that Princeton was the advocate of historical Calvinism in opposition to the modified and compromised Calvinism of a later time. Professor Hodge wrote the following:

The word *charis* means a favorable disposition or kind feeling and especially love as exercised toward the inferior, dependent, or unworthy. This is represented as the crowning attribute of the divine nature. Its manifestation is declared to be the grand end of the whole scheme of redemption. The Apostle teaches that predestination, election, and salvation are all intended for the praise of the glory of the grace of God, which He exercises toward us in Christ Jesus (Ephesian 1:3–6). He raises men from spiritual death and makes them sit together in heavenly places in Christ Jesus, that in the ages to come he might show the exceeding riches of his grace (Ephesians 2:6–7). Therefore, it is often asserted that salvation is of grace. The gospel is a system of grace. All its blessings are gratuitously bestowed. All is so ordered that in every step of the progress of redemption and in its consummation,

---

[135] *Manual of Theology,* book 7, *Doctrine Concerning Divine Grace,* chapter 4, section 1, "Election," 309.

the grace, or undeserved love of God, is conspicuously displayed. Nothing is given or promised on the ground of merit. Everything is an undeserved favor. That salvation was provided at all, is a matter of grace and not of debt. That one man is saved and another not, is to the subject of salvation, a matter of grace. All his Christian virtues, are graces, i.e., gifts. Hence, it is that the greatest of all gifts secured by the work of Christ, that without which salvation had been impossible, the Holy Ghost, in the influence which He exerts on the minds of men, has in all ages and in all parts of the Church been designated as divine grace. A work of grace is the work of the Holy Spirit. The means of grace are the means by which or in connection with which the influence of the Spirit is conveyed or exercised. By common grace, therefore, is meant that influence of the Spirit, which in a greater or less measure, is granted to all who hear the truth. By sufficient grace is meant such kind and degree of the Spirit's influence, as is sufficient to lead men to repentance, faith, and a holy life. By efficacious grace is meant such an influence of the Spirit as is certainly effectual in producing regeneration and conversion. By preventing grace is intended that operation of the Spirit on the mind, which precedes and excites its efforts to return to God. By the "gratia gratum faciens" is meant the influence of the Spirit which renews or renders gracious. Cooperating grace is that influence of the Spirit, which aids the people of God in all the exercises of the divine life. By habitual grace is meant the Holy Spirit as dwelling in believers or that permanent, immanent state of mind due to His abiding presence and power. Such is the established theological and Christian usage of this word. By grace, therefore, in this connection is meant the influence of the Spirit of God on the minds of men.[136]

B. C. Howell (1801–1868)

B. C. Howell served as the second president of the Southern Baptist Convention (from 1851 through 1858). He is described in *Cathcart's Baptist Encyclopedia* as "one of the ablest and most learned men in the South." The encyclopedia also claims that "no one exercised a greater or more beneficial influence within or outside of the church. His life was unspotted, his Christian course was marked by the highest virtues. His courtesy and kindness of heart made him a universal favorite, notwithstanding the fierce theological debates in which he was often engaged."

Regarding sovereign grace and the effectual call of the Spirit, within the context of election and predestination, he wrote the following:

The whole arrangement was, therefore, of His own sovereign grace, uninfluenced by human merit. But this conclusion is not only inferable from the facts before you. His entire sovereignty in this whole transaction is expressly affirmed in His Word: "Not by works of

---

[136] Charles Hodge, *Systematic Theology*, vol.1, Common Grace (Ravenio Books, 2014), 2:654–655.

righteousness which we have done, but according to His mercy He saved us, by the washing (purifying) of regeneration, and the renewing of the Holy Ghost; which He shed on us abundantly through Jesus Christ our savior; that being justified by His grace, we should be made heirs, according to the hope of eternal life.[137]

"Thus he secures your enlightenment, your regeneration, and your sanctification, for which when an apostle prays, he predicates his assurance of an answer, upon the faithfulness of God to his promise given in the covenant. . . . Faithful is He that calleth you, who also will do it."[138]

Joseph Charles Philpot (1802–1869)

Joseph Charles Philpot was known as The Seceder because he resigned from the Church of England in 1835 and became a "Strict and Particular Baptist." Afterward, he became the editor of the *Gospel Standard Magazine* and served in that capacity for twenty years. Educated at Oxford University, he was elected a fellow of Worcester College, and appeared to have a brilliant scholastic career before him. But he was brought into deep spiritual convictions, which led him into the ministry. He was baptized by John Warburton at Allington (Wilts). The rest of his life was spent ministering among the "Strict Baptists." For twenty-six years, he held a joint pastorate at Stamford (Lines) and Oakham (Rutland), while continuing as the editor of *The Gospel Standard,* where many of his sermons were first published. Regarding the doctrines under study here, he wrote the following in his magazine: "My desire is to exalt the grace of God; to proclaim salvation alone through Jesus Christ; to declare the sinfulness, helplessness and hopelessness of man in a state of nature; to describe the living experience of the children of God in their trials, temptations, sorrows, consolations and blessings."[139]

The following comments are from his sermon called "Blessings Imputed & Mercies Imparted" preached at Eden Street Chapel, Hampstead Road, London, on Sunday evening, August 17, 1845:

Now, in the text, the apostle traces out what brought them into this state of saintship, it is because of Him that you are in Christ Jesus. The expression refers to two distinct things. First, the original purpose of God and secondly, the execution of that purpose. Both are "of Him"—flowing out of Him, arising from him, purposed by Him in eternity, and executed by Him in time. "Of Him"—not of yourselves—"not of him that wills, nor of him

[137] R. B. C. Howell, *The Covenants* (Charleston: Southern Baptist Publication Society, 1855), 37–38.
[138] R. B. C. Howell, *The Covenants,* 42.
[139] https://www.monergism.com/sermons-j-c-philpot-10-volumes.

that runs," not by the exertion of creature intellect, not by the instrumentality of human operation, not by anything the creature has done, not by anything the creature can do. The apostle traces up the standing of Christ's people in Him to its origin—the eternal purpose and counsel of God. All that takes place in time he represents as flowing out of the eternal mind, and happening according to the original purpose and covenant plan of Jehovah. You will observe, then, that when the apostle speaks of these Corinthian believers as being "in Christ Jesus," he intends thereby to set forth their personal standing in the Son of God under two distinct points of view—First as originating in eternity and secondly as taking place in time. In other words, every believer has a twofold union with Christ; one from all eternity, which we may call an eternal or election-union; the other in time, through the Spirit's operation in his heart, which we may call a time or regeneration-union. Let us attempt to unfold these two kinds of union separately.

George Müller (1805–1898)

George Müller was a Christian evangelist and Director of the Ashley Down orphanage in Bristol, England, where he cared for 10,024 orphans over the course of his lifetime, depending totally and only on God by faith and secret prayer. He was well known for providing an education to the children under his care, to the point where he was accused of "raising the poor above their natural station in life." He also established 117 schools in various parts of the world, which offered Christian education to over 120,000 children, many of them being orphans.

Müller prayed about everything and expected each prayer to be answered, as he believed what he was doing was God's will. He read through the Bible two hundred times and was on his knees praying over what he read during a hundred of those readings. Müller wrote the following about how he came to believe in the doctrines of election, particular redemption, and final persevering grace while staying in Teignmouth, Devon in 1829:

> I had not before seen from the Scriptures that the Father chose us before the foundation of the world, and that in Him that wonderful plan of our redemption originated, and that He also appointed all the means by which it was to be brought about. Further, that to save us, the Son had fulfilled the law, to satisfy its demands, and with it also the holiness of God. He had borne the punishment due to our sins and had thus satisfied the justice of God. And further, that the Holy Spirit alone can teach us about our state by nature, show us the need of a Savior, enable us to believe in Christ, explain to us the Scriptures, help us in preaching, etc. It was my beginning to understand this latter point in particular, which had a great effect on me. For the Lord enabled me to put it to the test of experience, by laying aside commentaries and almost every other book and simply reading the word of

God and studying it. The result of this was, that the first evening that I shut myself into my room, to give myself to prayer and meditation over the Scriptures, I learned more in a few hours than I had done during a period of several months previously. But the particular difference was that I received real strength for my soul in doing so. I now began to try by the test of the Scriptures the things which I had learned and seen and found that only those principles which stood the test were really of value.[140]

Horatius Bonar (1808–1889)

Horatius Bonar was a Scottish churchman, hymn writer, and a poet educated in Edinburgh. As one of eleven children, he came from a long line of ministers who served a total of 364 years in the Church of Scotland. He married Jane Catherine Lundie in 1843, and five of their young children died in succession. Toward the end of their lives, one of their surviving daughters was left a widow with five small children and she returned to live with her parents. In 1853 Bonar earned the Doctor of Divinity degree at the University of Aberdeen. The following comments from Dr. Bonar come from his article "The Christian Treasury," which is a part of the publication called *The Life and Works of Horatius Bonar*:

> If Jewish or Gentile unbelief, and alienation from God were things which could be reached by moral persuasion, and human warmth; if men's souls were within our reach as completely as their bodies, then God's definite purpose as to salvation would be of little moment [importance]. But if the estrangement of humanity from God be a thing quite beyond man, and man's argument or eloquence; if the resistance of a human will be a thing of almost unconceivable potency, and if the subjugation of that will require the direct forthputting of Omnipotence, such as that which created heaven and earth, then God's purpose is the first and last thing to be considered in going forth to deal either with Jew or Gentile. Other considerations may light up a false fire and produce a fair seeming zeal, but only the knowledge of a divine purpose can bring a man into a right missionary position, fill him with missionary devotedness, and nerve him [give confidence] in the hour of disappointment or discomfort. "Even so Father—or so it seemed good in thy sight," was the truth on which the Son of God rested in the day of Israel's first rejection of His Word; and it is just on such a truth as this—a truth that lifts the divine purpose into its true place, that each of us, whether minister or missionary, must lean, in the day of apparent failure.
>
> The Pauline or if you like, the Calvinistic scheme, which connects all work for God with a definite purpose, and not with an indefinite wish, is that which alone can make us either comfortable or successful. Armed with this divine purpose, we feel ourselves invincible; nay,

---

[140] George Muller, *The Autobiography of George Muller* (Whitaker House; revised, updated edition, February 1, 1996), 39–40.

we are assured of being victorious. Having ascertained God's purpose, and adopted it as the basis of our operations, we feel that we are in sympathy with God while working for Him. And it is this sympathy, this oneness of mind with God, that cheers us and sustains. He ever wins who sides with God. We shall thus be better fitted for enduring hardness, for "spending and being spent" that is, for expending ourselves, till all that is in us is expended.[141]

Robert Murray McCheyne (1813–1843)

Robert Murray McCheyne was a Scottish gospel preacher who had a particular missionary interest in the Jews. While he was in Israel, revival broke out under the ministry of William Chalmers Burns. This revival was to continue through the remaining years of McCheyne's life. Even though McCheyne did not consider himself to be a writer, his spiritual devotion was expressed in his fifty-plus poems and hymns of which "Jehovah Tsidkenu" and "I am a Debtor" became famous. His only published book was a joint effort with Andrew Bonar called *The Narrative of a Mission of Inquiry to the Jews.* His poetry, art, and music were expressed in his sermons and writings, which included a volume of verses titled "Songs of Zion." Traveling severely strained McCheyne's health and he eventually developed a fever and contracted typhoid fever. As his life drew to a close, he continued to plead for the souls of his congregation in his prayers. He was not yet thirty years old when went to be with his Lord on March 25, 1843, and the vision of his most well-known hymn was realized, "When This Passing World Is Done." Regarding election and predestination, he wrote the following:

We are here taught that God is sovereign in choosing the souls that are saved. He is sovereign in choosing men, and not rebel angels. He is sovereign in choosing the countries that have the light of the gospel. All nations are equally lost and vile in the sight of God. He is sovereign in choosing the most unlikely persons to be saved. If my soul is saved, am I not bound to give thanks? If ministers are bound to thank God for the free salvation of their people, how much more are we bound to praise Him ourselves for saving us. I am no better than a rebel angel. Devils never rejected Christ as I have done, and yet He passed them by and saved me. I am no better than a Chinese or a Hindu, and yet grace has passed millions of them, and come to me. I was no better than the sinners around me, perhaps worse than most, and yet I trust I can say, "Thou hast delivered my soul from the lowest hell." Glory to God the Father, that He chose me before the world was. Glory to Jesus, that He passed by millions and died for me. Glory to the Holy Spirit, that He came out of free love and awakened me.[142]

---

[141] pp. 1334–1335 / Lux Publications, 1871
[142] Robert Murray McCheyne, "Sermons of Robert Murray McCheyne, Chosen to Salvation," #1—points 1–3 (Carlisle, PA: The Banner of Truth Trust), 127.

Patrick Hues Mell (1814–1888)

Patrick Hues Mell was one of the most influential educators and ministers in nineteenth-century Georgia. For almost fifty years he served as professor of ancient languages and chief administrator at Mercer University and the University of Georgia. He also held leadership roles in the Georgia Baptist and Southern Baptist Conventions. His greatest influence as a moderator of numerous religious and educational assemblies earned him the designation "prince of parliamentarians." Mell published the following books: *Baptism in Its Mode and Subjects* (1853), *Corrective Church Discipline* (1860), *A Manual of Parliamentary Practice* (1867), and *The Doctrine of Prayer* (1876). He also wrote articles and tracts on predestination and Calvinism. The following paragraphs are from his essay on Calvinism:

It is no inconsiderable argument in favor of the Calvinistic system that, as one of its effects, it presents God in a dignified and honorable aspect. It is surely a worthy view of God, to represent Him as a sovereign and efficient ruler, who accomplishes all His pleasure and is never thwarted; who is the author of everything good in His system and who is especially entitled to all the praise of our salvation. What a contrast is there between this system, and that which would represent Him as anxious and impotent—as waiting with solicitude for men to give Him a pretext to interpose; now, passing a decree in their favor, upon the supposition that they have furnished justifiable occasion, and then, reconsidering and reversing, when He has discovered that He acted on insufficient grounds; and all the while, surrounded by inextricable confusion, which, an invincible necessity prevents Him from abating, and which He must reluctantly content Himself with overruling, and directing to results that are attainable, since He cannot secure the highest and the best. Such a God, impotent, and subordinate, and changeable, dependent on contingencies that He does not ordain, and distracted by confusion that He cannot control, is not the God of Calvinism. Our God is in the heavens. He hath done whatsoever He pleased. For of Him, and through Him, and to Him, are all things. To whom be glory forever. Amen.

In conclusion, it becomes a serious and practical question—whether we should not make these doctrines the basis of all our pulpit ministrations. If this be, indeed, the gospel system, sustained by such arguments, and attested by such effects, every minister should be imbued with its spirit, and furnished with its panoply. It is not necessary, indeed, that we should present its truths, always in the form of dogmatic or polemic theology—though, even these should not be entirely neglected, if our people are not as yet, thoroughly indoctrinated—but our hearers should never be left in doubt as to the fundamental truths, that sinners are totally depraved, and utterly helpless that men must be regenerated by God's Spirit, and justified by the righteousness of Christ imputed to them, before they can obtain God's favor; that God's people are created by Him, in Christ Jesus, unto good works, which He had before ordained that they should walk in them, and that they are kept by God's power, through faith unto salvation, and that God is the sovereign ruler of the universe and the author of everything morally good, in the creature. In short, that the sinner has destroyed himself, but in God is his help. And surely, it will not impair the efficiency of the minister himself, for him ever to remember that his sufficiency is of God.[143]

John G. Paton (1824–1907)

John G. Paton was a Scottish Protestant missionary to the New Hebrides Islands of the South Pacific. Paton undertook an incredible work, which would show very little visible fruit for decades, but he was convinced of the absolute sovereignty of God to build His church. Paton was constantly under threat of death, but he preached faithfully to the cannibals of the New Hebrides, while raising his family there. As well as his missionary journeys, Paton raised great support for world missions at home in Scotland and inspired hundreds of missionaries to also take up the Great Commission and make disciples of all nations. He was a man who was visually attractive and bore his testimony with great power. He described himself as "a Presbyterian Evangelical Calvinist of the old Covenanter Reformed Church of Scotland." He wrote many pamphlets on missionary topics and to expose the evils of the Kanaka labor traffic, as well as opposing the French annexation of the New Hebrides in favor of British occupation. However, his autobiography made him famous and had tremendous sales because of the strength of his dangerous trials and tribulations on the islands of Tanna and Aniwa. Much of the book's success goes to the literary skill of his brother, Rev. James Paton, who died in Glasgow December 21, 1906.

Basil Manly Jr. (1825–1892)

Basil Manly, Jr. was the son of Basil Manly, Sr. (1798–1868), the well-known Baptist preacher and educator. The family moved to Tuscaloosa, Alabama, when Manly, Jr. was 12 years old, where his father served as president of the University of Alabama (1837–1855) for almost 20 years. Manly, Jr. was baptized at age 14 after reading a biography of Jonathan Edwards. He graduated from the University of Alabama and he was licensed to preach by the Baptist church at age nineteen. He enrolled at Newton Theological Institution in Massachusetts. After the Southern Baptist Convention was formed in 1845, Manly, Jr. transferred to Princeton Theological Seminary. Manly studied theology at under professors including Charles Hodge, a Presbyterian theologian and leading promoter of the Princeton theology, an orthodox Calvinist theological tradition that held sway from the founding of that institution in 1812 until the Fundamentalist-Modernist controversy during the

---

[143] J. H. Estill, "Calvinism: An Essay," public printer, Savannah, Georgia (1875).

1920s. Manly graduated from Princeton in 1847. With John Albert Broadus, William Williams, and James Petigru Boyce, he was instrumental in the formation of the Southern Baptist Theological Seminary in Greenville, South Carolina. He was one of the original four faculty members. The seminary was very important to the formation of the Southern Baptist convention. In 1877, the seminary moved to Louisville, Kentucky. Manly also wrote about forty hymns, many of which were printed in *The Baptist Psalmody* published in 1850, which he and his father edited together. The following quote about Manly and his father is from Dr. Michael A. G. Haykin who is a professor of church history at Southern Baptist Seminary and has written or edited more than twenty-five books:

> Basil Manly, Sr. and his son Basil Manly, Jr. played vital roles in shaping a number of the central institutions of the Southern Baptist community in its formative years in the nineteenth century, including the influential Southern Baptist Theological Seminary. Undergirding their churchmanship was a vigorous Calvinistic Baptist piety that was expressed in sermons and tracts, hymns and confessional statements, letters and diaries, all of which are represented in this timely volume of selections from their writings. Here we have a wonderful window onto the vista of nineteenth-century Southern Baptist life with all of its glorious strengths as well as its clear failings.[144]

James Petigru Boyce (1827–1888)

James Petigru Boyce was a Southern Baptist pastor, theologian, author, and seminary professor. He was educated at Brown University under Francis Wayland, whose evangelical sermons helped lead to Boyce's conversion. His father was considered the richest man in South Carolina at the time. Boyce also was educated at Princeton Theological Seminary under Charles Hodge, who led Boyce to appreciate Calvinistic theology. Boyce became a pastor, then a university professor, and finally the founder and first president of the Southern Baptist Theological Seminary, where he taught theology from 1859 until his death in 1888. Throughout his life, he promoted the importance of a theological education for all ministers. A year before his death, he published his *Abstract of Systematic Theology*. In the Preface he wrote, "This volume is published as a practical text book, for the study of the system of doctrine taught in the Word of God, rather than as a contribution to theological science." Boyce's views are rightly called Calvinistic or Reformed. He, like most early Southern Baptist leaders, was clearly convinced of the doctrines of sovereign grace. The following comments below from Boyce's abstract demonstrate his orthodox views of election

---

[144] The introduction in *Soldiers of Christ: Selections from the Writings of Basil Manly, Sr. and Basil Manly, Jr.*, Dr. Michael Haykin (Founders Press, July 28, 2009).

and predestination from Ephesians 2:1–13:

> The description of the condition of those who were dead in trespasses and sins, and in that state were quickened, proves that the quickening and salvation was due to no merit of their own. The texts thus exhibited under these three classes prove conclusively that not on account of their own merits, but because of the good pleasure of God, does He choose men. They have been presented at some length, because this is after all the point upon which all that is important in this controversy turns. For, although other matters are equally essential to the doctrine, the whole opposition arises from an unwillingness on the part of man to recognize the sovereignty of God, and to ascribe salvation entirely to grace. This proof, however, has been by no means exhausted, the attempt having been to select some only of the numerous passages, and mainly such as from their conciseness allow of presentation in full. Let the Scriptures be read with reference to this doctrine and every passage marked which indicates God's dealing with men as an absolute sovereign, and also every declaration which ascribes Election or the fruits of it to his choice and not to the will or acts of men, and every illustration afforded that this is God's usual method, and it will appear that scarcely any book of Scripture will fail to furnish testimony to the fact that in the acts of grace, no less than those of providence, God "doeth according to his will in the army of heaven and among the inhabitants of the earth." Dan. 4:3–5. (5.)
>
> Another important fact to be shown is the eternity of Election in opposition to the idea that it was in time. The proof on this point is twofold. There are (a) those passages which show that the Election took place before existence in this world or before the world began, and (b) those which actually declare that it was eternal. Between the two classes of passages there is really, however, very little difference, as from the nature of the case, what took place before time must have been in Eternity, and besides the object of proof of an eternal Election is simply to show that it was not dependent on human action, but simply on the will of God.[145]

John A. Broadus (1827–1895)

John A. Broadus was an American Baptist pastor and professor at the Southern Baptist Theological Seminary (then in Greenville, South Carolina, and in Louisville, Kentucky). He was one of the most famous preachers of his day. A. T. Robertson (the Greek Scholar) called him "one of the finest fruits of modern Christianity." Charles Spurgeon deemed him the "greatest of living preachers." A. H. Newman described Broadus as "perhaps the greatest man the Baptists have produced."

---

[145] Rev. James Petigru Boyce, DD, LLD, *Abstract of Systematic Theology*, chapter 30, "Election" (Founders Press, first published in 1887), 115–124.

Broadus was educated at home and at a private school. He taught in a small school before completing his undergraduate studies at the University of Virginia, and eventually became pastor of the Baptist church in Charlottesville. In 1859, he became professor of New Testament interpretation and homiletics at the new Southern Baptist Theological Seminary (where he later became the school's second president). During the Civil War, he served for a while as chaplain to Robert E. Lee's army in northern Virginia. He was a model author, teacher, preacher, scholar, seminary leader, and denominational statesman. His Calvinism is crucial in understanding nineteenth-century Southern Baptist theology and heritage. Here is one of his statements regarding the providence of God from his 1892 Southern Baptist catechism called *A Catechism of Bible Teaching*: "Both divine predestination and human freedom must be true from the very nature of God and man, and both are plainly taught in the Bible."[146]

Charles Haddon Spurgeon, The Prince of Preachers in Great Britain (1834–1892)

Charles Haddon Spurgeon was the British "Particular Baptist" preacher known as the Prince of Preachers. He was the most well-known leader in the Reformed Baptist tradition, defending the church in agreement with the 1689 London Baptist Confession of Faith. During his life, Spurgeon preached to around ten million people, often speaking up to ten times each week at different places. He was the pastor of the New Park Street Chapel (later called the Metropolitan Tabernacle) in London for thirty-eight years. In 1857, he started a charity organization which is now called Spurgeon's and works around the world. He also founded Spurgeon's College, which was named after him posthumously. He was a prolific author of many types of works including sermons, an autobiography, commentaries, books on prayer, devotionals, magazines, poetry, hymns, and more. Many sermons were transcribed as he spoke and were translated into many languages during his lifetime. His sermons were powerful and reached the hearts of people. His oratory skills held his listeners spellbound in the Metropolitan Tabernacle and many Christians have discovered Spurgeon's messages to be among the best in Christian literature. Here is one of his many statements about election and predestination, which he refers to here as his Calvinistic beliefs:

The old truth that Calvin preached, that Augustine preached, that Paul preached, is the truth that I must preach today, or else be false to my conscience and my God. I cannot

---

[146] *A Catechism of Bible Teaching,* "Lesson 2: Providence of God, Answer to Advanced Question 6 (John A. Broadus," American Baptist Publication Society (1892).

shape the truth. I know of no such thing as paring off the rough edges of a doctrine. John Knox's gospel is my gospel. That which thundered through Scotland must thunder through England again.[147]

Spurgeon: Election and Holiness

God has chosen to himself a people whom no man can number, out of the children of Adam—out of the fallen and apostate race who sprang from the loins of a rebellious man. Now, this is a wonder of wonders, when we come to consider that the heaven, even the heaven of heavens, is the Lord's. If God must have a chosen race, why did he not select one from the majestic orders of angels, or from the flaming cherubim and seraphim who stand around his throne? Why was not Gabriel fixed upon? Why was he not so constituted that from his loins there might spring a mighty race of angels, and why were not these chosen by God from before the foundations of the world!

What could there be in man, a creature lower than the angels, that God should select him rather than the angelic spirits? Why were not the cherubim and seraphim given to Christ? Why did he not take up angels? Why did he not assume their nature, and take them into union with himself? An angelic body might be more in keeping with the person of Deity, than a body of weak and suffering flesh and blood. There were something congruous if he had said unto the angels, "You shall be my sons." But, no! though all these were his own, he passes by the hierarchy of angels, and stoops to man! He takes up an apostate worm, and says unto him, "You shall be my son," and to myriads of the same race he cries, "you shall be my sons and daughters, by a covenant for ever." "But," says one, "It seems that God intended to choose a fallen people that he might in them show forth his grace. Now, the angels of course would be unsuitable for this, since they have not fallen." I reply, there are angels that have fallen; there were angels that kept not the first estate, but fell from their dignity. And how is it that these are consigned to blackness of darkness for ever? Answer me, you that deny God's sovereignty, and hate his election—how is it that angels are condemned to everlasting fire, while to you, the children of Adam, the gospel of Christ is freely preached?

"The only answer that can possibly be given is this—God wills to do it. He has a right to do as he pleases with his own mercy. Angels deserve no mercy: we deserve none."

Nevertheless, He gave it to us, and He denied it them. They are bound in chains, reserved for everlasting fire to the last great day, but we are saved. Why, if there were any reason to move God in his creatures, He would certainly have chosen devils rather than men—Had the angels been reclaimed, they could have glorified God more than we and they could have sang his praises louder than we can, clogged as we are with flesh and

---

[147] Charles H. Spurgeon, *"A Defense of Calvinism,"* from Tony Capoccia at the Bible Bulletin Board, www.biblebb.com.

blood. But passing by the greater, He chose the lesser, that He might show forth his sovereignty, which is the brightest jewel in the crown of his divinity!

Our Arminian antagonists always leave the fallen angels out of the question—for it is not convenient to them to recollect this ancient instance of election. They call it unjust, that God should choose one man and not another. By what reasoning can this be unjust, when they will admit that it was righteous enough in God to choose one race—the race of men, and leave another race—the race of angels, to be sunk into misery on account of sin? Brethren, let us be done with arraigning God at our poor fallible judgment seat! God is good and does righteousness. Whatever He does we may know to be right, whether we can see the righteousness or not. God's Election is marvelous indeed—God had unlimited power of creation. Now, if He willed to make a people who should be His favorites, who should be united to the person of His Son, and who should reign with Him, why did He not make a new race?

When Adam sinned, it would have been easy enough to strike the earth out of existence. He had but to speak and this round earth would have been dissolved, as the bubble dies into the wave that bears it. There would have been no trace of Adam's sin left, the whole might have died away and have been forgotten forever! But no! Instead of making a new people—a pure people who could not sin, instead of taking to himself creatures that were pure, unsullied, without spot—He takes a depraved and fallen people and lifts these up and that too, by costly means—by the death of His own Son, and by the work of His own Spirit; that these must be the jewels in His crown to reflect his glory forever!

Oh, singular choice! Oh, inexplicable Election! My soul is lost in your depths, and I can only pause and cry, "Oh, the goodness, oh, the mercy, oh, the sovereignty of God's grace!" Now, when you think that God has chosen you, you may well pause and say in the language of that hymn—"Pause, my soul! adore, and wonder! Ask, O why such love to Me?" Kings passed by and beggars chosen! Wise men left, but fools made to know the wonders of His redeeming love! Publicans and harlots sweetly compelled to come to the feast of mercy, while proud religious people are allowed to trust in their own righteousness, and perish in their vain boastings! God's choice will ever seem in the eyes of unrenewed men to be a very strange one—He has passed over those whom we should have selected, and He has chosen just the odds and ends of the universe, the men who thought themselves the least likely ever to taste of His grace! Before your sovereignty, I bow, great God, and acknowledge that You do as you wish, and that You give no account of your matters.[148]

---

[148] "Election and Holiness," sermon no. 303, volume 06, delivered on Sabbath Morning, March 11, 1860, by the Reverend C. H. Spurgeon at Exeter Hall, Strand—*Spurgeon's Sermons*, by Charles Haddon Spurgeon, ed. Anthony Uyl (Woodstock, Ontario: Devoted Publishing, 2017). The text of *Spurgeon's Sermons*, vol. 06, 1860, is all in the public domain.

A Feast for Faith

God does not work without a plan. God has not left the world to chance. There are some men who are always kicking against the doctrine of an eternal purpose and who grow angry if you assert that God has settled what shall occur. It is by the consent of all agreed that men are foolish if they work without a plan and yet they cry out when we insist that God also, in all his working, is fulfilling a well arranged design. Depend upon it, however, let men rebel against this truth as they will, that God has determined the end from the beginning. He has left no screw loose in the machine, He has left nothing to chance or accident. Nothing with God is the subject of an "if" or a "peradventure," but even the agency of man, free as it is, as untouched and undisturbed as if there were no God, even this is guided by His mysterious power, and works out thoroughly His own purpose in every jot and tittle.

God wings the thunderbolt, and shall He not guide the most passionate spirit? God puts a bit into the mouth of the whirlwind and shall He not control the most ambitious will? God takes care that even the sea shall come no farther than He bids it, and shall not the heart of man be equally subject to the Divine purpose? Yielding to man his free agency, giving to him his responsibility, leaving him as free as if there were no purpose and no decree, yet the eternal Jehovah works out His plans, and achieves His purpose to the praise of His glory.

Everything that has moved or shall move in heaven and earth and hell, has been, is, and shall be, according to the counsel and foreknowledge of God, fulfilling a holy, just, wise, and unalterable purpose! God is wonderful in His design and excellent in His working. Believer, God overrules all things for your good. The needs, be for all that you have suffered, have been most accurately determined by God. Your course is all mapped out by your Lord. Nothing will take Him by surprise. There will be no novelties to Him. There will be no occurrences, which He did not foresee and for which, therefore, He was not provided. He has arranged all and you have but to patiently wait and you shall sing a song of deliverance. Your life has been arranged on the best possible principles, so that if you had been gifted with unerring wisdom, you would have arranged a life for yourselves exactly similar to the one through which you have passed.

Let us trust God where we cannot trace Him. In the end, we shall read the whole of God's purpose as one grand poem and there will not be one verse in it that has a syllable too much, or a word too little. There will not be one stanza or letter redundant, much less one that is erased. But from beginning to end we shall see the master pen and the mastermind drawing forth the glorious array of majestic thoughts. And with angels, and seraphs, and principalities, and powers, shall burst forth into one mighty song, "Hallelujah! Hallelujah! Hallelujah! the Lord God Omnipotent reigns!" We shall see how from the first even to the last, the King has been ruling all things according to His own will.[149]

The Word "Chance"

"The word 'chance' should be forever banished from the Christian's conversation. Luck or chance is a 'base heathenish invention'! God rules and overrules all things and he does nothing without a motive."[150]

James Chalmers (1841–1901)

James Chalmers was a Scottish missionary-explorer, who served in Rarotonga in the Cook Islands for ten years and in New Guinea from 1877 until his brutal murder by cannibal tribesmen on April 4, 1901, during a missionary trip to Goaribari Island. In 1865, he was ordained a Minister in the Free Church of Scotland. The following year, with his bride of fifteen months, he was shipped off to Rarotonga, an island in the South Pacific.

Life was already well organized and structured on the island and the natives' prime time fun was fighting and indulging in drunken festivals involving gross immorality. Of course, young Chalmers put a stop to this. During his twenty-three years in New Guinea, Chalmers resided for short periods on the east coast at Suau, Port Moresby, Motumotu, and Saguane in the Fly River delta, but for certain periods of time he had no permanent home. His last station was Daru. From there, he set out with an associate named Oliver Tompkins, to establish a mission on Goaribari Island. Chalmers was a peculiar, but humane man with great personal charm, who counted among his friends, famous people as diverse as Robert Louis Stevenson and "Bully" Hayes, but his gift for genuine friendships was most evident in his relations with the New Guinea people to whom he was sincerely, emotionally, and tenderly devoted.

The Methodist missionary Dr. George Brown wrote, "Chalmers had consecrated himself to New Guinea and to that work he was loyal to the end." (Note: The Free Church of Scotland is "Calvinistic" or "Reformed" and claims the Westminster Confession of Faith as their confessional document.) In the excerpt below, from his sermon on Acts 27:22–31, Dr. Chalmers clearly articulates some of his thoughts on election and predestination, as he

---

[149] "A Feast for Faith," no. 715, by C. H. Spurgeon on Isaiah 28:29. Adapted from the C. H. Spurgeon Collection. Taken from The C. H. Spurgeon Collection, version 1.0, Ages Software. Only necessary changes have been made, such as correcting spelling errors, some punctuation usage, capitalization of deity pronouns, and minimal updating of a few archaic words. The content is unabridged. Additional Bible-based resources are available at www.spurgeongems.org.

[150] "The Voice of The Cholera," no. 705, Amos 3:3–6, a sermon delivered on Sunday Morning, August 12, 1866, by C. H. Spurgeon, at the Metropolitan Tabernacle, Newington.

comments on Acts 27:22, 31: "And now I exhort you to be of good cheer, for there shall be no loss of any man's life among you, but of the ship. Paul said to the centurion and to the soldiers, except these abide in the ship, ye cannot be saved."

The comparison of these two verses lands us in what may appear to many to be a very dark and unprofitable speculation. Now, our object in setting up this comparison, is not to foster in any of you a tendency to meddle with matters too high for us—but to protect you against the practical mischief of such a tendency. You have all heard of the doctrine of predestination. It has long been a settled article of our church. And there must be a sad deal of evasion and of unfair handling with particular passages, to get free of the evidence which we find for it in the Bible. And independently of Scripture altogether, the denial of this doctrine brings a number of monstrous conceptions along with it. It supposes God to make a world, and not to reserve in His own hand the management of its concerns. Though it should concede to Him an absolute sovereignty over all matter, it deposes Him from His sovereignty over the region of created minds, that far more dignified and interesting portion of His works. The greatest events in the history of the universe, are those which are brought about by the agency of willing and intelligent beings—and the enemies of the doctrine invest every one of these beings with some sovereign and independent principle of freedom, in virtue of which it may be asserted of this whole class of events, that they happened, not because they were ordained of God, but because the creatures of God, by their own uncontrolled power, brought them into existence. At this rate, even He to whom we give the attribute of omniscience, is not able to say at this moment, what shall be the fortune or the fate of any individual—and the whole train of future history is left to the wildness of accident. All this, carries along with it so complete a dethronement of God—it is bringing His creation under the dominion of so many nameless and undeterminable contingencies—it is taking the world and the current of its history so entirely out of the hands of Him who formed it—it is withal so opposite to what obtains in every other field of observation, where, instead of the lawlessness of chance, we shall find that the more we attend, the more we perceive of a certain necessary and established order—that from these and other considerations which might be stated, the doctrine in question, in addition to the testimonies which we find for it in the Bible, is at this moment receiving a very general support from the speculations of infidel as well as Christian philosophers. Assenting, as we do, to this doctrine, we state it as our conviction, that God could point the finger of His omniscience to every one individual amongst us, and tell what shall be the fate of each, and the place of each, and the state of suffering or enjoyment of each, at any one period of futurity however distant. Well does He know those of us who are vessels of wrath fitted for destruction, and those of us whom He has predestinated to be conformed to the image of His dear Son, and to be rendered meet for the inheritance. We are not saying that we, or that any of you could so cluster and arrange the two sets of individuals. This is one of the secret things which belongs to God. It is not our duty to be altogether silent about the doctrine of predestination—for the Bible is not silent about it, and it is our duty to promulgate and to hold up our testimony for all that we find there. But certain it is, that the doctrine has been so injudiciously meddled with—it has tempted so many ingenious and speculative men to transgress the limits of Scripture—it has engendered so much presumption among some, and so much despondency among others—it has been so much abused to the mischief of practical Christianity, that it were well for us all, could we carefully draw the line between the secret things which belong to God and the things which are revealed, and belong to us and to our children.[151]

James Gilmour (1843–1891)

James Gilmour was a was a Scottish Protestant missionary in China and Mongolia. His ancestors were Calvinist Christians. Gilmour won prizes in Latin, Greek, and English Literature. He got his bachelor's degree in 1867 and his master's degree in 1868. He received additional theological training at the Cheshunt Congregational Theological College (14 miles north of London). His early religious training at home bore great fruit, when he explained his conversion to Christianity during his university life. During his university days, he would go out in the evenings by himself and conduct open-air preaching services or share Christ with laborers along the roadside or in the fields. He also loved nature and the outdoors and would wander alone among the hills, woods, and glens, delighting in God's natural world and what it gave back to him.

He chose missionary service, because the workers abroad were so few compared to those at home, and he is quoted as saying, "To me the soul of an Indian seemed as precious as the soul of an Englishman, and the Gospel as much for the Chinese as the European." As he read the command of Jesus in Matthew to "go into all the word and preach," he saw a command to preach, but he saw it as coupled with the command to go into all the world. He served through the London Missionary Society and set sail from Liverpool, on February 22, 1870, upon the steamship *Diomed*. Once on board, he was appointed chaplain of the ship, and each night he talked to every member of the crew while on watch, and laid the matter of salvation so clearly before them that he afterward wrote, "All on board had repeated opportunities of hearing the Gospel as plainly as I could put it."

Gilmour reached Beijing, China on May 18, 1870, and settled right into his Chinese studies. During the summer of 1872, he and Joseph Edkins visited the sacred city of Wu Tai Shan, a famous place of Mongol pilgrimage. These people tried the zealous missionary

---

[151] Rev. Thomas Chalmers, DD and LLD, *Congregational Sermons*: vol. 2, sermon 8.

greatly. When he reached a new city, he would pitch his tent on a main thoroughfare, and from early in the morning until late at night, he ministered to the sick, preached, and talked to inquirers. During one eight month campaign, he saw about 6,000 patients, preached to nearly twenty-four thousand people, sold three thousand books, distributed forty-five hundred tracts, traveled 1,860 miles, spent about $200, and added that only two individuals openly confessed to believe in Christ. Gilmour made lonely, heroic efforts to preach the gospel to a people steeped in Lamaist forms of Buddhism. He would also spend summers with nomadic Mongols on the plains of Mongolia and spend winters with Mongols in Peking.

He longed for a helper on his field, but the society was unable to supply one. At last, when one did come, he was able to go home on furlough. When the tried and tested missionary reached England in 1889, he was so thin, and the marks of his struggles were so evident in his face, that his friends did not recognize him. He was delighted to be with his motherless boys, who had been sent home to be educated, after their mother's death.

His book, *Gilmour and His Boys*, has touched many a heart. After his restful furlough, he returned to Mongolia and continued his work. In April of 1891, he returned to Tianjin to attend the North China District Committee of the London Missionary Society. They honored him by appointing him chairman and he served them well. He was stricken suddenly with typhus fever and died on May 21, 1891. When the news of his death circulated in faraway Mongolia, strong, adult men wept like children, when they were told that their beloved Gilmour was no more. He worked and ministered in eastern Mongolia until his death at age forty-seven, after twenty-one years of missionary service.

(Endnote about the London Missionary Society: The founding of the broadly Calvinist London Missionary Society, originally just called the "Missionary Society" in 1795 was in fact the linear descendant of a proposal of 1772 made at Trevecca, Wales to send missionaries to prerevolutionary America's settlers and aboriginals.)[152]

Alexander Murdoch Mackay (1849–1890)

Alexander Murdoch Mackay was a Presbyterian missionary to Uganda. He studied at the Free Church Training School for Teachers at Edinburgh, then at Edinburgh University, and finally in Berlin. He displayed a great aptitude for mechanics and spent several years as a draftsman in Germany. In 1875, he offered his services as a missionary to the Church Missionary Society, was accepted, and sent to Zanzibar. King Mutesa (reigned 1856–84) had expressed an interest in receiving Christian missionaries.

[152] Kenneth J. Stewart, "Calvinism and Missions: The Contested Relationship Revisited," vol. 34, issue 1, point 1 (April 2009).

Mackay's sister, Alexina Mackay Harrison, wrote the book about his life called *Pioneer Missionary of the Church Missionary Society to Uganda*. This book is an account of Mackay's early life and his work in Uganda recounts Mackay's early successes in working with King Mutesa, who made Uganda a friend to Great Britain and promised never to fight Christianity. The book also reveals Mackay's struggles with King Mwanga, who succeeded King Mutesa and turned against the missionaries, and persecuted the Ugandan Christians until he was overthrown in 1888.

After the death of King Mutesa in 1884 and the martyrdom of Christians (both Protestant and Catholic) in 1886 by King Mwanga, Mackay moved to the south of Lake Victoria where he lived the rest of his life. Mackay was seen as a man of great spiritual understanding and practical skills. He translated the Gospel of Matthew into the Luganda language. He also used his engineering skills to help build roads, boats, and houses. Due to his courage, energy, and devotion—the mission in Uganda experienced great success. Very sadly though, he came down with a malarial fever, and only after four days with the fever, he died. Mackay passed into the presence of the Lord on 8th February 1890 at the age of 40 years. He never married and never once returned to his native Scotland for the fourteen years he served in Uganda. But during those fourteen years, he planted the seed of the gospel and principles of Christian and Scientific education that would in due time, become the foundation of the education enterprise of the Church of Uganda.

As a Presbyterian, Mackay shared the Reformed tradition within the Protestant faith, which traces its origins to the British Isles and particularly Scotland. Presbyterian churches get their name from their form of church government. Presbyterian doctrine and theology emphasize the sovereignty of God and the authority of the Scriptures. Presbyterian church government was ensured in Scotland by the Acts of Union in 1707, which created the kingdom of Great Britain. Presbyterians found in England usually have a Scottish connection and the Presbyterian denominations in Scotland hold to the theology of John Calvin and those who followed after him. Therefore, the incredible missionary zeal, ingenuity, and effectiveness demonstrated by Alexander Murdoch Mackay in Uganda, is a real testament to the burden for lost souls in the hearts of those led by the doctrines of grace.

33 ✦

Prominent Twentieth Century Christian Thinkers Who Affirmed the Decrees of Election & Predestination

This chapter will identify key figures of the 1900s who had influential lives in the worldwide body of Christ and who expressed their convictions regarding the twin doctrines of election and predestination.

A. H. Strong (1836–1921)

A. H. Strong was a Baptist minister and theologian who lived in America during the late nineteenth and early twentieth centuries and became a bedrock of Reformed Baptist theological education for several generations. While president of the Rochester Theological Seminary, he wrote his most influential book called *Systematic Theology*. Many see Strong as a four-point Calvinist who affirmed the Universal Atonement verses the traditional Limited Atonement, but here is a taste of his views on election and predestination: "Calvinism is the broadest of systems. It regards the divine sovereignty and the freedom of the human will, as the two sides of a roof, which come together at a ridgepole above the clouds. Calvinism accepts both truths. A system that denies either one of the two, has only half of a roof over its head."[153]

---

[153] Augustus Hopkins Strong, *Systematic Theology: A Compendium* (Valley Forge, PA: The Judson Press, 1907), 364.

Dr. Abraham Kuyper (1837–1920)

Dr. Abraham Kuyper was a Dutch Calvinist theologian, philosopher, and politician. As leader of the Anti-Revolutionary Party in the Netherlands, he served as Prime Minister of his country from 1901–1905. He believed a major part of his calling in life was the task of reconstructing the social structures of his native Holland on the basis of its Calvinistic heritage. He developed Neo-Calvinism, which emphasizes the sovereignty of Jesus over all pursuits and supports the idea that there is a grace given by God to all things in order to sustain the continued unfolding of creation. Kuyper wrote a number of books, including *Conservatism and Orthodoxy* (1870), *The Social Question and the Christian Religion* (1891), and *Common Grace* (1902).

He delivered six classic lectures on Reformation theology at Princeton Theological Seminary in 1898. He introduced Calvinism as a life system (not just a doctrinal system to be studied and debated), discussing its relationship to religion, politics, science, and art. According to Kuyper, Calvinism seeks to unify the cosmos under universal laws. He stated, "Predestination proves that a set of laws exists to govern the world and science is merely trying to figure them out." Kuyper defended Calvinism in the realm of art as well, writing a thorough and elegant explanation of this outlook on life. The collection is called "Lectures on Calvinism" and not lectures on Christianity, because he believed that Calvinism most truthfully and most completely articulates the biblical Christian faith, with the sovereignty of God and election and predestination as the foundation.[154]

James B. Gambrell (1841–1921)

James B. Gambrell was a Southern Baptist pastor, educator, and denominational leader who was born in South Carolina and raised in Mississippi. He also lived in Georgia and later moved to Texas. He was editor of *The Baptist Record* for fourteen years, president of Mercer University, editor of *The Baptist Standard*, and president of the Southern Baptist Convention from 1917–1921. Here is a taste of his clearly spoken views of the doctrines of grace:

> We may invigorate our faith and renew our courage by reflecting that divine power has always attended the preaching of doctrine, when done in the true spirit of preaching. Great revivals have accompanied the heroic preaching of the doctrines of grace, predestination, election, and that whole lofty mountain range of doctrines upon which Jehovah sits enthroned. Sovereign grace is in all things. God honors preaching that honors Him. There

[154] Professor A. Kuyper, "Lectures on Calvinism: The Stone Lectures of 1898," First Lecture, "Calvinism A Life System" (Princeton, NJ: Hoveker & Wormser Ltd., Fleming H. Revell, Oct. 10, 1898), 1–45.

is entirely too much milksop preaching nowadays, trying to cajole sinners to enter upon a truce with their Maker, quit sinning, and join the church. The situation does not call for a truce, but a surrender. Let us bring out the heavy artillery of heaven, and thunder away at this stuckup age as Whitefield, Edwards, Spurgeon and Paul did, and there will be many slain of the Lord, raised up to walk in newness of Life.[155]

B. B. Warfield (1851–1921)

Benjamin Breckinridge Warfield was professor of theology at Princeton Seminary from 1887 to 1921. Some conservative Presbyterians consider him to be the last of the great Princeton theologians before the split in 1929 that formed Westminster Theological Seminary and the Orthodox Presbyterian Church. His parents were originally from Virginia and were quite wealthy. His maternal grandfather was the Presbyterian preacher Robert Jefferson Breckinridge (1800–1871), the son of John Breckinridge, a former United States Senator and Attorney General. Warfield's uncle was John C. Breckinridge, the fourteenth vice president of the United States, and a Confederate general in the American Civil War. His brother, Ethelbert Dudley Warfield was a Presbyterian minister and college president.

At Princeton, his primary thrust (and that of the seminary) was the divine inspiration and authority of the Bible. He preached and believed the doctrine of "sola scriptura" (meaning that the Bible is God's inspired word, is the primary source of the Christian's authority, and is sufficient for the Christian to live his or her faith). These views were held in contrast to some of the reported emotionalism in revival movements, the rationalism of higher criticism in academia, and the heterodox teachings (opinions or doctrines at variance with official orthodox positions) of various new religious movements that were emerging at this time.

The seminary faithfully followed the Westminster Confession of Faith (the Reformed confessional tradition). Warfield's theology clearly mirrored the doctrines of sovereign grace. He believed that the sixteenth-century Reformers, as well as the seventeenth century Confessional writers, were simply and faithfully summarizing the content and application of Scripture. Below is one of his memorable paragraphs on predestination's importance in the Reformation:

Scarcely as the Reformation established, however, before the purity of its confession of the predestination of God began to give way. The first serious blow to it was given by the defection of Melanchthon to a synergistic conception of the saving act. As a result of the

---

[155] *James Bruton Gambrell, Ten Years in Texas*; "The Southern Baptist Denominational Leader as Theologian," Bill J. Leonard, *Baptist History and Heritage 16* (July 1980): 23–32, 61, 63; "*James Bruton Gambrell*," E. C. Routh, *Encyclopedia of Southern Baptists*, vol. 2.

consequent controversies, the Lutheran Churches were misled into seeking to define predestination as having sole reference to salvation, denying its obverse of reprobation. First of all," says the "Formula of Concord" (1576), it ought to be most accurately observed that there is a distinction between the foreknowledge and the predestination or eternal election of God. . . . This foreknowledge of God extends both to good and evil men, but nevertheless is not the cause of evil, nor is it the cause of sin. . . . But the predestination or eternal election of God extends only to the good and beloved children of God, and this is the cause of their salvation.

The grave inconsequence of this construction, of course, speedily had its revenge, and typical Lutheranism rapidly sank to the level of Romish indifference to predestination altogether, and of the Romish explanation of it as "*ex praevisa fide*." Meanwhile the Reformed continued to witness a better profession, partly no doubt, because of the greater depth of religious life induced in them by the severity of the persecutions they were called upon to undergo and partly no doubt, because of the greater height of religious thinking created in them by the example and impulse of their great leader—at once, as even Renan has been compelled to testify, the best Christian of his day and the greatest religious thinker of the modern world. The first really dangerous assault on what had now become distinctively the Reformed doctrine of predestination was delayed till the opening of the seventeenth century. In the meantime, though, no doubt, many individual Reformed thinkers had been more or less affected by a Lutheran environment, as in the lands of German speech, or by Romish remainders, as in England, as well as no doubt by the everywhere present rationalizing spirit which ever lays its stress on man's autocracy. Yet the Reformed Churches had everywhere compacted their faith in numerous creeds, in which the Reformed consciousness had expressed itself on the whole with remarkable purity. These now served as a barrier to the new attacks, and supplied strongholds in which the Reformed consciousness could intrench itself for future influence. The Arminian assault was therefore successfully met. And although, ever since, the evil seed then sown has produced a continuous harvest of doubt and dispute in the Reformed Churches until today—in a new age of syncretism of perhaps unexampled extension—it threatens to eat out all that is distinctive in the Reformed Confessions, nevertheless the Reformed sense of absolute dependence on the God of grace for salvation remains till today the dominant element in the thought of the Reformed Churches, and its theological expression in the complete doctrine of *praedestinatio duplex* retains its place in the hearts as well as in the creeds of a multitude of Reformed Christians throughout the world.[156]

---

[156] Benjamin Breckinridge Warfield, "Predestination in the Reformed Confessions," reprinted from *The Presbyterian and Reformed Review*, vol. 12. 1901, 49–128.

Lewis Sperry Chafer (1871–1952)

Lewis Sperry Chafer was the American theologian who founded and served as the first president of Dallas Theological Seminary and was an influential founding member of modern theological Dispensationalism. Chafer received a DD from Wheaton (1926), LittD, Dallas (1924), and ThD from the Aix-en-Provence, France, Protestant Seminary (1946). Through close association with Scofield, Chafer became confirmed in dispensational theology, and in 1913 he assisted Scofield in founding the Philadelphia School of the Bible, where he served as a Bible lecturer from 1914–1922.

In 1924, he moved to Dallas to pastor the First Congregational Church. With his friend W. H. Griffith Thomas, he cofounded the Evangelical Theological College, now Dallas Theological Seminary. Chafer served as its president and professor of systematic theology until his death in 1952. He was a prolific writer and is most noted for his popular book titled *Grace* (1922) and his *magnum opus* eight-volume *Systematic Theology* (1948). The following comments on the subject of human will and its relation to God's sovereign work in election and predestination are from his *Systematic Theology* first published in 1948. (Lewis Sperry Chafer, *Systematic Theology*, Kregel Publications / 1993 / Hardcover):

"When exercising his will, man is conscious only of his freedom of action. He determines his course by circumstances, but God is the author of circumstances. Man is impelled by emotions, but God is able to originate and to control every human emotion. Man prides himself that he is governed by experienced judgment, but God is able to foster each and every thought or determination of the human mind. God will mold and direct in all secondary causes until His own eternal purpose is realized" (Vol. I, p. 241).

"Men choose their course by what seems to them a free will and they glory in the fact that they are wise enough to adjust themselves to circumstances, but God is the Author of circumstances" (Vol. III, p. 169).

"It is reasonable to conclude that, as man by an act of his will renounced God at the beginning, in like manner he, by the act of his own will, must return to God. It matters nothing at this point that man cannot of himself turn to God and that he must be enabled to do so. In the end, though enabled, he acts by his own will and this truth is emphasized in every passage wherein the salvation of man is addressed to his will" (Vol. III, p. 210).

"It is thus demonstrated that the erroneous exaltation of the human ability in the beginning becomes man's effectual undoing in the end. Over against this, the man who is totally incompetent, falling into the hands of God, who acts in sovereign grace, is saved and safe forever" (Vol. III, p. 276).

"The two systems—Arminianism and Calvinism—are each consistent at this point within themselves. The Arminian contends that man is supreme and that God is compelled to adjust Himself to that scheme of things. The Calvinist contends that God is supreme and that man is called upon to be conformed to that revelation. The Arminian is deprived of the exalted blessing, which is the portion of those who believe the sublime facts of predestination, election, and the sovereignty of God, because he hesitates to embrace them in their full-orbed reality. Having incorporated into his scheme the finite human element, all certainty about the future is for the Arminian overclouded with doubts. Having made the purpose of God contingent, the execution of that purpose must be contingent. By so much the glorious divine arrangement, by which the ungodly may go to heaven, is replaced by the mere moral program in which only good people may have a hope" (Vol. III, p. 282).

Thomas Todhunter Shields (1873–1955)

Thomas Todhunter Shields was born in Bristol, England as the son of a Baptist pastor. Eventually Shields became a Canadian pastor. He was converted to Christ at an early age during a revival meeting in his father's church.[157]

After being educated in British universities he pastored a few churches in England before being called to the Jarvis Street Baptist Church in Toronto, Canada in 1910, where he served for forty-five years. He was also active with the Home Mission Board of the Baptist Convention of Ontario and Quebec, served as president of the Baptist Union of North America, vice president of the International Council of Christian Churches, president of the Union of Regular Baptist Churches of Ontario and Quebec, president of the Conservative Baptist Churches of Canada, president of the Canadian Council of Evangelical Christian Churches, and president of the Canadian Protestant League. In 1927 Dr. Shields organized the Toronto Baptist Seminary. He also was the author of a number of Christian books. As a Calvinist and the leading promoter of fundamental Christianity in Canada he came to be referred to as "the Spurgeon of Canada." In his sermon called "Kept by the Power of God" preached in 1925, he said, "I am a bit of a Calvinist myself. I mean by that, I believe in the sovereignty of God, that He chooses His people."[158]

Louis Berkhof (1873–1957)

Louis Berkhof was an American-Dutch Reformed theologian who produced works on systematic theology that were influential in seminaries and Bible colleges in the United States, Canada, Korea and with individual Christians in general throughout the twentieth

---

[157] Thomas Todhunter Shields, http://higherpraise.com/preachers/shields.htm.
[158] Thomas Todhunter Shields, sermon "Kept by the Power of God," in "The War of the Worlds: The Militant Fundamentalism of Dr. Thomas Todhunter Shields and the Paradox of Modernity," by Doug A. Adams, (2015), Electronic Thesis and Dissertation Repository, 2985, https://ir.lib.uwo.ca/etd/2985.

century. He said, "In the wounds of Jesus is predestination understood and found, and nowhere else."[159]

Harry A. Ironside (1876–1951)

Henry Allen "Harry" Ironside was a Canadian–American Bible teacher, preacher, theologian, pastor, and author who pastored Moody Church in Chicago from 1929 to 1948. He wrote the following:

> Thank God for such an assurance as that! God will not be defeated. His purpose will never fail of accomplishment. All that the Father giveth to Jesus shall come to Him. You do not like that, perhaps. You say you do not believe in election and predestination. Then you will have to tear a number of pages out of your Bible, for there are many of them which magnify God's sovereign electing grace.[160]

John Gresham Machen (1881–1937)

John Gresham Machen was one of America's most prominent Presbyterian theologians of the twentieth century, Machen was Professor of New Testament at Princeton Seminary between 1906 and 1929. He led the conservative revolt against modernist theology at Princeton (along with B. B. Warfield and John Murray) and finally left to establish the Westminster Theological Seminary in 1929 as a more orthodox alternative.

As the Northern Presbyterian Church continued to reject conservative attempts to enforce faithfulness to the Westminster Confession, Machen led a small group of conservatives out of the church to form the Orthodox Presbyterian Church. He is considered to be the last of the great Princeton theologians who stood up for Princeton as a conservative and Calvinistic influence upon Evangelical Christianity. His textbook on basic New Testament Greek is still used today in many seminaries, including PCUSA schools. When asked by *Literary Digest* how to pronounce his name, he answered, "The first syllable is pronounced like *May*, the name of the month. In the second syllable the *ch* is as in *chin*, with *e* as in *pen*: *may'chen*. In *Gresham*, the *h* is silent: *gres'am*."

Machen explained how the believer should think about God's choosing some and not others and praised the wonders of grace as follows:

---

[159] Louis Berkhof, *The History of Christian Doctrine* (Scotland: Banner of Truth, 1969 [first published 1937]), 317.
[160] H. A. Ironside, *The Gospel of John* (The Works of H. A. Ironside, Logos Bible Software, 1942).

Because we do not know what the reason is for God's choice of some and His passing by of others, that does not mean that there is no reason. As a matter of fact, there is without doubt an altogether good and sufficient reason. We can be perfectly sure of that. God never acts in arbitrary fashion. He acts always in accordance with infinite wisdom. All His acts are directed to infinitely high and worthy ends. We must just trust Him for that. We do not know why God has acted thus and not otherwise, but we know the One who knows and we rest in His infinite justice and goodness and wisdom. I think the Christian man glories in his ignorance of God's counsels at this point. He rejoices that he does not know. The hymns of the evangelical church are full of the celebrations of the wonder of God's grace. It is such a strange and utterly mysterious thing that God should extend His mercy to such sinners as we are. We deserved nothing, but His wrath and curse. It would have been completely just if we had been lost as others are lost. It is a supreme wonder that we are saved. We cannot see why it is. We could not possibly believe it unless it were written so plainly in God's Word. We can only rest in it as a supreme mystery of grace.[161]

Albert Benjamin Simpson (1884–1919)

Albert Benjamin Simpson[162] was the Canadian preacher and theologian who founded the Christian and Missionary Alliance (CMA). Before he was born, A. B. Simpson's mother consecrated him for the Christian ministry and to missions. He was baptized by the Canadian missionary, John Geddie, and many of his childhood heroes were among the greatest personalities of missionary history. About a decade later, he became interested in the evangelization of the world. Simpson was well known for his focus on global evangelism. His family's strict Calvinistic Scottish Presbyterian and Puritan background formed Simpson's view of his spiritual standing.

He was converted to Christ at the age of fifteen in 1859. After graduating from Knox College in Toronto in 1865, Simpson accepted his first pastorate at Knox Church in Hamilton, one of Canada's largest and most influential congregations. Simpson later left Canada for the US to pastor Presbyterian churches in Louisville, KY and New York City. After just two years in New York City, Simpson resigned from the Church to begin a gospel ministry targeted for new immigrants and the poor and uneducated people migrating into the city. He developed a deep compassion for the lost, and desired to evangelize them began to consume him.

Simpson was considered a very effective communicator and his writing was very Christ centered. He was a prolific writer and authored 101 books and countless hymns, period-

[161] J. Greshem Machen, *The Christian View of Man* (London: Banner of Truth Trust, 1937, 1965, British ed.), 70–71.
[162] Albert Benjamin Simpson, http://higherpraise.com/preachers/simpson.htm.

icals, booklets, articles, and curriculums over his lifetime. His influence went on to move the hearts of missionaries, pastors, and people of all denominations toward spreading the gospel in all nations. He wanted the CMA to be a spiritual association of believers who hungered to know the fullness of the blessing of the gospel, by working together effectively for the speedy evangelization of the world.

On October 28, 1919, Simpson slipped into a coma from which he never recovered. Family members recall that his final words were spoken to God in prayer for all the missionaries he had helped to send out into the world. One of his notable quotes about God's sovereign work in the salvation of the lost goes like this, "God is preparing His heroes and when the opportunity comes, He will fit them into their places in a moment, and the world will wonder where they came from."[163]

Arthur Pink (1886–1952)

Arthur Pink became a Christian in 1908 at the age of twenty-two. His conversion came from his father's patient admonitions from Scripture. Desiring to grow in his knowledge of the Bible, Pink moved to the United States to study at the Moody Bible Institute in Chicago. He pastored churches in Colorado, California, Kentucky, South Carolina, Australia, and England. In 1922, he started a monthly magazine titled *Studies in the Scriptures* that circulated among English-speaking Christians worldwide. In 1934, Pink began writing books and pamphlets. Pink died from anemia in Scotland in1952. After Pink's death, his works were republished by a number of publishing houses, like Banner of Truth Trust, Baker Book House, Christian Focus Publications, Moody Press, Truth for Today, and reached a much wider audience as a result.

Biographer Iain Murray wrote this about Pink: "The widespread circulation of his writings after his death made him one of the most influential evangelical authors in the second half of the twentieth century. His writing sparked a revival of expository preaching and focused readers' hearts on biblical living."

Pink's comments below, regarding the doctrines under study here, were always from his heart, as he was commenting on Luke 19:10, "For the Son of man is come to seek and to save that which was lost":

How different is this plain, positive and unqualified statement from the tale which nearly all preachers tell today! The story of the vast majority is that Christ came here to make salvation possible for sinners: He has done His part, now they must do theirs. To reduce

---

[163] From Mari-Anna Stainacke "My Ten Favorite Quotes by A. B. Simpson," Flowingfaith 2009-2020, 2 Cor. 4:18, http://www.flowingfaith.com/2016/07/my-ten-favorite-a-b-simpson-quotes.html.

the wondrous, finished, and glorious work of Christ to a merely making salvation possible is most dishonoring and insulting to Him. Christ came here to carry into effect God's sovereign purpose of election, to save a people already "His" (Matthew 1:21) by covenant settlement. There are a people whom God hath "from the beginning chosen unto salvation" (2 Thessalonians 2:13), and redemption was in order to the accomplishing of that decree. And if we believe what Scripture declares concerning the person of Christ, then we have indubitable proof that there can be no possible failure in connection with His mission. The Son of man, the Child born, was none other than "the mighty God" (Isaiah 9:6). Therefore, is He omniscient, and knows where to look for each of His lost ones. He is also omnipotent and so cannot fail to deliver when they are found.[164]

In his book, The Doctrine of Election, Pink wrote:

Election and predestination are but the exercise of God's sovereignty in the affairs of salvation and all that we know about them is what has been revealed to us in the Scriptures of Truth. The only reason why anyone believes in Election is because he finds it clearly taught in God's Word. No man, or number of men, ever originated this doctrine. Like the teaching of Eternal Punishment, it conflicts with the dictates of the carnal mind and is repugnant to the sentiments of the unregenerate heart. And like the doctrine of the Holy Trinity and the miraculous birth of our Savior, the truth of Election must be received with simple, unquestioning faith.[165]

Arthur Walkington Pink was a British Bible teacher who sparked a renewed interest in the exposition of Calvinism. Although he was virtually unknown in his own lifetime, Pink became one of the most influential evangelical authors in the second half of the twentieth century.

Alva J. McClain (1888–1968)

Alva J. McClain was the founder and first president of Grace Theological Seminary in 1937. Grace College was established eleven years later in 1948. Both the seminary and college were affiliated with the Fellowship of Grace Brethren Churches. The Brethren tradition was shaped by distinctive features from Pietism, as well as from the Anabaptist and Calvinist branches of the Protestant Reformation. They held a commitment to remain free from worldly conformity, while striving to remain relevant to the culture around them.

[164] A. W. Pink, Studies in the Scriptures, vol. 5 (Sovereign Grace Publishers, 1930–31), 152.
[165] Arthur Pink, The Doctrine of Election, chapter 2 (New York: Rotolo Media / A Great Christian Books publication, 2013), www.GreatChristianBooks.com.

Dr. McClain authored many short treatises, but will be remembered for his monumental work on Christian theology called The Greatness of the Kingdom. He is recognized and remembered as a scholar, theologian, educator, master teacher, and Christian gentleman. Below, are some basic challenges to election and McClain's answers to those challenges:

Doctrine of Election will discourage efforts to win the lost.

1. It ought to stimulate such work—because without election all would be lost—our only hope is in the sovereign God of Grace.
2. It is our duty to bear the testimony: whether men accept or reject it. Ezek. 2:7, 2 Tim 2:10.

God elects the means as well as the end. If God has elected some in Africa, He also has elected someone to go there with the message.

Election encourages sinners to sit down and do nothing.

1. If men neglect—it is certain they will be lost.
2. Any man can prove he is one of the elect by believing and obeying the Gospel.

There is no other way.

Election makes Christians proud and Pharisaical.

1. Actually, it humbles the true Christian. All he is and has is only by the Grace of our sovereign God.
2. A proud and haughty spirit is a sure mark of the non-elect (Matt 3:7–9).[166]

Martyn Lloyd-Jones (1899–1981)

Martyn Lloyd-Jones was a Welsh Protestant minister, preacher, and medical doctor who was influential in the Reformed wing of the British evangelical movement in the twentieth century. Lloyd-Jones is thought by many to be the most influential proponent of historic Calvinism in Britain in the twentieth century. For almost thirty years, he was the

[166] Alva J. McClain at Grace Theological Seminary 1937–1962, "Christian Theology Outlines," Subject 4—Salvation and the Christian Life, Doctrine of Calling, X. Some Questions and Problems, page 227–228. Copyright Information: It is the publisher's understanding that Dr. McClain's original Theology Outlines and student handouts used at Grace Theological Seminary, dated 1939–1963, are in the public domain from *https://www.scribd.com*.

minister of Westminster Chapel in London. Lloyd-Jones was strongly opposed to Liberal Christianity, which had become a part of many Christian denominations. He regarded Liberal Christianity as aberrant. He disagreed with the broad church approach and encouraged evangelical Christians (particularly Anglicans) to leave their existing denominations. He believed that true Christian fellowship was possible only among those who shared common convictions regarding the nature of the faith. Regarding our doctrines of election and predestination, some of his notable comments follow:

> I said that John Wesley was to me the greatest proof of Calvinism. Why? Because in spite of his faulty thinking he was greatly used of God to preach the gospel and to convert souls! That is the ultimate proof of Calvinism (predestination & election). So again, one of the greatest proofs of the truth of the doctrines emphasized by Calvin (what is known as Calvinism)—though I have already said I do not like these terms—is John Wesley. He was a man who was saved in spite of his muddled and erroneous thinking. The grace of God saved him in spite of himself. That is Calvinism! If you say, as a Calvinist, that a man is saved by his understanding of doctrine, you are denying Calvinism. He is not. We are all saved in spite of what we are in every respect. Thus, it comes to pass that men who can be so muddled, because they bring in their own human reason, as John Wesley and others did, are saved men and Christians, as all of us are, because it is "all of the grace of God" and in spite of us.[167]

Vance Havner (1901–1986)

> "God didn't save you to make you happy. That's a by-product. He saved you to make you holy. You were predestinated to be conformed to the image of God's Son."[168]

Dr. Vance Havner was a well-known Baptist preacher and author from North Carolina who started preaching at the age of fourteen and kept preaching until he died in 1986. Dr. Havner was a revivalist and authored nearly forty books during his ministry. Vance Havner's Reflections on the Gospels is a collection of devotionals that Dr. Havner wrote in the 1920s and 1930s. These were written as individual articles and eventually complied into this book by Michael Catt in 2004.

---

[167] Martyn Lloyd-Jones, *The Puritans: Their Origins and Successors*, chapter 5 (Published by The Banner of Truth, August 28, 2014).
[168] Vance Havner, *Reflections on the Gospels*. (Michael C Catt, 2004, published in the USA by CLC Publications).

Carl F. H. Henry 1913–2003)

Carl Ferdinand Howard Henry was an American evangelical Christian theologian who was born on Long Island and trained as a journalist. He earned two doctorates, including a PhD in theology from Boston University. Henry along with evangelist Billy Graham, founded the most influential magazine in evangelical circles in the second half of the twentieth century, *Christianity Today*. He also served as the magazine's first editor-in-chief, providing a solid intellectual voice for evangelical Christianity. In 1978, he signed the Chicago Statement on Biblical Inerrancy, which affirmed biblical inerrancy. In the early 1980s Henry was a founding board member of the Institute on Religion and Democracy. In 1983, he published the six-volume work titled *God, Revelation, and Authority* (Dallas, TX, Word Press). He taught at Northern Seminary, Fuller Seminary, Eastern Baptist Theological Seminary, Calvin Theological Seminary, and Trinity Evangelical Divinity School. In 1974, Henry accepted the position of Lecturer-at-large for World Vision International. The following two paragraphs are taken from Henry's book called *God Who Stands and Stays*:

> Any argument that God's election and provision of atonement automatically means universal salvation is without basis. Verses that imply God's sincere and strong wish for human salvation are not necessarily inconsistent with the divine election of only some to eternal life. Those who contend that it would impugn divine love and justice were God to elect only some fallen creatures without extending the same prerogatives to all are mistaken. Scripture gives no hint that the electing God provided divine salvation for the fallen angels. The fact that He provided salvation only for fallen humans does not reflect adversely either on divine love or on divine justice. God shows His love in electing some underserving human beings to salvation and His justice in redemptively passing over others who are equally underserving.
>
> God's election of only some does not imply that He ceases to be providential Lord of all the universe. Psalm 145:9 says that the Lord is good to all. Matthew 5:45 says that He makes His sun rise on the evil and on the good and sends rain on the just and the unjust. What the Bible affirms is man's hopeless moral and spiritual condition apart from God's election and God's provision of salvation in Christ.[169]

Loraine Boettner (1901–1990)

The truth of predestination should be preached for the comfort of believers. The doctrine of sovereign predestination should be publicly taught and preached in order that true be-

---

[169] Carl F. H. Henry, *God Who Stands and Stays* (Wheaton, IL: Crossway Books, 1999), 106–107.

lievers may know themselves to be special objects of God's love and mercy and that they may be confirmed and strengthened in the assurance of their salvation. For the Christian, this should be one of the most comforting doctrines in all the Scriptures. This doctrine of total inability which declares that men are dead in sin does not mean that all men are equally bad, nor that any man is as bad as he could be, nor that anyone is entirely destitute of virtue, nor that human nature is equal in itself, nor that man's spirit in inactive, and much less does it mean that the body is dead. What it does mean is that since the fall, man rests under the curse of sin, that he is actuated by wrong principles, and that he is wholly unable to love God, or to do anything meriting salvation. His corruption is extensive, but not necessarily intensive. It is in this sense that man, since the fall, is utterly indisposed, disabled, and made opposite to all good, wholly inclined to all evil. He possesses a fixed bias of the will against God and instinctively and willingly and turns to evil. He is an alien by birth and a sinner by choice. The inability under which he labors is not an inability to exercise volition, but an inability to be willing to exercise holy volitions. And it is this phase of it which led Luther to declare that 'free will' is an empty term, whose reality is lost and a lost liberty, according to my grammar, is no liberty at all.[170]

R. J. Rushdoony (1916–2001)

R. J. Rushdoony was a Calvinist philosopher, historian, and theologian and widely credited as the father of Christian Reconstructionism (See his "Institutes of Biblical Law") and an inspiration for the modern Christian home school movement. Many claim his teaching and writings exerted considerable influence on the Christian right. It has been said that Rushdoony probably had an IQ of around 200. For six days each week, he spent fourteen hours a day reading and studying. From the time he turned fourteen, he read one to three books a day and continued this habit for the rest of his life.

Rushdoony spent three years teaching the "Institutes of Biblical Law" and every lesson was recorded. These recordings were then sent to George Calhoun who faithfully maintained the tapes in the Mt Olive Tape Library for the last 35 years or so. Now they have been digitized and are presented at www.PocketCollege.com. The following paragraphs on predestination were a part of one of those recorded lessons:

Our subject in this period is predestination. Predestination is a very obvious fact. The necessity for discussing it is a moral fact even if man refuses to accept it, because it denies the ultimacy of man. In discussing predestination, therefore, certain things need to be pointed out.

---

[170] Loraine Boettner, *The Reformed Doctrine of Predestination* (Phillipsburg, NJ: Presbyterian and Reformed Publishing Company, 1991), 1.

First of all, the only real alternatives as we view the world are predestination or chance. Either everything is the product of chance, and chance rules the universe, or we have predestination. We cannot, without being guilty of self-contradiction, deny God and then insist that there is a world of order around us. The universe of order presupposes absolute order behind it, an absolute mind with an absolute purpose. So that it becomes a necessity for those who are consistent atheists or evolutionists or humanists to affirm chance, or to refuse to raise the question of order. When I was a student, a member of the University of California philosophy department admitted in a discussion that it was either chance or predestination. He said, moreover, 'if you allowed yourself'—he was talking to students who were pragmatic naturalists like himself—'if you allowed yourself to get into a discussion of origins with any Christian, you'd be the loser. So', he said, 'the thing to do is to say I refuse to raise the questions of origins, or of order. I simply take the order of the universe as a given. For granted. Just as you refuse to say, 'where did God come from?' I refuse to say, 'where did order in the universe come from'.' Now he was asked a second question which he refused to answer.

If we do that, have we not revised the same God of Scripture under the name of natural order in the universe? Have we not then transferred everything God is to the universe, so we have God without the name of God. You see, to believe that there is an order in the universe, and it is not from God, is to believe in greater miracles than any Christian believes in. Those who believe in chance, those who deny God, are the ones who truly have the greatest faith; and the most perverse of all faiths, the blindest of all faiths.

Then second, as we saw in our previous period, the doctrine of fiat creation requires predestination. Total creation means total control. At the council of Jerusalem, the apostle James said in Acts 15:18, "Known unto God are all his works, from the foundation of the world." Creation and history have no surprises for God. He planned it all, He made it all, He governs it all. To affirm predestination means to affirm total fiat creation and vice versa.

Then third, because God is the creator and the predestinator of all things, His predestination of all things is both universal and particular, because every detail is His handiwork as well as the overall purpose and plan. Election is thus both particular and general. All who are in covenant with Christ and in Christ are elected by God for redemption, and that redemption is both particular and general. It embraces the covenant people and it embraces the individuals.

In John 10:1–7 we are told that the good Shepherd knows his sheep, He calls them by name and he leads them. Both election and reprobation are a part of God's total government. Then fourth, because predestination is not only a necessary part of creation, but also of government, wherever sovereignty and government are claimed, there also predestination is claimed. If we say God is the Lord, then we believe God is the Creator, Governor, Predestinator, and the Lord of all things.

Wherever we say man is the Lord, then we say man must govern absolutely and pre-destinate absolutely.[171]

Dr. James Kennedy (1930–2007)

Dr. D. James Kennedy was the American pastor, evangelist, and Christian broadcaster who founded the Coral Ridge Presbyterian Church in Fort Lauderdale, Florida, where he was senior pastor from 1960 until his death in 2007. Kennedy also founded Evangelism Explosion International, Coral Ridge Ministries, the Westminster Academy in Fort Lauderdale, the Knox Theological Seminary, and the Center for Reclaiming America for Christ (a socially conservative political group). Dr. Kennedy related why he was a Presbyterian in this way: "I am a Presbyterian, because I believe that Presbyterianism is the purest form of Calvinism."[172]

In his book *Solving Bible Mysteries: Unraveling the Perplexing and Troubling Passages of Scripture*, he shared the following thoughts on predestination:

So God makes His sovereign selection from among the human race, a race of sinful and corrupt people, all of whom deserve condemnation. But God extends mercy to a vast multitude. He must be just, but He doesn't have to extend mercy to any. Those whom He selects are saved—a great number out of every tribe and tongue and nation. He sends His Spirit to them to draw them to Himself. For that is what predestination is a decision that our sovereign, gracious, loving Almighty God made from all eternity when He looked ahead to a world of lost and rebellious sinners. It's a decision He made to save a vast multitude of them through His Son, Jesus.[173]

In *Truths that Transform: Christian Doctrines for Your Life Today*, Kennedy wrote the following:

I am a Calvinist precisely because I love the Bible and the God of the Bible. The doctrines of the Calvinist theological system are the doctrines of the Bible. When you get to know what we actually believe, you may find you too are a Calvinist, especially if you love the Lord Jesus Christ and desire with all your heart to serve Him. As the respected Spurgeon stated: 'The longer I live the clearer does it appear that John Calvin's system is the nearest to perfection.'[174]

---

[171] Professor Dr. R. J. Rushdoony, *Systematic Theology*, Lesson 8 from the class recorded for Pocket College on "Knowing the Triune God," taught between 1960 and 1970.

[172] D. James Kennedy, *Why I Am a Presbyterian* (Fort Lauderdale: Coral Ridge Ministries, n.d.).

[173] D. James Kennedy, *Solving Bible Mysteries: Unraveling the Perplexing and Troubling Passages of Scripture* (Nashville: Thomas Nelson Inc. Complete Numbers Starting with 1, first edition, 2000), 30–31.

[174] D. James Kennedy, *Truths that Transform: Christian Doctrines for Your Life Today* (Grand Rapids, MI: F. H. Revell Co.), 1974.

R. C. Sproul, Sr. (1939–2017)

Robert Charles Sproul was an American Calvinist theologian, philosopher, author, and pastor. He founded Ligonier Ministries (named after the Ligonier Valley just outside of Pittsburgh where the ministry started as a study center for college and seminary students). Ligonier Ministries hosts several theological conferences each year, including the main conference held each year in Orlando, Florida at which Sproul was one of the primary speakers. Sproul was a passenger on the train wreck at Big Bayou Canot on September 22, 1993, when a barge hit the CSXT Big Bayou Canot bridge in northeast Mobile, Alabama, and derailed an Amtrak train killing forty-seven and injuring 103. It was the deadliest train wreck in Amtrak's history. Sproul often gave firsthand accounts of the story.

Sproul held a bachelor's degree from Westminster College in Pennsylvania, Master of Divinity degree from Pittsburgh-Xenia Theological Seminary, Doctors Degree from the Free University of Amsterdam, and a PhD from Whitefield Theological Seminary in Lakeland, Florida. He taught in numerous colleges and seminaries including the Reformed Theological Seminary and Knox Theological Seminary.

Sproul was a committed advocate of Calvinism in many of his printed, audio, and video publications. A dominant theme in many of teachings was the holiness and sovereignty of God. For information on his ministry and beliefs, visit his website at: www.ligonier.org. Below are a few of his most notable thoughts on election and predestination:

I once heard the president of a Presbyterian seminary declare, "I am not a Calvinist because I do not believe that God brings some people, kicking and screaming against their wills, into the kingdom, while he excludes others from his kingdom who desperately want to be there." I was astonished when I heard these words. I did not think it possible that the president of a Presbyterian seminary could have such a gross misconception of his own church's theology. He was reciting a caricature, which was as far away from Calvinism as one could get.

Calvinism does not teach and never has taught that God brings people kicking and screaming into the kingdom or has ever excluded anyone who wanted to be there. Remember that the cardinal point of the Reformed doctrine of predestination rests on the biblical teaching of man's spiritual death. Natural man does not want Christ. He will only want Christ if God plants a desire for Christ in his heart. Once that desire is planted, those who come to Christ do not come kicking and screaming against their wills. They come because they want to come. They now desire Jesus. They rush to the Savior. The whole point of irresistible grace is that rebirth quickens someone to spiritual life in such a way that Jesus is now seen in His irresistible sweetness. Jesus is irresistible to those who have been made alive to the things of God. Every soul whose heart beats with the life of God within it longs for the living Christ. All whom the Father gives to Christ come to Christ (John 6:37).[175]

So often when we struggle with the doctrine of predestination and election it is because our eyes are always fixed on the difficulty of resolving predestination with human freedom. The Bible, however, links them with salvation, which every Christian should find enormously comforting. Salvation is not an afterthought of God. The redemption of His people, the salvation of His church, my eternal salvation, these actions are not a postscript to the Divine activity. Instead, from the very foundation of the world, God had a sovereign plan to save a significant portion of the human race, and He moves heaven and earth to bring it to pass.[176]

In Tabletalk magazine, Sproul wrote the following:

Some have argued from Romans 8:29 that predestination is based on God's foreknowledge in the sense that God looked down the corridors of time, and saw who would freely choose to believe, and then predestinated them. This position assumes that foreknowledge here only means "knows in advance." In the Bible, however, knowledge is often used in a sense of personal intimacy, as when Adam "knew" Eve and she conceived a son (Genesis 4:1).

God's foreknowledge is linked to His foreloving. We see in Romans 8:30 that everyone who was "foreknown" was also "predestined, called, justified, and glorified." Does God glorify everyone? Does God justify everyone? No. Clearly then, in terms of what this passage is dealing with, God does not call everyone, does not predestine everyone, and does not foreknow everyone. In Romans 8:29–30, "foreknowledge" must have the sense of intimacy and personal calling and can refer only to God's elect. God's predestination does not exist in a vacuum and it is not simply for the purpose of saving us from sin. Verse 29 shows us the goal or purpose of salvation: that we might be conformed to the likeness of His Son. Ultimately, the reason God has saved you and me is for the honor and glory of His Son, "That He might be the firstborn." The goal in creation is that God would give as a gift to His Son many who are reborn into Christ's likeness.[177]

Dr. John MacArthur (1939–Present)

God did not draw straws. He didn't look down the corridor of time to see who would choose Him before He decided. Rather, by His sovereign will He chose who would be in the body of Christ. The construction of the Greek verb used indicates God chose us for

[175] R. C. Sproul, *Chosen by God* (Carol Stream, IL: Tyndale Momentum Publishing, 1994), 97.
[176] R. C. Sproul, *The Purpose of God: An Exposition of Ephesians* (Christian Focus Publications, 1994), 23.
[177] R. C. Sproul, *Tabletalk* (Sanford, FL: Ligonier Ministries, 1989). *Tabletalk* Magazine was formed in 1977 by Ligonier Ministries to provide a substantive study tool for believers.

Himself. That means God acted totally independent of any outside influence. He made His choice totally apart from human will and purely on the basis of His sovereignty. It probably ought to be the first thing you teach a young believer. Now that you come to Christ, this is what I want you to know, you were saved by the sovereign grace of God who stepped into your life in the midst of your death and blindness and gave you life and sight and picked you up and brought you into His Kingdom. Sheer grace has done this for you. That, I think, is the first thing you should say to a new convert. This is, if in fact, you are faithful to the confession you have made, if in fact your love for Christ and desire to honor, to worship and to obey Him continues to grow, this will be an ongoing evidence that God has wrought a miracle in your life. And because of that, you need to know this is really important, that you should live a life of gratitude for a work has been done in you which you did not deserve and did not earn.[178]

John Fullerton MacArthur Jr. is an American pastor and author known for his internationally syndicated Christian teaching radio program Grace to You. He has been the pastor-teacher of Grace Community Church in Sun Valley, California, since February 9, 1969. He is also the current president of The Master's University in Newhall, California, and The Master's Seminary in Los Angeles, California.

Hugh Ross, Canadian-American Astrophysicist (1945–Present)

Einstein gave grudging acceptance to "the necessity for a beginning" and eventually to "the presence of a superior reasoning power," but never did he accept the doctrine of a personal God. Two specific obstacles blocked his way. According to his journal writings, Einstein wrestled with a deeply felt bitterness toward the clergy, toward priests in particular, and with his inability to resolve the paradox of God's omnipotence and man's responsibility for his choices. "If this being is omnipotent, then every occurrence, including every human action, every human thought, and every human feeling and aspiration is also His work; how is it possible to think of holding men responsible for their deeds and thoughts before such an almighty being? In giving out punishment and rewards He would to a certain extent be passing judgment on Himself. How can this be combined with the goodness and righteousness ascribed to Him?"[179]

Seeing no solution to this paradox, Einstein, like many other powerful intellects through the centuries, ruled out the existence of a personal God.

---

[178] John MacArthur Jr., "Who Chose Whom," sermon GTY65, Dec. 1, 1997, https://www.gty.org/library/sermons-library/GTY65/who-chose-whom.

[179] Hugh Ross, *The Fingerprint of God* (Los Angeles, CA: Promise Publications, 1991), 59.

Wayne Grudem (1948–Present)

Wayne A. Grudem is the evangelical theologian, seminary professor, and author who cofounded the Council on Biblical Manhood and Womanhood and served as the general editor of *The ESV Study Bible*. Grudem holds a BA from Harvard University, an MDiv from Westminster Theological Seminary, and a PhD from the University of Cambridge.

After teaching and serving as the Chairman of the Department of Biblical and Systematic Theology at Trinity Evangelical Divinity School for twenty years, Gruden became the Research Professor of Theology and Biblical Studies at Phoenix Seminary in 2001. He served on the committee overseeing *The English Standard Version* translation of the Bible, and from 2005 to 2008, he served as General Editor for the *ESV Study Bible* (which was named "2009 Christian Book of the Year" by the Evangelical Christian Publishers Association). He edited (with John Piper) *Recovering Biblical Manhood and Womanhood*, which was named "Book of the Year" by *Christianity Today* in 1992. He is the author of *Systematic Theology: An Introduction to Biblical Doctrine*, which advocates a Calvinistic soteriology, the verbal plenary inspiration and inerrancy of the Bible, the body-soul dichotomy in the nature of man, and the complementarian view of gender relationships. The following excerpt is from Grudem's *Systematic Theology*:

Quite commonly people will agree that God predestines some to be saved, but they will say that He does this by looking into the future and seeing who will believe in Christ and who will not. If He sees that a person is going to come to saving faith, then He will predestine that person to be saved. In this way, it is thought, the ultimate reason why some are saved and some are not lies within the people themselves, not within God. All that God does in His predestining work is to give confirmation to the decision He knows people will make on their own. The verse commonly used to support this view is Romans 8:29: "For those whom He foreknew He also predestined to be conformed to the image of His Son." But this verse can hardly be used to demonstrate that God based His predestination on foreknowledge of the fact that a person would believe. The passage speaks rather of the fact that God knew persons ("those whom He foreknew"), not that He knew some fact about them, such as the fact that they would believe. It is a personal, relational knowledge that is spoken of here. God, looking into the future, thought of certain people in saving relationship to Him and in that sense, He "knew them" long ago. This is the sense in which Paul can talk about God's "knowing" someone. For example, in 1 Corinthians 8:3: "But if one loves God, one is known by Him." Similarly, He says, "but now that you have come to know God, or rather to be known by God . . ." (Gal. 4:9). When people know God in Scripture, or when God knows them, it is personal knowledge that involves a saving relationship. Therefore, in Romans 8:29, "those whom He foreknew" is best understood to mean, "those whom He long ago thought of in a saving relationship to Himself." The text actually says nothing about God foreknowing or foreseeing that certain people would believe, nor is that idea mentioned in any other text of Scripture.

Sometimes people say that God elected groups of people, but not individuals to salvation. In some Arminian views, God just elected the church as a group, while the Swiss theologian Karl Barth (1886–1968) said that God elected Christ, and all people in Christ. But Romans 8:29 talks about certain people whom God foreknew ("those whom he foreknew"), not just undefined or unfilled groups. And in Ephesians Paul talks about certain people whom God chose, including himself: "He chose us in him before the foundation of the world" (Eph. 1:4). To talk about God choosing a group with no people in it is not biblical election at all. But to talk about God choosing a group of people means that He chose specific individuals who constituted that group. It seems best, for the previous four reasons, to reject the idea that election is based on God's foreknowledge of our faith. We conclude instead that the reason for election is simply God's sovereign choice—He "destined us in love to be his sons" (Eph. 1:5). God chose us simply because He decided to bestow His love upon us. It was not because of any foreseen faith or foreseen merit in us. This understanding of election has traditionally been called "unconditional election." It is "unconditional" because it is not conditioned upon anything that God sees in us that makes us worthy of His choosing us.[180]

Howard Ahmanson, Jr. (1950–Present)

Howard Ahmanson, Jr. was the son of Dorothy Johnston Grannis and the American financier Howard F. Ahmanson, Sr. Howard Ahmanson, Sr. died when his son was eighteen and Ahmanson Jr. inherited a large fortune of 300 million dollars. He then went to Occidental College and earned a degree in economics. Then he toured Europe but returned because of arthritis. He earned a master's degree in linguistics at the University of Texas at Arlington and became a Calvinist in the 1970s. *TIME Magazine* covered the Ahmansons in 2005 of the 25 Most Influential Evangelicals in America, classifying them as "the financiers."

Below, is a story his wife shared about an experience Ahmanson had, after previously considering the doctrines theologically, which confirmed his belief in election and predestination from a practical perspective. His former college roommate tried to convince Ahmanson that certain people would go to hell if Ahmanson did not give him money to open a surf shop and use the shop to witness to non-Christians who came in. Ahmanson

---

[180] Wayne Grudem, *Systematic Theology* (Leicester, England: InterVarsity Press, and Grand Rapids, MI: Zondervan Publishing House, 1994, 2000), 674–79.

was able to see that making another frail human like himself responsible for the eternal destiny of other people was just not right. "In that very hour, according to his wife, he became a full-fledged Calvinist, giving himself to Calvin's doctrine of predestination, which holds that God "elects" individuals for salvation based on factors beyond their control."[181]

Don Fortner (1950-2020)

Don Fortner was a Reformed Baptist Pastor at Grace Baptist Church of Danville, Kentucky. He spoke about God's elect in the excerpts from two sermons below:

'THEY SHALL BE MY PEOPLE'
by Don Fortner (1950-2020)
'THEY SHALL BE MY PEOPLE': Jeremiah 24:7: And I will give them a heart to know me, that I am the Lord and they shall be my people, and I will be their God. For they shall return unto me with their whole heart. There are some men and women in this world whom God has chosen to salvation from eternity, who must and shall be saved (John 15:16; 2 Thess. 2:13). There is a multitude, scattered among the fallen sons of Adam, in every age, in every nation who must be saved. The number of God's elect is so great that no man can calculate it, though it always appears as only a remnant at any given time. The number is unalterably fixed by God. All the elect must be saved. Nothing can prevent their salvation. The Lord Jesus Christ has made atonement for the sins of God's elect and redeemed them from the curse of the law by His own precious blood (Gal. 3:13). All of God's elect, having been redeemed by the blood of Christ, shall be called from death to life by the irresistible power and almighty grace of God through the Holy Spirit (Gal. 3:13–14; Psa. 65:4; 110:3). Repentance toward God, faith in Christ, and eternal life are the results of the Spirit's call. These are things effectually wrought in God's elect by his almighty grace. There is specific day appointed by God in which each of His elect will be called to life and faith in Christ by the gospel (Psalm 110:3, Ezekiel 16:68). God will see to it that the sinner whom He has chosen will be in the place he has ordained, with his heart thoroughly prepared to receive the gospel, at the appointed time. And He will send His Word to that sinner in the irresistible power and grace of the Holy Spirit. In that day, God says, regarding every chosen, redeemed sinner, 'They shall be my people'."[182]

---

[181] Max Blumenthal, "Avenging Angel of the Religious Right," found at: https://www.salon.com/2004/01/06/ahmanson. The entire article is a great read on the life of Howard Ahmanson Jr.
[182] "THEY SHALL BE MY PEOPLE," Radio Message #814 by Don Fortner, Reformed Baptist Pastor at Grace Baptist Church of Danville, Kentucky / DonFortner.com

'THE PURPOSE OF GOD'

by Don Fortner

The Lord our God is a God of purpose—absolute and unalterable purpose. God's purpose must and shall be accomplished. Before the world was made, before time began, Almighty God sovereignly purposed all that comes to pass. Everything that is, has been, and shall hereafter be, was purposed by God from eternity. Everything in the universe is moving toward the predestined end of God's eternal purpose with absolute, precision and accuracy. Everything that comes to pass in time was purposed by our God in eternity.

The purpose of God is eternal.

The purpose of God includes all things.

The purpose of God has for its particular design the spiritual and eternal benefit of God's elect. Everything God has purposed is for the ultimate, spiritual, and eternal blessedness of his covenant people. The purpose of God is immutable and sure. That which comes to pass in time is exactly what God purposed from eternity.

In its ultimate end, God's purpose will accomplish the eternal salvation of his elect and the glory of His own great name.

All God's elect shall be saved. Not one of Christ's sheep shall perish. Every sinner redeemed by blood shall be saved by grace and crowned with glory. The purpose of God demands it. The law of God demands it. Justice satisfied, cannot punish those for whom it has been satisfied.[183]

Al Mohler (1959–Present)

Richard Albert Mohler, Jr. is an American theologian and the ninth president of the Southern Baptist Theological Seminary in Louisville, Kentucky. Mohler is the former host of *The Albert Mohler Program*, a nationwide radio show devoted to engaging contemporary culture with Christian beliefs. He is a member of the board of *Focus on the Family* and a member of the Council on Biblical Manhood and Womanhood. *Christianity Today* recognized Mohler as a leader among American evangelicals and *TIME* called him the "reigning intellectual of the evangelical movement in the U.S."

Mohler has presented lectures or addresses at a variety of conservative evangelical universities, including Wheaton College and Samford University. Mohler is an evangelical and an exclusivist, which means that he believes Jesus is the only way through which an individual can attain salvation or have a relationship with God the Father. As a Calvinist, Mohler believes that human salvation is a free gift from God, which cannot be earned by

---

[183] 'THE PURPOSE OF GOD' audio sermon by Don Fortner at DonFortner.com: http://www.donfortner.com/sermon_notes/basic_bible_doctrineseries/Doctrine%20 014%20%20The%20Purpose%20of%20 God.htm

human action or will, and is only given to the elect. He has publicly expressed this position with respect to Judaism, Islam, and Catholicism.

He recently stated that "any belief system, any world view, whether it's Zen Buddhism, Hinduism, Marxism, or dialectical materialism for that matter, that keeps people captive and keeps them from coming to faith in the Lord Jesus Christ, is a demonstration of Satanic power" (March 17, 2006 edition of Fox News *The O'Reilly Factor)*. He believes Muslims are motivated by demonic power, and in the months after the September 11, 2001 attacks, Mohler characterized Islamic views of Jesus as false and destructive. The following is a quote from Dr. Mohler titled "Southern Baptist Theological Seminary's Response to the Baptist General Convention of Texas Seminary Study Committee Report":

> All Southern Baptists are Calvinists of one sort or another. Anyone who believes in the perseverance of the saints or the security of the believer has Calvinist elements in his or her theology. Those who established the SBC were Calvinists, as were early leaders of the BGCT. Southern Seminary's Abstract of Principles reflects that Calvinist influence, as does the Baptist Faith and Message (and the New Hampshire Confession of Faith, on which it is based). In the modern era, as in the founding generation, Southern Baptists have included those who were more Calvinistic, and those who were less Calvinistic. Nevertheless, strong Calvinist elements have been present in the Southern Baptist mainstream throughout our history. The Abstract of Principles requires all professors to believe in total depravity, unconditional election, and perseverance. The Seminary does not require professors to hold a specific view of the extent of the atonement or effectual calling. Southern Seminary's faculty hold differing positions on these questions, as do Southern Baptists at large. . . . If Calvinism is not to be tolerated by BGCT leadership, then they should make clear their own theological convictions in a responsible manner. Further, they must apologize to BGCT titans such as B. H. Carroll and J. B. Gambrell, who were clear about their own Calvinist convictions.[184]

Ligon Duncan, American Presbyterian Pastor (1960–Present)

I well remember as a fifteen-year-old boy at my grandparents' house, reading through Ephesians 1 with grandmother and granddad and my aunt and the family for our morning devotions. And at the end of those devotions, knowing that my grandmother did not share my same love for Calvinistic doctrine, even though the word "predestination" had popped up a couple of times in that passage, I knew that I should keep quiet. After about thirty seconds of awkward silence my grandmother could resist it no longer and she said to me,

[184] You can find more of this article online at: http://sbcvoices.com/r-albert-mohler-jr-answers-the-calvinism-criticism/#sthash.ll4a38J4.dpuf.

"Now, Ligon, we're Southern Baptist and we don't believe in predestination."

Now with all the tact of a fifteen-year-old, I restrained myself from engaging in a theological dialogue and said very diplomatically, "Grandmother, you do believe in predestination. It's just that you think it means something different than what we as Presbyterians believe that it means." She immediately responded, "Son, you don't understand. We're Southern Baptist and we don't believe in predestination."

And I quickly responded again, "But, Grandmother, you do believe in predestination. The word is there in Ephesians 1. It's just that you think it means something like, God foresees that we are going to choose him, and I believe it means that God ordains that we are going to choose him." And she quickly responded, "Son, you don't understand. We're Southern Baptist and we don't believe in predestination!"

I realized about fifteen years later that my grandmother had two controlling beliefs: The Bible is true and predestination is not true. And therefore, there is no place in the Bible that teaches predestination. It doesn't matter if the Bible uses the word or not.

Let me quickly say that I am not bashing Southern Baptists. Actually, there was a time when the Southern Baptists used to believe exactly what Presbyterians believe regarding predestination and election. In fact, many Southern Baptists today believe what we believe about God's sovereignty, predestination and election.

Furthermore, election is still in all the Baptist confessions. Look at the Philadelphia Confession, the New Hampshire Baptist Confession, and the abstract principles of the Southern Baptist Theological Seminary. Southern Baptists and Presbyterians used to agree on this entirely. There has just been a collective amnesia among some Baptists for the last hundred years or so on this topic. The point is that we sometimes have a hard time swallowing God's election. It makes us uncomfortable.[185]

Dr. Duncan is pastor of the First Presbyterian Church in Jackson, Missouri. The text for this sermon is at https://www. fpcjackson.org/resource-library/sermons/the-purpose-of-god.

James Robert White (1962–Present)

James Robert White is the director of Alpha and Omega Ministries, an evangelical Reformed Christian apologetics organization based in Phoenix, Arizona. He is the author of more than twenty books and has engaged in over 100 moderated debates. He has a BA from Grand Canyon College, an MA from Fuller Theological Seminary, and a ThM, a ThD and a DMin from Columbia Evangelical Seminary. He has served as a professor of Greek, Hebrew, systematic theology, and various apologetics topics at Golden Gate Bap-

---

[185] Dr. J. Ligon Duncan, "The Purpose of God," sermon on Romans 8:28–30, July 22, 2001.

tist Theological Seminary's extension campus in Arizona and the unaccredited Columbia Evangelical Seminary.

White is also a critical consultant for the Lockman Foundation's New American Standard Bible. His debates have covered topics such as Calvinism, Roman Catholicism, Islam, Mormonism, the King James Only movement, Jehovah's Witnesses, and Atheism. His debate opponents have included scholars such as Bart Ehrman, John Dominic Crossan, and Marcus Borg and popularizers such as Dan Barker and John Shelby Spong. White has also been an elder of Phoenix Reformed Baptist Church in Phoenix, AZ, since 1998. For more information on Dr. White or his books and debates, see his website at http://aomin. org. Below are several of White's comments on election and predestination from his book, *Debating Calvinism: Five Points, Two Views*, coauthored by James White and Dave Hunt, published by Multnomah (2004):

> In the final analysis, I have peace with God because **God in eternity past chose this undeserving sinner** and **placed His grace and love upon me**. There can be no other consistent, biblical, and God-glorifying answer. This is sovereign freedom, divine grace, and it leads inexorably to the truth of unconditional election. (*Debating Calvinism,* p. 95, emphasis mine.)
>
> Why should we give thanks to God upon hearing of the faith of fellow believers, if in fact having faith in Christ is something that every person is capable of having **without any gracious enablement by God**? (*Debating Calvinism,* p. 20, emphasis mine.)
>
> No more soul-destroying doctrine could well be devised than the **doctrine that sinners can regenerate themselves, and repent and believe just when they please**. (*Debating Calvinism,* p. 90, emphasis mine.)
>
> Every works-oriented system must deny God His kingship over the creature and must give to man abilities and powers beyond his sinful state, so that in the final analysis God's power can be "channeled" through human structures, whether they be rituals, sacraments, or even the very popular concept of "decisionalism," the idea that man, by his autonomous will, **controls the very work of the triune God in salvation**. (*Debating Calvinism,* p. 99, emphasis mine.)
>
> There is no basis in the Bible for asserting that **God's love** knows no **levels, kinds, or types**. Just the opposite is true. (*Debating Calvinism,* p. 267, emphasis mine.)[186]

---

[186] Another great source for White's views on God's sovereign work in salvation is his book *The Sovereign Grace of God: A Biblical Study of the Doctrines of Calvinism* (Reformation Press Edition, 2003).

Michael Scott Horton (1964–Present)

Michael Scott Horton has been the Professor of Theology and Apologetics at Westminster Seminary in California since 1998, Editor-in-Chief of *Modern Reformation Magazine*, and president and host of the nationally syndicated radio broadcast, *The White Horse Inn*. Both *Modern Reformation* magazine and *The White Horse Inn* radio broadcast are now entities under the umbrella of White Horse Media, whose offices are located on the campus of Westminster Seminary in California. After being raised in an Arminian Southern Baptist church, Horton adopted Calvinistic beliefs during high school and began attending the Philadelphia Conference on Reformed Theology, where he met James Montgomery Boice, R. C. Sproul and J. I. Packer.

Horton received a BA degree from Biola University, his MA from Westminster Seminary California and his PhD from Wycliffe Hall, Oxford and Coventry University. He also completed a Research Fellowship at Yale Divinity School. In 1996, *Christianity Today* included him on their list of "Up & Comers: Fifty Evangelical Leaders 40 and Under." Horton has written and edited more than fifteen books. His best-known title may be *Putting the Amazing Back into Grace: An Introduction to Reformed Theology*, from which the following affirmation of election and the doctrines of grace was taken: "God's choice is not based on anything in us—even our decision to accept the gospel. After all, we accept the gospel only because God has accepted us in Christ through election. So our salvation is based on a decision God made in eternity past, without respect to our personal choices or actions. Hence, salvation is by grace alone."[187]

For more information on Dr. Horton and his writings, go to: www.whitehorseinn.org.

John Piper (1964–Present)

"The teaching of Scripture on election has been controversial. But I believe with all my heart that it is precious beyond words and a great nourishment for the Christlikeness of faith. If I understand the teaching of the Bible, God has pleasure in election. To know that this is true, and to know why it is, is to see another facet of the glory of God. And that sight is the power to make us holy and happy people."[188]

Philip Graham Ryken (1966–Present)

Philip Graham Ryken is the eighth and current president of Wheaton College in Wheaton, Illinois. Ryken received a BA from Wheaton College in 1988, with a double major

---

[187] M. S. Horton, *Putting the Amazing Back into Grace* (Nashville: Thomas Nelson, 1991), 207.
[188] John Piper, *Five Points: Towards a Deeper Experience of God's Grace*, chapter 6 (Scotland, UK: Christian Focus Publications, Geanies House, Fearn, Tain, Ross-Shire), 2013.

in English literature and philosophy. He also completed a Master of Divinity from Westminster Theological Seminary in 1992, and a PhD in historical theology from University of Oxford in 1995. He is a member of the Alliance of Confessing Evangelicals, serving as a member of the Alliance Council, which features his expository preaching on its weekly national radio and internet broadcast, *Every Last Word*. He has written over thirty books on a wide variety of Christian subjects, one of which is *The Doctrines of Grace: Rediscovering the Evangelical Gospel* with James Montgomery Boice and R. C. Sproul.

Ryken has also coauthored a series of commentaries on individual books of the Bible with R. Kent Hughes. Ryken and his father, literary scholar Leland Ryken, have worked together to produce a study Bible, and the father-son team worked with James Wilhoit to write *Ryken's Bible Handbook*, which focuses on the literary genres and styles in each book of the Bible. Below are some of his thoughtful considerations of election and predestination:

> Theologians sometimes speak of "double predestination," which means that according to God's decree, some sinners will never repent and thus finally will be lost in their sins. Strictly speaking, double predestination is not a biblical term, for the Bible nowhere speaks of anyone being predestined to hell. It reserves the verb "predestine" (*proorizo*) for the salvation of sinners unto eternal life. However, even if it is not a biblical term, double predestination expresses a biblical truth. If God has made an advance decision about which people He will save from their sins, He has also made an advance decision about which people He will leave in their sins (Romans 1:28). The theological term for this is "reprobation." It means that when God stablished His plan of salvation, He decided to pass some sinners by.
>
> Election is best understood in hindsight, for it is only after coming to Christ that one can know for sure whether one has been chosen in Christ. Those who make a decision for Christ find that God made a decision for them in eternity past. It is like the words of the anonymous nineteenth-century hymn: I sought the Lord, and afterward I knew He moved my soul to seek Him, seeking me; it was not that I found, O Savior true; no, I was found of Thee.[189]

From Moody Bible Institute

The story is told of a group of theologians who were discussing the tension between predestination and free will. Things became so heated that the group broke up into two opposing factions. But one man, not knowing which to join, stood for a moment trying to decide. At last he joined the predestination group. "Who sent you here?" they asked. "No one sent me" he replied. "I came of my own free will." "Free will!" they exclaimed. "You

---

[189] Philip Graham Ryken, *Assured by God,* ed. Burk Parsons (P&R, 2006), 44–46. Used by permission.

can't join us! You belong with the other group!" So he followed their orders and went to the other clique. There someone asked, "When did you decide to join us?" The young man replied, "Well, I didn't really decide, I was sent here." "Sent here!" they shouted. "You can't join us unless you have decided by your own free will!"[190]

---

[190] *Today in the Word* (August 1989): 35. *Today in the Word* is a publication of Moody Bible Institute.

34

Confessions of Faith that Affirm the Decrees of Election and Predestination

This chapter is dedicated to what is referred to as "Confessions of Faith" that have arisen at crucial times of church history and spiritual reformation and more specifically how these important statements of faith address various issues within the two doctrinal considerations of this book, which are election and predestination. Hopefully, this will help you see the importance of election and predestination from the 1500's through today. Before looking at these confessions of faith, let us define a confession of faith using the definition found in the online edition of the Encyclopedia Britannica.[191]

> **Confession of faith**: A formal statement of doctrinal belief ordinarily intended for public avowal by an individual, a group, a congregation, a synod, or a church; confessions are similar to creeds, although usually more extensive. They are especially associated with the churches of the Protestant Reformation. A brief treatment of confessions of faith follows.

---

[191] https://www.britannica.com/topic/confession-of-faith-theology.

Quotes from the "Heidelberg Catechism of 1563"

Written in 1563, the Heidelberg Catechism originated in one of the few pockets of Calvinistic faith in the Lutheran and Catholic territories of Germany. Originally created as a teaching instrument to promote Christian unity in the Palatinate, the catechism quickly became a guide for preaching as well. It is a very user friendly and personalized confession of faith, eminently deserving of its popularity among Reformed churches to the present day. The catechism is structured in a question and answer format with thirty-four questions and answers with supporting Bible verses for each answer. The following questions and answers refer only to the depravity of man.[192]

Question & Answer 5

Q. Can you live up to all this perfectly?

A. No. I have a natural tendency to hate God and my neighbor.

Romans 3:9–20, 23, 1 John 1:8, 10, Genesis 6:5, Jeremiah 17:9, Romans 7:23–24 and 8:7, Ephesians 2:1–3, Titus 3:3.

Question & Answer 6

Q. Did God create people so wicked and perverse?

A. No. God created them good and in His own image, that is, in true righteousness and holiness, so that they might truly know God their creator, love him with all their heart, and live with God in eternal happiness, to praise and glorify him.

Genesis 1:31, Genesis 1:26–27, Ephesians 4:24, Colossians 3:10, Psalm 8.

Question & Answer 7

Q. Then where does this corrupt human nature come from?

A. The fall and disobedience of our first parents, Adam and Eve, in Paradise. This fall has so poisoned our nature that we are all conceived and born in a sinful condition.

Genesis 3, Romans 5:12–19, Psalm 51:5.

Question & Answer 8

Q. But are we so corrupt that we are totally unable to do any good and inclined toward all evil?

---

[192] From the Heidelberg Catechism of 1563, the First Part "Of the Misery of Man" found online at: https://www.blueletterbible.org/study/ccc/heidelberg/ofTheMiseryOfMan.cfm.

A. Yes, unless we are born again by the Spirit of God.

Genesis 6:5 and 8:21, Job 14:4, Isaiah 53:6, John 3:3–5.

Question & Answer 9

Q. But doesn't God do us an injustice by requiring in His law what we are unable to do?

A. No, God created human beings with the ability to keep the law. They, however, provoked by the devil, in willful disobedience, robbed themselves and all their descendants of these gifts.

Genesis 1:31, 3:6, 3:13, John 8:44, Romans 5:12–19, Ephesians 4:24.

Quotes from the "Westminster Confession of 1646"

The Westminster Confession of Faith was drawn up by the 1646 Westminster Assembly as part of the Westminster Standards to be a confession of the Church of England. In 1643, the English Parliament called upon "learned, godly and judicious Divines," to meet at Westminster Abbey in order to provide advice on issues of worship, doctrine, government, and discipline of the Church of England. Their meetings, over a period of five years, produced the confession of faith, as well as a *Larger Catechism* and a *Shorter Catechism*. For almost four centuries, various churches around the world have adopted the Confession and the catechisms as their standards of doctrine, subordinate only to the Bible.

The Westminster Confession of Faith was modified and adopted by Congregationalists in England in the form of the Savoy Declaration (1658). Likewise, the Baptists of England modified the Savoy Declaration to produce the Second London Baptist Confession (1689). English Presbyterians, Congregationalists, and Baptists would together (with others) come to be known as Nonconformists, because they did not conform to the Act of Uniformity (1662) establishing the Church of England as the only legally approved church, though they were in many ways united by their common confessions, built on the *Westminster Confession*. The following section of the *Westminster Confession* expresses its view on "election and predestination":[193]

God from all eternity did by the most wise and holy counsel of His own will freely and unchangeably ordain whatsoever comes to pass: . . . By the decree of God, for the manifestation of His glory, some men and angels are predestinated unto everlasting life, and others foreordained to everlasting death. These angels and men, thus predestinated and

[193] The summary data on the "Westminster Confession of 1646" was drawn from the following online source: https://www.britannica.com/topic/Westminster-Confession.

foreordained, are particularly and unchangeably designed and their number is so certain and definite that it cannot be either increased or diminished. Those of mankind that are predestinated unto life, God, before the foundation of the world was laid, according to His eternal and immutable purpose, and the secret counsel and good pleasure of His will, hath chosen in Christ, unto everlasting glory, out of His free grace and love alone, without any foresight of faith or good works, or perseverance in either of them or any other thing in the creature, as conditions, or causes moving him thereunto . . . The rest of mankind God was pleased . . . to ordain them to dishonor and wrath for their sin . . . Chap. III, p 1–7.

All those whom God hath predestinated unto life, and those only, He is pleased, in His appointed and accepted time, effectually to call by His Word and Spirit out of that state of sin and death, in which they are by nature, to grace and salvation by Jesus Christ . . . This effectual call is of God's free and special grace alone, not from any thing at all foreseen in man, who is altogether passive therein . . . Others, not elected, although they may be called by the ministry of the Word, . . . yet they never truly come to Christ, and therefore cannot be saved . . . Chap. X, p. 1–4.[194]

Quotes from the "Scots Confession of 1560"

The Scots Confession was written in 1560 by six leaders of the Protestant Reformation in Scotland, coincidentally all named John.[195] The Confession was the first Book of Faith for the Protestant Scottish Church. The Six Johns were Knox, Spottiswoode, Willock, Row, Douglas and Winram. Although the Confession and its accompanying documents were really the product of the joint effort of the six Johns, it's authorship is customarily credited to John Knox. The following section of chapter 8 of the Scots Confession express its view on "election and predestination":

For that same Eternal God and Father, who of mere grace elected us in Christ Jesus His Son, before the foundation of the world was laid, 1) appointed Him to be our Head, 2) our Brother, 3) our Pastor, and great Bishop of our souls. 4) But because that the enmity betwixt the justice of God and our sins was such that no flesh by itself could or might have attained unto God, 5) it behooved that the Son of God should descend unto us, and take Himself a body of our body, flesh of our flesh, and bone of our bones, and so become the perfect mediator betwixt God and man, 6) giving power to so many as believe in Him

---

[194] https://www.blueletterbible.org/study/ccc/westminster/index.cfm.

[195] Please see the following sites for more complete details on what the "Scotts Confession" is about and how it came to be:
https://reformationhistory.org/scotsconfessionoffaith.html
https://en.wikipedia.org/wiki/Scots_Confession
https://theancientpaths.org/2012/01/17/the-scots-confession-of-1560.

to be the sons of God, 7) as Himself does witness: I pass up to my Father and unto your Father, to my God, and unto your God, 8) By which most holy fraternity, whatsoever we have lost in Adam is restored to us again, 9) And for this cause are we not afraid to call God our Father, 10) not so much that [because] He has created us (which we have common with the reprobate), as for that He has given to us His only Son to be our brother, and 11) and given unto us grace to acknowledge and embrace Him for our only mediator, as before is said.

It behooved further the Messiah and Redeemer to be very God and very Man, because He was to underlie the punishment due for our transgressions, and to present Himself in the presence of His Father's judgments, as in our person, to suffer for our transgression and disobedience, by death, to overcome him that was author of death. But because the only Godhead could not suffer death, neither yet could the only man head overcome the same, He joined both together in one person, that the imbecility [weakness] of the one should suffer, and be subject to death (which we had deserved), and the infinite and invincible power of the other (to wit, of the Godhead) should triumph and purchase to us life, liberty, and perpetual victory. And So we confess, and most undoubtedly believe.[196]

1. Ephesian 1:11 / Matthew 25:34
2. Ephesians 1:22–23
3. Hebrews 2:7–8, 11–12 / Psalm 22:22
4. Hebrews 13:20 / 1 Peter 2:24, 5:4
5. Psalm 130:3, 143:2
6. 1 Timothy 2:5
7. John 1:12
8. John 20:17
9. Romans 5:17–19
10. Romans 8:15 / Galatians 4:5–6
11. Acts 17:26
12. Hebrews 2:11–12
13. 1 Peter 3:18 / Isaiah 53:8
14. Acts 2:24 / John 1:2 / Acts 20:20 / 1 Timothy 3:16 / John 3:16

Quotes from the "Canons of Dort of 1619"

The Canons of Dort or Canons of Dordrecht, officially called *The Decision of the Synod of Dort on the Five Main Points of Doctrine in Dispute in the Netherlands*, is the judgment

---

[196] You can be read the actual text online at http://apostles-creed.org/wp-content/uploads/2014/07/Scots_Confession_1560.pdf.

of the National Synod held in the Dutch city of Dordrecht in 1618–1619. At the time, Dordrecht was mostly referred to in English as *Dort*. Today the Canons of Dort are a part of the *Three Forms of Unity*, one of the confessional standards of many of the Reformed churches around the world, including the Netherlands, South Africa, Australia, and North America.[197]

The following section of the *Canons of Dort* express their views on "election and predestination."[198]

First Head of Doctrine:

- **Divine Election and Reprobation**

FIRST HEAD: ARTICLE 1. As all men have sinned in Adam, lie under the curse, and are deserving of eternal death, God would have done no injustice by leaving them all to perish and delivering them over to condemnation on account of sin, according to the words of the apostle: "that every mouth may be silenced and the whole world held accountable to God." (Rom 3:19). And: "for all have sinned and fall short of the glory of God," (Rom 3:23). And: "For the wages of sin is death" (Rom 6:23).

FIRST HEAD: ARTICLE 2. But in this the love of God was manifested, that He "sent his one and only Son into the world, that whoever believes in him shall not perish but have eternal life." (1 John 4:9, John 3:16).

FIRST HEAD: ARTICLE 3. And that men may be brought to believe, God mercifully sends the messengers of these most joyful tiding to whom He will and at what time He pleases; by whose ministry men are called to repentance and faith in Christ crucified. "How, then, can they call on the one they have not believed in? And how can they believe in the one of whom they have not heard? And how can they hear without someone preaching to them? And how can they preach unless they are sent?" (Rom 10:14–15).

FIRST HEAD: ARTICLE 4. The wrath of God abides upon those who believe not this gospel. But such as receive it and embrace Jesus the Savior by a true and living faith are by Him delivered from the wrath of God and from destruction, and have the gift of eternal life conferred upon them.

FIRST HEAD: ARTICLE 5. The cause or guilt of this unbelief as well as of all other sins is no wise in God, but in man himself; whereas faith in Jesus Christ and salvation through Him is the free gift of God, as it is written: "For it is by grace you have been saved, through faith—and this not from yourselves, it is the gift of God" (Eph 2:8). Likewise:

---

[197] For a great introduction and overview of the "Canons of Dort of 1619, please see https://www.crcna.org/welcome/beliefs/confessions/canons-dort.
[198] The text can be found in "The Canons of Dort" (1618–1619), by Synod of Dort (May 4, 2014).

"For it has been granted to you on behalf of Christ not only to believe on him, but also to suffer for him" (Phil 1:29).

FIRST HEAD: ARTICLE 6. That some receive the gift of faith from God, and others do not receive it, proceeds from God's eternal decree. "For known unto God are all his works from the beginning of the world" (Acts 15:18, AV). "who works out everything in conformity with the purpose of his will" (Eph 1:11). According to which decree He graciously softens the hearts of the elect, however obstinate, and inclines them to believe; while He leaves the non-elect in His just judgment to their own wickedness and obduracy. And herein is especially displayed the profound, the merciful, and at the same time the righteous discrimination between men equally involved in ruin; or that decree of election and reprobation, revealed in the Word of God, which, though men of perverse, impure, and unstable minds wrest it to their own destruction, yet to holy and pious souls affords unspeakable consolation.

FIRST HEAD: ARTICLE 7. Election is the unchangeable purpose of God, whereby, before the foundation of the world, He has out of mere grace, according to the sovereign good pleasure of His own will, chosen from the whole human race, which had fallen through their own fault from the primitive state of rectitude into sin and destruction, a certain number of persons to redemption in Christ, whom He from eternity appointed the Mediator and Head of the elect and the foundation of salvation. This elect number, though by nature neither better nor more deserving than others, but with them involved in one common misery, God has decreed to give to Christ to be saved by Him, and effectually to call and draw them to His communion by His Word and Spirit; to bestow upon them true faith, justification, and sanctification; and having powerfully preserved them in the fellowship of His son, finally to glorify them for the demonstration of His mercy, and for the praise of the riches of His glorious grace; as it is written "For he chose us in him before the creation of the world to be holy and blameless in his sight. In love, He predestined us to be adopted as his sons through Jesus Christ, in accordance with his pleasure and will—to the praise of his glorious grace, which he has freely given us in the One he loves." (Eph 1:4–6). And elsewhere: "And those he predestined, he also called; those he called, he also justified; those he justified, he also glorified." (Rom 8:30).

FIRST HEAD: ARTICLE 8. There are not various decrees of election, but one and the same decree respecting all those who shall be saved, both under the Old and New Testament; since the Scripture declares the good pleasure, purpose, and counsel of the divine will to be one, according to which He has chosen us from eternity, both to grace and to glory, to salvation and to the way of salvation, which He has ordained that we should walk therein (Eph 1:4, 5; 2:10).

FIRST HEAD: ARTICLE 9. This election was not founded upon foreseen faith and the obedience of faith, holiness, or any other good quality or disposition in man, as the prerequisite, cause, or condition of which it depended; but men are chosen to faith and to the obedience of faith, holiness, etc. Therefore, election is the fountain of every saving good, from which proceed faith, holiness, and the other gifts of salvation, and finally eternal life itself, as its fruits and effects, according to the testimony of the apostle: "For he chose us (not because we were, but) in him before the creation of the world to be holy and blameless in his sight." (Eph 1:4).

FIRST HEAD: ARTICLE 10. The good pleasure of God is the sole cause of this gracious election, which does not consist herein that out of all possible qualities and actions of men God has chosen some as a condition of salvation, but that He was pleased out of the common mass of sinners to adopt some certain persons as a peculiar people to Himself, as it is written: "Yet, before the twins were born or had done anything good or bad—in order that God's purpose in election might stand: not by works but by him who calls—she (Rebekah) was told, 'The older will serve the younger.' Just as it is written: 'Jacob I loved, but Esau I hated.'" (Rom 9:11–13). "When the Gentiles heard this, they were glad and honored the word of the Lord; and all who were appointed for eternal life believed." (Acts 13:48).

FIRST HEAD: ARTICLE 11. And as God Himself is most wise, unchangeable, omniscient, and omnipotent, so the election made by Him can neither be interrupted nor changed, recalled, or annulled; neither can the elect be cast away, nor their number diminished.

FIRST HEAD: ARTICLE 12. The elect in due time, though in various degrees and in different measures, attain the assurance of this their eternal and unchangeable election, not by inquisitively prying into the secret and deep things of God, but by observing in themselves with a spiritual joy and holy pleasure the infallible fruits of election pointed out in the Word of God—such as, a true faith in Christ, filial fear, a godly sorrow for sin, a hungering and thirsting after righteousness, etc.

FIRST HEAD: ARTICLE 13. The sense and certainty of this election afford to the children of God additional matter for daily humiliation before Him, for adoring the depth of His mercies, for cleansing themselves, and rendering grateful returns of ardent love to Him who first manifested so great love toward them. The consideration of this doctrine of election is so far from encouraging remissness in the observance of the divine commands or from sinking men in carnal security, that these, in the just judgment of God, are the usual effects of rash presumption or of idle and wanton trifling with the grace of election, in those who refuse to walk in the ways of the elect.

FIRST HEAD: ARTICLE 14. As the doctrine of election by the most wise counsel of

God was declared by the prophets, by Christ Himself, and by the apostles, and is clearly revealed in the Scriptures both of the Old and the New Testament, so it is still to be published in due time and place in the Church of God, for which it was peculiarly designed, provided it be done with reverence, in the spirit of discretion and piety, for the glory of God's most holy name, and for enlivening and comforting His people, without vainly attempting to investigate the secret ways of the Most High (Acts 20:27; Rom 11:33f; 12:3; Heb 6:17f).

FIRST HEAD: ARTICLE 15. What peculiarly tends to illustrate and recommend to us the eternal and unmerited grace of election is the express testimony of sacred Scripture that not all, but some only, are elected, while others are passed by in the eternal decree; whom God, out of His sovereign, most just, irreprehensible, and unchangeable good pleasure, has decreed to leave in the common misery into which they have willfully plunged themselves, and not to bestow upon them saving faith and the grace of conversion; but, permitting them in His just judgment to follow their own ways, at last, for the declaration of His justice, to condemn and punish them forever, not only on account of their unbelief, but also for all their other sins. And this is the decree of reprobation, which by no means makes God the Author of sin (the very thought of which is blasphemy), but declares Him to be an awful, irreprehensible, and righteous Judge and Avenger thereof.

FIRST HEAD: ARTICLE 16. Those in whom a living faith in Christ, and assured confidence of soul, peace of conscience, an earnest endeavor after filial obedience, a glorying in God through Christ, is not as yet strongly felt, and who nevertheless make use of the means which God has appointed for working these graces in us, ought not to be alarmed at the mention of reprobation, nor to rank themselves among the reprobate, but diligently to persevere in the use of means, and with ardent desires devoutly and humble to wait for a season of richer grace. Much less cause to be terrified by the doctrine of reprobation have they who, though they seriously desire to be turned to God, to please Him only, and to be delivered from the body of death, cannot yet reach that measure of holiness and faith to which they aspire; since a merciful God has promised that He will not quench the smoking flax, nor break the bruised reed. But this doctrine is justly terrible to those who, regardless of God and of the Savior Jesus Christ, have wholly given themselves up to the cares of the world and the pleasures of the flesh, so long as they are not seriously converted to God.

FIRST HEAD: ARTICLE 17. Since we are to judge of the will of God from His Word, which testifies that the children of believers are holy, not by nature, but in virtue of the covenant of grace, in which they together with the parents are comprehended, godly parents ought not to doubt the election and salvation of their children whom it pleases God to call out of this life in their infancy (Gen 17:7; Acts 2:39; 1 Cor 7:14).

FIRST HEAD: ARTICLE 18. To those who murmur at the free grace of election and the just severity of reprobation we answer with the apostle "But who are you, O man, to talk back to God?" (Rom. 9:20), and quote the language of our Savior: "Don't I have the right to do what I want with my own?" (Matt 20:15). And therefore, with holy adoration of these mysteries, we exclaim in the words of the apostle: "Oh, the depth of the riches of the wisdom and knowledge of God! How unsearchable his judgments, and his paths beyond tracing out! Who has known the mind of the Lord? Or who has been his counselor? Who has ever given to God, that God should repay him? For from him and through him and to him are all things. To him be the glory forever! Amen." (Rom. 11:33–36).

Quotes from the "Second Helvetic Confession of 1566"

This Confession expresses the maturing theology of the Reformed churches of Switzerland in the years following the Reformation and is assuredly a Protestant document. It not only distances the Swiss Reformed churches from Roman Catholicism, but also expresses many of the emerging points of emphasis in Protestantism. It was written by Heinrich Bullinger, a Swiss pastor who emerged as a leading Reformed theologian after the death of Ulrich Zwingli, who had been one of the leaders of the Reformation in Switzerland. The following section of *The Second Helvetic Confession* express it's view on "election and predestination."[199]

Chapter 10: Of the Predestination of God and the Election of the Saints (2nd Helvetic Confession)

God has elected us out of grace: From eternity, God has freely and of His mere grace, without any respect to men, predestinated or elected the saints whom He wills to save in Christ, according to the saying of the apostle, "God chose us in him before the foundation of the world" (Eph. 1:4). And again: "Who saved us and called us with a holy calling, not in virtue of our works but in virtue of his own purpose and the grace which he gave us in Christ Jesus ages ago, and now has manifested through the appearing of our Savior Christ Jesus" (2 Tim. 1:9 f.).

We are elected or predestinated in Christ: Therefore, although not on account of any merit of ours, God has elected us, not directly, but in Christ, and on account of Christ, in order that those who are now ingrafted into Christ by faith might also be elected. But those who were outside Christ were rejected, according to the word of the apostle, "Examine yourselves, to see whether you are holding to your faith. Test yourselves. Do you not realize that Jesus Christ is in you? Unless indeed you fail to meet the test!" (2 Cor. 13:5).

[199] For a fuller description of the "The Second Helvetic Confession," please see the pdf at https://ammooni. ga/file-ready/second-helvetic-confession.

We are elected for a definite purpose: Finally, the saints are chosen by God for a definite purpose, which the apostle himself explains when he says, "He chose us in Him for adoption that we should be holy and blameless before Him in love. He destined us for adoption to be His sons through Jesus Christ that they should be to the praise of the glory of his grace" (Eph. 1:4 ff.).

We are to have a good hope for all: And although God knows who are His, and here and there mention is made of the small number of elect, yet we must hope well of all, and not rashly judge any man to be a reprobate. For Paul says to the Philippians, "I thank my God for you all" (now he speaks of the whole Church in Philippi), "because of your fellowship in the Gospel, being persuaded that He who began a good work in you will bring it to completion at the day of Jesus Christ. It is also right that I have this opinion of you all" (Phil. 1:3 ff.).

Whether few are elect: And when the Lord was asked whether there were few that should be saved, He does not answer and tell them that few or many should be saved or damned, but rather He exhorts every man to "strive to enter by the narrow door" (Luke 13:24): as if He should say, It is not for you curiously to inquire about these matters, but rather to endeavor that you may enter into heaven by the straight way.

What in this matter is to be condemned: Therefore, we do not approve of the impious speeches of some who say, "Few are chosen, and since I do not know whether I am among the number of the few, I will enjoy myself." Others say, "If I am predestinated and elected by God, nothing can hinder me from salvation, which is already certainly appointed for me, no matter what I do. But if I am in the number of the reprobate, no faith or repentance will help me, since the decree of God cannot be changed. Therefore, all doctrines and admonitions are useless." Now the saying of the apostle contradicts these men: "The Lord's servant must be ready to teach, instructing those who oppose him, so that if God should grant that they repent to know the truth, they may recover from the snare of the devil, after being held captive by him to do his will" (2 Tim. 2:23 ff.).

Admonitions are not in vain, because salvation proceeds from election: Augustine also shows that both the grace of free election and predestination, and also salutary admonitions and doctrines, are to be preached (*Lib. de Dono Perseverantiae,* cap. 14 ff.).

Whether we are elected: We therefore find fault with those who outside of Christ ask whether they are elected. And what has God decreed concerning them before all eternity? For the preaching of the Gospel is to be heard, and it is to be believed; and it is to be held as beyond doubt that if you believe and are in Christ, you are elected. For the Father has revealed unto us in Christ the eternal purpose of His predestination, as I have just now shown from the apostle in 2 Tim. 1:9–10. This is therefore above all to be taught and considered, what great love of the Father toward us is revealed to us in Christ. We must hear what the Lord himself daily preaches to us in the Gospel, how He calls and says: "Come to me all who labor and are heavy laden, and I will give you rest" (Matt. 11:28). "God so loved the world, that he gave His only Son, that whoever believes in Him should not perish, but have eternal life" (John 3:16). Also, "It is not the will of my Father that one of these little ones should perish" (Matt. 18:14). Let Christ, therefore be the looking glass, in whom we may contemplate our predestination. We shall have a sufficiently clear and sure testimony that we are inscribed in the Book of Life if we have fellowship with Christ, and He is ours and we are His in true faith.

Temptation in regard to predestination: In the temptation in regard to predestination, than which there is scarcely any other more dangerous, we are confronted by the fact that God's promises apply to all the faithful, for He says: "Ask, and everyone who seeks, shall receive" (Luke 11:9 f.). This finally we pray, with the whole Church of God, "Our Father who art in heaven" (Matt. 6:9), both because by baptism we are ingrafted into the body of Christ, and we are often fed in His Church with His flesh and blood unto life eternal. Thereby, being strengthened, we are commanded to work out our salvation with fear and trembling, according to the precept of Paul.[200]

Quotes from the "London Baptist Confession of 1689"

The 1689 London Baptist Confession of Faith was written by sovereign grace Baptists in England, to give a formal expression of the Reformed and Protestant Christian faith, with a distinctive Baptist perspective. This Confession, like the Westminster Confession of Faith (1646) and the Savoy Declaration (1658), was written by evangelical Puritans who were concerned that their particular church organization reflect what they perceived to be biblical teaching.[201]

The following section of *The London Baptist Confession* expresses its views on "election and predestination."[202]

---

[200] For Selected print and online resources for chapter 10, "Of the Predestination of God and the Election of the Saints" (2nd Helvetic Confession) please see:
- An English translation of *Fidei ratio* by George Joye, 1548. At Early English Books Online (available through BYU);
- *Zwingli and Bullinger: Selected Translations*, Library of Christian Classics, vol. 24. Ed. G. W. Bromiley. Philadelphia: Westminster Press, 1953.
- –HBLL Stacks BR 346 .A24.

[201] For relevant background information on this confession and how it came to be, please see https://www.theopedia.com/london-baptist-confession-of-1689.

[202] The entire 1689 London Baptist Confession of Faith can be read at https://www.1689.com/confession.html.

Chapter 3: Of God's Decree

God hath decreed in Himself, from all eternity, by the most wise and holy counsel of His own will, freely and unchangeably, all things, whatsoever comes to pass; yet so as thereby is God neither the author of sin nor hath fellowship with any therein; nor is violence offered to the will of the creature, nor yet is the liberty or contingency of second causes taken away, but rather established; in which appears His wisdom in disposing all things, and power and faithfulness in accomplishing His decree. (Isaiah 46:10; Ephesians 1:11; Hebrews 6:17; Romans 9:15, 18; James 1:13; 1 John 1:5; Acts 4:27, 28; John 19:11; Numbers 23:19; Ephesians 1:3–5.)

Although God knoweth whatsoever may or can come to pass, upon all supposed conditions, yet hath He not decreed anything, because He foresaw it as future, or as that which would come to pass upon such conditions. (Acts 15:18; Romans 9:11, 13, 16, 18.)

By the decree of God, for the manifestation of His glory, some men and angels are predestinated, or foreordained to eternal life through Jesus Christ, to the praise of His glorious grace; others being left to act in their sin to their just condemnation, to the praise of His glorious justice. (1 Timothy 5:21; Matthew 25:34; Ephesians 1:5, 6; Romans 9:22, 23; Jude 4.)

These angels and men thus predestinated and foreordained, are particularly and unchangeably designed, and their number so certain and definite, that it cannot be either increased or diminished. (2 Timothy 2:19; John 13:18.)

Those of mankind that are predestinated to life, God, before the foundation of the world was laid, according to His eternal and immutable purpose, and the secret counsel and good pleasure of His will, hath chosen in Christ unto everlasting glory, out of His mere free grace and love, without any other thing in the creature as a condition or cause moving Him thereunto. (Ephesians 1:4, 9, 11; Romans 8:30; 2 Timothy 1:9; 1 Thessalonians 5:9; Romans 9:13, 16; Ephesians 2:5, 12.)

As God hath appointed the elect unto glory, so He hath, by the eternal and most free purpose of His will, foreordained all the means thereunto; wherefore they who are elected, being fallen in Adam, are redeemed by Christ, are effectually called unto faith in Christ, by His Spirit working in due season, are justified, adopted, sanctified, and kept by His power through faith unto salvation; neither are any other redeemed by Christ, or effectually called, justified, adopted, sanctified, and saved, but the elect only. (1 Peter 1:2; 2 Thessalonians 2:13; 1 Thessalonians 5:9, 10; Romans 8:30; 2 Thessalonians 2:13; 1 Peter 1:5; John 10:26; John 17:9; John 6:64.)

The doctrine of the high mystery of predestination is to be handled with special prudence and care, that men attending the will of God revealed in His Word, and yielding obedience thereunto, may, from the certainty of their effectual vocation, be assured of their eternal election; so shall this doctrine afford matter of praise, reverence, and admiration of God, and of humility, diligence, and abundant consolation to all that sincerely obey the gospel. (1 Thessalonians 1:4, 5; 2 Peter 1:10; Ephesians 1:6; Romans 11:33; Romans 11:5, 6, 20; Luke 10:20.)

Chapter 5: Of Divine Providence (The London Baptist Confession continued)

God the good Creator of all things, in His infinite power and wisdom doth uphold, direct, dispose, and govern all creatures and things, from the greatest even to the least, by His most wise and holy providence, to the end for the which they were created, according unto His infallible foreknowledge, and the free and immutable counsel of His own will; to the praise of the glory of His wisdom, power, justice, infinite goodness, and mercy. (Hebrews 1:3; Job 38:11; Isaiah 46:10, 11; Psalms 135:6; Matthew 10:29–31; Ephesians 1:11.)

Although in relation to the foreknowledge and decree of God, the first cause, all things come to pass immutably and infallibly; so that there is not anything befalls any by chance, or without His providence; yet by the same providence He ordereth them to fall out according to the nature of second causes, either necessarily, freely, or contingently. (Acts 2:23; Proverbs 16:33; Genesis 8:22.)

God, in His ordinary providence maketh use of means, yet is free to work without, above, and against them at His pleasure. (Acts 27:31, 44; Isaiah 55:10, 11; Hosea 1:7; Romans 4:19–21; Daniel 3:27.) The almighty power, unsearchable wisdom, and infinite goodness of God, so far manifest themselves in His providence, that His determinate counsel extendeth itself even to the first fall, and all other sinful actions both of angels and men; and that not by a bare permission, which also He most wisely and powerfully boundeth, and otherwise ordereth and governeth, in a manifold dispensation to His most holy ends; yet so, as the sinfulness of their acts proceedeth only from the creatures, and not from God, who, being most holy and righteous, neither is nor can be the author or approver of sin. (Romans 11:32–34; 2 Samuel 24:1, 1 Chronicles 21:1; 2 Kings 19:28; Psalms 76;10; Genesis 1:20; Isaiah 10:6, 7, 12; Psalms 1:21; 1 John 2:16.)

The most wise, righteous, and gracious God doth oftentimes leave for a season His own children to manifold temptations and the corruptions of their own hearts, to chastise them for their former sins, or to discover unto them the hidden strength of corruption and deceitfulness of their hearts, that they may be humbled; and to raise them to a more close and constant dependence for their support upon Himself; and to make them more watchful against all future occasions of sin, and for other just and holy ends. So that whatsoever befalls any of His elect is by his appointment, for his glory, and their good. (2 Chronicles 32:25, 26, 31; 2 Corinthians 12:7–9; Romans 8:28.)

As for those wicked and ungodly men whom God, as the righteous judge, for former sin doth blind and harden; from them He not only withholdeth His grace, whereby they might have been enlightened in their understanding, and wrought upon their hearts; but sometimes also withdraweth the gifts which they had, and exposeth them to such objects as their corruption makes occasion of sin; and withal, gives them over to their own lusts, the temptations of the world, and the power of Satan, whereby it comes to pass that they harden themselves, under those means which God useth for the softening of others. (Romans 1:24–26, 28; Romans 11:7, 8; Deuteronomy 29:4; Matthew 13:12; Deuteronomy 2:30; 2 Kings 8:12, 13; Psalms 81:11, 12; 2 Thessalonians 2:10–12; Exodus 8:15, 32; Isaiah 6:9, 10; 1 Peter 2:7, 8.)

As the providence of God doth in general reach to all creatures, so after a more special manner it taketh care of His church, and disposeth of all things to the good thereof. (1 Timothy 4:10; Amos 9:8, 9; Isaiah 43:3–5)

Chapter 10: Of Effectual Calling (The London Baptist Confession continued):

Those whom God hath predestinated unto life, He is pleased in His appointed, and accepted time, effectually to call, by His Word and Spirit, out of that state of sin and death in which they are by nature, to grace and salvation by Jesus Christ; enlightening their minds spiritually and savingly to understand the things of God; taking away their heart of stone, and giving unto them a heart of flesh; renewing their wills, and by His almighty power determining them to that which is good, and effectually drawing them to Jesus Christ; yet so as they come most freely, being made willing by His grace. (Romans 8:30; Romans 11:7; Ephesians 1:10, 11; 2 Thessalonians 2:13, 14; Ephesians 2:1–6; Acts 26:18; Ephesians 1:17, 18; Ezekiel 36:26; Deuteronomy 30:6; Ezekiel 36:27; Ephesians 1:19; Psalm 110:3; Song of Solomon 1:4.)

This effectual call is of God's free and special grace alone, not from anything at all foreseen in man, nor from any power or agency in the creature, being wholly passive therein, being dead in sins and trespasses, until being quickened and renewed by the Holy Spirit; he is thereby enabled to answer this call, and to embrace the grace offered and conveyed in it, and that by no less power than that which raised up Christ from the dead. (2 Timothy 1:9; Ephesians 2:8; 1 Corinthians 2:14; Ephesians 2:5; John 5:25; Ephesians 1:19, 20.)

Elect infants dying in infancy are regenerated and saved by Christ through the Spirit; who worketh when, and where, and how He pleases; so also—are all elect persons, who are incapable of being outwardly called by the ministry of the Word. (John 3:3, 5, 6; John 3:8.)

Others not elected, although they may be called by the ministry of the Word, and may have some common operations of the Spirit, yet not being effectually drawn by the Father, they neither will nor can truly come to Christ, and therefore cannot be saved: much less can men that receive not the Christian religion be saved; be they never so diligent to frame their lives according to the light of nature and the law of that religion they do profess. (Matthew 22:14; Matthew 13:20, 21; Hebrews 6:4, 5; John 6:44, 45, 65; 1 John 2:24, 25; Acts 4:12; John 4:22; John 17:3.)

Quotes from The Baptist Faith and Message of 2000

On June 14, 2000, the Southern Baptist Convention adopted a revised summary of faith.[203]

The following section of the *Baptist Faith and Message* expresses its view on "election" below.[204]

V. God's Purpose of Grace

Election is the gracious purpose of God, according to which He regenerates, justifies, sanctifies, and glorifies sinners. It is consistent with the free agency of man and comprehends all the means in connection with the end. It is the glorious display of God's sovereign goodness and is infinitely wise, holy, and unchangeable. It excludes boasting and promotes humility.

All true believers endure to the end. Those whom God has accepted in Christ, and sanctified by His Spirit, will never fall away from the state of grace, but shall persevere to the end. Believers may fall into sin through neglect and temptation, whereby they grieve the Spirit, impair their graces and comforts, and bring reproach on the cause of Christ and temporal judgments on themselves; yet they shall be kept by the power of God through faith unto salvation.

(Genesis 12:1–3; Exodus 19:5–8; 1 Samuel 8:4–7, 19–22; Isaiah 5:1–7; Jeremiah 31:31ff.; Matthew 16:18–19; 21:28–45; 24:22, 31; 25:34; Luke 1:68–79; 2:29–32; 19:41–44; 24:44–48; John 1:12–14; 3:16; 5:24; 6:44–45, 65; 10:27–29; 15:16; 17:6, 12, 17–18; Acts 20:32; Romans 5:9–10; 8:28–39; 10:12–15; 11:5–7, 26–36; 1 Corinthians 1:1–2; 15:24–28; Ephesians 1:4–23; 2:1–10; 3:1–11; Colossians 1:12–14; 2 Thessalonians 2:13–14; 2 Timothy 1:12; 2:10, 19; Hebrews 11:39–12:2; James 1:12; 1 Peter 1:2–5, 13; 2:4–10; 1 John 1:7–9; 2:19; 3:2.)[205]

---

[203] See http://www.sbcec.net/baptist-faith-and-message/introduction.

[204] This section is taken from http://www.hsbchurch.com/Misc_Images/Hsbchurch.com_misc_image49318.pdf.

[205] http://www.sbc.net/bfm.

SUMMARY AND CONCLUSION

Well, what can I say? If you have reached this page in your journey through this book, you have read and thought about a lot of things. Whatever conclusions you may have come to about election and predestination and God's sovereign power in your salvation, I want to thank you for allowing me the privilege of sharing these concepts with you. I am grateful for the time and effort you made to study these topics and issues.

If you ever want to discuss any of these doctrines, please contact me at the email address below. I would count it a blessing to hear from you.

In the meantime, I want to conclude by restating the goal of the book, which is the supernatural freedom that each born-again Christian can experience through his or her experimental knowledge and spiritual understanding of election and predestination—planned, orchestrated, implemented, and fulfilled though God's sovereign love and grace. These truths are a resting place, for a believer kept by the power of Christ in this life and sealed by the Holy Spirit until the day of redemption.

Thanks again!

Yours in Christ,

Gene Gobble
gene@gobblefamily.com

APPENDIX 1

George Whitefield's Letter to John Wesley about Election and Predestination

Below is a letter from George Whitefield to the Reverend John Wesley in answer to Mr. Wesley's sermon titled "Free Grace," based upon Galatians 2:11: "But when Peter was come to Antioch, I withstood him to the face, because he was to be blamed":

I am very well aware what different effects publishing this letter against the dear Mr. Wesley's Sermon will produce. Many of my friends who are strenuous advocates for *universal redemption* will immediately be offended. Many who are zealous on the other side will be much rejoiced. They who are lukewarm on both sides and are carried away with carnal reasoning will wish this matter had never been brought under debate. The reasons I have given at the beginning of the letter, I think are sufficient to satisfy all of my conduct herein. I desire therefore that they who hold election would not triumph, or make a party on one hand (for I detest any such thing)—and that they who are prejudiced against that doctrine be not too much concerned or offended on the other. Known unto God are all his ways from the beginning of the world. The great day will discover why the Lord permits dear Mr. Wesley and me to be of a different way of thinking. At present, I shall make no enquiry into that matter, beyond the account which he has given of it himself in the following letter, which I lately received from his own dear hands:

London, August 9, 1740
Reverend and very dear Brother,
God only knows what unspeakable sorrow of heart I have felt on your account since

I left England last. Whether it be my infirmity or not, I frankly confess that Jonah could not go with more reluctance against Nineveh, than I now take pen in hand to write against you. Was nature to speak, I had rather die than do it and yet if I am faithful to God and to my own and others' souls, I must not stand neutral any longer. I am very apprehensive that our common adversaries will rejoice to see us differing among ourselves. But what can I say? The children of God are in danger of falling into error. Nay, numbers have been misled, whom God has been pleased to work upon by my ministry, and a greater number are still calling aloud upon me to show also my opinion. I must then show that I know no man after the flesh, and that I have no respect to persons, any further than is consistent with my duty to my Lord and Master, Jesus Christ.

This letter, no doubt, will lose me many friends and for this cause perhaps God has laid this difficult task upon me, even to see whether I am willing to forsake all for him, or not. From such considerations as these, I think it my duty to bear a humble testimony, and earnestly to plead for the truths which I am convinced, are clearly revealed in the Word of God. In the defense whereof, I must use great plainness of speech, and treat my dearest friends upon earth with the greatest simplicity, faithfulness, and freedom, leaving the consequences of all to God.

For some time before and especially since my last departure from England, both in public and private, by preaching and printing, you have been propagating the doctrine of universal redemption. And when I remember how Paul reproved Peter for his dissimulation, I fear I have been sinfully silent too long. O then be not angry with me, dear and honored Sir, if now I deliver my soul, by telling you that I think in this you greatly err. 'Tis not my design to enter into a long debate on God's decrees. I refer you to Dr. Edwards his Veritas Redux (this refers to a work by Dr. John Edwards of Cambridge, not Jonathan Edwards, the famous American pastor-theologian), which, I think is unanswerable—except in a certain point, concerning a middle sort between elect and reprobate, which Edwards condemns.

I shall only make a few remarks upon your sermon, titled "Free Grace." And before I enter upon the discourse itself, give me leave to take a little notice of what in your Preface you term an indispensable obligation to make it public to all the world. I must own, that I always thought you were quite mistaken upon that head.

The case (you know) stands thus: When you were at Bristol, I think you received a letter from a private hand, charging you with not preaching the gospel, because you did not preach up election. Upon this you drew a lot: the answer was "preach and print." I have often questioned as I do now, whether in so doing, you did not tempt the Lord. A due exercise of religious prudence, without [the drawing of] a lot, would have directed you in that matter. Besides, I never heard that you enquired of God, whether or not election was a gospel doctrine. But, I fear, taking it for granted [that election was not a biblical truth], you only enquired whether you should be silent or preach and print against it.

However, this be, the lot came out "preach and print." Accordingly, you preached and printed against election. At my desire, you suppressed the publishing of the sermon whilst I was in England, but you soon sent it into the world after my departure. O that you had kept it in! However, if that sermon was printed in answer to a lot, I am apt to think, one reason why God should so suffer you to be deceived, was, that hereby a special obligation might be laid upon me, faithfully to declare the Scripture doctrine of election, that thus the Lord might give me a fresh opportunity of seeing what was in my heart, and whether I would be true to his cause or not as you could not, but grant he did once before, by giving you such another lot at Deal.

The morning I sailed from Deal for Gibraltar [2 February 1738], you arrived from Georgia. Instead of giving me an opportunity to converse with you, though the ship was not far off the shore, you drew a lot and immediately set forward to London. You left a letter behind you, in which were words to this effect: "When I saw [that] God, by the wind which was carrying you out, brought me in, I asked counsel of God. His answer you have enclosed." This was a piece of paper, in which were written these words, "Let him return to London." When I received this, I was somewhat surprised. Here was a good man telling me he had cast a lot and that God would have me return to London. On the other hand, I knew my call was to Georgia, and that I had taken leave of London and could not justly go from the soldiers, who were committed to my charge. I betook myself with a friend to prayer. That passage in 1 Kings 13 was powerfully impressed upon my soul, where we are told that the Prophet was slain by a lion when he was tempted to go back (contrary to God's express order) upon another Prophet's telling him God would have him do so. I wrote you word that I could not return to London. We sailed immediately.

Some months after, I received a letter from you at Georgia, wherein you wrote words to this effect: "Though God never before gave me a wrong lot, yet, perhaps, he suffered me to have such a lot at that time, to try what was in your heart. I should never have published this private transaction to the world, did not the glory of God call me to it." It is plain you had a wrong lot given you here, and justly, because you tempted God in drawing one. And thus, I believe it is in the present case. And if So let not the children of God who are mine and your intimate friends, and also advocates for universal redemption, think that doctrine true—because you preached it up in compliance with a lot given out from God.

This, I think, may serve as an answer to that part of the Preface to your printed sermon, wherein you say, "Nothing but the strongest conviction, not only that what is here advanced is the truth as it is in Jesus, but also that I am indispensably obliged to declare this truth to all the world." That you believe what you have written to be truth, and that you honestly aim at God's glory in writing, I do not in the least doubt. But then, honored Sir, I cannot but think you have been much mistaken in imagining that your tempting God, by casting a lot in the manner you did could lay you under an indispensable obligation to any action, much less to publish your sermon against the doctrine of predestination to life.

I must next observe, that as you have been unhappy in printing at all upon such an imaginary warrant, so you have been as unhappy in the choice of your text. honored Sir, how could it enter into your heart to choose a text to disprove the doctrine of election out of Romans 8, where this doctrine is so plainly asserted? Once I spoke with a Quaker upon this subject, and he had no other way of evading the force of the apostle's assertion than by saying, "I believe Paul was in the wrong." And another friend lately, who was once highly prejudiced against election, ingenuously confessed that he used to think St. Paul himself was mistaken or that he was not truly translated.

Indeed, honored Sir, it is plain beyond all contradiction that St. Paul, through the whole of Romans 8, is speaking of the privileges of those only who are really in Christ. And let any unprejudiced person read what goes before and what follows your text, and he must confess the word "all" only signifies those that are in Christ. And the latter part of the text plainly proves what I find, dear Mr. Wesley, will by no means, grant. I mean the final perseverance of the children of God: "He that spared not his own Son, but delivered him up for us all, [i.e., all Saints] how shall he not with him also freely give us all things?" (Rom. 8:32). He shall give us grace, in particular, to enable us to persevere, and everything else necessary to carry us home to our Father's heavenly kingdom.

Had any one a mind to prove the doctrine of election, as well as of final perseverance, he could hardly wish for a text more fit for his purpose than that which you have chosen to disprove it! One who did not know you would suspect that you were aware of this, for after the first paragraph, I scarce know whether you have mentioned [the text] so much as once through your whole sermon. But your discourse, in my opinion, is as little to the purpose as your text, and instead of warping, does but more and more confirm me in the belief of the doctrine of God's eternal election.

I shall not mention how illogically you have proceeded. Had you written clearly, you should first, honored Sir, have proved your proposition: "God's grace is free to all." And then by way of inference [you might have] exclaimed against what you call the horrible decree. But you knew that people (because Arminianism, of late, has so much abounded among us) were generally prejudiced against the doctrine of reprobation, and therefore thought if you kept up their dislike of that, you could overthrow the doctrine of election entirely. For, without doubt, the doctrine of election and reprobation must stand or fall together.

But passing by this, as also your equivocal definition of the word grace, and your false definition of the word free, and that I may be as short as possible, I frankly acknowledge: I believe the doctrine of reprobation, in this view, that God intends to give saving grace, through Jesus Christ, only to a certain number, and that the rest of mankind, after the fall of Adam, being justly left of God to continue in sin, will at last suffer that eternal death which is its proper wages.

This is the established doctrine of Scripture and acknowledged as such in the seventeenth article of the Church of England, as Bishop Burnet himself confesses. Yet dear Mr. Wesley absolutely denies it. But the most important objections you have urged against this doctrine as reasons why you reject it, being seriously considered, and faithfully tried by the Word of God, will appear to be of no force at all. Let the matter be humbly and calmly reviewed, as to the following heads:

First, you say that if this be so (i.e., if there be an election) then is all preaching vain. It is needless to them that are elected. For they, whether with preaching or without, will infallibly be saved. Therefore, the end of preaching to save souls is void with regard to them. And it is useless to them that are not elected, for they cannot possibly be saved. They, whether with preaching or without, will infallibly be damned. The end of preaching is therefore void with regard to them likewise. So that in either case our preaching is vain and your hearing also vain (page 10, paragraph 9).

O dear Sir, what kind of reasoning—or rather sophistry—is this! Hath not God, who hath appointed salvation for a certain number, appointed also the preaching of the Word as a means to bring them to it? Does anyone hold election in any other sense? And if so how is preaching needless to them that are elected, when the gospel is designated by God Himself to be the power of God unto their eternal salvation? And since we know not who are elect and who reprobate, we are to preach promiscuously to all. For the Word may be useful, even to the non-elect, in restraining them from much wickedness and sin. However, it is enough to excite to the utmost diligence in preaching and hearing, when we consider that by these means, some, even as many as the Lord hath ordained to eternal life, shall certainly be quickened and enabled to believe. And who that attends, especially with reverence and care, can tell but he may be found of that happy number?

Second, you say that the doctrine of election and reprobation directly tends to destroy holiness, which is the end of all the ordinances of God. For (says the dear mistaken Mr. Wesley), "It wholly takes away those first motives to follow after it, so frequently proposed in Scripture. The hope of future reward, and fear of punishment, the hope of heaven, and the fear of hell, et cetera."

I thought that one who carries perfection to such an exalted pitch as dear Mr. Wesley does, would know that a true lover of the Lord Jesus Christ would strive to be holy for the sake of being holy, and work for Christ out of love and gratitude, without any regard to the rewards of heaven or fear of hell. You remember, dear Sir, what Scougal says, "Love's a more powerful motive that does them move." But passing by this, and granting that rewards and punishments (as they certainly are) may be motives from which a Christian may be honestly stirred up to act for God, how does the doctrine of election destroy these motives? Do not the elect know that the more good works they do, the greater will be their reward? And is not that encouragement enough to set them upon, and cause them to persevere in working for Jesus Christ? And how does the doctrine of election destroy holiness? Whoever preached any other election than what the apostle preached, when he said, "Chosen . . . through sanctification of the Spirit?" (2 Thess. 2:13). Nay, is not holiness made a mark of our election by all that preach it? And how then can the doctrine of election destroy holiness?

The instance which you bring to illustrate your assertion, indeed dear Sir, is quite impertinent. For you say, "If a sick man knows that he must unavoidably die or unavoidably recover, though he knows not which, it is not reasonable to take any physic at all." Dear Sir, what absurd reasoning is here? Were you ever sick in your life? If so did not the bare probability or possibility of your recovering, though you knew it was unalterably fixed that you must live or die, encourage you to take physic? For how did you know but that very physic might be the means God intended to recover you by?

Just thus it is as to the doctrine of election. I know that it is unalterably fixed (one may say) that I must be damned or saved, but since I know not which for a certainty, why should I not strive, though at present in a state of nature, since I know not but this striving may be the means God has intended to bless, in order to bring me into a state of grace?

Dear Sir, consider these things. Make an impartial application and then judge what little reason you had to conclude the 10th paragraph, page 12, with these words: "So directly does this doctrine tend to shut the very gate of holiness in general, to hinder unholy men from ever approaching thereto, or striving to enter in thereat."

"As directly," you say, "does the doctrine tend to destroy several particular branches of holiness, such as meekness, love, et cetera." I shall say little, dear Sir, in answer to this paragraph. Dear Mr. Wesley, perhaps has been disputing with some warm narrow-spirited men that held election, and then he infers that their warmth and narrowness of spirit was owing to their principles? But does not dear Mr. Wesley know many dear children of God, who are predestinarians, and yet are meek, lowly, pitiful, courteous, tenderhearted, kind, of a Catholic spirit, and hope to see the most vile and profligate of men converted? And why? Because they know God saved themselves by an act of His electing love and they know not, but He may have elected those who now seem to be the most abandoned.

But, dear Sir, we must not judge of the truth of principles in general, nor of this of election in particular, entirely from the practice of some that profess to hold them. If so I am sure much might be said against your own. For I appeal to your own heart, whether or not you have not felt in yourself or observed in others, a narrow-spiritedness, and some dis-union of soul respecting those that hold universal redemption. If so then according to your own rule, universal redemption is wrong, because it destroys several branches of holiness, such as meekness, love, et cetera. But not to insist upon this, I beg you would observe that your inference is entirely set aside by the force of the apostle's argument, and the language which he expressly uses in Colossians 3:12–13: "Put on therefore, as the elect of God, holy and beloved, bowels of mercies, kindness, humbleness of mind, meekness, longsuffering, forbearing one another, and forgiving one another, if any man have a quarrel against any: even as Christ forgave you, so also do ye."

Here we see that the apostle exhorts them to put on bowels of mercy, kindness, humble-ness of mind, meekness, longsuffering, et cetera, upon this consideration: namely, because they were elect of God. And all who have experientially felt this doctrine in their hearts feel that these graces are the genuine effects of their being elected of God.

But perhaps dear Mr. Wesley may be mistaken in this point and call that passion which is only zeal for God's truths. You know, dear Sir, the Apostle exhorts us to "contend ear-nestly for the faith once delivered to the saints" (Jude 3). Therefore, you must not condemn all that appear zealous for the doctrine of election as narrow-spirited, or persecutors, just because they think it their duty to oppose you. I am sure, I love you in the bowels of Jesus Christ and think I could lay down my life for your sake, but yet dear Sir, I cannot help strenuously opposing your errors upon this important subject, because I think you warmly, though not designedly, oppose the truth, as it is in Jesus. May the Lord remove the scales of prejudice from off the eyes of your mind and give you a zeal according to true Christian knowledge!

Third, says your sermon, "This doctrine tends to destroy the comforts of religion, the happiness of Christianity, et cetera." But how does Mr. Wesley know this, who never believed election? I believe they who have experienced it will agree with our seventeenth article, that the godly consideration of predestination and election in Christ, is full of sweet, pleasant, unspeakable comfort to godly persons, and such as feel in themselves the working of the Spirit of Christ, mortifying the works of the flesh, and their earthly members, and drawing their minds to high and heavenly things, as well because it does greatly establish and confirm their faith of eternal salvation to be enjoyed through Christ, as because it doth fervently kindle their love toward God," et cetera. This plainly shows that our godly Reformers did not think election destroyed holiness or the comforts of religion. As for my own part, this doctrine is my daily support. I should utterly sink under a dread of my impending trials, were I not firmly persuaded that God has chosen me in Christ from before the foundation of the world, and that now being effectually called, he will allow no one to pluck me out of his almighty hand.

You proceed thus: "This is evident as to all those who believe themselves to be reprobate or only suspect or fear it, all the great and precious promises are lost to them, they afford them no ray of comfort."

In answer to this, let me observe that none living, especially none who are desirous of salvation, can know that they are not of the number of God's elect. None but the unconverted, can have any just reason so much as to fear it. And would dear Mr. Wesley give comfort or dare you apply the precious promises of the gospel, being children's bread, to men in a natural state, while they continue so? God forbid! What if the doctrine of election and reprobation does put some upon doubting? So does that of regeneration. But, is not this doubting a good means to put them upon searching and striving and that striving, a good means to make their calling and their election sure?

This is one reason among many others why I admire the doctrine of election and am convinced that it should have a place in gospel ministrations and should be insisted on with faithfulness and care. It has a natural tendency to rouse the soul out of its carnal security. And therefore, many carnal men cry out against it. Whereas universal redemption is a notion sadly adapted to keep the soul in its lethargic sleepy condition and therefore, so many natural men admire and applaud it.

Your thirteenth, fourteenth and fifteenth paragraphs come next to be considered. "The witness of the Spirit," you say, "experience shows to be much obstructed by this doctrine." But, dear Sir, whose experience? Not your own. For in your journal, from your embarking for Georgia to your return to London, you seem to acknowledge that you have it not and therefore you are no competent judge in this matter. You must mean then the experience of others. For you say in the same paragraph, "Even in those who have tasted of that good gift, who yet have soon lost it again (I suppose you mean lost the sense of it again) and fallen back into doubts and fears and darkness, even horrible darkness that might be felt, et cetera." Now, as to the darkness of desertion, was not this the case of Jesus Christ himself, after he had received an unmeasurable unction of the Holy Ghost? Was not his soul exceeding sorrowful, even unto death, in the garden? And was he not surrounded with a horrible darkness, even a darkness that might be felt, when on the cross he cried out, "My God! My God! why hast thou forsaken me?"

And that all his followers are liable to the same, is it not evident from Scripture? For, says the Apostle, "He was tempted in all things like as we are" (Heb 4:15) so that he might be able to succor those that are tempted (Heb. 2:18). And is not their liableness thereunto, consistent with that conformity to him in suffering, which his members are to bear (Phil. 3:10)? Why then should persons falling into darkness, after they have received the witness of the Spirit, be any argument against the doctrine of election?

Yet you say, "Many, very many of those that hold it not, in all parts of the earth, have enjoyed the uninterrupted witness of the Spirit, the continual light of God's countenance, from the moment wherein they first believed, for many months or years, to this very day." But how does dear Mr. Wesley know this? Has he consulted the experience of many, very many in all parts of the earth? Or could he be sure of what he hath advanced without sufficient grounds, would it follow that their being kept in this light is owing to their not believing the doctrine of election? No, this [doctrine], according to the sentiments of our church, "greatly confirms and establishes a true Christian's faith of eternal salvation through Christ" and is an anchor of hope, both sure and steadfast, when he walks in darkness and sees no light; as certainly he may, even after he hath received the witness of the Spirit, whatever you or others may unadvisedly assert to the contrary.

Then, to have respect to God's everlasting covenant and to throw himself upon the free distinguishing love of that God who changeth not, will make him lift up the hands that hang down, and strengthen the feeble knees. But without the belief of the doctrine of election and the immutability of the free love of God, I cannot see how it is possible that any should have a comfortable assurance of eternal salvation. What could it signify to a man whose conscience is thoroughly awakened and who is warned in good earnest to seek deliverance from the wrath to come, though he should be assured that all his past sins be forgiven and that he is now a child of God, if notwithstanding this, he may hereafter become a child of the devil and be cast into hell at last? Could such an assurance yield any solid, lasting comfort to a person convinced of the corruption and treachery of his own heart, and of the malice, subtlety and power of Satan? No! That which alone deserves the name of a full assurance of faith is such an assurance as emboldens the believer, under the sense of his interest in distinguishing love, to give the challenge to all his adversaries, whether men or devils and that with regard to all their future, as well as present, attempts to destroy—saying with the Apostle in Rom. 8:33–39, "Who shall lay anything to the charge of God's elect? It is God that justifieth. Who is he that condemneth? It is Christ that died, yea rather, that is risen again, who is even at the right hand of God, who also maketh intercession for us. Who shall separate us from the love of Christ? Shall tribulation, or distress, or persecution, or famine, or nakedness, or peril, or sword? As it is written, For thy sake we are killed all the day long. We are accounted as sheep for the slaughter. Nay, in all these things we are more than conquerors through him that loved us. For I am persuaded, that neither death, nor life, nor angels, nor principalities, nor powers, nor things present, nor things to come, nor height, nor depth, nor any other creature, shall be able to separate us from the love of God, which is in Christ Jesus our Lord."

This, dear Sir, is the triumphant language of every soul that has attained a full assurance of faith. And this assurance can only arise from a belief of God's electing everlasting love. That many have an assurance they are in Christ today, but take no thought for or are not assured they shall be in him tomorrow—nay to all eternity—is rather their imperfection and unhappiness than their privilege. I pray God to bring all such to a sense of his eternal love, that they may no longer build upon their own faithfulness, but on the unchangeableness of that God whose gifts and callings are without repentance. For those whom God has once justified, He also will glorify.

I observed before, dear Sir, it is not always a safe rule to judge of the truth of principles from people's practice. And therefore, supposing that all who hold universal redemption in your way of explaining it, after they received faith, enjoyed the continual uninterrupted sight of God's countenance, it does not follow that this is a fruit of their principle. For that I am sure has a natural tendency to keep the soul in darkness forever, because the creature thereby is taught that his being kept in a state of salvation is owing to his own free will. And what a sandy foundation is that for a poor creature to build his hopes of perseverance upon? Every relapse into sin, every surprise by temptation, must throw him "into doubts and fears, into horrible darkness, even darkness that may be felt."

Hence, it is that the letters which have been lately sent me by those who hold universal redemption are dead and lifeless, dry and inconsistent, in comparison of those I receive from persons on the contrary side. Those who settle in the universal scheme, though they might begin in the Spirit, (whatever they may say to the contrary) are ending in the flesh, and building up a righteousness founded on their own free will—whilst the others triumph in hope of the glory of God and build upon God's never-failing promise and unchangeable love, even when His sensible presence is withdrawn from them.

But I would not judge of the truth of election by the experience of any particular persons. If I did (O bear with me in this foolishness of boasting), I think I myself might glory in election. For these five or six years, I have received the witness of God's Spirit; since that, blessed be God, I have not doubted a quarter of an hour of a saving interest in Jesus Christ, but with grief and humble shame I do acknowledge I have fallen into sin often since that. Though I do not—dare not—allow of any one transgression, yet hitherto I have not been (nor do I expect that while I am in this present world I ever shall be) able to live one day perfectly free from all defects and sin. And since the Scriptures declare that there is not a just man upon earth (no, not among those of the highest attainments in grace) that doeth good and sinneth not (Eccl. 7:20), we are sure that this will be the case of all the children of God.

The universal experience and acknowledgment of this among the godly in every age is abundantly sufficient to confute the error of those who hold in an absolute sense that after a man is born again he cannot commit sin. Especially since the Holy Spirit condemns the persons who say they have no sin as deceiving themselves, as being destitute of the truth, and as making God a liar (1 Jn. 1:8, 10). I have been also in heaviness through manifold temptations and expect to be often so before I die. Thus, were the apostles and primitive Christians themselves. Thus was Luther, that man of God, who as far as I can find, did not peremptorily at least, hold election, and the great John Arndt was in the utmost perplexity, but a quarter of an hour before he died, and yet he was no predestinarian.

And if I must speak freely, I believe your fighting so strenuously against the doctrine of election and pleading so vehemently for a sinless perfection are among the reasons or culpable causes, why you are kept out of the liberties of the gospel, and from that full assurance of faith which they enjoy, who have experimentally tasted, and daily feed upon God's electing, everlasting love.

But perhaps you may say that Luther and Arndt were no Christians, at least very weak ones. I know you think meanly of Abraham, though he was eminently called the friend of God, and I believe also of David, the man after God's own heart. No wonder, therefore, that in a letter you sent me not long since, you should tell me that no Baptist or Presbyterian writer whom you have read knew anything of the liberties of Christ. What? Neither Bunyan, Henry, Flavel, Halyburton, nor any of the New England and Scots Divines? See, dear Sir, what narrow-spiritedness and want of charity arise from your principles, and then do not cry out against election any more on account of its being "destructive of meekness and love."

Fourth, I shall now proceed to another head. Says the dear Mr. Wesley, "How uncomfortable a thought is this, that thousands and millions of men, without any preceding offense or fault of theirs, were unchangeably doomed to everlasting burnings?"

But whoever asserted, that thousands and millions of men, without any preceding offense or fault of theirs, were unchangeably doomed to everlasting burnings? Do not they who believe God's dooming men to everlasting burnings, also believe, that God looked upon them as men fallen in Adam? And that the decree which ordained the punishment first regarded the crime by which it was deserved? How then are they doomed without any preceding fault? Surely Mr. Wesley will own God's justice in imputing Adam's sin to his posterity. And also, after Adam fell, and his posterity in him, God might justly have passed them all by, without sending His own Son to be a Savior for anyone. Unless you heartily agree to both these points, you do not believe original sin aright. If you do own them, then you must acknowledge the doctrine of election and reprobation to be highly just and reasonable. For if God might justly impute Adam's sin to all, and afterward have passed by all, then he might justly pass by some. Turn on the right hand, or on the left, you are reduced to an inextricable dilemma. And, if you would be consistent, you must either give up the doctrine of the imputation of Adam's sin, or receive the amiable doctrine of election, with a holy and righteous reprobation as its consequent. For whether you can believe it or not, the Word of God abides faithful: "The election hath obtained it, and the rest were blinded" (Rom. 11:7).

Your seventeenth paragraph on page sixteen, I pass over. What has been said on the ninth and tenth paragraphs, with a little alteration, will answer it. I shall only say, it is the doctrine of election that most presses me to abound in good works. I am willing to suffer all things for the elect's sake. This makes me to preach with comfort, because I know salvation does not depend on man's free will, but the Lord makes willing in the day of his power, and can make use of me to bring some of His elect home, when and where He pleases.

But, fifth, you say, "This doctrine has a direct manifest tendency to overthrow the whole Christian religion." For say you, "Supposing that eternal, unchangeable decree, one part of mankind must be saved, though the Christian revelation were not in being."

But dear Sir, how does that follow? Since it is only by the Christian revelation that we are acquainted with God's design of saving His church by the death of His Son. Yea, it is settled in the everlasting covenant that this salvation shall be applied to the elect through the knowledge and faith of Him. As the prophet says in Isaiah 53:11, "By his knowledge shall my righteous servant justify many." How then has the doctrine of election a direct tendency to overthrow the whole Christian revelation? Who ever thought that God's declaration to Noah, that seedtime and harvest should never cease, could afford an argument for the neglect of plowing or sowing? Or that the unchangeable purpose of God, that harvest should not fail, rendered the heat of the sun, or the influence of the heavenly bodies unnecessary to produce it? No more does God's absolute purpose of saving His chosen preclude the necessity of the gospel revelation, or the use of any of the means through which he has determined the decree shall take effect. Nor will the right understanding, or the reverent belief of God's decree, ever allow or suffer a Christian in any case to separate the means from the end, or the end from the means.

And since we are taught by the revelation itself that this was intended and given by God as a means of bringing home His elect, we therefore receive it with joy, prize it highly, use it in faith, and endeavor to spread it through all the world, in the full assurance that wherever God sends it, sooner or later, it shall be savingly useful to all the elect within its call.

How then, in holding this doctrine, do we join with modern unbelievers in making the Christian revelation unnecessary? No, dear Sir, you mistake. Infidels of all kinds are on your side of the question. Deists, Arians, and Socinians arraign God's sovereignty and stand up for universal redemption. I pray God that dear Mr. Wesley's sermon, as it has grieved the hearts of many of God's children, may not also strengthen the hands of many of his most avowed enemies!

Here I could almost lie down and weep. "Tell it not in Gath, publish it not in the streets of Askelon; lest the daughters of the Philistines rejoice, lest the daughters of the uncircumcised triumph" (2 Sam. 1:20).

Further, you say, "This doctrine makes revelation contradict itself." For instance, say you, "The assertors of this doctrine interpret that text of Scripture, Jacob have I loved, but Esau have I hated, as implying that God in a literal sense, hated Esau and all the reprobates from eternity!" And, when considered as fallen in Adam, were they not objects of his hatred? And might not God, of His own good pleasure, love or show mercy to Jacob and the elect—and yet at the same time do the reprobate no wrong? But you say, "God is love. And cannot God be love, unless He shows the same mercy to all?

Again, says dear Mr. Wesley, "They infer from that text, 'I will have mercy on whom I will have mercy,' that God is merciful only to some men, viz. the elect and that He has mercy for those only, flatly contrary to which is the whole tenor of the Scripture, as is that express declaration in particular, 'The Lord is loving to every man, and His mercy is over all His works'."

And so it is, but not His saving mercy. God is loving to every man. He sends His rain upon the evil and upon the good. But you say, "God is no respecter of persons" (Acts 10:34). No! For everyone, whether Jew or Gentile, that believeth on Jesus, and worketh righteousness, is accepted of him. "But he that believeth not shall be damned" (Mk. 16:16). For God is no respecter of persons, upon the account of any outward condition or circumstance in life whatever; nor does the doctrine of election in the least suppose Him to be so. But as the sovereign Lord of all, who is debtor to none, He has a right to do what He will with His own, and to dispense His favors to what objects He sees fit, merely at His pleasure. And His supreme right herein is clearly and strongly asserted in those passages of Scripture, where He says, "Moses, I will have mercy on whom I will have mercy, and I will have compassion on whom I will have compassion" (Rom. 9:15, Exod. 33:19).

Further, from the text, "the children being not yet born, neither having done any good or evil, that the purpose of God according to election might stand, not of works, but of Him that calleth; it was said unto her [Rebekah], The elder shall serve the younger" (Rom. 9:11–12)—you represent us as inferring that our predestination to life in no way depends on the foreknowledge of God.

But who infers this, dear Sir? For if foreknowledge signifies approbation, as it does in several parts of Scripture, then we confess that predestination and election do depend on God's foreknowledge. But if by God's foreknowledge you understand God's foreseeing some good works done by His creatures as the foundation or reason of choosing them and therefore electing them, then we say that in this sense predestination does not any way depend on God's foreknowledge.

But I referred you, at the beginning of this letter, to Dr. Edwards's Veritas Redux, which I recommended to you also in a late letter, with Elisha Coles on God's sovereignty. Be pleased to read these, and also the excellent sermons of Mr. Cooper of Boston in New England (which I also sent you) and I doubt not, but you will see all your objections answered. Though I would observe, that after all our reading on both sides the question, we shall never in this life be able to search out God's decrees to perfection. No, we must humbly adore what we cannot comprehend, and with the great Apostle at the end of our enquiries cry out, "O the depth of the riches both of the wisdom and knowledge of God! How unsearchable are His judgments, and His ways past finding out! For who hath known the mind of the Lord? Or who hath been His counsellor?" (Rom. 11:33–34)—or with our Lord, when He was admiring God's sovereignty, "Even so, Father: for so it seemed good in Thy sight" (Matthew 11:26).

However, it may not be amiss to take notice, that if those texts, "The Lord is . . . not willing that any should perish, but that all should come to repentance" (2 Pet. 3:9) and "I have no pleasure in the death of the wicked; but that the wicked turn from his way and live" (Ezek. 33:11)—and such like—be taken in their strictest sense, then no one will be damned.

But here's the distinction. God taketh no pleasure in the death of sinners, so as to delight simply in their death; but He delights to magnify His justice, by inflicting the punishment which their iniquities have deserved. As a righteous judge who takes no pleasure in condemning a criminal, may yet justly command him to be executed, that law and justice may be satisfied, even though it be in his power to procure him a reprieve.

I would hint further, that you unjustly charge the doctrine of reprobation with blasphemy, whereas the doctrine of universal redemption, as you set it forth, is really the highest reproach upon the dignity of the Son of God, and the merit of His blood. Consider whether it be not rather blasphemy to say as you do, "Christ not only died for those that are saved, but also for those that perish."

The text you have misapplied to gloss over this, see explained by Ridgely, Edwards, Henry, and I purposely omit answering your texts myself so that you may be brought to read such treatises, which under God, would show you your error. You cannot make good the assertion that Christ died for them that perish without holding (as Peter Bohler, one of the Moravian brethren, in order to make out universal redemption, lately frankly confessed in a letter) that all the damned souls would hereafter be brought out of hell. I cannot think Mr. Wesley is thus minded. And yet unless this can be proved, universal redemption, taken in a literal sense, falls entirely to the ground. For how can all be universally redeemed, if all are not finally saved?

Dear Sir, for Jesus Christ's sake, consider how you dishonor God by denying election. You plainly make salvation depend not on God's free grace, but on man's free will. And if thus, it is more than probable, Jesus Christ would not have had the satisfaction of seeing the fruit of His death in the eternal salvation of one soul. Our preaching would then be vain, and all invitations for people to believe in him, would also be in vain.

But, blessed be God, our Lord knew for whom He died. There was an eternal compact between the Father and the Son. A certain number was then given Him as the purchase and reward of His obedience and death. For these He prayed (Jn. 17:9) and not for the world. For these elect ones, and these only, He is now interceding, and with their salvation He will be fully satisfied.

I purposely omit making any further particular remarks on the several last pages of your sermon. Indeed, had not your name, dear Sir, been prefixed to the sermon, I could not have been so uncharitable as to think you were the author of such sophistry. You beg the question, in saying that God has declared, (notwithstanding you own, I suppose, some will be damned) that He will save all—i.e., every individual person. You take it for granted (for solid proof you have none) that God is unjust, if He passes by any, and then you exclaim against the "horrible decree": and yet, as I before hinted, in holding the doctrine of original sin, you profess to believe that he might justly have passed by all.

Dear, dear Sir, O be not offended! For Christ's sake, be not rash! Give yourself to reading. Study the covenant of grace. Down with your carnal reasoning. Be a little child and then, instead of pawning your salvation, as you have done in a late hymn book, if the doctrine of universal redemption be not true; instead of talking of sinless perfection, as you have done in the Preface to that hymn book, and making man's salvation to depend on his own free will, as you have in this sermon; you will compose a hymn in praise of sovereign distinguishing love. You will caution believers against striving to work a perfection out of their own hearts, and print another sermon the reverse of this, and entitle it "Free Grace Indeed." Free, not because free to all, but free, because God may withhold or give it to whom and when He pleases.

Till you do this, I must doubt whether or not you know yourself. In the meanwhile, I cannot but blame you for censuring the clergy of our church for not keeping to their articles, when you yourself by your principles, positively deny the ninth, tentth and seventeenth.

Dear Sir, these things ought not so to be. God knows my heart, as I told you before, so I declare again, nothing but a single regard to the honor of Christ has forced this letter from me. I love and honor you for His sake and when I come to judgment, will thank you before men and angels, for what you have, under God, done for my soul.

There, I am persuaded, I shall see dear Mr. Wesley convinced of election and everlasting love. And it often fills me with pleasure to think how I shall behold you casting your crown down at the feet of the Lamb, and as it were filled with a holy blushing for opposing the divine sovereignty in the manner you have done. But I hope the Lord will show you this before you go hence. O how do I long for that day! If the Lord should be pleased to make use of this letter for that purpose, it would abundantly rejoice the heart of, dear and honored Sir,

Your affectionate, though unworthy brother and servant in Christ,
George Whitefield[206]

---

[206] Arnold A. Dallimore, *George Whitefield: The Life and Times of the Great Evangelist of the Eighteenth-Century Revival,* vol. I and 2 (Banner of Truth, 1970).

Iain Murray's Historical Background on Whitefield and Wesley

The following article first appeared in the 1960 edition of *Whitefield's Journals*, published by the Banner of Truth Trust.[207] Here Iain Murray discusses the historical background that led to George Whitefield's famous letter to John Wesley.

The occasion and background of Whitefield's letter to Wesley requires a few words of explanation. From the time of his conversion in 1735, Whitefield had been profoundly conscious of man's entire depravity, his need of the new birth, and the fact that God can save and God alone. Describing an experience which occurred a few weeks after his conversion, he wrote: "About this time God was pleased to enlighten my soul, and bring me into the knowledge of His free grace . . ." Strengthened by his reading of the Scriptures, the Reformers and the Puritans, Whitefield gradually grasped the great related chain of truths revealed in the New Testament—the Father's electing love, Christ's substitutionary death on behalf of those whom the Father had given Him, and the Spirit's infallible work in bringing to salvation those for whom it was appointed. These doctrines of free grace were the essential theology of his ministry from the very first and consequently the theology of the movement which began under his preaching in 1737.

When Whitefield returned to England at the end of 1738, after his first visit to America, he found that the awakening in London had been furthered by the conversion and subsequent ministry of the Wesleys. Immediately they began to work together. Under Whitefield's preaching the revival spread to Bristol and the West country in February and March 1739, and when he left that area at the beginning of April 1739, John Wesley was given the oversight of the work. But before three months had elapsed it began to be evident that there had not been the same doctrinal development in the Wesleys on all points mentioned above. The fact is that while John Wesley had at his conversion in May 1738 accepted evangelical views on sin, faith, and the rebirth, he had at the same time retained his preconversion opinions on the doctrines of predestination and the extent of the atonement. As the religious influences, which had molded Wesley prior to his conversion were

---

[207] Whitefield's letter to Wesley was added to the *Banner of Truth Trust* edition of *The Journals* for these reasons: a) It was written during the period covered in [The Journals] and best illustrates Whitefield's views on several important points of doctrine. The letter is therefore an important aid to a full understanding of his ministry, b) It explains references in *The Journals* which would otherwise be obscure and reveals a principal reason why Whitefield returned to England in 1741. He feared the results of the controversy which had broken out since his departure, c) *The Journals* show Whitefield and the Wesleys working in close cooperation. It is well known that this cooperation terminated in 1741. Without a knowledge of this letter the cause of that momentous separation cannot be rightly understood, and d) Copies of this letter have become extremely scarce and, in view of the contemporary prevalence of the same errors which Whitefield here opposes, it is highly relevant to the present situation.

High Anglican, it is not surprising that these opinions were Arminian and not orthodox.[208] His views on these points were not part of his new evangelical experience but arose, as Howell Harris declared to him, "from the prejudices of your education, your books, your companions, and the remains of your carnal reason."[209]

The first hint that this doctrinal difference might lead to serious results occurs in a letter of Whitefield's to Wesley on June 25, 1739: "I hear, honored sir, you are about to print a sermon on predestination. It shocks me to think of it. What will be the consequences, but controversy? If people ask me my opinion, what shall I do? I have a critical part to act, God enable me to behave aright! Silence on both sides will be best. It is noised abroad already, that there is a division between you and me. Oh, my heart within me is grieved . . ."[210]

On July 2, 1739, Whitefield wrote further to Wesley on this subject, terminating his letter with another appeal:

"Dear, honored sir, if you have any regard for the peace of the church, keep in your sermon on predestination. But you have cast a lot. Oh! my heart, in the midst of my body, is like melted wax. The Lord direct us all! . . ."[211]

On Whitefield's departure from England in August 1739, Wesley immediately published this sermon. Titled "Free Grace," it professed to be founded upon Romans 8:32, and was printed as a 12 mo. pamphlet in twenty-four pages. Annexed to it was a hymn by Charles Wesley on *Universal Redemption*. It was this sermon which occasioned Whitefield's reply (reprinted above). But it is interesting to note that although Wesley's sermon was published in August 1739, Whitefield's reply is dated December 24, 1740, and was not published till early 1741. The reasons for this delay are probably as follows: (1) By the correspondence[212] which passed between Whitefield and Wesley in 1740 it is evident that Whitefield longed to avoid an open breach and still hoped that his friend might be brought to a clearer understanding of the truth. Such sentences as the following are typical of Whitefield's attitude: "How would the cause of our common Master suffer by our raising disputes about particular points of doctrines! . . . For Christ's sake, let us not be divided amongst ourselves. . . . Avoid all disputation. Do not oblige me to preach against you; I had rather die . . .," (2) It is evident that while on his second visit to America, Whitefield devel-

[208] The statement of Dr. H. B. Workman is significant: "Whitefield linked the Evangelical movement to Puritanism; Wesley linked it to Laud, for Laud was one of the founders of the Arminian movement." (*The Methodist Times*, in the issue commemorating the bicentenary of Whitefield's birth, December 1914.)
[209] L. Tyerman, *The Life and Times of John Wesley.* vol. 1, 315.
[210] Ibid., 277. It was Wesley's practice at this period sometimes to decide on questions of guidance by casting lots.
[211] Ibid., 313.
[212] Tyerman gives lengthy extracts from this correspondence and the quotations which follow will be found in pp. 313–322.

oped stronger views on the issues which this controversy involved. Before he left England in August 1739, he had been satisfied to counsel "silence" on these doctrines and they were not at that time conspicuous in his preaching. As late as March 1740, he wrote to Wesley: "Provoke me to it as much as you please, I intend not to enter the lists of controversies with you on the points wherein we differ . . ." But before the year had ended Whitefield went back on this decision, the reason apparently being that he had come to see the seriousness of these questions in a new light. He could thus remain silent no longer. On September 25, 1740, he wrote to Wesley: "What a fond conceit is it to cry up perfection, and yet cry down the doctrine of final perseverance. But this and many other absurdities, you will run into, because you will not own election. . . . O that you would study the covenant of grace! . . . O that you would not be too rash and precipitant! If you go on thus, honored sir, how can I concur with you? It is impossible. I must speak what I know. . . ." On February 1, 1741, he says further: "I must preach the gospel of Christ, and that I cannot now do, without speaking of election. . . ."

The reasons for Whitefield's more decided attitude are not hard to find. Firstly, during 1740, he had made close friendships with such American evangelicals as the Tennents and Jonathan Edwards,[213] and through them he was doubtless led into a deeper understanding of Puritan theology and its relevance to evangelism and revivals. He also witnessed the outstanding blessing on their preaching. Secondly, as the year 1740 advanced, the reports that he received from his friends like John Cennick and Howell Harris made it increasingly obvious that harm and divisions were being wrought by the Wesley's insistence on their Arminian views (Wesley's pamphlet, "Set the Nation Disputing.") As Harris wrote to Wesley: "You grieve God's people by your opposition to electing love and many poor souls believe your doctrine simply because you hold it." A situation had developed in which it was imperative that Whitefield should declare his mind and do something to arrest the drift from evangelical orthodoxy.

The outcome of Whitefield's return to England in March 1741 and the publication of his reply to Wesley was an inevitable separation. Henceforth, the evangelical forces engaged in the revival movement were divided and a new party of Arminian evangelicals emerged for the first time in British church history. Due to the eminence, of the Wesleys, this new form of evangelical faith has exerted a widespread influence even down to the present day. The contemporary strength of this influence can be judged from the manner in which

---

[213] Tyerman's comments on this fact are interesting [Ibid., 312 and *Life of Whitefield*, vol. 1, 274–275], but Tyerman needs to be read with care on matters relating to Whitefield's theology. He is glaringly inconsistent when he says: "Whitefield worked himself into a fume, and wrote his pamphlet in answer to Wesley," for elsewhere he says, "The spirit breathing in this letter is beautiful!" (Compare *Life of Whitefield*, vol. 1, 471, with his *Life of Wesley*, vol. 1, 351.)

George Whitefield, with his great predecessors (the Reformers and Puritans), have been forgotten. Indeed, it would not be too much to say that Whitefield's views, as expressed in his letter to Wesley, would appear to many to be quite alien to the evangelicalism that is commonly believed in today.

Some evangelical writers have sought to minimize the division between Whitefield and Wesley by referring to their "minor differences." An impression is given that Whitefield abandoned the strong conviction he had about Arminianism in 1741. In proof of this we are referred to the fact that in 1742 their personal friendship was in measure resumed. But all this is misleading. The truth is that Whitefield rightly made a distinction between a difference in judgment and a difference in affection. It was in the former sense that he differed from the Wesleys and that difference was such that, as Tyerman writes, it "led them to build separate chapels, form separate societies, and pursue to the end of life, separate lines of action . . . the gulf between Wesley and Whitefield was immense."[214] But while their public cooperation was thus seriously disturbed, his personal affection for the Wesleys as Christians, was preserved to the last.[215]

In this respect, Whitefield teaches us a needful lesson. Doctrinal differences between believers should never lead to personal antagonism. Error must be opposed even when held by fellow members of Christ, but if that opposition cannot coexist with a true love for all saints and a longing for their spiritual prosperity, then it does not glorify God nor promote the edification of the church.

---

[214] Tyerman's comments on this fact are interesting [Ibid., 312 and *Life of Whitefield*, vol. 1, 274–275], but Tyerman needs to be read with care on matters relating to Whitefield's theology. He is glaringly inconsistent when he says: "Whitefield worked himself into a fume, and wrote his pamphlet in answer to Wesley," for elsewhere he says, "The spirit breathing in this letter is beautiful!" (Compare *Life of Whitefield*, vol. 1, 471, with his *Life of Wesley*, vol. 1, 351.)

[215] He had cause to write at a later date: "I have been supplanted, despised, censured, maligned, judged by and separated from my nearest, dearest friends." (*Works of George Whitefield*, ed. Gillies, vol. 2, 466.) But Whitefield was too great to contend for personal prominence. The legend of England before and after Wesley began to originate from this time.

APPENDIX 2

Additional Resources

For an additional list of American theologians who affirm the doctrines of predestination and election, please see this online link:

http://en.wikipedia.org/wiki/Category: American_Calvinist_and_Reformed_ theologians.

The list of scientists below from the sixteenth and seventeenth centuries (listed at the website below) are reported to be individuals who believed in the traditional understandings of election and predestination (http://www.adherents.com/largecom/fam_calvin. html).

If you have interest in researching their scientific accomplishments and/or their Christian perspectives, you can do your own online search on any of those listed below:

Adriaan Anthonisz
Gaspard Bauhin
Jean Bauhin
Isaac Beeckman
Govard Bidloo
Willem Janszoon Blaeu
Hermann Boerhaave
Pierre Borel
Abraham Bosse
Ismael Boulliau
Louis Bourguet
Henry Briggs
Franco Burgersdijk
Ludolphvan Ceulen

Jacob Christmann
Volcher Coiter
Oswald Crollius
Jean-Pierre de Crousaz
Cunradus Dasypodius
Jan Cornets De Groot
Joseph Duchesne
Thomas Erastus
Henry Gellibrand
Konrad Gesner
Albert Girard
Johann Heinrich Glaser
Johannes Goedaert
John Graunt
Nehemiah Grew
Theodore Haak
Samuel Hartlib
Nicolaas Hartsoeker
Clopton Havers
Denis Henrion
Jakob Hermann
Hendrikvan Heuraet
Janvan Heurne
Wilhelm Homberg
Johannesvan Horne
Jeremiah Horrocks
Martinus Hortensius
Jan Hudde
Christiaan Huygens
John Jonston
Bartholomew Keckermann
Emanuel Koenig
Guy de LaBrosse
Philipvan Lansberge
Antonivan Leeuwenhoek
Nicaise LeFebvre

Nicolas Lemery

Pierre Magnol

Georg Markgraf

Jacob Metius

Adriaan Metius

Abraham De Moivre

Robert Moray

Samuel Morland

Sebastian Muenster

Johannes von Muralt

John Napier

Bernard Nieuwentijt

Richard Norwood

Henry Oldenburg

Bernard Palissy

Denis Papin

John Pell

William Petty

Johann Conrad Peyer

Willem Piso

Bartholomeo Pitiscus

Felix Platter

Peter Ramus

John Ray

Guillaume Rondelet

Frederik Ruysch

Angelo Sala

Joseph Saurin

Johann Jakob Scheuchzer

Franzvan Schooten

Olivier de Serres

Robert Sharrock

Hans Sloane

Willebrord Snel

Adriaanvanden Spiegel

Jan J. de J. Stampioen

George Starkey
Simon Stevin
Jan Swammerdam
Thomas Sydenham
Franc de le Boe Sylvius
Willem Ten Rhyne
Nicolaas Tulp
William Turner
Theod. Turquet de Mayerne
Adriaan Vlacq
John Wallis
John Webster
Johann Jakob Wepfer
Thomas Wharton
John Wilkins
John Winthrop

Order Information

To order additional copies of this book, please visit
www.redemption-press.com.
Also available on Amazon.com and BarnesandNoble.com
or by calling toll-free 1-844-2REDEEM.

CPSIA information can be obtained
at www.ICGtesting.com
Printed in the USA
LVHW062041220321
682094LV00025B/278